Canal

Canal Fever

The Ohio & Erie Canal,
from Waterway to Canalway

Fever

Edited by Lynn Metzger and Peg Bobel,
with illustrations by Chuck Ayers

Kent State University Press   Kent, Ohio

Lake Erie
CLEVELAND
FIRST SECTION OF OHIO & ERIE CANAL OPENS JULY 4, 1827
AKRON
OHIO
Canal
NATIONAL ROAD EXITS OHIO BY 1837
COLUMBUS
1833
ZANESVILLE
1826
TO VANDALIA ILL.
Ohio & Erie
PORTSMOUTH
Ohio River
TO WHEELING BY 1818
EXTENSION DELAYED UNTIL 1825

CONSTRUCTION
OF ERIE CANAL
JULY 4, 1817-OCT. 26, 1825
Lake Ontario
Erie Canal
BUFFALO
ALBANY
Hudson River
NEW YORK
PENNSYLVANIA
NEW YORK
CUMBERLAND
MARYLAND
ONAL ROAD
BALTIMORE

Frontis: Ohio's canals, connected by Lake Erie to New York's Erie Canal, became a transportation system that opened Ohio for settlers and commerce. (Drawing by Chuck Ayers.)

Library of Congress Catalog Card Number 2008051859

ISBN 978-1-60635-013-3

Manufactured in the United States of America

LIBRARY OF CONGRESS CATALOGING-IN-PUBLICATION DATA

Canal fever : the Ohio & Erie Canal, from waterway to canalway / edited by Lynn Metzger and Peg Bobel, with illustrations by Chuck Ayers.

p. cm.

Includes index.

ISBN 978-1-60635-013-3 (hardcover : alk. paper) ∞

1. Ohio and Erie Canal (Ohio)—History. I. Metzger, Lynn. II. Bobel, Peg.

HE396.033C36 2009

386'4809771—dc22 2880051859

British Library Cataloging-in-Publication data are available.

13 12 11 10 09 5 4 3 2 1

Contents

Preface and Acknowledgments

There have been three canal fevers in northeast Ohio. First came the excitement generated by the building and opening of the Ohio & Erie Canal, beginning in 1825; second was the frequent occurrence of the disease labeled "canal fever" that afflicted canal builders and their families; and the third, still rampant, is completely good for one's health. Fueled by the many potential benefits of preserving the canals, many grassroots organizations and public and private entities have had the fever since the mid-1980s. The result of this latest fever was the creation of the Ohio & Erie Canal National Heritage Corridor in 1996. Now called the Ohio & Erie Canalway, it is a designated linear swath of land extending 110 miles from Cleveland to New Philadelphia. The Canalway features the historic canal and its signature Towpath Trail and provides recreation, education, historic preservation, natural resource protection, and economic development in the region.

This canal fever, in book form, takes the reader on a journey through 185 years on those 110 miles. It is a journey from the time the Ohio & Erie Canal was built, through years of operation, floods, and ultimate demise as a transportation system; then through the era of disuse and abuse; and into the canal's current renaissance as a recreational, educational, and economic resource for northeast Ohio. The chapters, all written specifically for this book, use original sources, interviews, and old stories to connect the canal's past life to its present one.

We hope people in the communities within and surrounding the Ohio & Erie Canalway will enjoy a case of canal fever and the book will be a resource for all those interested in the story of the Canalway to explain what a canal is, why it was built, and how we now have this Towpath Trail. Of course the best medicine for canal fever is to get out on that trail and visit the Canalway.

The discussions leading to this book began in 1998, between historian Sam Tamburro and anthropologist Lynn Metzger researching the canal in the Village of Clinton. Their conversations, concepts, and research led to deciding the topics, recruiting the contributing authors, and convincing Peg Bobel to coedit the manuscript. A grant from the Ohio & Erie Canal Association supported the prepublication work.

We would still be moving at the canal-boat rate of four miles an hour, were it not for the help and support of family, colleagues, and friends. We are deeply grateful for all the individuals who gave their time and talent to help bring this book to life. We are especially grateful to Sam Tamburro, whose vision helped to form the contents of the book and who contributed so much. We also shared this journey with friend and totally committed canal buff illustrator Chuck Ayers, who not only selected and organized the images for the book, but he contributed his research skills as well. The other contributing authors have brought additional expertise, depth, and variety to the book. We wish to thank George Knepper, Jack Gieck, Joe Hannibal, Sabina Thomas, Michael Noll, Kathy Fernandez, Rick Sicha, Roger Grant, Rob Bobel, Glenn Harper, Bob Downing, Russ Musarra, Rory Robinson, and Dan Rice for their contributions. We are also grateful to all the individuals listed in the appendix who allowed us to interview them about their roles in developing the Canalway.

We wish to thank the Kent State University Press editors Mary Young and Joanna Hildebrand Craig for their wise and supportive guidance and Erin Holman for sharp-eyed copyediting. Were it not for their help, the book would have been unliftable.

So many others have helped along the way. John Miller, retired University of Akron archivist, and Steve Paschen of the Kent State University Archives helped with both research and humor. We are immensely grateful to friend and mentor Delmus Williams, University of Akron Libraries, for his advice and good cheer. Others read parts of the manuscript for content and clarity—especially Linda Whitman, University of Akron archeologist; Sally Longville, retired Akron educator; and Mary Metzger Croft, reading specialist. And then there is Jim King, of Angel Falls Coffee Company who cheerfully checked on our progress as we used hours of table space. All authors need a friendly café.

Of course we are grateful to the many family members and friends who had to listen to us talk about this project for years. The deepest thanks, however, go to our spouses, Rob Bobel and Ed Metzger. They helped with field trips, research, and information gathering; debated fine points of content; and provided food and spirits when most needed. Most of all, they sustained their own and bolstered our senses of humor. It has been a huge advantage to us and this book that they both also have severe and unrelenting cases of canal fever.

Part 1

The Historic Ohio & Erie Canal

Chapter 1

The History of the Ohio & Erie Canal

SAM TAMBURRO

In the twenty-first century, it is difficult to grasp the significance of the canal era to U.S. and Ohio history. The period seems far removed, even quaint in its complexities. However, the canal system that developed in the nineteenth century created a commercial network that revolutionized trade and travel in the United States. Nowhere are these connections more evident than the nexus between New York's Erie Canal and Ohio's Ohio & Erie Canal.

The Ohio & Erie Canal and its link with the Erie Canal created an interrelated regional economy. Eastern seaboard farms could not compete with the fertile land of the Old Northwest. The reduced shipping costs provided by the canal systems enticed easterners to buy plentiful western agricultural produce because it was more economical than growing their own. And the Old Northwest, a rapidly developing area, provided an excellent market for manufactured goods. As a result, the East Coast began to focus on mass production of manufactured goods, and it had ample workforce numbers of displaced farmers to work in factories. A symbiotic production-consumption relationship was established between the two geographic areas.

The importance of an extension of the canal system into Ohio was not lost on the Erie Canal investors. A capital-impoverished frontier state in the early nineteenth century, Ohio turned to New York financiers to partially fund its internal improvement project. New York banking houses underwrote the initial $400,000 state bond issue. New York businessman John Jacob Astor also loaned the State of Ohio $1 million at 6 percent interest to support the Ohio & Erie Canal's construction. It is clear that the New York business community understood the economic potential of Ohio and the Old Northwest, and they sought to capitalize on it through ground-level investment.

When the Ohio & Erie Canal groundbreaking ceremony occurred at the Licking Summit on July 4, 1825, it was not a coincidence that New York governor DeWitt Clinton, the "Father of the Erie Canal," lifted the first spade of dirt. He also made a speech there that echoed the importance of a United States interconnected through internal improvements. Clinton boasted to the crowd: "See what my country has done in her juvenile state! And if She has achieved this gigantic enterprise in infancy, what will she not effect in the maturity of her strength, when her population becomes exuberant and her whole territory in full cultivation. And your sister states, and the civilized world, will be astonished."[1]

The Ohio & Erie Canal's connection with the Erie Canal influenced far more than the region's economy. In the first half of the nineteenth century, Ohio's population migration and settlement patterns, politics, social issues, architecture, and culture were all affected by the connectivity of the Ohio & Erie Canal. This is the historical context in which the Ohio & Erie Canal must be viewed. Subsequent chapters of this book explore many of these aspects of the canal in greater detail.

In 1818, Governor Ethan Allen Brown urged the Ohio legislature to begin surveys for canals from Lake Erie to the Ohio River, and with the

Early versions of the state seal depicted a canal boat (Henry Howe, *Historical Collections of Ohio*).

passage of the Ohio Survey Law of 1822, several were conducted in the following years. The final route of the Ohio & Erie Canal combined parts of two of the originally proposed routes surveyed: the northern portion of the Cuyahoga-Muskingum line, and the southern portion of the Scioto Valley line. Beginning at Cleveland, the Ohio & Erie Canal ran down the Cuyahoga Valley to the Portage Summit, lifted by forty-two locks in thirty-eight miles to reach the summit at Akron, 395 feet above Lake Erie. From this point, the canal followed the Tuscarawas Valley south to Roscoe Village, where the Tuscarawas River joins the Walhonding River to form the Muskingum River.[2] From here, the canal turned to the west toward the center (and the capital) of the state, and the Licking Valley. In this stretch, several aqueducts, feeders, and reservoirs were needed to engineer the canal through the topography. South from Columbus, the canal followed the Scioto River Valley to Circleville and Chillicothe, to the terminus at Portsmouth.

Ground was broken on July 4, 1825, and by July 4, 1827, the northern section between Cleveland and Akron was completed. Alfred Kelley, attorney and former mayor of Cleveland, served as acting commissioner on the northern section of the canal, which encompassed the canal north of Newark. The engineering of the Ohio & Erie Canal was patterned after that of New York's Erie Canal. The canal's prism was forty feet wide (at water level) and four feet deep, and its locks were ninety feet long and fifteen feet wide. Many of the canal's initial engineers came from New York, but locals quickly filled additional positions.

Several Ohio engineers directed the large construction project, including Francis Cleveland, Jessie L. Williams, and Richard Howe. In 1825, Howe was appointed resident engineer on the northern division of the canal, which stretched from Cleveland to Massillon, and served in that position until the 1850s. Resident engineers, like Howe, were responsible for directing the labor force. Howe built his home in downtown Akron; involved in civic activities in Akron, Howe proved to be instrumental in politicking for Akron to be the western terminus of the Pennsylvania & Ohio Canal, a feeder canal connecting with the Pennsylvania Mainline Canal in New Castle, Pennsylvania. His home still stands in downtown Akron and is being restored by the Ohio & Erie Canalway Coalition. Jack Gieck, canal historian and engineer, gives a full discussion of both the engineers and the engineering of the canal in chapter 2.

Immigrants, especially Irish and German, provided the bulk of the labor on the construction of the Ohio & Erie Canal. However, many local farmers joined the construction ranks during winter. At times the state also used convict labor—for instance, in 1827 Ohio released a number of prisoners from its state penitentiary to build the Columbus Feeder.[3] Dangerous working conditions and illness characterized the job. Historian Peter Way notes that in the summer of 1825, typhoid broke out among Ohio canal laborers digging the basin at Cleveland; the disease spread down the Cuyahoga Valley and resulted in seventeen deaths.[4] The role of the common laborer and more on immigrant history are discussed by George Knepper in chapter 3, Kathleen Fernandez in chapter 6, and Lynn Metzger in chapter 15.

Completed in 1832 and stretching 309 miles from Cleveland to Portsmouth, the infrastructure of the Ohio & Erie Canal system was substantial. The canal maintained approximately 151 lift locks and 7 guard locks, 23 aqueducts, and numerous ancillary structures such as towpaths, waste weirs, floodgates, and wasteways. The total cost of the Ohio & Erie Canal was $4.3 million, making it less expensive than any other canal of similar length in America.[5] The state funded the canal's construction by having Canal Fund Commissioners sell bonds to banking houses in Ohio, New York, and Europe. Additional funding for the project came from the federal government through land grants: 1,100,351 acres of federal land were given to the State of Ohio for canal use. This land was sold at two dollars per acre, and the proceeds used for the construction of the canal. The U.S. government made the grant on the condition that it would never be charged a toll for use of the canals.[6]

The pace of life in Ohio changed significantly after the opening of the Ohio & Erie Canal. Travelers on the canal were able to cross the state in approximately eighty hours, a dramatic improvement over a trip by horseback. However, it would be a mistake to characterize canal travel as luxurious or romantic. Most travelers found canal travel monotonous because of the lack of an appealing view: generally, packet boats sat below the level of the towpath, and the canal banks were covered with thick vegetation.[7] In addition, the accommodations on canal boats left much to be desired.

George Combe, a visitor from England in 1838, described his sleeping quarters in disturbing detail. He writes: "The beds were arranged in three tiers along the walls. During the day the beds, consisting of mattresses, sheets, pillows, and cotton quilts, were piled one above another. . . . The smell of animal effluvia, when they were unpacked, was truly horrid . . . they [the beds] were saturated with the perspiration of every individual who had used them since the commencement of the season, or probably from the time they were first taken on board."[8]

A few travelers, such as Maximilian, Prince of Wied, recorded their journeys in great detail. Chapter 5, by Joseph T. Hannibal, Sabina F. Thomas, and Michael G. Noll, presents a new translation of Prince Maximilian's journey on the Ohio & Erie Canal. Such observant travelers also left a valuable record of what the Ohio region's natural history was like at the time. See Joe Hannibal's chapter 4 for a clear and detailed look at that natural history.

Canal travel was also unpredictable. A heavy rain could rupture an embankment, leaving a canal dry for long periods. Because canals were artificial, self-contained waterways, there was little drainage or circulation of water. As a result, water often became stagnant. Poorly drained places like canals were collectively recognized as unhealthy. One traveler described the Ohio & Erie Canal: "Carrion often float on the surface [and] miasmata are generated, all which must render a residence near the bank unhealthy. It is in fact a nursery of fever and ague."[9]

Nonetheless, eastern settlers and new immigrants boarded canal boats to migrate to Ohio for a better life. U.S. Census statistics confirm that after 1820 significant population growth occurred in counties through which the Ohio & Erie Canal passed. Until the canal's completion, the state's principle population centers were located in or near the Ohio River Valley. By 1850, there was a definite immigration pattern in Ohio related to the Ohio & Erie Canal: counties that the canal bisected had higher

Lumber was an important product hauled on the canal (Historic Print Collection, National Park Service).

populations of foreign immigrants than others in the state.[10] Glenn Harper takes a fresh look at these settlement patterns and the resulting architecture and landscape of the canal region in chapter 11.

The Ohio & Erie Canal rapidly transformed the economy of Ohio. It carried more trade than any other internal Ohio waterway. In 1851, the zenith of the canal's operation, 2,529,342 bushels of wheat arrived at Cleveland, and 645,730 barrels of flour, 1 million bushels of corn, 3 million bushels of coal, and 11 million pounds of merchandise were shipped south. According to Ronald E. Shaw's *Canals for a Nation,* more grain came into Cleveland from the interior of the state than from the Cuyahoga Valley or the Lake Erie shore.[11] Much of the wheat and flour came from the Scioto, Muskingum, and Tuscarawas River Valleys. John G. Clark, in his book *Grain Trade in the Old Northwest,* argues that wheat and flour exports from Newark, Dresden, Roscoe, Dover, Massillon, and Akron constituted almost all of the receipts in Cleveland. Akron served as a regional milling center and milled most of its wheat into flour, sending 376,000 barrels of flour to Cleveland in 1846 and 1847.

As a result of the Ohio & Erie Canal opening, the state's farming economy rapidly evolved from a subsistence- to a market-based one. The Ohio & Erie Canal's role in the facilitation of the market revolution in the U.S. economy during the early part of the nineteenth century cannot be understated.[12] Similar to New York's Erie Canal, the Ohio & Erie Canal played a significant role in the establishment of a market economy by providing a mechanism (improved transportation) for specialized production and economies of scale based on comparative advantage, setting the stage for the Industrial Revolution. As canal historian Jack Gieck has pointed out, by the mid-nineteenth century, the Ohio & Erie Canal had transformed Ohio from an agrarian frontier wilderness into a prosperous agricultural and industrial commonwealth.[13]

The opening of the Ohio & Erie Canal, with its connection to the Erie Canal, shifted the local economy paradigm, creating a "national economy." The Ohio & Erie Canal was the first transportation system extended into the Old Northwest, and it facilitated the entrenchment of the new economy. Moreover, with the addition of branch canals like the Pennsylvania & Ohio and the Sandy & Beaver during the 1830s, the Ohio & Erie profited from traffic on the Pennsylvania Mainline Canal, a major rival of the Erie Canal.

The same comparative advantage developed in the northern section of the canal between Canal Dover and Cleveland, which now compromises the Ohio & Erie National Heritage Canalway. Cities like Cleveland, Akron, and Massillon saw the development of an industrial base, while other areas, mostly in the southern section, focused on agricultural production.

The impact of the Ohio & Erie Canal on the development and growth of towns and villages along its route was profound. See chapter 10, in which I explore the history of Navarre. In chapter 8, Richard Sicha takes an in-depth look at Cleveland's history and its relationship to the canal. Peg Bobel and Lynn Metzger have gathered recollections of canal life in chapter 7.

The Zoarites were instrumental in the construction of the Ohio & Erie Canal through their community, south of Bolivar. In fact, the canal construction saved this communal society of German Separatists when they avoided foreclosure on their land by contracting to dig the canal, which was located on the west and opposite side of the river from Zoar. (Kathleen Fernandez in chapter 6 shows how the development of Zoar, founded before the coming of the canal, was intertwined with its development.) The citizens of Zoar developed lands on both sides of the river and used the canal as a source of transportation and a link to the outside world.

Without question, Cleveland was the business end of the Ohio & Erie Canal. In 1851, near the bridge at the foot of Seneca Street (now West Third Street), the State of Ohio installed a weigh lock—a specialized lock that weighed freight boats to assess tolls. A canal boat would enter the lock and rest on a cradle attached to a weighing mechanism. After water drained from the lock, the gross weight of the boat was determined, then the empty weight was subtracted to obtain the weight of the cargo itself. The Cleveland Weigh Lock remained the only one on the entire length of the canal.

During the canal era, many of Cleveland's residents were merchants, artisans, or craftsmen in small shops and industries. The city's main business interests focused on shipping and exchange. In 1836, almost two thousand vessels called Cleveland Harbor home; it provided employment opportunities for forwarding and commission merchants, dock laborers, and ship carpenters. Cleveland was also home to several industries such as iron foundries, steam engine factories, soap and candle factories, carriage manufacturers, and breweries.[14]

Akron, the seat of Summit County, also developed a strong manufacturing base because of its proximity to the Ohio & Erie Canal. In 1846, the city was home to twenty stores, four woolen mills, two blast furnaces, and five flour mills. After the Civil War, its milling industry grew exponentially, and the city became the headquarters for Quaker Oats.

Other communities along the canal centered on smaller milling operations. Massillon maintained several forwarding warehouses and attracted local Tuscarawas Valley farmers' shipments of wheat, earning it the title "Wheat City." Gristmills could be found in nearly every town of substance along the Ohio & Erie Canal.

Other industries, such as mining and boat building, prospered along the canal. Small villages like Independence and Peninsula had thriving sandstone mining operations that shipped their goods on the canal. Much of the stone was ground into millstones for the numerous gristmill operations along the system. The Village of Clinton, with its proximity to the mining area of Rogues' Hollow, shipped tons of coal to Akron and Cleveland. The Villages of Boston and Peninsula and the City of Akron were homes to large canal boat–building operations that provided most of the boats along the northern division of the Ohio & Erie Canal.

The success of the canal spurred the construction of numerous feeder canals, or side canals that connected to the Ohio & Erie on an east-west axis. These are the feeder canals associated with the Ohio & Erie: Ohio City Canal, Pennsylvania & Ohio Canal, Middlebury Branch Canal, Sandy & Beaver Canal, Nimishillen & Sandy Canal, Zoar Feeder & Sidecut, Trenton Feeder, Walhonding Canal, Dresden Sidecut, Muskingum River Improvement, Granville Feeder, Hocking Canal, and Columbus Feeder. Driven by economic speculation, many of the feeders, like the Walhonding Canal, were financial disasters. Others, such as the Nimishillen & Sandy Canal, were never completed. Three feeders of consequence within the present-day boundaries of the Ohio & Erie National Heritage Canalway were the Pennsylvania & Ohio Canal (P&O), the Sandy & Beaver Canal, and the Zoar Feeder & Side cut.

Completed in 1840, the P&O Canal stretched eighty-two miles, from Akron to New Castle, Pennsylvania, where it connected with the Beaver Division of the Pennsylvania Mainline Canal. In Akron, the P&O connected with the Ohio & Erie just south of Lock 1 at the Lower Basin. It passed through numerous towns in the Western Reserve such as Cuyahoga Falls, Franklin Mills (Kent), Ravenna, and Youngstown. And it was an economic success and a much-needed financial stimulus for Akron, whose economy was lagging after the Panic of 1837. First envisioned by Ohio & Erie Canal surveyor James Geddes, in 1823, the P&O Canal connected Akron with the coal-rich Mahoning Valley, and it functioned for ten years without competition from railroads and profited from its east-west connection. Much of the canal's ruins have been removed from the Akron landscape; however, there are remnants of sites in the eastern

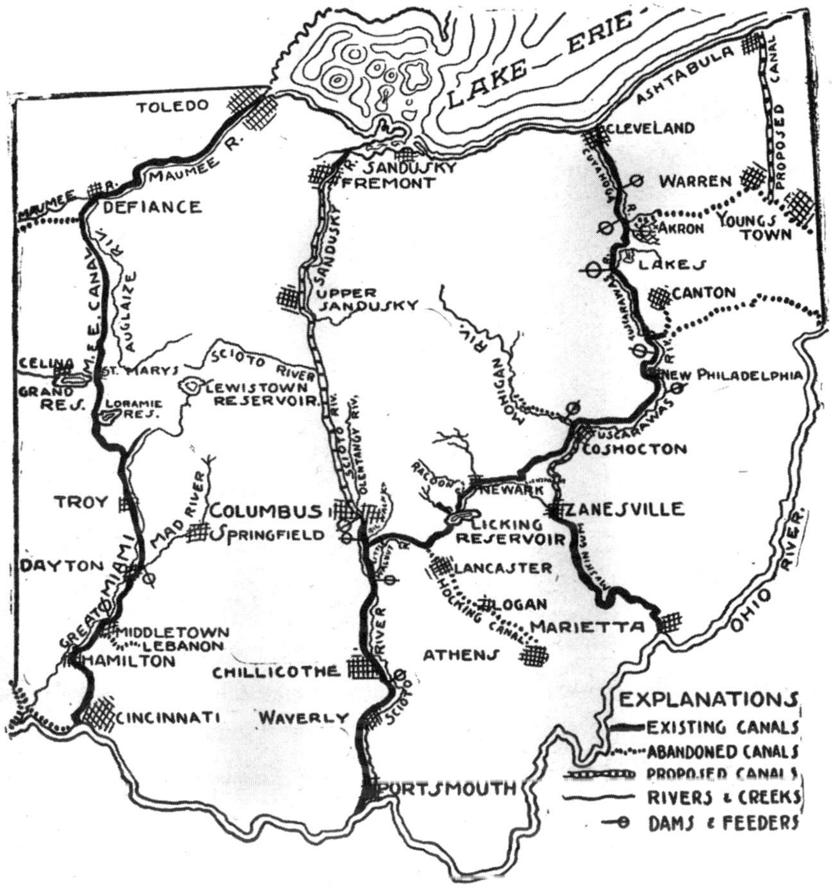

Although the earliest and most active, the Ohio & Erie Canal was not the only one in the state (Louis Baus Canal Photograph Collection, Ohio Archaeological and Historical Society Publications, University of Akron Archival Services).

section of the system. Only thirty-five miles south, the Sandy & Beaver Canal, a parallel feeder, proved much less successful.

Similar to the Pennsylvania & Ohio Canal, the Sandy & Beaver was designed to connect to the Ohio & Erie Canal. From Bolivar it headed east to the Ohio River, and from there it was to connect with the Pennsylvania Mainline Canal at the Big Beaver River; however, that portion was never completed. The history of the construction and operation of the Sandy & Beaver Canal is fraught with engineering setbacks and disappointments, engagingly described by Jack Gieck in chapter 2. Construction began in 1834, and the canal design called for one hundred locks and seven aqueducts to span the ninety miles between the east and west termini. Operated as a private enterprise, the canal's stock sold quickly with anticipation of connecting Bolivar with New Lisbon (Lisbon), a burgeoning community that was home to Rebecca Furnace, a rolling mill and nail-making factory. Since it had access to natural resources and a transportation connection to the Ohio & Erie Canal to the west and the Ohio River and Pennsylvania Mainline Canal to the east, many thought New Lisbon was destined to become the next Pittsburgh. But the predictions of prosperity did not come to fruition.

A series of financial setbacks and engineering mistakes significantly delayed the completion of the Sandy & Beaver Canal. The Panic of 1837 crippled the project and resulted in a 90 percent layoff, reducing the canal's workforce from two thousand to less than two hundred.[15] The Sandy & Beaver also required two tunnels to take it through the ridge dividing the Big Sandy and Little Beaver watersheds. The Little Tunnel was completed in 1846, and the Big Tunnel was finished in 1848, nearly eight years after the P&O Canal. Ironically, the water level at the summit was not sufficient to carry regular traffic, delaying the opening until 1850. The Sandy & Beaver Canal would operate only for two years, when the Cold Run Reservoir, the summit's water source, collapsed, sending a flood of water to the valley below. Fortunately, the people living in the valley were forewarned, but property loss was significant, and public opinion rapidly turned against the canal. The Sandy & Beaver Canal Company went bankrupt in 1853, and its canal lands were sold off to pay overdue debts. Today, much of the remains of the canal still exist. The Village of Magnolia, approximately ten miles east of Bolivar, contains several resources related to the Sandy & Beaver Canal, including a section of the canal prism and a lock and the still-operating Elson grain mill. (For more on Magnolia, see the sidebar in chapter 14.)

After the Civil War, the Ohio & Erie Canal fell into decline. The Ohio Board of Canal Commissioners became a political patronage appointment, and, as a result, political problems impeded the efficient operation of the canal. Many believed that the state ran the canal ineffectually and that transportation needs were best met by private railroads. In chapter 9, H. Roger Grant discusses the intricacies of the railroad-canal relationship.

In places where railroad operations were in direct competition with the Ohio & Erie Canal, they devastated the canal. For instance, by the early 1850s, Clevelanders saw the opening of two railroads: the Cleveland, Columbus & Cincinnati Railroad and the Cleveland & Pittsburgh. The negative effect on the Ohio & Erie Canal was virtually instantaneous. In 1839, approximately twenty thousand people arrived in Cleveland via the canal. By 1855, four years after the Cleveland, Columbus & Cincinnati Railroad opened in Cleveland, far fewer passengers entered the city on a canal boat. The effects on the commercial shipments on the Ohio & Erie Canal were equally harsh. In 1856, as a result of railroad competition, the net revenues from the canal system fell below zero for the first time.[16]

In 1861, the state leased most of the Ohio & Erie Canal to private lessees for a ten-year period. By the time the leases expired, many sections of the canal were in disrepair. Interest in canal commerce in Cleveland waned. In fact, local politicians, railroad promoters, and business leaders began publicly discussing the future of the Ohio & Erie Canal. Arguments against the canal ranged from the unsanitary condition of its stagnant water to the enormous value of the property and its potential as a railroad corridor through the Cuyahoga Valley. In November 1872, the Cleveland City Council passed a resolution to appoint a committee to negotiate for the rights of the Cleveland section of the Ohio & Erie Canal with its current lessee. In the following year, the committee submitted a contract for the acquisition of canal lands. In December 1873, the city council approved the contract and authorized the payment of $125,000 to the state for canal lands within the city limits.

The City of Cleveland quickly sold its canal development rights to the Valley Railway Company, who used the canal right-of-way for its new railroad line. As construction on the Valley Railway began, the Ohio & Erie Canal bed was filled with rail ballast to hold tracks. The remnants of the canal in Cleveland soon began to disappear. Cleveland, realizing that it could still make a profit from the Ohio & Erie Canal, retained its role as northern terminus of the system. As part of the purchase, the city relocated the nearby weigh lock and Lock 42 to a place near the foot of Dille Street along Independence Road, barely within the city limits.

The state's private leasing, which raised approximately $20,000 a year, restored a scant margin of profit to the canal from 1861 to 1877. However, the private companies failed to perform routine maintenance. During the leasing period, locks had deteriorated and several areas of the canal's banks had washed out, flooding adjacent farmland.[17]

By 1877, the Ohio & Erie Canal had ceased functioning as a transportation system from Cleveland to Portsmouth. Several sections of the system were inoperable and in need of major repairs. In the southern section of the Ohio & Erie Canal, squatters had moved onto canal lands. The part of the Ohio & Erie Canal south of Circleville had become useless and unnavigable. However, several sections, especially in the northern division of the canal, operated locally, filling short-haul needs. As late as 1880, the Cleveland Stone Company's quarry in Independence and Peninsula quarries shipped cut sandstone blocks and millstones on the Ohio & Erie

Where the Canal Meets the Road

GLENN HARPER

Imagine for a moment that you are a passenger on a canal boat traveling the Ohio & Erie Canal from Portsmouth to Cleveland, 150 years ago. The placid water of the canal has made for a relatively quiet and uneventful trip. Suddenly, just south of the little town of Hebron, a cloud of dust envelops an approaching bridge over the waterway. As the boat draws closer, you hear the clamor and clatter of wagons, livestock, and people, a discordant mingling of sounds, in stark contrast to the tranquility of your mode of travel. You have just reached the junction of the canal and the National Road, the nation's first federally funded interstate highway and the most important land route to the west throughout much of the nineteenth century.

Today it is hard to imagine the impact of these two corridors of culture and commerce on the settlement and development of Ohio. People flooded the highway, bringing their customs, languages, building traditions, religions, and farming practices. Both the road and the canal provided transportation and access for Ohio products to the burgeoning eastern markets and enabled the state's citizens to play an important role in the affairs of the new nation. On a smaller scale, the road and canal not only helped the fledgling Licking County village prosper, they also dictated the actual layout of its rectangular grid of streets and individual lots. The map illustrates how the east side of the village was platted parallel to the canal while west side lots paralleled the National Road, identified on the map as Main Street. The intersection of Basin Street (named for the canal basin near this site) and Main Street

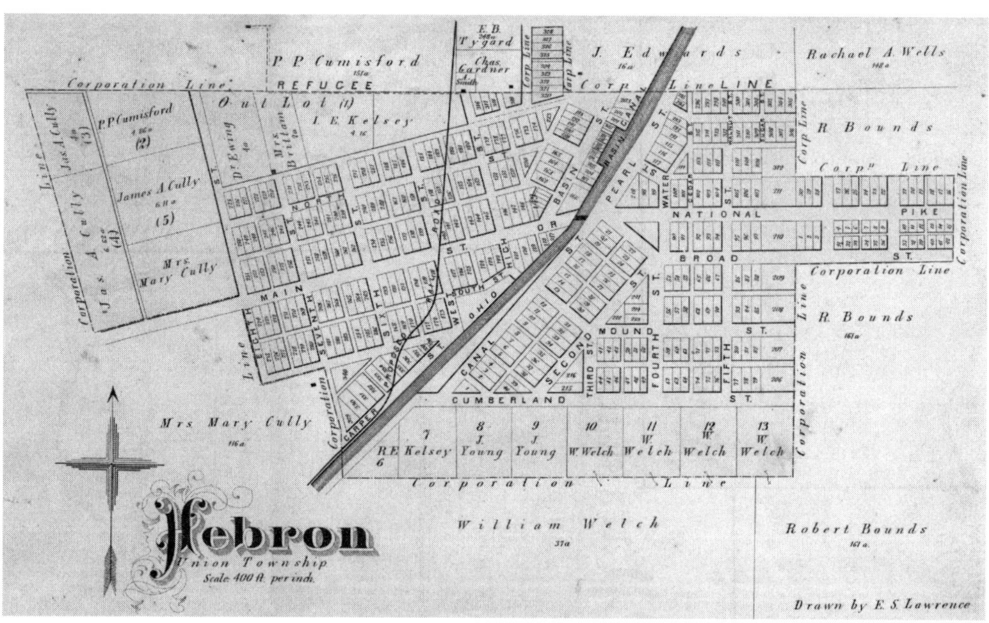

The National Road and the Ohio & Erie Canal intersected in Hebron (*New Historical Atlas of Licking County Ohio*, 1875).

Canal. Cuyahoga Valley farmers also used the canal for local shipments of their produce, even after the opening of the Valley Railway in 1880.

In 1888, Ohio's governor Joseph B. Foraker established a new canal commission to determine correct boundaries and to recover canal right-of-ways from squatters. In the 1890s, the Ohio Board of Public Works contracted for a complete survey of Ohio canal lands to determine which lands were rightfully under state ownership. As a result of the survey, two comprehensive series of maps were drawn of the Ohio & Erie Canal lands; these still remain the definitive primary source for determining the canal lands and associated structures.

From 1904 to 1909, the state made an attempt at rehabilitating the Ohio & Erie Canal to improve its operational ability. In chapter 12, Peg Bobel takes a detailed look at the final years of the canal, including this period of rehabilitation. The entire Ohio & Erie Canal was slated for repairs; however, the earliest efforts focused on the northern section of the canal,

---

(the National Road) clearly shows the angle at which the canal and the road met.

The canal and the road have something else in common: in a remarkable coincidence of Ohio history, groundbreaking for these two great internal improvements occurred on the same day, July 4, 1825. Construction of the National Road in Ohio began in St. Clairsville, the seat of Belmont County, opposite the courthouse. The road was conceived by Albert Gallatin, secretary of the treasury under Thomas Jefferson, and was authorized by Congress in 1806. Construction of the road fulfilled the country founders' desire for an all-weather road across the Allegheny Mountains.

Construction began in Cumberland, Maryland, in 1811 and reached the Ohio River at Wheeling, West Virginia (then Virginia) in 1818. The National Road was constructed through Ohio in the 1820s and 1830s, reaching Zanesville in 1830, Columbus in 1833, and Springfield in 1838. To pay for the road in Ohio, Congress allocated 5 percent of the net proceeds from the sale of Ohio lands. It was estimated that the average cost per mile (including three inches of broken stone and masonry bridges and culverts) would be about $3,400.

Groundbreaking for the canal occurred at the Licking Summit (now Heath) in Licking County, a few miles north of Hebron. Canal engineer John Forrer had prepared some ground where the canal was to pass and where the public and invited dignitaries, including New York governor DeWitt Clinton, father of that state's Erie Canal, and Ohio governor Jeremiah Morrow, gathered to commemorate the occasion.

Ironically, the road and the canal suffered a similar fate, overshadowed by the railroad as a faster and more efficient mode of travel even before they were finished. Their declines throughout the later decades of the nineteenth century also paralleled each other. Today the similarities continue. Both have received national recognition and are undergoing a revival as heritage tourism destinations for a new generation of travelers.

from Cleveland to Dresden. State construction crews, along with several subcontractors, completed the work at a cost of approximately $2 million. Unfortunately, the rehabilitation efforts only made it as far as Dresden before political support and funding ran out.

Some have argued that the rehabilitation efforts represent an attempt to compete with railroad traffic. However, the specifications and capacity of the Ohio & Erie Canal were not increased by the rehabilitation project, which would seem counter to the railroad competition theory. How could a canal system that was outmoded in the 1850s compete with railroads in the early twentieth century? Others have suggested that the state rehabilitation project served to preserve the canal as a water source for industries. The exact motivation for the rehabilitation effort remains a historical question.

Massive flooding in 1913 permanently ended the operation of the Ohio & Erie Canal as a connected transportation system. In March 1913, after a winter of record snowfall, spring rains led to massive flooding statewide. Torrents of water destroyed aqueducts and locks and washed out several sections of canal embankment, flooding nearby towns. In Akron, in an attempt to save the B. F. Goodrich plant from flooding, Lock 1 was dynamited, releasing a wall of water down the Cuyahoga Valley; the cascade caused devastating damage to the villages downstream.

After this flood, the Ohio & Erie Canal ceased to function as a complete transportation resource, but industries continued to use canal water for their operations. American Steel & Wire, later U.S. Steel, maintained a long-term hydraulic lease on the canal through the Cuyahoga Heights and Valley View area to utilize the water for its factory in Cleveland. American Steel & Wire performed routine maintenance on the canal and ancillary structures such as the Mill Creek and Tinker's Creek aqueducts. In Akron, the B. F. Goodrich Company used the canal water for the cooling process in manufacturing rubber, as did Firestone Tire and Rubber, which took water from the Summit Lake section. The City of Akron used a portion of the Ohio & Erie Canal's right-of-way to run a trunk sewer line to its treatment plant in the Cuyahoga Valley. Constructed in 1928, the massive sewer line obliterated Locks 21, 22, and 23 in the Old Portage area.

Sections of the canal still were used for recreational activities and excursion trips. For example, Canal Fulton utilized its section recreationally. In the 1930s, the Works Progress Administration built a replica lock tender's house adjacent to Lock 4, south of Canal Fulton. The Ohio Conservation Division invested in stocking the Canal Fulton section with fish for anglers; and during the 1970s, a replica packet boat, the *St. Helena II*, began to offer boat rides to visitors. Peg Bobel and Lynn Metzger explore recreational and other uses of the canal in chapter 13, drawing on historic documents and memoirs.

Eventually, responding to public advocacy led by Ralph Regula, the Stark County Commissioners acquired all the canal lands in that county from the State of Ohio. This increased local advocacy for protection of the canal and towpath and began to focus attention on both the canal's historic importance and recreational potential in the region. In chapter 14, Bob Downing and Russ Musarra delve into this period of renewed interest in the canal, looking at the canal towns that began to preserve their history and the preservation pioneers who led the effort.

Several other initiatives in the second half of the twentieth century supported the protection of the Ohio & Erie Canal. The Cuyahoga Valley National Recreation Area was established in 1974 as a National Park Service unit, providing federal protection of land and resources, including the Ohio & Erie Canal, which bisects the park. The Ohio Historical Society promoted and expanded its operations at Zoar Village, creating expanded interest in the canal's heritage. Finally, in 1996, the U.S. Congress designated the section of the Ohio & Erie Canal from Cleveland to Dover–New Philadelphia a National Heritage Corridor, now known as the Ohio & Erie National Heritage Canalway. The intent of the designation is to help local entities protect and use historic, cultural, and recreational resources for community benefit, while raising regional and national awareness of the Ohio & Erie Canal's importance. We end this book with a brief look at this latest canal fever, who has it and why they do, and how it is affecting northeast Ohio.

Human and natural forces have had a significant impact on the canal, towpath, and associated structures of the Ohio & Erie Canal in the National Heritage Canalway. In particular, interstate construction has obliterated several portions of the canal. In the north, the construction of Interstates 271, 80, and 77, and State Routes 21 and 800 affected large sections of the Ohio & Erie Canal. Railroad construction and community infrastructure improvements have also taken their toll on the remnant canal structures.

However, substantial elements of the canal remain evident on the landscape. The canal prism, locks, aqueducts, floodgates, waste weirs, and other associated structures are still visible. Surveys identify numerous structures, sites, and ruins associated with the canal. Sections of the Ohio & Erie Canal with the highest degree of historic integrity in the National Heritage Canalway are the sections between Cuyahoga Heights and Cuyahoga Valley National Park; in the Canal Fulton area; and in Zoar. This remaining physical evidence, along with museums, visitor centers, the Ohio & Erie Canal Towpath Trail, and exhibits along the trail, transports today's visitors to the time when Ohio as we know it was emerging from the wilderness of the wild west.

NOTES

1. U.S. Department of the Interior, *Proposed Ohio and Erie Canal: Suitability/Feasibility Study* (Denver, Colo.: National Park Service, 1975), 15.

2. Ronald E. Shaw, *Canals for a Nation: The Canal Era in the United States, 1790–1860* (Lexington: Univ. Press of Kentucky, 1990), 127.

3. Peter Way, *Common Labor: Workers and the Digging of North American Canals, 1780–1860* (Baltimore: Johns Hopkins Univ. Press, 1997), 99.

4. Ibid., 155.

5. Shaw, *Canals for a Nation*, 127.

6. George Perkins, "Ohio Canal: An Account of Its Completion to Chillicothe," *Ohio Archeological and Historical Quarterly* 34.4 (Oct. 1925): 597–604.

7. John A. Jakle, *Images of the Ohio Valley: A Historical Geography of Travel, 1740 to 1860* (New York: Oxford Univ. Press, 1977), 30.

8. George Combe, *Notes on the United States of North America, during a Phrenological Visit in 1838–39–40* (Philadelphia: Carey & Hart, 1841), 338, cited in Jakle, *Images of the Ohio Valley*, 29.

9. Cyrus P. Bradley, "Journal of Cyrus P. Bradley," *Ohio Archeological and Historical Quarterly* 15 (1906): 230.

10. H. G. H. Wilhelm, *The Origin and Distribution of Settlement Groups: Ohio 1850* (Athens: Ohio Univ. Press, 1982), 74–75.

11. Shaw, *Canals for a Nation*, 133.

12. See Charles Sellers, *The Market Revolution: Jacksonian America, 1815–1846* (New York: Oxford Univ. Press, 1992); Paul E. Johnson, *A Shopkeepers' Millennium: Society and Revivals in Rochester, New York* (New York: Hill & Wang, 1978).

13. Jack Gieck, *A Photo Album of Ohio's Canal Era, 1825–1913* (Kent: Kent State Univ. Press, 1988), 270.

14. Icon Architecture, *Ohio & Erie Canal National Heritage Corridor Management Plan*, 2 vols. (Boston: Icon Architecture, 2000), 2:4–5.

15. Gieck, *A Photo Album of Ohio's Canal Era*, 202.

16. Ibid., 270.

17. Ibid.

Chapter 2

Building the Canals

The Engineers

JACK GIECK

When he raised his glass at gatherings, George Washington was known for toasting "Success to the Navigation of the Potomac!" An experienced surveyor and mapmaker, Washington was president of the Potomack Canal Company, chartered in 1785, before he was president of the United States. The canal he championed at the time was to be a bypass around the Great Falls of the Potomac River, opening up the waterway to commercial traffic. But George Washington was also the one to first suggest a canal to run from Lake Erie to the Ohio River. And he actually made such a proposal to the Virginia House of Burgesses before the Revolutionary War—not as a shortcut but as a transportation artery that would provide an outlet for the produce of Ohio farms and encourage the development of northeast Ohio territory.

Even then, canals had an ancient heritage. The construction of China's Grand Canal began about 500 B.C., the year Nebuchadnezzar created his Royal Canal of Babylon, connecting the Tigris and Euphrates Rivers. (Actually, Nebuchadnezzar rebuilt a canal that had first been dug a thousand years earlier.) Indeed, the well-known Suez Canal, which connects the Mediterranean Sea with the Gulf of Suez and the Red Sea, follows a route that had been periodically restored by such famous rulers as Xerxes I and Ptolemy II ever since it was first excavated in the nineteenth or twentieth century B.C.E. But these canals were all simple ditches, adequate for floating boats through flat country between bodies of water with essentially equal elevation; it would be impossible for them to transport boats across Ohio's rolling countryside.

For canal boats to climb up intervening hills or to descend into valleys would require the invention of hydraulic elevators called locks. Canal locks first appeared on European canals in the thirteenth century C.E., in the Netherlands; however, locks had been invented by the Chinese three hundred years earlier so that construction of that country's Grand Canal could continue—as it would grind on for another three centuries.

By contrast, Ohio's first canal, the 309-mile Ohio & Erie Canal, would be completed in only seven years, a remarkable accomplishment achieved entirely with the muscle power of mules and men—and the talents of a handful of canal engineers. The Ohio Canal, as it was called for short, was the first and most successful of what would become a network of Ohio waterways—813 miles of them. In a state whose few roads were little more than muddy trails and whose rivers couldn't be used for freight because they were too shallow in summer and often became raging torrents in spring, the canals would become the interstates of the day—albeit with a speed limit of only four miles an hour, to prevent the wake of the boats from washing out the clay banks.

Ohio's canal era was born at a time when the entire state's population was less than 300,000—considerably smaller than the population of Cleveland today. Moreover, most of these early settlers lived in the southern part of the state along the river systems. To get their crops to market, some farmers built rafts and floated their wheat, corn, flour, oats, and salt pork down the Scioto, the Miami, and the Muskingum Rivers into the Ohio River, then west, down the Ohio to its confluence with the Mississippi, south of St. Louis—often all the way to the international port of New Orleans. But northeastern Ohio at that time had few inhabitants; the land was still a forested wilderness.

So the initial objective of the Canal Act, passed by Ohio's general assembly in 1825 after years of study, was to encourage development of the interior of the state by providing the Ohio farmers with access to New York and eastern markets, as well as to the Ohio River and the South. With an outlet to Lake Erie, they would be able to ship their produce by lake schooner (or later, by lake steamer) to Buffalo, then on the Erie Canal across New York State to the Hudson River. Some imaginative Ohio politicians with limited knowledge of the state's topography envisioned a canal running diagonally from Cincinnati to the state's northeast corner. But wiser heads realized there would be no way to keep such a canal full of water.

Historian George W. Knepper points out in *Ohio and Its People:*

> Canals can go only where natural watercourses are available to keep the channels full. This reality limited the principal north-south routes to three main stems and two potential branches. In the west was the line defined by the Great Miami-Auglaize-Maumee; in the center the Scioto-Sandusky; and in the east the Muskingum-Tuscarawas-Cuyahoga. . . . Each of these three main routes followed ancient Indian pathways that crossed the Continental Divide separating the northward from the southward-flowing rivers. For the canal builders it was essential that water be available at the high point where the canal crossed the Divide.[1]

Prudently, the Board of Canal Commissioners appointed by the legislature employed James L. Geddes, an experienced surveyor and one of the nation's most prominent civil engineers. Geddes had made his reputation on New York's Erie Canal. He began running his study of Ohio topography in April 1822, surveying some nine hundred miles of lines in eight months, much of it through primeval wilderness.

The commission hoped Geddes would prove the practicality of a canal running from Cincinnati eastward to the Scioto River Valley and then north to Lake Erie via the Muskingum River (passing through as many settled regions of the state as possible, to garner political support). But, as Knepper further explains, "To the surprise of nearly everyone, there was insufficient water on the Scioto-Sandusky watershed to sustain a canal." So Geddes concentrated his onsite instrument studies on a meandering route that stretched from the Scioto east to the Muskingum, then north to Lake Erie by way of either the Black River or the Cuyahoga. The latter route would eventually become that of the Ohio & Erie Canal.[2]

But Geddes couldn't complete the job because of his unfinished responsibilities to the Canal Commission of New York State, where the Erie Canal was still under construction. The Erie's middle section, from Utica to Salina, had been completed in 1820, and its eastern section through the Mohawk Valley would be finished in 1823. But the canal from Buffalo to the Hudson River would not be opened for another two years.

Finally, the first boat to make it all the way through from Lake Erie to the Hudson left Buffalo on October 26, 1825, carrying a load of dignitaries from Buffalo and New York City—including, of course, the state's governor, DeWitt Clinton, whose campaign promise of 1817 had been derided by opponents as "Clinton's folly." A week later, greeted along the way by clanging bells, booming cannon, and the cheers of ecstatic crowds, having descended 571 feet from the water level of the lake, the *Seneca Chief* completed its historic 363-mile voyage at last, reaching the Hudson River just north of Albany. Here, Clinton and his entourage boarded a steamboat to carry them down the river into New York City, where, triumphantly, the governor poured a barrel of Lake Erie water into New York Harbor—a symbolic marriage of the waters, illustrated in more than one popular painting. The completion of the Erie Canal made the future even brighter for the future Ohio & Erie Canal; since the two canals were linked by Lake Erie, goods could move from central Ohio to the Hudson River and then New York City.

A few months earlier, on July 4, Clinton had helped a fellow governor launch a similar project when he joined Ohio governor Jeremiah Morrow near Newark, Ohio, to break ground for the Ohio & Erie Canal. The resulting scene, assembled partly from contemporary accounts, has been described as follows:

> The Fourth of July crowd at Licking Summit milled about in the hot afternoon sunshine. Most of those present had driven over from nearby Newark. But some had booked stagecoach passage from as far away as Cleveland to hear the famed Erie Canal pioneer, Governor DeWitt Clinton of New York, on the same platform with Ohio's governor Jeremiah Morrow, and that brilliant young orator, Thomas Ewing. . . .
>
> Straining to make himself heard above the confusion, Governor Clinton concluded his speech at last and, accepting a ceremonial shovel passed up to the platform by a sergeant of the Chillicothe Blues, descended the steps and plunged it into the earth. As the first spadeful of dirt landed in the wooden wheelbarrow, a roar of approval rose from the crowd—but was immediately drowned out by a rolling thunder of field cannon as a loading and firing contest commenced between the various artillery companies present.
>
> . . . Governor Morrow took the spade from Governor Clinton and lifted the second shovelful of earth into the wheelbarrow. Suddenly a scuffle broke out among several prominent citizens over who would have the honor of digging the next spadeful of dirt. Then, fortunately, a second spade appeared—and then a third—and in a moment the wheelbarrow was full. And as the prize cargo was wheeled away by a beaming militia captain, many in the cheering throng "wept manly tears of joy."[3]

Two weeks later, on July 21, the drama was repeated for a new audience in Middletown, Ohio, where the two governors broke ground for the Miami Canal between Cincinnati and Dayton.

Two of the state's canal commissioners took up the task that James Geddes had left earlier. A young Cleveland lawyer-entrepreneur, Alfred Kelley (who had earlier become president of the Commercial Bank of Cleveland), left his law practice for eight years to complete Geddes's survey for the Ohio & Erie and to manage construction of the northern and central portions of the canal. He was assisted by Micajah T. Williams, a businessman from Cincinnati who had participated in an 1823 survey of the potential Sandusky Valley route. Kelley and Williams were the managing commissioners. Williams would supervise construction of the southern part of the Ohio & Erie Canal and develop a plan for the sixty-six-mile Miami Canal to be constructed between Cincinnati and Dayton.

Williams's Miami Canal would be extended north incrementally over the next two decades, finally reaching Toledo in 1845. In what amounted to a political coup, the Ohio State Legislature had secured permission to link up with (and essentially appropriate) a segment of Indiana's existing 465-mile Wabash & Erie Canal from Fort Wayne to Toledo—the last eighty-six miles of which had been built in Ohio. In a slyly worded public announcement, the Ohio Board of Public Works proclaimed that "for the sake of convenience," the resulting composite waterway would be called the "Miami & Erie Canal." It would provide western Ohio farmers with access to both Lake Erie and Ohio River markets, at last—thirteen years after completion of the Ohio & Erie, but with no further digging.

Knepper has observed:

> Kelley and Williams were remarkable public servants. They prepared for their task by spending months working with Erie Canal engineers in New York State until they knew every detail of canal construction and operation.
>
> Back in Ohio Kelley and Williams literally got on their horses and rode the routes, checking to make certain that the work was up to specification. Kelley carried an iron rod with which he prodded suspicious spots, thus uncovering occasional shoddy workmanship.[4]

The rod became Kelley's trademark. Supervisors and workers could spot him a mile away.

Why, it might be asked, considering the importance and the magnitude of these projects, had they been given to a lawyer and a businessman instead of to professional engineers? The fact is, there were no engineering schools in the United States in 1825 except for the United States Military Academy at West Point and Norwich University, a private military college. Formal education for civilian engineers was unknown in the United States when Ohio's canal systems were conceived, and there wouldn't be a U.S. engineering degree granted by a technical school until 1835, at Rensselaer Polytechnic Institute. None of today's engineering societies, organized to share data and establish national engineering standards, were established until late in the nineteenth century. So canal engineers in the early part of the century got their education the hard way. Kelley and Williams prepared themselves by apprenticing on New York's Erie Canal—one still under construction. It was the best training they could have had; during its construction, the Erie Canal trained a generation of canal engineers.

The task undertaken by the two managing commissioners would be formidable. In its 309 miles, crossing two summits (one at Akron, the other at Newark), the Ohio & Erie would require 151 lift locks to accomplish 1,218 feet of elevation changes between Lake Erie and the Ohio River. There would be twenty-three aqueducts and twenty-five culverts to bridge intersecting rivers and streams, as well as three slackwaters, where the new waterway would descend into a river—sometimes using its channel for several miles before climbing out on the opposite shore through a river lock and returning to an excavated ditch.

Kelley and Williams delegated much of the detailed survey and layout work to such experienced canal engineers such as David S. Bates, Samuel Forrer, Sebried Dodge, and Richard Howe. Typical of this group was Samuel Forrer, who began his career as a rodman. A rodman is a surveyor's assistant who carries the calibrated stadia rod (also called a "leveling rod"), which looks like a white, heavy-duty, six-foot ruler with large black numbers and a sliding marker. He places the base of the rod on the exact spot specified by the surveyor, who directs the operation by waving his arms while sighting through the telescope on his transit, mounted on a tripod situated on an established benchmark. The telescope has internal crosshairs, which the surveyor aligns horizontally with the edge of the stadia rod and vertically on its sliding marker. After leveling the bubbles on his instrument, the surveyor can pinpoint locations and precisely measure elevations. To measure physically the distance along the ground between benchmarks, the team used a sixty-six-foot surveyor's chain containing a hundred links. Today, some older maps and property deeds still report distances in "chains" and "links."

Transit with surveyor's chain on a tripod, used in surveying early Akron (Simon Perkins Collection, Summit County Historical Society; photo by Rob Bobel).

Progressing through the classic civil engineering curriculum of the time, Sam Forrer graduated from rodman to surveyor in 1818, eventually becoming an engineer, then a contractor, and finally a canal commissioner. He devoted his life to building and maintaining Ohio's canals, establishing an unchallenged record of more than fifty years in canal service, before his retirement in 1873.[5] Canal engineers, thus, were surveyors, designers, planners, and managers. They laid down detailed specifications that would be followed by the stone masons, carpenters, blacksmiths, and other craftsmen who would construct the locks, aqueducts, and culverts

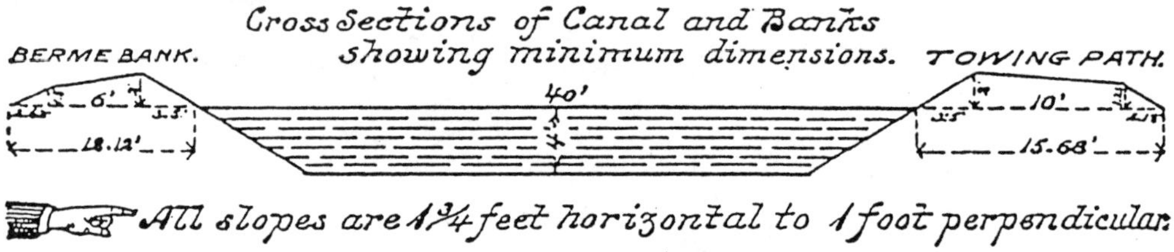

Consistency in size and shape of the canal was critical for the boats to move through efficiently (Ohio Canal Commission, 1902).

and hydraulic feeders, bridges, and other structures; and they supervised the digging of the canal channel itself.

The cross section of the canal (called its prism because of its trapezoidal shape) was not just a crudely dug ditch. Uniform specifications required that it be no less than twenty-eight feet wide at the bottom, with sloping sides that provided forty feet of width at the water level to give boats ample room to pass each other. The water was to be a minimum of four feet in depth. One of the banks was to have a ten-foot-wide towpath, nearly always between the canal and the river it paralleled.[6]

In practice, the ditch was dug five to twelve feet deep, and its width was from 50 to 150 feet. To make them as waterproof as possible, workers lined the banks and bottom with clay—but not before grubbing and clearing the banks of all porous stone, brush, and other vegetation that might contribute to leakage. But leaks would prove to be a constant problem. In the wild, uninhabited countryside, it would be necessary to employ men to patrol the canal and with straw plug muskrat holes in the banks (the berm and towpath).

To provide the most practical route with the fewest number of locks, the engineers decided that the canals would follow the relatively flat, though often tortuous, river valleys—usually at an elevation several feet above the river level. The canals would crawl up out of one river valley and descend into the next one through a system of locks. These locks were built as rectangular stone channels, usually ninety feet long and fifteen feet wide (to be able to pass boats that were fourteen feet wide), and they were up to twenty feet deep, depending upon the lift. Lock walls were built of huge blocks of squarely cut stone, usually quarried nearby. Consequently, the locks were mostly sandstone on the Ohio & Erie and limestone on the Miami & Erie (although at Defiance, on the Miami & Erie, they were constructed entirely of wood because of the scarcity of stone there). Lock stones were tuck-pointed with lime mortar to waterproof them.

Each canal lock was closed at both ends by wooden whaler gates (the name probably taken from the giant cargo portals on whaling vessels), which closed in a "V," pointing upstream so that the head of water pressure kept them closed. These gates were usually made of hardwood, often white oak, and they were opened and closed by boat crewmen leaning their backs against their long handles of heavy timber sweeps while digging in their heels. Hinges and other lock hardware were made of wrought iron. When closed, the gates turned the lock chamber into a pair of versatile dams.

Locks worked by gravity, and they operated like hydraulic elevators. Near the base of each pair of gates was a metal wicket, or butterfly valve, that was opened or closed by iron crank handles at the top of each gate. With the gates closed, opening the wicket in the lower gate drained the lock, causing the level of the impounded water to fall to the downstream level.

If a boat was going upstream, the lower gates could be opened and the boat drawn inside. Closing the wicket in the lower gate and opening the one in the upper gate would let water in to refill the lock, lifting the boat to the upstream level. When the two levels were equal, the upper gates could be opened and (after rehitching the mules) the boat could continue on its way. The process would be reversed for a boat going downstream. Most locks had a lift of six to ten feet, although there were exceptions. Deep Lock, twenty-five miles south of Cleveland on the Ohio & Erie, had a seventeen-foot lift.

Locks with a high lift posed a special problem for boats traveling upstream. Opening the wicket in the upper gate (which could be well above the boat's top deck when the water in the lock was still at downstream level) would shower water down on any passengers or crew members on deck near the bow. To cope with this annoyance, an internal sluiceway was built into the wall of locks like the ones in Akron's chain of Cascade Locks—nearly all of which have a lift of ten feet. On the upstream side, ahead of the upper gate and below the waterline, a two-foot-square opening can be seen in the lock wall. This hole was covered by a wooden sluice gate. When the gate was opened, water entered an internal passageway built into the lock, flowing down the sluiceway and coming back out into the lock chamber below the waterline—resulting in dryer crews and happier passengers. Locks having this feature also had the standard butterfly valves in the gates, however, since the problem didn't exist when boats were going downstream.

During periods of less than peak traffic, to keep the backed-up water from flowing over the tops of the gates and creating a different set of problems, each lock had a bypass channel, or wasteway, a stone-lined ditch that carried excess water around the lock. This water flowed back into the canal below the lower gates.

For a lift of ten feet, each time a lock was operated, more than thirteen thousand cubic feet of water would be released—about one hundred thousand gallons lost downstream. To provide for the passage of a hundred boats a day, the maximum the planners believed a lockmaster could handle (if, indeed, a lock had a lockmaster; most did not), their calculations showed that an average flow of fifteen hundred cubic feet per minute would have to be provided from a source upstream of all the locks in the system. But, taking evaporation losses and inevitable leakage into account, knowledgeable engineers concluded that at least ten times this amount would be required. With a uniform flow of boat traffic both ways, it would theoretically have been possible to double this hundred-a-day capacity, but as the *Second Annual Report of Canal Commissioners* primly observed in 1824, "It would be extremely vexatious to compel a boat to wait until one should arrive to pass in the opposite direction."[7]

The statement assumed a politeness that rarely existed between boat crews. Although rules were established to govern upstream/downstream priority into a lock, in practice, the matter would sometimes be settled by a fistfight—or, much more fun, a duel, with driving sticks, between competitive teenage muleskinners balanced precariously on the top edges of the gates. The dunked loser's boat was second.

To supply anticipated water needs, canal engineers dammed the Great Salt Lick and surrounding swamp south of Newark at the Ohio & Erie's southern summit. The reservoir thus created was called Buckeye Lake. To provide for the higher northern summit, which is actually on the continental divide, the engineers dammed and enlarged a chain of small, interconnected natural lakes located close to the headwaters of the Tuscarawas River. These lakes formed the Portage Lakes Reservoir, encompassing about a thousand acres of water on three levels.[8]

Portage Lakes water still enters the nine-mile summit of the Ohio & Erie between the Tuscarawas and Cuyahoga River Valleys, opposite Young's Tavern on Akron's Manchester Road. Standing on the canal bank near the tavern, one can sometimes see the water dividing and flowing both ways. That which flows to the left goes north, eventually into the Cuyahoga River, into Lake Erie, over Niagara Falls and into Lake Ontario, then down the St. Lawrence River into the North Atlantic Ocean. The water that goes to the right goes south, flowing into the Ohio River,

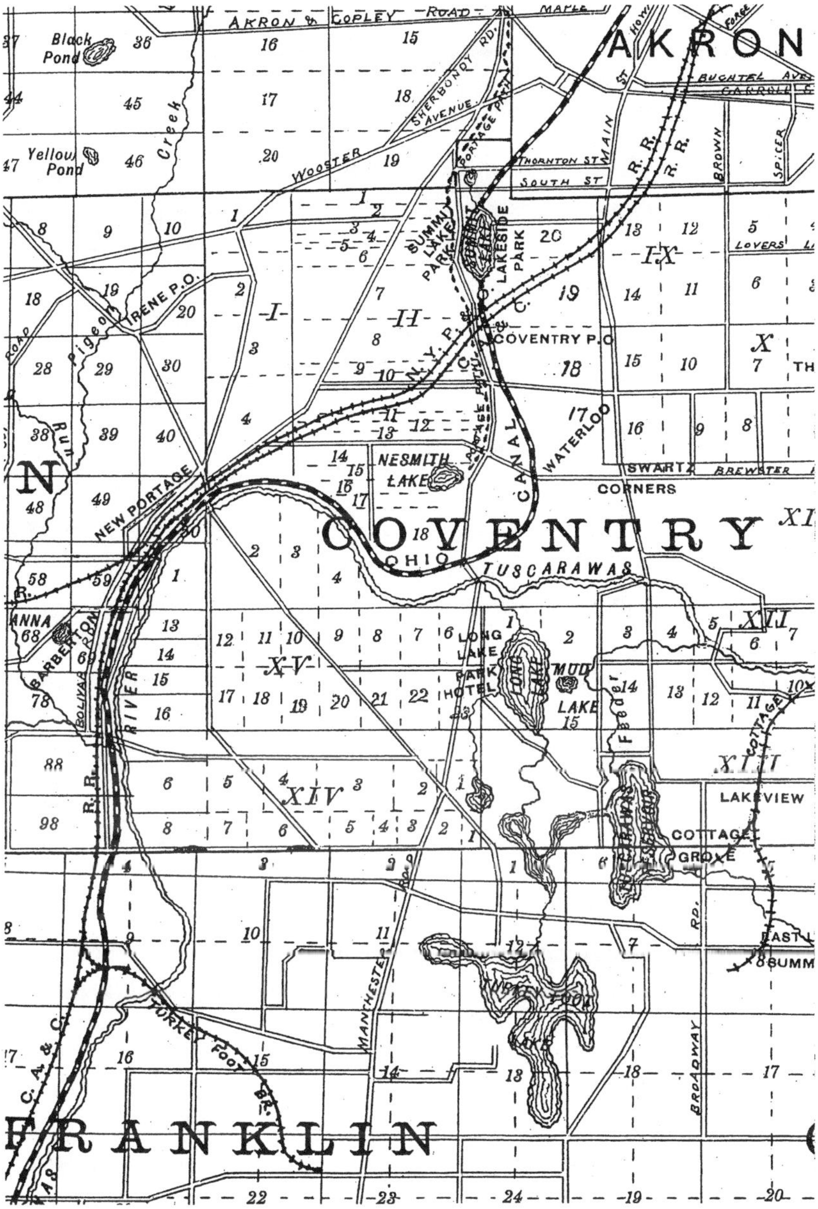

Portage Lakes in 1874. These were natural lakes near Akron that were enlarged to serve as a major canal reservoir (*Atlas of Summit County*, 1874).

west to the Mississippi River, and ultimately down the Mississippi into the Gulf of Mexico.

In the western part of the state, the water needs of what eventually became the Miami & Erie Canal were served by three reservoirs, of which Grand Lake St. Marys was the largest, the others being Loramie and Lewiston reservoirs. Supplementing these were a number of dams on creeks and rivers that raised the water level high enough to permit it to flow into the canal through a feeder.

When there were hills in the path of planned canal routes that turned out to be higher than any available water sources, the problem was solved with a radical excavation called a deep cut. The longest of these cuts is on the Miami & Erie south of Spencerville. This continuous six-thousand-foot trench, from five to fifty-two feet deep with a constant water level, was blasted through the blue-clay ridge that separates the Auglaize River Valley from the Saint Marys watershed. The Miami & Erie Deep Cut is on the National Register of Historic Places.

The Pennsylvania & Ohio Canal also had a deep cut at its Ravenna summit, which otherwise would have been starved for water. That cut was nearly five thousand feet long and was more than forty feet deep in places. Something similar was done on the Ohio & Erie when surveyors found that Summit Lake, south of Akron, was significantly higher than the planned nine-mile summit between Akron's Lock 1 and Wolf Creek Lock in what would become Barberton. In fact, the Summit Lake level was even higher than the Portage Lakes Reservoir outlet that was to serve the northern section of the canal from Akron north to Cleveland as well as locks to the south of the Akron Summit. Dredging the canal channel north from Summit Lake to Lock 1, the spring-fed lake was partially drained, which dropped its level by eight feet and reduced its area by 75 percent. Thereafter, the water flow could operate the forty-four locks required to get down 395 feet to the level of Lake Erie.[9]

Even more daring was the construction of two tunnels on the Sandy & Beaver Canal, a privately financed seventy-three-mile spur running east from the Ohio & Erie at Bolivar—much of it blasted through solid rock. The two tunnels made it possible to shorten the Sandy & Beaver by seventeen miles and to lower the water level sufficiently so feeders from adjacent streams could be used.

Locks had an unintended consequence: they caused towns. Since passengers and crews were delayed about twenty minutes while the mules were unhitched and the locks were operated by some of the members of the boat crew, those on board, both passengers and crew, would often debark to stretch their legs. So a lock was a natural location for a general store, such as the Mustill Store at Akron's Lock 15 on the Ohio & Erie, or a saloon, as the one at New Portage. Other enterprises followed, including an occasional gambling parlor or brothel. On the Miami & Erie, the lockmasters, underpaid public servants, frequently supplemented their incomes by not only operating stores but also offering overnight lodging for canalers on the second floors of their residences. Deeper locks were frequently the locations of gristmills, which used the waterpower available in the bypass channel—water otherwise wasted over a spillway.

Towns often grew up around these nuclei. A staircase of locks—fifteen in a single mile—was required to climb the last hundred feet of the 395-foot ascent from Lake Erie to the canal's summit between the Cuyahoga and Tuscarawas River Valleys. Thus, negotiating these locks would delay passengers and crews half a day. Convinced that this would encourage the growth of a major city, General Simon Perkins of Warren successfully lobbied the canal commissioners to put the locks on his and Paul Williams's property. Perkins was a representative of a Connecticut land company who had acquired 1,003 acres for himself simply by paying back taxes on the land—a total of $4.07. He registered his town plat in Warren, the county seat, in 1825, naming it "Akron," from the Greek word for "high place," giving the state a canal right-of-way down the middle of his town map, thus assuring its growth.

The development of waterpower was a more powerful stimulus for Akron's growth. In 1832, Dr. Eliakim Crosby, a physician who was also an entrepreneur and a competent hydraulic engineer, built a dam on the Little Cuyahoga River in the Village of Middlebury (near today's Goodyear headquarters) to divert water into a two-mile mill race he and his partners created. Crosby's Ditch ran down the edge of the Little Cuyahoga Valley to what is Akron's Main Street today, turning south at that point to what would be named Mill Street. Here, the race turned west to power Crosby's newly constructed Old Stone Mill at Lock 5—the largest and, at that point, most modern gristmill in Ohio.

Having turned the wheels of Crosby's Stone Mill, the effluent water flowed north down a steep grade, becoming the Cascade Race in a channel parallel to the canal and about ten feet higher in elevation. Dropping nearly one hundred feet between Locks 9 and 16, the Cascade Race powered a string of industries, the same water turning one waterwheel after another as it made its way down the slope before flowing through a 550-foot tunnel under North Street—ultimately finding its way back into the Little Cuyahoga River from whence it came.

There would be basins between most of the locks in this industrial valley. These were the parking lots for the canal boats that served the five cupola furnaces, several gristmills, a textile mill, a furniture factory, and a distillery—all turned by the waterpower of Crosby's Ditch. An example to note: after the Civil War, one of the finest and most technologically up-to-date industries in the valley was built by German immigrant Ferdinand Schumacher, another entrepreneur-inventor—who later became famous for founding the American breakfast food industry by introducing oatmeal to the American market. Schumacher converted a former woolen mill at Lock 14 into a gristmill that was even bigger and more modern than Crosby's Stone Mill. It was Schumacher's fourth Akron mill, and it had an overshot wheel. William Perrin admiringly describes the operation of the Cascade Mill:

> The water power is ample at all seasons. It has a head and fall of 38 feet. The power is derived from an iron overshot wheel, 35 feet in diameter with a 10-foot face. This immense wheel weighs 37 tons, and yet, being well balanced, it revolves on its shaft as steadily and smoothly as if it were made of the lightest wood. The wheel contains a series of 96 steel buckets, having a total weight of 16,000 pounds. Each bucket is made of a single sheet of cold-rolled steel one-eighth of an inch in thickness. . . . [10]

Schumacher's Cascade Mill was famous for its power derived from an iron overshot wheel. This circa 1880s photo shows the mill after it added coal power (Summit County Historical Society Collection, Special Collections Division, Akron Summit County Public Library).

> The water supply flows through a 6-foot subterranean tube, to an iron standpipe rising about 18 feet to the level of the basin, and flowing from an iron tank 26 feet long, 8 feet wide and 4½ feet high, to the iron gate, which gauges and delivers it to the buckets at the apex of the wheel.[11] From spur-wheels, connected with a 12-foot pulley, by a 40-inch leather-double belt 120 feet long, power is communicated to the line-shaft over a 10-foot pulley, whence the 12 run of burrs are operated by quarter-twist belts.[12]

Less than a decade after having spent a fortune building his state-of-the-art waterpower system, the prescient Schumacher recognized the emerging age of steam, and the Cascade Mill boasted the tallest smokestack in the valley. It is evidence of Schumacher's technical wisdom, for one ton of water falling one mile releases about the same amount of energy as the burning of one pound of coal.[13]

Directly related to the canal and shipping, the Village of Cascade was established in 1833, with its center at Howard and Market Streets. After the Pennsylvania & Ohio Canal was put through to Akron in 1840 (from a point on the Ohio River near Pittsburgh), connecting with the Ohio & Erie in a basin at Lock 1, additional warehouses began to line both canals. The Pennsylvania & Ohio ran down the center of Akron's Main Street, utilizing a widened section of Crosby's Ditch. Soon Cascade was connected to Simon Perkins's first Akron, located one mile to the south, next to the basin in which the two canals had their junction.

Following Ohio's river valleys as they did, canals frequently crossed intersecting tributary streams. And sometimes they had to bridge major rivers, when the topography made it necessary for the canals to change sides. Centuries earlier, canal aqueducts had been developed in England, Wales, and in continental Europe to cope with challenges like these. A canal aqueduct is a bridge filled with water to float canal boats across a depression in the canal channel. Most were constructed as rectangular wooden flumes or troughs that fitted into stone channels at the end of stone abutments built into the banks of the stream to be crossed—essentially a larger version of the channels for conveying fresh water built originally by the Romans. If it had a long span over a wide river, the center portion of the aqueduct was usually supported by one or more stone piers whose foundations were firmly anchored in the river bottom. In building their aqueducts, Ohio's canal engineers were guided by European standards and techniques, researched by Robert Fulton, who sailed to England to study Old World canal technology. Famed for inventing the steamboat, he rarely gets credit for his consuming interest in canals and his significant contribution to canal engineering in America.

But American engineers also came up with innovations of their own. To minimize sagging of the wooden flume between piers under the constant weight of canal water (a weakness that can be seen in many antique photos), some aqueducts were built with roofs, which made them look like covered bridges. These roofs not only protected the structure from the weather but also added substantial rigidity (what engineers call "bending strength") to the resulting box-beam cross section.

Nineteenth-century photographs also reveal that Ohio's canal builders frequently used the rigidity of triangles in designing their aqueducts, often adding diagonal "Y" members of heavy timber that reached out at thirty- or forty-five-degree angles from supporting piers and abutments to help support the bottom of the rectangular trough. The long, slim Sandy & Beaver Aqueduct over the Tuscarawas River at Bolivar was built entirely of wood—even the abutments. Instead of stone piers, the flume was supported by nine clusters of tall vertical posts about the size of telephone poles. Each of these, a total of thirty-six vertical poles, sprouted supporting "Y" members on both sides that formed a triangle with the wooden flume to which it was fastened. The finished structural network was composed of more than a hundred rigid wooden triangles.

An aqueduct carried the Ohio & Erie over the Tuscarawas River. The stone piers are still in the river (Louis Baus Canal Photograph Collection, University of Akron Archival Services).

In contemporary photographs, the result appears as a long, skinny bridge that, despite its fragile, spindly look and its heavy burden of water, was straight as a ruler.

Permitting wider unsupported spans for these water bridges, the Howe arch bears the name of its inventor, veteran canal engineer Richard Howe. His wooden truss was a curved parabolic beam built into the sides of the wooden flume. Further rigidity was added to the rainbow-shaped arch by a lattice of triangularizing diagonals. Howe's truss was used in the design of the famous Great Miami River Aqueduct on the Miami Canal.

But the grandest of all Ohio aqueducts was the Great Circleville Aqueduct, which crossed the broad Scioto River about halfway between Columbus and Chillicothe. This magnificent roofed tunnel was 425 feet long and 20 feet wide. After almost a century of service, when the southern portion of the Ohio & Erie was finally abandoned in 1911, the long, cozy corridor was drained to become a gambling house—one apparently ignored by Circleville police, not unlike later floating gambling casinos on the Mississippi River. The structure eventually burned and fell into the river, allegedly an act of revenge by a sore loser.

Perhaps the most ingenious construction, however, one that provided maximum strength and rigidity with minimum weight, was the invention of German immigrant John Augustus Roebling (1806–1869), whose mind ran to using steel cable in tension instead of relying on the bending strength of heavy wooden timbers or the compressive strength of stone. Roebling was probably one of the first American engineers to understand stress analysis, an invaluable engineering tool pioneered by Thomas Young. After establishing the validity of his mathematically sophisticated designs, Roebling built a plant to manufacture steel cable in Trenton, New Jersey.

John Roebling had begun his career on eastern canals, but he used his unique concept in Ohio on the aqueduct spanning the Auglaize River on the Miami & Erie near Melrose. Unlike his later suspension bridges, which hung from twisted steel catenaries, the cables on Roebling's aqueducts were stretched in tension in a trapezoidal pattern beneath the aqueduct's channel to limit its bending under the weight of the water. Roebling went on to use his technology to build the famous Great Suspension Bridge across the Ohio River at Cincinnati in 1865–67, and he designed New York's Brooklyn Bridge.

All aqueducts had the same defect, however: they leaked. They required constant maintenance to avoid losing precious water. Most had forgivable dribbles in summer; but in winter, when the water expanded as it froze, ice pushed out the sides of the wooden conduit, developing a curtain of icicles that often became a frozen waterfall. Although these walls of ice were sometimes pictured as winter wonderlands on local postcards, they were an annual disaster for canal engineers who had to hire extra crews every spring to repair the damage so the canal could open—knowing they would face exactly the same problem the next year.

An alternative to the wooden aqueduct, which minimized this problem, was the stone culvert. Culverts took much more labor to build, but they were usually immune to leakage and were largely maintenance free. Most culverts were built as single arches across relatively narrow streams, the stones laid over a temporary curved wooden frame between the abutments. After the stone structure was complete, the supporting frame was removed and the interior channel was covered with earth, then lined with waterproofing clay. The result looked something like today's highway culverts.

There was yet another way to cross a waterway: slackwater navigation. This made it possible to cross a wide river without building either an aqueduct or a culvert. At a slackwater, a boat exited the canal channel through a guard lock and was simply poled or towed across the river. Usually, a dam was built downstream to assure sufficient river water depth during all seasons, and, ideally, a bridge was built for the mules (who otherwise rode on board while the boat was poled across). Sometimes, to bypass a rocky cliff (as at Black Hand Gorge on the Ohio & Erie), or to avoid the expense of digging several miles of canal, the river channel became the canal channel for some distance. It became a useful expedient on the Pennsylvania & Ohio at Franklin Mills (now Kent), and at several points on the Hocking. The Muskingum River Improvement was entirely slackwater. And, in a sense, the crossing of Summit Lake south of Akron on the Ohio & Erie was slackwater navigation. Here, however, the mules did not get a break from towing the boat across the water. In fact, their job became more difficult, as they struggled to keep their balance while pulling the tow rope on the floating wooden footbridge—which, depending on the weight and number of the animals in the mule team, sometimes just barely floated. The cost reduction for a slackwater system was sometimes not great, however, as taller, more elaborate dams often had to be built downstream and a system of river locks constructed upstream, to compensate for greater water-level differences between the canal and the river.

As the immense Ohio & Erie project neared completion in 1832, engineers had problems keeping eager canal captains off the new waterway until they were ready to open it for traffic. Navigating the first boat on a new canal segment was a coveted prize. Typical is the story recounted by the Ross County Historical Society about how one entrepreneur suddenly turned canal captain was literally carried away with his zeal. James Emmitt, the wealthiest man in Waverly and a local political power, personally funded a party to welcome the water into the town. Water welcoming had been a major excuse for celebration in a number of communities on the path of the watered part of the canal as it crept south. Emmitt was so excited by the canal's imminent completion into his town that he forgot his politics and fed everyone—Whigs, Democrats, and nonpartisans alike.

The segment between Chillicothe and Waverly had been built through a gravelly loam, and the water took its time coming down as some of it soaked into the porous canal bed. This delayed the festive meal several hours, during which celebratory drinking continued. When the water finally arrived, with two boats right behind, Emmitt bought one of them on the spot for $600. He immediately loaded the *Thomas Worthington* with friends and cast off—vowing to be the first boat to reach Portsmouth, the canal's southern terminus on the Ohio River.

But Emmitt didn't quite make it; he ran out of water about two miles short of his goal. A legend insists that Emmitt's newly acquired boat, responding to his urging, at times got ahead of the water. More likely, the water continued to soak into the dry, porous canal bed faster than the flow replenished it, leaving Emmitt's boat high and dry. His adventure resulted in public censure by the canal engineers for using the waterway before it was officially opened; likely Emmitt would feel that his immortality in legend made it all worthwhile.[14]

More than half of the 813 miles of canals that ran through Ohio at the height of its canal era consisted of the two main trunks, the 309 miles of the Ohio & Erie Canal and another 250 miles of the Miami & Erie. The remainder was made up of no less than twenty-nine considerably shorter canals that included sidecuts, branch canals, and feeders. And then there was the tiny, three-mile Milan Canal southeast of Sandusky, which permitted Lake Erie schooners to sail up the Huron River through the canal's two locks, into the Milan Basin. By 1847, Milan was second only to the Russian port of Odessa in shipping wheat.

Economic impacts like this had been making news for years as new canals were opened. Until 1827, when Alfred Kelley's contractors finished the thirty-nine-mile segment of the Ohio & Erie from the Akron Summit down to Lake Erie, Cleveland merchants had been selling about a thousand barrels of flour a year to Buffalo traders. But in 1828, the first full year that portion of the Ohio Canal was open, they sold 250,000 barrels.

Similar statistics can be found all over the state, documenting the effects of the new waterways as each one came to life.

The results accomplished by Ohio's canal engineers—these self-educated visionaries, planners, builders, innovators—exceeded even the ambitious objectives of the state's politicians. By midcentury, the wilderness State of Ohio had become the third most populous in the union. Between 1826 and 1858 the price of wheat paid to Ohio farmers rose from fifty cents a bushel to over a dollar, corn went from twenty-five cents to seventy cents during the same period, while coffee, salt, sugar, and other imported staples dropped in price. Property values in the thirty-seven canal counties increased fourteen times.

Legends grew up around some of the colorful figures responsible for this remarkable growth. Edward Hall Gill, an Irish immigrant who was one of the designers of the Sandy & Beaver Canal and became its first chief engineer, was one of these. The Sandy & Beaver ran east to the Ohio River from its junction with the Ohio & Erie at Bolivar. It was originally intended as a competitor to the Pennsylvania & Ohio, which was being built less than fifty miles to the north. Gill's 1834 engineering plan included the construction of the Sandy & Beaver's daring 1,060-yard Big Tunnel and 600-yard Little Tunnel, to shorten the route by seventeen miles. But the privately financed canal took almost twenty years to complete because of continuing cash-flow problems during the depression of the 1830s.

Gill lost patience in 1837 and left when work was halted and 90 percent of his workers were laid off. During his three-year watch, however, he established his reputation as a stern boss with an unswerving passion for excellence. His specifications were long, detailed, and demanding. The locks he built were constructed like monuments. Their massive stone blocks were sawed and notched so that the staircase risers on both sides of the gates were of precisely even heights. Steps near the top were decorated with sculptured ends. Contractors were told that work was to be done at their risk, and they were warned that they would not be paid until their jobs were completed and approved. Gill was absolutely intolerant of "ardent spirits" (in an age when a jigger of whiskey a day was customarily part of a canal laborer's pay), and he made it known that an intoxicated laborer would be summarily fired. His prohibition was more often honored in the breach, however, since there were no fewer than twelve saloons in Dungannon, a town fortuitously located between the two tunnels—both of which would remain under construction for more than a decade.

Typical of Gill's resourcefulness and innovation, when a twenty-inch vein of high-grade bituminous coal was discovered during excavation of the Little Tunnel, he had it mined and conveyed to steam engines he brought in to haul away rock spoil from the Big Tunnel—pressing his eighty-foot vertical air vents into service as mine shafts. But not all the rock was discarded. Limestone was separated and burned in a kiln to convert it into quick lime mortar for tuck-pointing and waterproofing his locks.

For all his authoritarian sternness, Gill is said to have had a tender side. People tell how he cherished his only daughter, Gretchen—especially after his wife's death and burial at sea during their voyage from Europe during the family's immigration to the United States. According to the legend, when little Gretchen died of malaria during construction of a lock above Sprucevale, her father had a crypt built into the wall of the lock, and had her entombed there for years. When Gill decided to return to Ireland, however, he had her body removed from the crypt and took it with him for burial in the town of her birth. But then, in a final tragedy, Gill's ship encountered a storm on his return voyage, and all aboard were lost.

Author Max Gard put it thus: "E. H. Gill and little Gretchen joined their wife and mother in the waters of the Atlantic. Little Gretchen's monument is the lock near Sprucevale where she was entombed. Everyone who knows of this lock knows it as 'Gretchen's Lock.' The pilgrims who wish to make the trip . . . will be rewarded with a view of the open crypt where Gretchen slept for a while."[15]

Subsequent research by historian T. Gibson Hobbs Jr. of Lynchburg, however, revealed that Gill died in Virginia after serving as superintendent of several railroads in that state. He had, in fact, arrived in the United States as an unmarried teenager and later married a woman from Pennsylvania, but the Gills had no children.[16] Doing such crass, heartless violence to endearing, traditional romanticism almost calls for an apology. That Gretchen never lived seems somehow sadder than the legend of her death. But such is the stuff of which canal lore is made.

It would be unforgivable to leave this chronicle of the truly remarkable achievements of Ohio's intrepid canal builders on such a note. A more appropriate conclusion might be an account of the festivities that surrounded the long-delayed opening of Edward Gill's Big Tunnel. And this story, the reader is assured, is said to be altogether true. The event comes off as a kind of metaphor for the history of the Sandy & Beaver and, indeed, for much of Ohio's canal era.

The celebration was scheduled for New Year's Day 1848, two years after completion of the Little Tunnel and nearly eight years after the Sandy

& Beaver's rival, the Pennsylvania & Ohio Canal, was finished and operating. Gill, of course, had long since left the scene. Crowds lined both sides of the waterway in front of the yawning tunnel entrance. Raising their voices and their bottles in celebratory toasts and firing guns into the air (gunpowder and alcohol being the twin lubricants for all signal events during canal construction), they saluted those lucky enough to be aboard the colorfully decorated, overloaded boat as it began moving toward the tunnel entrance.

Since the tunnel had been blasted through three thousand feet of solid rock eighty feet below the crest of the ridge that had blocked its path, it had been impossible to build a towpath inside. So the mules rode on board, together with all of the dignitaries that could be mustered in the surrounding countryside, scores of other passengers who insisted on being aboard this first boat poled through the Big Tunnel, and a brass band that played so loudly that it was difficult to hear the gunfire.

The vessel was propelled by another Gill invention, a tow rope more than half a mile long, which wound onto a winch at the far end of the tunnel. The winch was turned by a single mule on a treadmill, but Gill's gear gave the animal a mechanical advantage. As the boat disappeared into the darkness, its lanterns began lighting the walls of the man-made cave. The band could be heard by the crowds at both ends of the tunnel as the boat crept along.

Suddenly, about halfway through, the heavily laden boat came to a scudding halt. Its keel had run aground. It had probably encountered a spot where the uneven depth of the stone floor was less than the prescribed four-foot minimum—for the tunnel had not been completed under the command of perfectionist Edward Gill. Undaunted, the band played on, wiping out any attempt at communication as the blare of the instruments reflected off the stone walls, echoing throughout the length of the tunnel. Locals insist that it was the sound that caused the huge rock to crash down from the tunnel ceiling, blocking any further progress of the boat.

One of the boat's crew, as it happened, was scheduled to be married that afternoon, but he had not been willing to miss this historic event. He had only one option. Vaulting over the side of the boat, he waded, nearly chest deep at times, through the remainder of the tunnel, astonishing the waiting crowd at the far end, who had expected a boat to emerge. The marriage took place later that day.

It was two more years before a canal boat came out of the far end of the Big Tunnel, making the canal fully operational at last in 1850. But the life of the Sandy & Beaver ended abruptly only two years later when its Cold Run Reservoir collapsed, stranding a number of boats on the summit level. Those boats never moved again because the Cold Run Reservoir would never be rebuilt. For a new interstate transportation network was creeping into Ohio—one offering speeds ten times as fast as well as one that didn't freeze up in winter. The steel rails of American railroads were beginning to cobweb the nation.

NOTES

1. George W. Knepper, *Ohio and Its People* (Kent: Kent State Univ. Press, 1989), 149.

2. Ibid.

3. Jack Gieck, *A Photo Album of Ohio's Canal Era, 1825–1913* (Kent: Kent State Univ. Press, 1988), xiv.

4. Knepper, *Ohio and Its People,* 149.

5. Frank W. Trevorrow, *Ohio's Canals* (Oberlin: Privately printed, 1973), 23.

6. Gieck, *A Photo Album of Ohio's Canal Era,* 5.

7. Ibid., 13.

8. George W. Knepper, *Akron, City at the Summit* (1981; rpt., Akron: Summit County Historical Society, 1994), 30.

9. The original forty-four locks were later reduced to forty-two when a new river lock was constructed upstream on the Cuyahoga River.

10. William Henry Perrin, *History of Summit County* (Chicago: Baskin & Battey, 1881), 48. The diameter of this wheel is specified as thirty-six feet in Karl H. Grismer's *Akron and Summit County* (Akron: Summit County Historical Society, 1952). In either case, a "head and fall of 38 feet" (greater than the diameter of the overshot wheel) is not physically possible.

11. The size of the effluent opening in a dam near the top of the hill suggests that his pipe may have been a four-foot-diameter (bell and spigot) ceramic sewer pipe.

12. Perrin, *History of Summit County,* 48.

13. A ton of water, 2,000 lb., falling 5,280 ft. would generate 10,560,000 ft. lbs. of work (2,000 x 5,280), which is equivalent to 13,569 Btu. A good grade of bituminous coal yields 15,000 Btu per pound.

14. See Gieck, *A Photo Album of Ohio's Canal Era.*

15. See Max Gard and William Vodrey Jr., *The Sandy and Beaver Canal* (East Liverpool: East Liverpool Historical Society, 1952).

16. T. Gibson Hobbs Jr., private correspondence with the author, 1986.

Chapter 3

Mucking Through

Common Labor on the Ohio & Erie Canal

GEORGE KNEPPER

The State of Ohio was still young and poor when it embarked on construction of a massive canal system connecting Lake Erie with the Ohio River. We honor those who conceived that system, planned it, found funds to finance it, and managed its construction. We know their names.

The forgotten man in canal history is the common laborer, the largely unskilled worker who cleared trees, grubbed brush, muscled rocks, and, above all, dug the great ditches. His tools were not ledger books and legal documents; they were pick, shovel, scoop, axe, and wheelbarrow. His office was a pit or a mucky ditch.

Why has so little been written about this essential contributor to canal construction? The reasons are obvious. Common laborers were without personal distinction. They worked in crews, performing repetitive, uninspiring work, their individual contribution concealed in the mass. A shovelful of dirt was just a shovel full of dirt. The common laborer might be a local farmer, a member of his family, or his hired hand. As work progressed, however, the common laborer on the Ohio & Erie Canal was usually an unlettered Irish immigrant.

A lack of documentation limits his story. Illiterate workers could not keep diaries or journals. If someone wrote letters for them, they have been lost. Newspapers seldom, if ever, treated them as individuals, rather lumped them together under the rubric of canal worker or, more simply, "Irish." These diggers may have lacked individual distinction, but their collective role in building the state's canal system was monumental. In

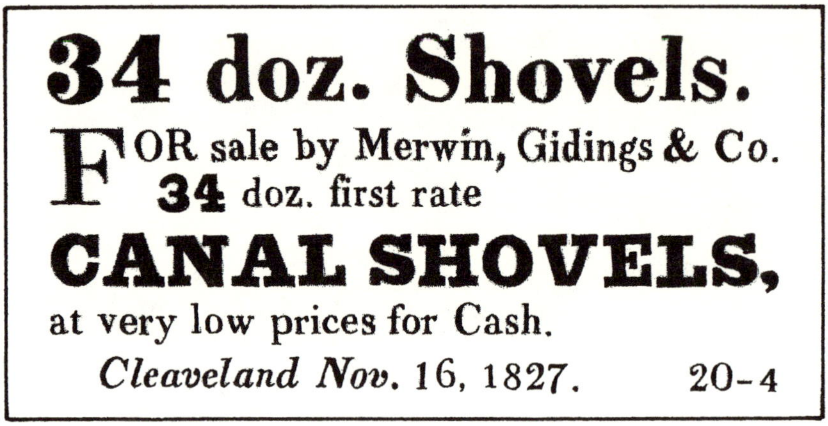

Canal shovels were being advertised in the *Cleveland Herald* after the Cleveland to Akron section of the canal opened (National Park Service).

telling their story, a first step is to identify how they fit in the chain of command: Who above them determined their destiny?

America's first canals were built by private enterprise. From 1817 to 1825, however, the State of New York demonstrated how a public entity could manage the intricacies of canal construction by building the Erie Canal across more than 350 miles of sparsely populated central and western New York. No private company of that era could undertake such an extensive and risky venture, so the state assumed the burden, planning the route, setting construction goals, and finding funds to finance it.

Ohio, still largely a wilderness in the early 1820s, followed New York's lead, making canal construction a state responsibility and profiting from the experience of her eastern neighbor. In 1822, the Ohio General Assembly created the Ohio Board of Canal Commissioners, whose seven members were all men of distinction. The commission authorized feasibility studies, selected routes later confirmed by the state legislature, and served as the prime contractor. In that guise, the commissioners hired surveyors and engineers to lay out routes, divide them into manageable-sized lots, write specifications and cost estimates for each job lot, put the jobs out for bids, award contracts, provide oversight for quality performance on fulfilling each contract, and pay the contractors for approved work.

Two of the commissioners, Alfred Kelley and Micajah T. Williams, spent months along the Erie Canal learning the intricacies of canal building. Kelley supervised work on the northern two-thirds of the Ohio & Erie, and Williams was responsible for the southern third. More than others, they assured the quality that marked the 309-mile canal connecting Portsmouth on the Ohio with Cleveland on Lake Erie.[1]

The General Assembly also appointed a three-man Canal Fund Commission to sell state-backed canal bonds in eastern money markets. Money from bond sales was deposited in Ohio banks—for the Ohio & Erie, the banks chosen were the Bank of the Western Reserve at Warren and the Bank of Lancaster in the Fairfield County town of that name. Worker's wages ultimately were paid from accounts in these banks.[2]

The contractor was the key player in canal construction. Anyone could try his hand at winning a contract, but competition was fierce, especially in the early years. Scores of experienced contractors, fresh from work on the Erie Canal, sought to win contracts on the Ohio & Erie. The large pool of bidders allowed commissioners to contract for work below cost estimates. Some would-be contractors submitted character references, but experience proved these unreliable. Jobs demanding skilled labor—building locks, aqueducts, sluices, and the like—went to experienced men, but inexperienced farmers living along and near the canal route could win contracts for unskilled jobs as small as preparing one half-mile of the ditch.[3]

Contractors were true risk capitalists. They hired workers and provided them with room, board, and tools. Few had deep pockets. Typically, they worked on the economic edge and could be pressed into debt by disease, bad weather, and bad breaks. Most were honest businessmen, but honest men might default when subject to costly, unanticipated blows.

Hard-pressed contractors occasionally abandoned their responsibilities, leaving their workers unpaid. In 1827, numerous contractors on Portage Summit abandoned their work without paying laborers, creating morale problems that discouraged local residents from signing on as canal labor. The canal commission finished the work using state crews. It is little wonder that work was abandoned on the Portage Summit, for construction problems in that area were uncommonly difficult to overcome and many contractors had been too optimistic in submitting their bids. Canal historian Harry N. Scheiber estimated that from 12 to 15 percent of Ohio's canal contracts were abandoned.[4]

A good contractor, considerate of his crew and skilled in handling their capriciousness, was a father figure of sorts. If he were Irish like his crew, he knew to select men from a common Irish background so as to minimize intramural fighting over matters of honor and turf. Contractors also reduced friction by working alongside their men. Peter Way, perhaps the most analytical of writers on the subject, states that Irish workers regarded their contractors as "padrones" who looked after their interests and represented them to management.[5]

Men from many different backgrounds worked on the Ohio & Erie. Resident farmers were well represented, especially in the early stages of construction, but the dominant figure in the pits and ditches was the Irish immigrant. Others, with the exception of immigrant Germans, were too few to attract much attention. Skilled jobs were dominated by local craftsmen and immigrant English, Scots, and Welsh. A newcomer to the Akron region in 1838 found a job on the Pennsylvania & Ohio Canal, then under construction. He liked little about the experience except the money. In a letter to his Massachusetts home, he wrote, "There is Dutch [Germans] a plenty, Irish, Scotch, Welch, English, French, Yankees, and plenty of rattlesnakes." People only stayed around, he wrote, "for the sake of work on the canal." Although he wrote the letter several years after the Ohio & Erie was completed, the same variety of mankind was attracted to canal work during its construction.[6]

Mention common labor on the canals, and the Irish immigrant comes to mind. Seldom does one think of farmers doing the scut work of canal building, although they did so by the hundreds. It was reasonable for a farmer whose lands lay astride or near the canal right-of-way to contract for a half-mile or more of ditching. He had a crew ready at hand—his sons, hired hands, and neighbors. By living at home and eating his own food, he reduced costs and minimized the disease and disorder associated with immigrant encampments.

Farmers knew all about clearing trees and brush, grubbing out stumps, plowing, and digging. For the farmer, canal work was an extension of farmwork, with one great advantage: it paid cash. This was a boon to farmers in cash-starved pioneer Ohio. In his normal downtime, the farmer could earn enough to pay his taxes and other obligations requiring cash.

Work on the Ohio & Erie commenced in July 1825, with most of the effort concentrated in the thirty-eight-mile stretch between Portage Summit (now part of Akron) and Cleveland. Lock 1 at Portage Summit was 395 feet higher than the Cuyahoga's mouth at Cleveland. Forty-four locks were required to allow boats to negotiate this difference in elevation. Fifteen of these formed a staircase in the first mile and a half north of Lock 1, calling for much skilled labor—carpenters, stone masons, iron workers, and the like—who sometimes worked alongside, but did not fraternize with, the Irish work gangs.

By late November about two thousand workers, many of them recently employed on the Erie Canal, were thought to be working in the Akron-Cleveland stretch. A Cleveland newspaper welcomed the "daily arrival of . . . hardy sons of Erin" as they joined local farmers in getting work underway. Some five hundred Irish were reported to be living in Cleveland's Flats early in 1826.[7]

The "sons of Erin" had plenty to do along the Cuyahoga. In addition to the usual problems attending ditching, engineers created new challenges for both skilled and unskilled labor. The Cuyahoga River was "turned out of its course, and a new channel . . . formed, in four different places, to make room for, and give security to the canal." In this stretch, "protection walls" were required to keep the river from eroding canal banks. We are not told how, or of what material, they were made, but one can be fairly certain that their construction required scores of common laborers.[8]

While assuring a channel north of Lock 1 created special problems, a different set of concerns faced workers digging the ditch south of Lock 1. To create a satisfactory summit level for the canal, the water level of Summit Lake, a natural spring-fed body just south of Lock 1, was reduced by nine feet, exposing large stretches of muck that had to be removed prior to digging the channel. Intense effort was required to stabilize banks and towpath, and one can be sure this work fell to the Irish diggers. Near the south end of the reduced lake, stabilization was impossible, so carpenters constructed a floating wooden towpath, anchored to the lake bottom, along which horses and mules towed boats across open water. Much of this work was performed in the unusually wet winter and spring of 1827–28, in what canal commission reports referred to as the section "extending through the swamps from Summit Lake to the Tuscarawas." The deluge, said the report, had an effect that was "peculiarly embarrassing and greatly retarded progress of the work." Labor in such conditions, as we shall note, was central to the brief and troubled lives of many a canal worker.[9]

Excess moisture also plagued construction on the southern reaches of the Ohio & Erie between Chillicothe and the Ohio River. Floods and high water were perennial problems on this stretch, and the fractious Ohio River washed out every attempt to maintain a lock connecting the canal directly to the river. Disease was also prevalent along this stretch, and an 1832 cholera epidemic seriously diminished worker ranks and frightened off potential replacements.[10]

Major construction efforts were also involved in building reservoirs holding reserve water supplies designed to keep the canal full on its two highest points—Portage Summit and Licking Summit. Swamps surrounding small natural lakes were enclosed by large earthen dikes and then flooded from adjoining water supplies. At Portage Summit, water was diverted through a long race from the Tuscarawas River, creating East and West Reservoirs, parts of the modern Portage Lakes just south of Akron. Impounded waters south of Newark became known as Buckeye Lake, which developed into a resort and playground region of enduring value. The heavy work of earth moving and channeling was performed in large part by unskilled diggers.[11]

Several canal sections were dug by people other than the Irish. In Tuscarawas County, men and women of the utopian community of Zoar contracted to dig the canal through their property. Men dug, and women hauled the dirt away in tubs. In this communal setting, arrangements for cooking, child care, and other necessities were already in place. Money earned from canal labor allowed Zoarites to pay off the mortgage on their land. Special crews were also used to dig the Columbus feeder, nearly twelve miles long, connecting the capital city with the Ohio & Erie mainline. Prisoners from the Ohio Penitentiary in Columbus had sentences commuted for volunteering to do the hard work of canal digging. Deputies guarded the men at their work stations.[12]

The Irish canal digger has been stereotyped almost to the point of caricature. Though many Irish shared certain predispositions and attitudes, there was more diversity among them than is commonly appreciated. Many who worked on the Ohio & Erie had worked for a number of years in America before coming to Ohio. The more provident among them had earned enough money to establish families and carry on at least a modicum of normal family life in spite of the precarious conditions in which they lived. Prudent workers were valued for the stability they brought to labor gangs dominated by footloose young men, yet many of these still were moved by passion and drink and faced the same demons that captured their unmarried brethren. Common labor was recruited by the contractor. It was wise to hire Irish from a common Old World background, men originally from the same county, for emotional ties to one's home turf remained strong, and Irish clannishness persisted in America.

Terms of employment were simple. In 1825–26, the contractor furnished room, board, tools, a wage of thirty cents per day, and a daily jigger of whiskey. Some furnished blankets, and, when work conditions were trying or the crews had to meet strict deadlines, an additional whiskey ration might be added. As work progressed on the Ohio & Erie, death from accidents or disease and competition from other canal projects, the National Road extension through Ohio, and the lure of available farmwork led to worker shortages. Wages and whiskey rations rose in response as contractors tried to hold on to their workforce.

For the construction crews, housing and food and room and board were an enterprise in their own right. For unmarried men, room was a bunk in a dormitory that provided little more than shelter. These minimal structures could be knocked apart and transported to the next job.

Married men with wives and children lived in shanties. These, too, were primitive buildings without amenities, yet families continued to live in them long after construction had moved along. Shantytowns developed where significant concentrations of workers were required. They tended to be Irish ghettoes, shunned by neighbors as a blight on the land.

Cleveland had a shantytown along the Flats, located on each side of the Cuyahoga River. Akron's shantytown, nicknamed Dublin, was located near and along the lip of the Little Cuyahoga Valley on the developing city's near north side. This community endured long after canal construction passed on. At Roscoe (later Coshocton), a semipermanent shantytown appears to have been somewhat more integrated into the community than was true elsewhere.[13]

Shanties were crude, but they differed little from much of the nearby housing. Poverty was endemic in the less settled parts of Ohio in the 1820s and 1830s. The standard of living improved after the Ohio & Erie opened isolated portions of the state to new markets. Improved economic conditions even reached the shantytowns, allowing the prudent and fortunate families living there to participate in the general trend of upward economic mobility.

Shanties were designed for the short haul. They were the temporary housing of their day, but temporary housing has a way of becoming permanent, as persons remembering the "temporary" housing of the World War II era can attest. Transients and the homeless often occupied shanties abandoned by canallers as work moved along. A local Akron area tradition maintains that abandoned worker shanties at New Portage (later Barberton) were occupied briefly by Mormons migrating from their Kirtland homes to new locations in the West.[14]

One thinks the rough life of the canal worker was only for men; and so it was in large part. Women, however, performed much of the support work, as hired hands and sole proprietors. Contractors hired workers' wives and neighborhood women as cooks, laundresses, and clothing menders. Wages paid for these services were minimal, well below those paid the men building the great ditch. For married women, however, the wages were a welcome supplement to family income and helped families climb up from the lowest levels of the economic ladder. Contractors often employed their own wives and daughters.[15]

Entrepreneurial women set themselves up in business operating boardinghouses where men, willing to pay, could get better fare than that provided in their employment agreement. Laundry, mending, and similar services were also available for a fee. Women who cared more for their income than for their reputation operated grog shops—shanties set up as taverns. Then there is the question of prostitution. Did it exist in an organized way while the canal was still under construction? Records are largely silent on this point, but if history is any guide, it existed whether organized or not. Whenever large bodies of men gathered with money in pocket, or in the offing, enterprising women were certain to follow. Once the canals were carrying traffic, prostitutes could be found at certain wayside taverns and "boardinghouses," according to local tradition.

The common laborer's work routine varied little insofar as it involved ditch digging. With pick, shovel, and scoop, he slogged away, filling endless wheelbarrows with dirt and muck. Moving loaded barrows out of deep ditches was tricky, as the boards up which they were pushed often rose at a steep angle. To minimize slippage on treacherous boards, workers attached iron creepers to their shoes, but injuries persisted nonetheless.[16]

Workers did the final grading in the ditch and along the berms with horse- or oxen-drawn scoops and scrapers. These tools did not work well in muck, so hand labor put on the finished touches. Dirt and muck removed from the ditch were used to build up the berms and the towpath that always, with few exceptions, ran along the river side of the canal.[17]

A final step in the ditching process was puddling the bottom and sides with dense clay to prevent leakage. Clay was pressed into the dirt with long rods, a monotonous and tiring job done poorly unless workers were watched. Leaks could prove devastating if left unattended, and poor workmanship could not be tolerated. Even muskrat holes in the embankments were promptly filled by boys paid a pittance for their efforts.

Canal construction proceeded as weather permitted. Limited work was done in winter, but the ditching season ran from spring thaw to winter freeze. A normal workday was twelve to fifteen hours, sunrise to sunset. Brief rest stops featured the water boy with his pail and dipper or the jigger boss with his whiskey measure. Work proceeded daily except Sunday and occasionally Saturday. Workers were paid only for days worked. When a job shut down because of disease, accident, or management dictate, it was the workers' tough luck.

Before a contractor was paid for finished work, the job had to be inspected and approved by an engineer or, as in a limited number of cases, by a commissioner. Alfred Kelley inspected work on the Ohio & Erie. He was well qualified, having spent months along the Erie Canal learning all the intricacies of construction. He rode the line, checking construction as it progressed and evaluating the finished work. He is said to have carried a long iron rod with which he probed suspicious-looking spots on bank and berm to see if they were watertight. When the rod met little resistance, he ordered surface dirt removed, for a favorite trick of a shoddy contractor or poor workman was to fill a cavity with brush covered with a thin layer of dirt. Repairs were ordered on the spot. (For more on Kelley, see chapter 2.)

The lifestyle of the canal digger has been described through too narrow a focus. Rowdiness was common in the camps, but many kept apart from the ensuing melees. Cooler and more prudent men left the roughhousing to those who reveled in it. Clannishness was at the root of altercations involving men from different Irish backgrounds. Workers were quick to defend supposed slights to their honor or origins with fists, cudgels, or whatever came to hand, and they formed secret societies to better defend their turf and to coerce concessions from employers.

The belligerence that sprang from offended honor was fueled by alcohol. The "Irish curse" of excessive drink was endemic in barracks and shantytowns. When fired with alcohol, altercations among workers were apt to turn lethal, confirming outsiders' disdainful attitudes toward canallers. However, the Irish were certainly not alone in their abuse of alcohol. Whiskey was the great lubricator of pioneer life, used by women as well as men, children as well as adults, clergy as well as laity, black people as well as white people.

In pioneer Ohio, workmen expected a whiskey ration as a normal part of their employment. Not until the shocking personal and social costs of excessive drinking became apparent were the first fumbling steps taken to curb the ubiquitous use of alcohol. Some of the earliest efforts occurred in the Western Reserve close by the Ohio & Erie. Deacon David Hudson, founder of the town of that name, and Colonel Simon Perkins of Akron were among the first employers to withhold the whiskey ration, much to the disgust of their employees. Among canallers, Alfred Kelley is said to have tried urging temperance, but with little success. By the late 1820s, temperance societies began to appear in the Western Reserve, but they were removed from direct contact with canallers. In time, the Father Mathew Temperance Society, founded in England to address the "special" needs of the Irish, appeared in the United States, not soon enough, however, to help the Irish digging the Ohio & Erie.

Contractors contributed to their own problems by occasionally extending the whiskey ration for men working in unusually difficult circumstances. Those working in water got more pay and more whiskey, up to five or six jiggers of whiskey per day. (The measure of a "jigger" varies; it appears to have been a generic term rather than a precise measure, at least along the canals.) Peter Way relates the story of a former jigger boss to whom someone remarked that workers must have been drunk all the time. "You wouldn't expect them to work on the canal if they were sober, would you?" he replied.[18]

After hours and on free days, men continued to quench their thirst. Rotgut whiskey, some of it nearly lethal, was available for twenty to twenty-five cents a gallon. If one preferred convivial drinking, grog shops were ready at hand. Looking back from a modern perspective, it is remarkable that alcohol's toll was not even greater than it was.

Drink was devastating, but disease was the wholesale killer of canal workers. There are no reliable numbers, not even good estimates of the number who died while building the canals. Smallpox, typhoid fever, and cholera swept along the route, killing the canal digger and his neighbor indiscriminately. Epidemics took such a toll on the workforce that construction ceased, sometimes for months, before fear abated. In 1825, typhoid fever struck in the Cleveland basin; in 1827, it was again typhoid, this time near Massillon, and "black-tongue fever" near Akron; smallpox hit Roscoe in 1829; cholera wreaked havoc near Roscoe and farther south in 1832, and it reached Cleveland in 1834. Ague was the common name given a form or stage of malaria, with symptoms that included chills, fever, and sweating at reoccurring intervals.

> Of all the ills to which the new country was heir, ague was the most common. So inescapable was it that many people refused to regard it as a disease, but considered it like hard work, a concomitant of the frontier. "He ain't sick, he's got the ager," was the usual view. The symptoms were unmistakable: yawnings and stretching, a feeling of lassitude, blueness of the fingernails, then little cold sensations which increased until the victim's teeth chattered in his jaws and he "felt like a harp with a thousand strings." After an hour or so warmth returned, then came raging heat with racking head pains and aching back. The spell ended with copious sweating and a return to normality, then the world looked bright and happy again.[19]

R. Carlyle Buley provides descriptions of treatments for the canal-borne illnesses: "To cure the dumb ague, some thought it was necessary to bring on the shakes. 'Carry then your patient in the passage between the two cabins—strip off all his clothes that he may lie naked in the cold air and upon a bare sacking—and then and there pour over and upon him successive buckets of cold spring water, continue until he has a decided and pretty powerful smart chance of a shake.' Wet sheets wrapped

Ayer's Ague Cure.

A poisoned atmosphere, whether it originates in the vapors which arise from decaying vegetable matter on newly ploughed lands, from the noxious mists which overhang swamps and ponds, from the "deadly sewer-gas" from polluted wells, from open cesspools,—whatever tends to poison and make unhealthful the air we breathe, is all summed up in the one word Malaria. When this poison is lodged in the system, the effect is exhibited in diseases known as **FEVER and AGUE, CHILL FEVER, "MALARIA," DENGUE,** or **"BREAKBONE FEVER," INTERMITTENT, BILIOUS,** and **TYPHOID FEVERS,** diseases which ordinary modes of treatment fail to reach. The specific for every variety of Malarial disorder is AYER'S AGUE CURE. It cures with certainty, and no injurious effect whatever can arise from its use. AYER'S AGUE CURE is a vegetable product; it contains no mineral, nor anything in the least harmful to the system, and the ingredients are so nicely and exactly adjusted, proportionately, as to impart the full effect of each, making it the best compound it is possible to produce. Accompanying each bottle are printed directions, to which due regard must be given, thus rendering the AGUE CURE a protection for travelers and residents in Malarial districts.

☞ AYER'S AGUE CURE is sold by all Druggists and Dealers in Medicine.

"To cure the dumb ague, some thought it was necessary to bring on the shakes" (*Ayer's American Almanac*, 1895).

around the sufferer were also used to drive out the fever. If pneumonia resulted, the cure was bleeding, tartar emetic, and calomel."[20]

The epidemics were noteworthy for their intensity, the effect magnified by constant close contact between tired, malnourished, dispirited canal workers and their families in the shantytowns. Most canalers were left to their own resources when illness struck. Doctors (nearly anyone claiming some medical training) were scarce in the interior of Ohio, and their services were preempted by locals who knew them. Failing to get the service of a doctor might not have been all that bad, for in their primitive appreciation of the causes and cures of illness, pioneer physicians sometimes did more harm than good. Large doses of calomel, ipecac, and mercury could kill a healthy man, let alone one prostrate with fever. It was said the pioneer doctor killed quick but healed slow. Most were well-intentioned men. They, and the women who assisted them, were often heroic in efforts to stem epidemics, but, heroic or not, few doctors appear to have had much direct contact with the ills of the canaller.[21]

There were exceptions. Dr. Samuel Lee treated canal workers near Roscoe for the assorted cuts, bruises, and splinters common to their lot. He prescribed whiskey for malaria, countering some of the nasty stuff patients swallowed. Not long after work was completed on the Ohio & Erie, quinine became available for treating malaria, greatly easing the burden posed by this all but ubiquitous disease.[22]

How many workers died along the canal? There are no statistics, and, furthermore, during epidemics canal workers, whether local men or Irish, suffered the same anonymous burials. Canal historians have singled out the Irish when dealing with death, for they dominated the roughest jobs, worked in the worst conditions, lived the least healthy lifestyles, and had the fewest resources to combat trouble. Guesses as to their mortality run the gamut from "a dead Irishman for every yard of canal constructed in northwest Ohio," an estimate that seems excessive even though work in the Great Black Swamp in that region was especially lethal, to "one Irish for every three miles of canal bed."[23]

Canalside cemeteries and isolated graves along the ditch were common. During the 1832 cholera epidemic near Roscoe, "funeral barges, draped in black, gathered in the dead in the morning and deposited them at canal side cemeteries where grave diggers paid off punishment by handling the corpses." Akron's "Dublin" was adjacent to a cemetery discovered in the mid-nineteenth century while excavations were being made for a railroad. This forgotten plot most likely contained Irish graves.[24]

Death and disease reduced the worker pool, and the fear they inspired kept men away from affected regions, contributing to labor shortages and elevating wages. Competition from other construction projects and the chance to secure employment away from the canal also had an effect on wages. Diggers earning $8 per month in 1825–26 were paid $16 in 1829 and $18 in 1832. Contractors sought workers through newspaper advertisements and by circulating flyers extolling job benefits. One wonders how such written appeals affected illiterate workers. Naturally, word of mouth was still the most effective recruiting device.[25]

Each month the canal commission paid contractors for finished work that had passed inspection. An engineer estimated the amount of work completed in each job. Payroll funds were drawn from the Bank of the Western Reserve and the Bank of Lancaster, which served as repositories for funds the commission had received from bond sales. Since state-chartered banks controlled the money supply during the canal-building era, each bank issued its own paper notes under guidelines set forth in its charter. Some state banks were poorly managed or engaged in scams. Both of the banks relied on by commissioners for holding deposits scheduled for the Ohio & Erie were well-run businesses whose notes passed at face value. Ohio's record, on the whole, was quite good when compared to some other states. When contractors got their money from the commission, they paid their workers in bank notes; therefore, if notes failed to pass at par value, the worker absorbed the ultimate loss.[26]

The amount due each worker depended on the number of days worked and the nature of the job. Extra pay, the kind later generations would call hardship pay, went to men doing the most dangerous or uncomfortable jobs—working in water, cutting through rock, and the like. Compared to other employment, canal work paid well. The catch was its uncertainty and inherent dangers.

Had the canal workforce been fully transient, moving en masse to new jobs as old ones were completed, conflict and other social frictions between worker and local citizen might have been minimized, but shantytowns often endured well beyond completion of particular jobs. Outsiders regarded them as roistering, alcoholic places to be avoided. In 1828, William Case of Cleveland noted that canal construction "brought a great many irregular-drinking and rowdy persons" to town. Not all of them left when their work was completed. Some stayed on, especially if they had families and had found ways to eke out a living. Thus, their cultural traits were carried on in emerging cities and towns along the canal route.[27]

Those who lingered in shantytowns occasionally committed serious crimes. Far more common, however, were the petty crimes—small-time thievery, chicken stealing, petty assault, and riotous behavior. It is unfair to point solely to the Irish, although they contributed at least their fair share of deviant behavior. The early nineteenth century was a far rougher time in which to live and work than later generations can imagine. Much that today would be criminal behavior was simply part of the crudity of existence in the 1820s and 1830s. The environment was rough, and it bred rough people. This truth about early pioneer days in Ohio tends to be overlooked, because the people who wrote the letters, journals, and diaries from which we learn of the times separated themselves as much as possible from unruly illiterates. Newspapers did a better job of exposing the harsh realities, but few towns had newspapers in the first few decades of the nineteenth century.

P. P. Cherry, in *The Western Reserve and Early Ohio* recounts this story:

> While the canal was building Ambrose King was constable and with a warrant went to arrest an Irish laborer for some offense. He found him in an unfinished lock-pit above Old Portage in company with a gang of other working men, who, . . . refused to permit the arrest, surrounded him, threatening his life. Armed with spades and cudgels they cornered him in the lock. With only a horse pistol for defense, he warned them to desist; but, instead they made a charge, when he fired, the ball striking one of them on his rib, glancing off without inflicting a serious wound. Being very active, he sprang up the steep bank and ran for his life. He was followed, overtaken, knocked down and beaten with clubs until supposed to be dead. His friends hearing of the affray sent a wagon for him, put him in it and started for Akron followed by the workmen. . . . Meeting a physician they halted while an examination was made and King pronounced yet alive.
>
> "Then," shouted an excited Irishman standing by, "we will kill him yet," striking a blow at his head with a long club but the horses were frightened and started off and the blow missed its mark. Then the furious laborer turned on a German standing by and with a sweeping blow of his club struck him on the head, from which he fell as if shot. . . . This aroused indignation and vengeance to its highest pitch. Next the militia company was called out, armed with rifles and ammunition; a bottle of whiskey was passed around and a battle and bloodshed was imminent. Just then a rider came dashing up, his horse covered with dust and foam. He was a contractor and

> had just heard of the difficulty and asked for time to hold a consultation with his employees hoping to induce a surrender without resistance. He rode down and . . . explained what folly it would be to resist, that every man would be shot down if necessary, to make the arrest. They laid down their weapons, surrendered and were marched to Middlebury for safe keeping, where the militia stood guard till the trial and conviction of their leader. As King recovered the penalty was not severe and peace was again restored.[28]

It is easy to overlook the Irish families that minded their own business and worked to better their lots in life. One step in securing a better life was to leave canal labor, which was stigmatized as "the roughest of rough labor performed by the lowest of the low Irish immigrants and slaves."[29] As the completed sections of the Ohio & Erie brought more people and some prosperity to interior Ohio, job options appeared to canal diggers and their wives. Men might find farm labor, serve as draymen, work in the mills and nascent factories, and the like, while women served as domestics in "quality" homes. Initially, such jobs might pay less than canal labor, but they tended to be steadier, year-round, and performed in a healthier environment than canal labor.

One notable Irish contribution to the culture of early Ohio was the Roman Catholic Church. Catholics other than canallers may have initiated much of the early development, but it was certainly helped by large numbers of Irish canal workers and their families. The church was central to Irish life, and from an early time, they received its rites in their far-flung concentrations along the great ditch.

Like members of the dominant Protestant denominations, Catholics employed circuit riders, in their case, itinerant priests who traveled long distances on horseback to serve their faithful. In northeastern Ohio, the best known of these priests, Father John Henni, rode initially from Cincinnati to tend his flock. It appears that he later rode from Doylestown (Wayne County) where Saints Peter & Paul emerged in 1827 as the first parish in what was to become the Cleveland diocese. However, Cleveland's first parish, Saint Mary's in the Flats, traces its beginning to 1826 in response to that small town's growing Irish population. Akron's first parish, Saint Vincent de Paul, traces its origins to services in private homes before organization in 1843–44. At the time, most of Akron's Irish were, or had been, associated with the canal.[30]

The Irish canal workers and their counterparts in mines and mills were but the first outside group to enter Ohio with little more to offer other than their muscle and willingness to work. Those who came later—the "new" immigrants composed of European factory and mine workers, southern white Appalachians, southern black people—experienced some of the same rejection and some of the same learning experiences that the Irish canallers pioneered.

Initially set apart by their culture, these newcomers, too, made their way into fuller participation in American society. Even as those who built the canals opened Ohio to a larger world, so those who followed, through labor in mines and mills, opened it to a leadership role in a nascent global economy.

NOTES

1. A brief, convenient summary of the Ohio & Erie's organizational phases is in Jack Gieck, *A Photo Album of Ohio's Canal Era, 1825–1913* (Kent: Kent State Univ. Press, 1988), xiii–xix, 1–11.

2. George W. Dial, "The Construction of the Ohio Canals," *Ohio Archeological and Historical Society Publications* 13 (1904): 469.

3. For character references, see John Kilbourne, comp., *Public Documents Concerning the Ohio Canals, Which Are to Connect Lake Erie with the Ohio River, Comprising a Complete Official History of These Great Works of Internal Improvement, from Their Commencement Down to the Close of the Session of the Legislature of 1831–32* (Columbus: Isaac N. Whiting, 1832), 249.

4. Harry N. Scheiber, *Ohio Canal Era: A Case Study of Government and the Economy, 1820–1861* (Athens: Ohio Univ. Press, 1969), 48–49. See also Peter Way, *Common Labour: Workers and the Digging of North American Canals, 1780–1860* (Cambridge: Cambridge Univ. Press, 1993), 73.

5. Way, *Common Labour,* 68.

6. T. J. Partridge to Alvan A. Patridge [*sic*], Talmedge [*sic*], Nov. 4, 1838, vertical files, Summit County Historical Society, Akron.

7. Scheiber, *Ohio Canal Era,* 45. David D. Van Tassel and John J. Grabowski, eds., *The Encyclopedia of Cleveland History* (Bloomington: Indiana Univ. Press, 1987), xxiii.

8. Kilbourne, *Public Documents,* 237. Erosion is still a problem more than 170 years later along the Towpath Trail in Cuyahoga Valley National Park.

9. Gieck, *A Photo Album of Ohio's Canal Era,* 80. To reduce the lake level, some 230,000 cubic yards of muck was loaded on scows and removed. Doubtless the Irish did most of the labor. See also the *[Ohio] Board of Canal Commissioners Report,* Jan. 6, 1829, 323.

10. Scheiber, *Ohio Canal Era,* 52.

11. Gieck, *A Photo Album of Ohio's Canal Era,* 13–14.

12. For Zoar, see ibid., 6. For prison labor, see Kilbourne, *Public Documents*, 266–67, and Ernest Teagarden, "Builders of the Ohio Canal, 1825–1832," *Inland Seas* 19.2 (Summer 1963): 97.

13. Van Tassel and Grabowski, *Encyclopedia*, xxiii; Samuel Lane, *Fifty Years and Over of Akron and Summit County* (Akron: Beacon Job Department, 1892), 39; Lorle Porter, *Roscoe: Generation—Regeneration* (Coshocton: Roscoe Village Foundation, 1991), 44.

14. The tradition remains undocumented, but Mormons were familiar with New Portage and had traveled there. See Scott H. Faulring, ed., *An American, Prophet's Record: The Diaries and Journal of Joseph Smith* (Salt Lake City: Signature Books, 1989), 28.

15. Lorle Porter reports that the wife of a West Lafayette contractor, under contract to feed workers, used a barrel of flour a day baking bread in her outdoor beehive ovens (*Roscoe*, 44).

16. Teagarden, "Builders," 99.

17. T. H. Findley claims the horse scraper was not "invented" until its use in grading railroad right-of-ways ("One Canaller's Enthusiasm," *Towpaths* 11.2 [1973]: 16). Teagarden disagrees ("Builders," 99).

18. See Way, *Common Labour*, for fighting (11) and for jigger boss (183–84). For Kelley's efforts, see Teagarden, "Builders."

19. R. Carlyle Buley, *The Old Northwest: Pioneer Period, 1815–1840* (Indianapolis: Indiana Univ. Press, 1950), 244.

20. Ibid.

21. Ibid., 245.

22. Porter, *Roscoe*, 25.

23. For the high estimate, see Findley, "One Canaller's Enthusiasm." For the low estimate, see William D. Ellis, "How Came the Irish to Dig the Canals?" *Towpaths* 3 (1965): 1.

24. Porter, *Roscoe*, 46; Lane, *Fifty Years*, 233.

25. Teagarden, "Builders," 98.

26. Dial, "Construction," 469. Notes paid workers on the Miami & Erie Canal were discounted 2.5 percent. Some of the larger contractors paid workers with scrip, vouchers redeemable at the contractors' stores. See Way, *Common Labour*, 119.

27. Van Tassel and Grabowski, *Encyclopedia*, xxiii.

28. P. P. Cherry, *The Western Reserve and Early Ohio* (Akron: R. L. Fouse, 1921), 289–91.

29. Way, *Common Labour*, 10.

30. Van Tassel and Grabowski, *Encyclopedia*, 860. See also "String of Pearls" (Cleveland: Catholic Diocese of Cleveland, 1997), and Lane, *Fifty Years*, 207.

Chapter 4

Natural History, Natural Resources, and the Ohio & Erie Canal

JOSEPH T. HANNIBAL

The main purpose of building the Ohio & Erie Canal was to create a route for local agricultural products to reach eastern markets. Indeed, an early 1900s history of Ohio agriculture notes that "the opening of the Ohio and Erie Canal is the most clearly defined epoch-making event in our agricultural history."[1] But the canal had an effect on many natural features and natural resources of the canal corridor as well.

The location of the Ohio & Erie Canal was chosen in great part because of a favorable natural setting, mostly a series of bottom lands along the valleys of the Cuyahoga, Tuscarawas, Licking, and Scioto Rivers. Advantageous geological conditions and abundant supplies of good quarry stone were additional factors that favored a north-south canal route along these rivers. Also, the well-known lakes and wetlands along the continental divide that separated the Cuyahoga and Tuscarawas Rivers at Akron promised to provide abundant supplies of water for the canal.[2] The Licking Summit, farther south on the Ohio & Erie Canal, was more problematic and required the construction of a reservoir, Buckeye Lake.

The canal, in turn, had a profound effect on its natural setting. The completed Ohio & Erie Canal provided a passageway for the movement of people; animals; plants; and forest, agricultural, and manufactured products through the state. The canal and the lakes formed or enlarged to water it provided new or expanded habitats for aquatic organisms. The canal acted as a water bridge between natural aquatic systems, and so it affected the movement of native and non-native organisms through the region.

The canal facilitated the exploitation of the natural resources of the surrounding areas. Wood from the forests along the canal was cut for lock foundations, timber, charcoal, and even matchsticks. Stone quarries were developed along the canal, and deposits of coal and iron were mined within the region. Geologists and others noted the potential for production of local geological resources, such as stone and coal. The production of dimension stone for the canal provided a jumpstart to the building stone industry in a region accustomed to building with wood. It also gave an early impetus to the cement industry and, later, the concrete industry.

The canal also facilitated the movement of natural resources and other material goods from outside the area via links to Lake Erie, New York's Erie Canal, and other bodies of water. Changes brought about directly or indirectly by the canals were so profound that the Ohio canals have come to symbolize the end of the Ohio frontier.[3]

This discussion of the geology, natural history, and natural resources of the Ohio & Erie Canal is based on personal observations, discussions with colleagues, and a review of literature from a number of disciplines. It also builds on the published work of early naturalists, surveyors, and geologists, including such notable nineteenth-century Ohio scientists as naturalist Jared Potter Kirtland (1793–1877) and geologist John Strong Newberry (1822–1892), and the more recent work of biologists Milton Trautman, Marvin Roberts, and Ronald Stuckey.[4] Some information is based on the work of observers and scientists from outside Ohio, including the great canal proponent DeWitt Clinton (1769–1828), who published on canal natural history, and W. B. Langbein, who published on the hydrogeology and environmental aspects of the Erie Canal in the 1970s.[5]

Bedrock and sediments are the foundation of the natural history of the canal. The bedrock of eastern Ohio consists of a series of shales, siltstones, and sandstones, with minor amounts of calcareous (limestone and related) rocks, which are of the Late Devonian (about 360 million years old) through Early Permian (about 280 million years old) periods. The rocks occur in layers named based on their lithology, typically the dominant or characteristic rock type, for instance "sandstone," and the name of a place, for instance, "Berea," yielding the name Berea Sandstone. The surface rock in eastern Ohio varies from one part of the region to another. In the north and west parts, the older rock layers generally are at the surface and at lower elevations, while to the south and southeast the younger rock layers are at the surface and are at higher elevations.

The geologists working for the first Ohio Geological Survey of 1837–38 and subsequent surveys made many notes and measurements related to the Ohio & Erie Canal. Their observations began shortly after the Ohio & Erie Canal was completed and can be found in reports published as early as 1838.[6] The canal is shown on 1838 and subsequent maps published by the Ohio Geological Survey.[7] The building of the canal, coincidentally, affected the survey itself. The first Ohio Geological Survey was discontinued after only a short time; the lack of state funding for continuation of this first survey has been blamed on the expenses of the canal, but there are other possible reasons for the discontinuation as well.[8] The survey resumed in the 1870s, and the Ohio & Erie Canal is prominently shown on geological maps published by the survey early in that decade. These include geologic maps of Cuyahoga, Summit, and Tuscarawas Counties.[9] These county geologic maps of the 1870s show streams, the canal, and railways, but no roads.

The routes of the canals took advantage of river valleys whenever possible. The rivers were both a water source and a drain for excess water. The river floodplains and the terraces along the rivers were relatively flat, with gentle gradients or slopes. Alluviums, river-bottom sediments of the floodplains and terraces, were mostly level, soft, and easy to dig, especially compared to bedrock. In northeastern Ohio, these alluvial deposits are

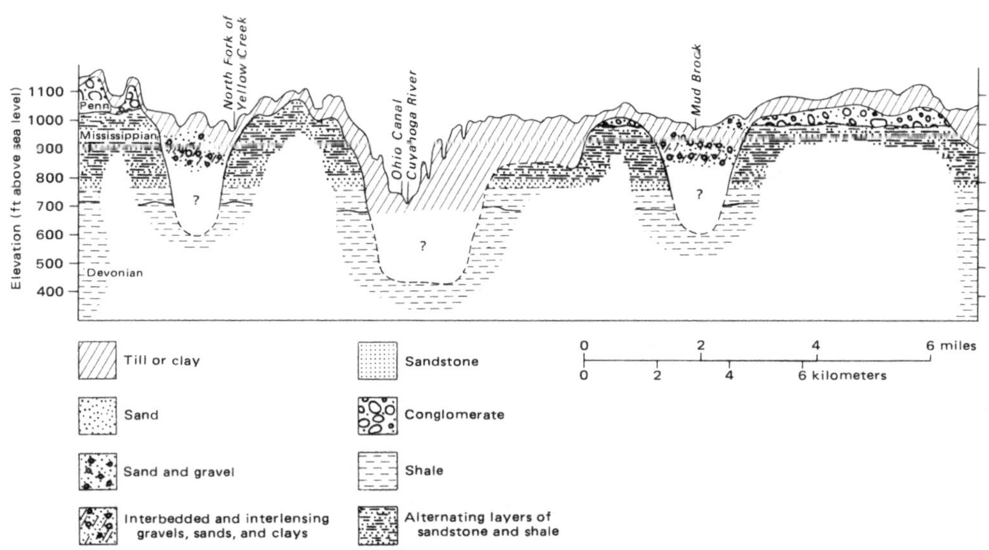

This cross-section shows the distribution of subsurface rocks and sediments across central Summit County. Three preglacial valleys, filled mostly with glacial sediment, are shown. The Ohio & Erie Canal passes through the preglacial valley in the middle of the cross-section (Originally from R. C. Smith and G. W. White, *The Ground Water Resources of Summit County, Ohio: Ohio Division of Water Bulletin*, 1953. Reproduced courtesy of the Ohio Division of Geological Survey).

composed of clay, silt, and sand, along with gravel and cobbles. Engineer Nathan Roberts reported that the proposed Cuyahoga and Tuscarawas route was "located on ground very favorable for a canal, being mostly along alluvial bottoms, or on plains, of a soil composed of sandy or gravelly loam, which can be, in most places, readily excavated by the plough and scraper."[10] Most of the stretch of the Ohio & Erie Canal between Cleveland and New Philadelphia was constructed in alluvial deposits of the Cuyahoga and Tuscarawas Rivers.

Many of the alluvial deposits in the river bottoms are superimposed, more or less, on old, buried prehistoric river valleys that have been filled by glacial sand and gravel. The great depth of some of these old valleys became apparent in the 1800s, as holes were bored for pilings and salt wells and as part of the exploration for coal, oil, and gas. John Newberry, for example, noted these ancient channels in the Tuscarawas Valley: "In the valley of the Tuscarawas an extensive series of borings has been made for coal, and these have revealed the fact that this stream is now running far above its former bed, and that it does not accurately follow the line of its ancient valley."[11] Salt wells drilled at Canal Dover reached the bottom of the buried valley at 175 feet below stream level. At Zoar, the bottom of the preglacial valley is about 120 feet below the level of the canal. Along much of the canal route in Cuyahoga County, the preglacial valley is about one hundred feet or so deep below the canal, and at places in Summit County the canal is estimated to be about three hundred feet above the bottom of a preglacial valley.[12] Newberry called the line of the Ohio & Erie Canal through the watershed divide at Akron an "old watergap," as it ran through the valley of a predecessor of the present Cuyahoga River.[13]

As the canal prisms were dug, the glacial sediments that had buried the old valleys occasionally yielded fossil remains of Ice Age animals. Cleveland geologist and historian Charles Whittlesey noted two instances of this. A portion of a trunk of a mastodon or mammoth was found at Massillon during excavation of the Ohio & Erie Canal, and during construction of the Sandy & Beaver Canal, mammoth and mastodon bones, a bear tooth, and a prehistoric horse tooth were found in the buried valley just beneath Sandy Creek.[14]

At most points between Akron and Canton, the canal cuts through glacial deposits. At a few places, however, the canal cuts through or very near to bedrock. The canal just nicks a Chagrin Shale outcrop at Boston in Cuyahoga Valley National Park. Outcrops of the shale can also be seen alongside the Cuyahoga River at Lock 29. Originally this lock was built with timbers only five feet above the shale bedrock; a new foundation of

Outcrops of Chagrin Shale bedrock can be seen alongside the Cuyahoga River near Lock 29 (photo by Rob Bobel).

concrete was added in 1905.[15] To the north, the Peninsula feeder at Lock 30 has a bedrock foundation. In Akron, the Meadville Formation (siltstone and shale) floors part of the bottom of the canal prism just north of Lock 12 along the stairstep Cascade Locks in Cascade Valley Metro Park. Newberry described a coal-bearing rock outcrop at Lock 17 in Tuscarawas County.[16] The most famous bedrock along the canal, however, was at Black Hand Gorge near Newark.

The relatively low amount of bedrock versus unconsolidated alluvial and glacial material along the canal route was very advantageous. Canal engineers knew from experience along the Erie Canal that cutting through large expanses of bedrock was expensive. They correctly expected that the Ohio & Erie would cost less to excavate. The prediction was that "the ground for making a canal across the state of Ohio is much more favorable than that over which the New York canal is now making. And although there would be more lockage on the Ohio canal than on the New York canal, yet it is believed that it can be made at less expense than an equal distance of the New York canal. There would not have to be that heavy expence [*sic*] incurred in excavating rock that is encountered on the New York canal."[17]

Due to upgrades in material and other factors, the cost of the Ohio & Erie Canal proved to be more than originally estimated, but it was less per mile than the Erie or any other canal in the United States.[18]

Being located in a river valley also meant that the canal would pass through relatively saturated sediment and thus would be expected to leak less than would be the case in drier areas. Ohio & Erie Canal documents put it this way: "A line of canal conducted along the bottom of a valley or on the lowest ground in its vicinity, expends but little water by leakage. The banks though porous being once saturated with water which find no lower level to which it can escape, permit no water to pass off."[19] The very saturated alluvial sediments on the floodplain (flats) of the Cuyahoga River at Cleveland, however, posed a problem for the canal engineers and delayed the planned opening of the outlet terminus of the canal into the Cuyahoga River.[20]

The position of the canal in river valleys had system-wide disadvantages as well. The biggest problem was being located on or just above floodplains, since these floodplains would—upon occasion—flood. Flooding was more common in topographically lower portions of the canal and where the canal was very close to or below the level of adjacent rivers. A second challenge was that aqueducts had to be constructed to carry the canals across tributaries flowing into the rivers along which the canal ran.

Flooding would periodically wash out sections of the canal. The *Cleaveland Herald* of July 12, 1834, for instance, reported "material injury" due to rain along the Ohio & Erie Canal, mainly because the canal aqueduct over Raccoon Creek in Newark had been washed away. The dams of the canal system were also frequently breached or otherwise damaged by floodwaters. They were not adequately engineered for large flows of water, and the wood dams were especially susceptible to flood damage. The greatest of all the canal floods, that of March 1913 (discussed in greater detail in chapter 12), caused great devastation and in essence was the end of the Ohio & Erie as a thoroughfare for goods.

The canal's location alongside rivers also created problems for the canal because rivers tend to meander, eroding banks on outside curves (cutbanks) and depositing sediment on inside curves (pointbars). A river, in its meandering, naturally eroded adjacent canal embankments.

Canals themselves are like artificial rivers. They were built with some curves, because they followed natural contours to some extent, but they were straighter than the rivers alongside which they followed. Thus, canals also would create cutbanks and pointbars were it not for linings and continued removal of silt and mud. Clay mixed with gravel, known as puddle, was used to line the Ohio & Erie Canal where necessary. Much of that lining material must have been glacial (known in olden times as "bowlder clay"). Canal walls were also reinforced when necessary with wood or stone to prevent erosion.

In the early years, hand laborers cleared the canal of gravel bars in the spring when the canal was drained.[21] Later, state boats were added for maintenance of the canal, and steam dredges were used once that technology became practical. Dredging was a time-consuming process. For instance, in 1908, when the canal was undergoing extensive renovation, it took eight months to dredge the section from Everett to Howard Street in Akron, a distance of about ten miles.[22] Bars were sometimes cleared by opening downstream lock gates in order to release a lock full of water at one time, a method known as swelling.[23]

The moving water in the canal, like that in parts of the canal today, would have been brown. Maximilian, Prince of Wied (see chapter 5), poetically referred to the "beautiful dark brown mirror" of the canal. The color was caused by the suspended load of fine sediment carried by the current. Sediment was brought into the canal from feeder streams, the upstream reaches of the canal itself, and water flowing into the sides of the canal from the surrounding area. Siltation of locks and the canal prism itself could be a serious problem, since mud and gravel bars could hinder canal travel. Locally famed Johnnycake Lock in Cuyahoga Valley National Park is named for an incident in which a canal boat was grounded due to siltation of the canal. This reportedly led to the crew subsisting on johnnycakes (cornbread baked on a griddle) for several days. Similarly, the derivation of the nickname Mudcatcher Lock for Lock 25 is self-explanatory.

Some gravel bars reoccurred at the same locations despite canal maintenance, some even earning names. Occasionally, small streams fed directly into the canal. Such feeder streams had mud catchers to forestall siltation. One such mud catcher along the Galley Run canal feeder is located north of Route 82 and can be seen from the canal towpath.

The waves generated by the wake of canal boats, especially those moving over the speed limit of four miles per hour, would affect the movement of the sediment accumulating on the sides and bed of the canal prism. The waves and turbulence caused increased erosion of the sides of the canal banks and moved deposits along the floor of the canal. This also necessitated frequent dredging. Sediment would, of course, also have found its way to the canal termini in Cleveland and Portsmouth, adding to the sediment load of the rivers at the ends of the canal.

Silt and mud remaining in the canal prism after the end of the canal era has actually helped preserve a number of the locks. The wood substructure of a lock is preserved in wet sediment, at least in part due to low oxygen conditions; when such foundations are exhumed, they tend to decay. Aqueducts and other structures along rivers have not fared as well, except where they have been maintained, because they are subjected to the erosive power of the rivers.

Construction of the Ohio & Erie Canal altered the natural drainage of the land it passed through. The land immediately adjacent to the canal—that is, the canal berm and the towpath—was angled away from the canal when possible to provide drainage. The natural flow of streams near the canals was also altered by the presence of the canal. Canals diverted surface water by blocking surface drainage from areas just above the canal prism. Some of the water from the area surrounding the canal, including water that otherwise may have made its way into the stream alongside the canal, would have flowed through porous material into the canal, depending on the permeability of the canal lining. Water also could move through the subsurface from the canal into the surrounding sediment.

More important, feeders and dams further altered the landscape. To create a feeder, a dam was constructed across a river and the water diverted through a control gate and channel to the canal. Feeders helped maintain the water level in the canal but lowered the amount of water in the natural streams. However, outseepage, or leakage of water from the canal prism, which was usually above the level of the stream or river, could provide groundwater flow that would augment the rivers and streams during dry seasons.[24] In Cuyahoga Valley National Park, both a working feeder and an abandoned feeder can be seen. There was also a feeder dam across the Tuscarawas River in Trenton, today's Tuscarawas.[25]

Dams built as part of the canal system impeded the migration of fish, an effect obvious in Ohio by 1839.[26] Some dams on rivers adjacent to the canals were built to create slackwaters, places where boats could cross from one side to the other, using the river as part of the canal system. The dam was necessary to maintain the river water at a constant level. Slackwaters were created on the canal route where the bedrock was thick and resistant, thus saving the effort of cutting a canal prism through bedrock. The most famous of the slackwater reaches of the Ohio & Erie Canal was at Black Hand Gorge in the Newark area. Another similar slackwater reach was created at Kent (then Franklin Mills) in Portage County, along the route of the Pennsylvania & Ohio Canal, a tributary canal of the Ohio & Erie Canal.[27]

Dams were also built to create or enlarge lakes used as water supplies for the canals. It was necessary to find a source to provide adequate water for the two high areas of the Ohio & Erie Canal. Akron was the highest of the two. The city is perched atop the continental divide that separates the watershed of the Great Lakes and the St. Lawrence River from the watershed of the Mississippi River. In Summit County, this divide separates the watershed of the Cuyahoga River and its tributaries from the watershed of the Tuscarawas and its tributaries. Natural lakes and wetlands in the Akron area were an attractive factor in the positioning of the Ohio & Erie Canal route.

The lakes on the divide were formed on the top of a buried valley, and within a great complex of kames (knobby, layered glacial deposits). The lakes, in their pre-canal configurations, were natural kettle lakes. These are glacial in origin, formed in the waning stages of the Ice Age as large chunks of ice were buried in glacial sediments just beyond the glacial boundary in what is known as glacial outwash. When these ice chunks melted, water-filled depressions known as kettle lakes were formed. The sediments surrounding these lakes are typical of glacial outwash: interbedded gravels, sands, and clays.[28] The land around the lake complex would have included a large area of wetlands, consisting in part of kettle lakes that had been filled in over time with peat and marl (limy mud). Extensive tamarack (*Larix laricina*) bogs could be found in the Summit wetlands and along the margins of the lakes. These bogs contained sphagnum (*Sphagnum* sp.) and American cranberry (*Vaccinium macrocarpon*), as well as an assortment of other bog plants.

Native Americans used a mile-long portage to cross the divide in Akron during times of high water. This portage pathway (one of the main portage routes in the area) connected the Cuyahoga River and the Tuscarawas River systems via Summit Lake and the associated wetlands from Summit Lake southward. At Akron, canal engineers linked together the complex of summit lakes and wetlands, which they called an "extensive wet swamp," to form what became known as the Portage Lakes Reservoir.[29] The lake complex was expanded even more in the late nineteenth century and during the period of canal reconstruction at the beginning of the twentieth, forming a complex of regulated lakes, most now part of Portage Lakes State Park.

By 1905, the interconnected system of lakes consisted of Summit Lake, Long Pond, East and West Reservoirs, and Turkeyfoot Lake with its two small appendages, Rex Lake and Mud Lake. Turkeyfoot Lake, the irregularly shaped (hence the name) body of water, was a creation of the canal engineers. Tamarack bogs along it were known for the large numbers of cranberries that grew in them. The wetlands around Turkeyfoot Lake have been greatly reduced by residential development.

Some lakes were enlarged with dams, while Summit Lake was actually lowered to reach canal level and to save the cost of adding another pair of locks. The canal crossed Summit Lake itself, with mule or horse drivers using a floating boardwalk towpath. The lowering of the water level and concomitant reduction in the size of the lake probably devastated the tamarack bog that once existed there. Travelers in the 1830s, however, including Maximilian and Dr. Samuel P. Hildreth, noted the tamaracks that had not yet disappeared.[30] Later, structures built along the lake, including an amusement park, were the coup de grace. The impenetrable tamarack swamp noted by the surveyors was gone. After these alterations, Summit Lake began to fill in with sediment. A core taken of that sediment records increasing amounts of trace metals due to anthropogenic (human) impact from the 1830s until the early 1970s.[31] Also, the mingling of water from one side of the divide with that of the other, which was created by the canal crossing the continental divide, set a precedent that has broader implications today.

The system of lakes used to water the Akron Summit did function well. Watering of the other summit on the Ohio & Erie Canal, the Licking Summit, was not as reliable. There, by means of a dike, canal engineers had changed a swampy wetland known as the Buffalo swamp into a canal reservoir, the Licking Reservoir, or Buckeye Lake, arguably the best-known lake along the Ohio & Erie Canal. When the swamp was diked and the peats in the wetland rose, they formed what became a famous floating island in the lake, which still exists today.[32]

The Ohio & Erie Canal had several major effects on plants and animals along its path. These included providing new habitat for aquatic and semiaquatic organisms; providing a link, or corridor, by crossing watershed divides and allowing organisms to spread from Lake Erie to the Ohio River and vice versa; and increasing the number of non-native species brought by Europeans into the region.

The canal provided habitat for aquatic and semiaquatic organisms preadapted for the type of habitats found in and along the canal prism. The gradient of the canal was quite low (one inch to the mile along the level portions), and the canal bottoms of the Ohio & Erie Canal were typically muddy or sandy.[33] Compared to natural rivers, the water flow in the canal was fairly slow and constant. Because of decreased turbulence, the amount of dissolved oxygen in the canal was less than that of natural streams. (Some oxygen, however, was introduced during the release of water at canal gates.) The canals were also periodically dewatered for repairs and cleaning, especially in the spring. This was not good for the fish population, but it made it quite easy to catch fish for eating.[34]

The canal waters were rich in nutrients, which included the human waste from those who traveled on the canal boats, and certainly some mule and horse manure as well. The level of toxicity, however, was probably relatively low during the early years of the canal because of the constant inflow of oxygenated water into the canal from feeder streams.[35] Industrial growth along the canal led to increased pollutants, from sawmill sawdust to a host of industrial waste, including heavy minerals; the canal was a convenient dumping ground. Feeder streams and lakes also became more polluted over the years of canal operation.

Canals are well-known avenues for dispersal of aquatic and semiaquatic plants. While there were already wetlands that would have probably allowed some floral and faunal exchange along the continental divide in Summit County, construction of the Ohio & Erie Canal across the divide provided a clear corridor for the migration of aquatic plants and animals. Ronald L. Stuckey and D. P. Salamon determined that the non-native narrow-leaved cattail, *Typha angustifolia*, probably spread westward and southward via New York and Ohio canals, following the canal across the divide in Summit County.[36] In 1992, Marvin L. Roberts and Ronald Stuckey investigated in detail the distribution of aquatic and wetland plants in relation to the Ohio canals.[37] Their study involved surveys of literature, including accounts of early botanists, examination of specimens in herbariums, and work in the field. They found that some northern species, such as the rigid arrowhead *Sagittaria rigida*, and wild rice, *Zizania aquatica*, may have made their way south via the Ohio & Erie Canal. Conversely, they noted southern species such as the swamp rose-mallow, *Hibiscus mosheutos*, may have migrated in the opposite direction along the canal.

The canals did more than allow an interchange of northern and southern plants; they also facilitated the spread of non-native species. Eurasian—that is, alien or introduced—organisms were imported, mostly unintentionally, by the Europeans moving into and beyond northeastern Ohio. A large proportion of the plants found in Ohio today are alien, including one-third of the composites (a family of plants including daisies and sunflowers). The existence of alien plants was recognized by the early botanists of the area, including John L. Riddell, who, in his 1835 "Synopsis of the flora of the western states," noted species that were introduced or probably introduced.[38] The pastiche of non-native and endemic plants and animals found in today's Canalway is the result.

Lush vegetation accumulated in the canals, feeder lakes, and waste weirs. Sedges (*Cyperus* spp.), bulrush (*Scirpus* spp.), water-lily (*Nymphaea* sp.), bur-reed (*Sparganium eurycarpum*), arrowhead (*Sagittaria rigida*), and cattail (*Typha* spp.) were probably among these plants; they are common today along parts of the canals and feeder lakes. Special machines were devised to cut down vegetation, then known as canal grass, as often as four or five times a year. (Experiments have shown that mowing such emergent vegetation can be quite effective.)

Vegetation in the canals, while anathema to canal boats, must have been a boon to certain fish and other animals. Some molluscs, for instance, are preadapted to canals.[39] Chief among these are freshwater mussels, or unionids. Published reports and museum specimens indicate thriving and/or diverse unionid communities in parts of the canal complex. They have been reported from the Ohio & Erie Canal by a number of observers from the early years of the canal to the present. In 1834, Maximilian noted what seems to be the giant floater, *Pyganodon grandis* (Say), at two places along the Ohio & Erie Canal (see chapter 5). Hildreth devoted a section of his report on his 1835 trip along the Ohio & Erie Canal to bivalves. He wrote: "The canal promises to be of great importance to conchologists, as well as to agriculturalists. Wherever there is 'a feeder' putting into the canal from the main streams, as for instance the Tuscarawas, Licking or Scioto, the bottom of the canal is literally covered at this time with the most perfect and beautiful specimens of bivalve shells. This is especially the fact at Zoar, Newark and Chilicothe. The soft sediment, and the absence of any current to abrade their surfaces, preserves them with their delicate markings unharmed."[40]

In an 1838 publication, Cleveland naturalist Jared Potter Kirtland noted the occurrence of the mussel *Unio declivis* in the Ohio & Erie Canal.[41] Almost seventy years later, in a catalog of Ohio molluscs, biologist Victor Sterki noted the occurrence of several mussel species in the Ohio & Erie Canal, including *Pyganodon grandis,* which he found both at Canal Winchester and near Cleveland.[42] Sterki hypothesized that the canals "were great routes for molluscs," noting that the mussel *Elliptio complanata* probably followed the canal across the divide.[43] The giant floater, in particular, has been reported from the Ohio & Erie Canal by both early and recent workers. If the canal were to have an official mussel, this would be it.

The occurrence of unionids in the canal has implications for the distribution of fish, since the larval form of the mussel (glochidia) must attach to the gills of host fish during part of the unionid life cycle, with specific species of mussels attaching to specific species of fish. *P. grandis* is spread by several types of fish, including yellow perch (*Perca flavescens*), a fish Kirtland thought spread via the canal. Interestingly, *Pyganodon grandis* has its highest glochidia release in winter when the canal would be partially frozen and inconsistently watered, not an optimal time for the release.

The canals must have also opened habitat and routes for aquatic or semiaquatic insects; however, travelers along the canals did not make much note of insects (for an exception, see Maximilian's remark about butterflies in chapter 5). Mosquitoes must have readily bred in temporary ponds and standing waters during and after canal construction. Mosquitoes have been blamed for causing the disease that killed many workers during the construction of the canal.[44] The disease has been identified as malaria, which is spread by mosquitoes, but typhoid fever and cholera, a result of poor sanitation, probably killed many more of the workers. In 1832, cholera was epidemic in North America, spread by contaminated food and water. Midges (chironomidae) also almost certainly colonized the canal as soon as it was opened.

Crayfish would have been preadapted to canal environments. It is likely that both the Ohio & Erie Canal and the Erie Canal provided habitat and served as a distribution corridor for these crustaceans. *Orconectes rusticus*, a common species of crayfish with a widespread distribution, is thought to have arrived in the Lake Erie Basin after 1800. When canals are superimposed on zoologists Roger F. Thoma and Raymond F. Jezerinac's distribution maps of Ohio crayfish, interesting correlations result. Thoma believes that this crayfish entered Lake Erie via the Miami & Erie Canal.[45] It is also possible that the crayfish crossed the watershed along the Ohio & Erie Canal. The disturbance of habitats, including stripping of forests adjacent to the canals, would also have favored some species of crayfish over others.

Fish must have been one of the first kind of organisms to colonize the canal waters. The canal and its reservoirs provided new habitat and allowed fish to expand their range. Kirtland hypothesized about the effect of the canals on fish, especially the yellow perch and the hickory shad (*Chatoessus elipticus*, now known as *Dorosoma cepedianum*). In an early Ohio Geological Survey publication, Kirtland reported:

> The yellow perch is found in Lake Erie and most of the small lakes in the northern parts of the State, but did not exist in the waters of the Ohio until it found its way into them through the midium [*sic*] of the Ohio canal. . . . As soon as the Pennsylvanian and Ohio canal shall be completed, a new and more convenient thorough-fare for this fish to extend its migration will be opened, and as it abounds in the small lakes connected with feeders of that canal on the summit-level, it will, without doubt, soon stock all the northern branches of the Ohio.[46]

In 1859, Kirtland noted that the hickory shad was plentiful in Lake Erie and wrote that it had "doubtless reached the Lake through the Ohio Canal."[47] All of Kirtland's specific hypotheses about fish and the canals have not been accepted by later biologists, but the general concept of the canals having some effect was investigated further by famed Ohio fish expert Milton B. Trautman. In his classic 1981 book, *Fishes of Ohio*, Trautman noted the relationship of the Ohio canals to the distribution

Fish were one of the first kind of organisms to colonize the canal and have attracted anglers ever since (Louis Baus Canal Photograph Collection, University of Akron Archival Services).

of certain fish and included the canals on maps showing fish species distribution.[48] He also published a report specifically on canals.[49] Trautman recorded the spread of yellow perch (but only to Buckeye Lake along the canal, not to the Ohio River, as Kirtland had predicted). Trautman also observed, for instance, the unquestionable influence of the canals on the distribution of the northern largemouth black bass (*Micropterus salmoides salmoides*) in Ohio. Trautman later argued that the greatest effect of the Ohio canals was that they allowed some northern Ohio fish to extend their range southward.

The canal lakes, including Buckeye Lake along the Ohio & Erie Canal, were important commercial fisheries during the second half of the nineteenth century. Later, fish hatcheries were established around the state, some associated with the canal (for example, at Zoar) and with canal lakes. Today, Hebron State Fish Hatchery is located along the old canal system in Licking County near Buckeye Lake. Part of the water used at the Hebron facility is brought from Buckeye Lake via the canal.

In 1834, Maximilian noticed turtles, bull frogs, tree frogs, and swimming snakes along the stretch of the canal between Fulton and Akron. All of these can be found along the Towpath Trail in Cuyahoga Valley National Park today.[50] Mudpuppies (several types of salamanders that live in mud under water) probably also lived in the canals, because canals have been implicated in their spread in New York State.

Snakes were not appreciated at all in canal days. Kirtland noted that workmen excavating the canal prism for the Ohio & Pennsylvania Canal had killed many copperheads.[51] Cyrus P. Bradley, reporting on an 1835 trip, described water snakes in a less than admiring tone and, indeed, killing snakes seemed to be customary on and along the North American canals.[52]

Bird distribution might have also been affected by the canals and, even more, the deforestation and vegetation changes that accompanied and followed their building. Supposedly, bobolinks moved into Ohio with the expansion of open lands in the 1800s. They were not found in the Western Reserve in the early 1800s and may have expanded with the increase in grasslands that accompanied deforestation.[53]

Muskrats (*Ondatra zibethicus*) found the canals to their liking. The muddy, nutrient-rich water was replete with aquatic vegetation and mussels (favorite foods) and cattails (construction materials for muskrat homes). These large rodents were not appreciated along canals because they caused damage to the canal walls as they tunneled into banks to build entryways into their homes. DeWitt Clinton described the muskrat as the "most formidable foe" of canals.[54] As always, rats (*Rattus norwegicus*) and house mice (*Mus musculus*) accompanied the Europeans and their grain crops. Clinton also worried about rats "taking up their habitations in houses adjacent to the canals" and the effect of their burrowing on the walls of the Erie Canal. Kirtland later noted the expanding range of the Norway rat "extending itself in every direction, especially along the shores of our canals and navigable streams."[55]

Changes in the canal after it ceased to be used for transportation, including abandoning of sections of the canal, rewatering sections, draining for repairs, changing water flow, and reforestation of some of the banks, have also affected organisms. Although the canal was more riverlike when being actively used, the canal is more lakelike today along some stretches, resulting in changes such as in the unionid mussel distributions.[56] Large populations of duckweed (*Lemna* sp.) can also be found in stagnant areas of canal locks (for example, Deep Lock in Cuyahoga Valley National Park) and would not have been as common in flowing water.

Today, with the development of other modes of transportation, the transport of alien organisms continues, with the canals being the recipients rather than the mode of transmission. New plants and organisms have appeared in and along the canals and canal feeder lakes, even though the entire canal has not been continuously watered since the great flood of 1913. Today, the water-loving aliens *Phragmites* (*Phragmites australis*), Japanese knotweed (*Polygonum cuspidatum*), and the notorious purple loosestrife (*Lythrum salicaria*) are found in the canal prism and along the canal, but, with the possible exception of purple loosestrife, introduction into this area occurred long after the heyday of the canals. And zebra mussels (*Dreissena polymorpha*) were introduced into the Portage Lakes in the late 1990s, probably in the bilgewater of pleasure craft that had previously been used in Lake Erie. *Oxidus gracilis*, the hothouse millipede, can occasionally be found in large numbers along the canal. These water-loving millipedes can sometimes be seen swarming on canal locks and nestled in cracks in the balance beams. The timing of the arrival of this millipede in Ohio is not known, but by 1928 it was noted as a pest of greenhouses throughout Ohio.[57] It is capable of withstanding prolonged submersion in water.[58]

The Ohio & Erie Canal both used and facilitated various natural resources. Water was the chief resource used, since the canal provided a ready source for water-powered processes. The water of the canal was much more reliable than that of most streams in the region. Numerous mills as well as many iron furnaces were constructed alongside the canal or along millraces connected with the canal and were noted by early travelers.

The canal also facilitated the deforestation of the region. In 1800, the vegetation of northeastern Ohio in the current Canalway region was primarily mixed oak, mixed mesophytic (that is, a mix of species with none particularly dominant), and oak-sugar maple.[59] To the south of this region, the forest types varied. The land immediately adjacent to most of the canal, however, was dominated by river-bottom, floodplain species. This was especially true on the river side of the canal. In Cuyahoga County, these species included black walnut, cherry, mulberry, oaks, poplar, tulip trees, elm, hickory, maple, sycamore, ash, willow, and buckeye.[60] A variety of shrubs and herbaceous vegetation could be found in the understory of the woods and in clearings and wetlands.

The canals created demand for wood products in their construction, particularly white oak, *Quercus alba,* which was preferred for foundations and flooring.[61] Canal boats were also constructed of white oak and white pine. More important, canals provided a cost-effective method for transporting lumber, and products made from it, for a variety of uses. Waterpower from the canals could also be used for sawmills. The lumber industry boomed in Ohio from at least 1838 through sometime into the 1860s, by which time much of the state had been deforested. Early industry also used charcoal produced from the forests to fuel iron furnaces.

Forests adjacent to the canals were among the first cut down, primarily for farm fields (fertile river-bottom lands were extremely desirable for farms). Initially, trees were burnt or girdled, but later they were cut for lumber. The change from forest to farmland seems to have been viewed favorably by most people. While traveling along a stretch of the Ohio & Erie Canal adjacent to the Tuscarawas River in 1835, Hildreth described the countryside as being "moderately hilly, and clothed with dense forests, which are every where fast falling before the axe of the woodman, and rich wheat fields, orchards and meadows are occupying their place."[62] Maximilian, however, disdained the wanton destruction of forests, noting the charred tree stumps along the canal route. John Quincy Adams likewise decried the deforestation he saw along the Ohio & Erie Canal during a trip in November 1843. He recorded this, between entries for Massillon and Zoar: "We see we are in a beautiful country, with a deep, rich soil, but much of it along the borders of the canal is woodland, and much with the

While lumber mills thrived along the canal, some observers decried the loss of Ohio's extensive forests (Cuyahoga Valley National Park Historic Print Collection, National Park Service).

wood cut down, and the stumps standing, like the pins of a bowling-green, and presenting an aspect rather of desolation than of plenty."[63]

Deforestation and nineteenth-century agricultural techniques must have increased clay and silt runoff into the feeder streams of the canal and thus also into the canal itself. Soil conservation was rare; adjacent forested land was cleared when fertility declined on farmsteads.[64] This deforestation resulted in denuding of the soil as well, creating entryways for exotic plants adapted to living in disturbed habitats.

During the nineteenth century, there was a concern that deforestation was having an effect on the hydrologic cycle, decreasing rainfall and thus potentially affecting the amount of water available for canals.[65] While arguments can be marshaled to support or refute such an effect, it was probably not significant.

Eastern Ohio had abundant stone for use in locks and other canal structures. The exploitation of these stone deposits provided stimulus to the stone industry in the area, and the completion of the canal system facilitated the movement of stone from the quarries to other areas. Several of the sandstone layers in eastern Ohio, including the Berea Sandstone (known historically as the Berea Grit), Sharon Conglomerate (known historically as the Conglomerate and also as the Sharon Formation), Massillon Sandstone, Black Hand Sandstone, and Buena Vista Sandstone, have proved to be good dimension stones, that is, rock split or sawn into shapes for construction. Berea Sandstone, due to its durability and its advantageous location in relation to the canal, was the most famed of these.

The stone used for the Ohio & Erie Canal was obtained from the Devonian through Pennsylvanian bedrock of the region.[66] Most of the stone used was sandstone, but some of the less pebbly layers of conglomerate were used as well. Stone used for structures along the northern stretch of the Ohio & Erie Canal was primarily local. Indeed, the local supply of stone was so great that the cost of the segment from the Portage Summit to Cleveland was under budget. An 1825 report in the *Cleaveland Herald* found that "even the most experienced Lock builders have been deceived in the ease with which stone can be procured and fitted for building locks."[67]

Alfred Kelley's published newspaper advertisements and notices for stone and stonework did not specify stone by name. Published advertisements for proposals, notices of acceptance, and contracts between parties involved with quarrying and cutting the stone did not specify which layers of rock were to be quarried for the Ohio & Erie Canal.[68] Even when copies of contracts are available for study, it is difficult, if not impossible,

Local Berea Sandstone was used to rebuild Lock 29 in 1880–82 (photo by Joseph T. Hannibal).

to be sure of where exactly stone was quarried and, therefore, what rock layer was quarried. Thus, unless a stone structure still exists, it is difficult to know exactly what rocks were used in its construction.

With some exceptions, most canal structures have undergone one or more major renovations, many involving replacement of stone with other stone or concrete, further obscuring determination of the original stone type. But original stone usually remains in the lower section of locks, even those extensively rebuilt with concrete in the early 1900s. Lock 38, next to the National Park Service's Canal Visitor Center, was restored with modern concrete in 1991–92, but still some original stone can be seen at the lower and northern ends of the lock.[69]

Berea Sandstone was used for most of the stonework visible today in the locks between Cleveland and Akron. Based on the location of individuals contracted to supply stone, it is possible that Euclid Bluestone, a very fine–grained sandstone found stratigraphically below the Berea Sandstone, may have been used, at least in part, for some of the northernmost locks. Based on the stone seen in locks today and in existing records, Berea Sandstone was also the stone of choice when locks were rebuilt along the northern part of the Ohio & Erie Canal during the last decades of the canal's operation. For instance, Peninsula Stone Company, a quarrier of Berea Sandstone, supplied the stone used for the reconstruction of Lock 29 in Peninsula in 1880–82.[70]

Outcrops of suitable Berea Sandstone were—and still are—located near and uphill of the canal. The stone was transported downhill by wagon or later by short train lines to the canal. In an 1873 report, Newberry wrote, "At Peninsula the Berea grit has been extensively quarried for many years. The base of the formation is here from 30 to 60 feet above the canal, so that the quarries are worked with facility, and their product shipped with comparatively little expense."[71] Later, in 1888, Henry Howe noted, "Near Peninsula, in the northern part of Summit County, on the west bank of the Cuyahoga River, is a valuable outcrop of the Berea grit which has been very extensively quarried in the past, and shipped by canal to Cleveland and thence by lake to various lake ports, principally to Buffalo, New York. The base of the Berea grit is here several feet above the canal. The stone is still shipped quite extensively by canal, and also by the Valley railroad. The principal market at present is Akron."[72] The situation was similar at Independence, Ohio, where outcrops were near the canal, although not as near as those at Peninsula.

By virtue of its extensive, well-preserved quarry walls and its location within an excellent park system, Deep Lock Quarry, a Berea Sandstone quarry now part of Metroparks, Serving Summit County, is the best known of the canal-era quarries in Ohio. It is one of several in the Peninsula area and was likely one source of stone for some of the original locks.

The Sharon Conglomerate is a Pennsylvanian deposit that crops out in the Akron area. It was a well-known building stone quarried at various locations in Akron and its vicinity.[73] One of the Akron quarries was along Quarry Street (renamed Bowery Street in the 1870s), now part of the downtown business district. The Sharon Conglomerate was used for canal structures as well as buildings and foundations in Akron and elsewhere, for example, in the lower part of the Mustill Store in Cascade Locks Park in Akron. Pebbly Sharon Conglomerate can also be seen in the spillway adjacent to Lock 14 in the park. Less pebbly parts of this rock unit (sometimes known as the Sharon Sandstone) were preferred to more pebbly layers. The pebbles, however, can distinguish this stone from Berea Sandstone, and it is typically coarser than Berea Sandstone.

The Sharon Conglomerate was also used for the original Lock 2 in Clinton, but the locks at Clinton were redone in concrete in 1908. Pieces of the original lock are piled up in places alongside Lock 2, and some original stone protrudes from the sides of the lock on the outer edge near the Towpath Trail. The sand grains in the stone are medium to coarse in size. Some of the stone has a purplish coloration, and pebbles, usually 2 mm to 2 cm long, can be seen in some of the blocks.

Massillon Sandstone, another Pennsylvanian sandstone that occurs stratigraphically just above the Sharon Conglomerate in the southern area of Akron and elsewhere, was used in Akron's Lock 2 north reconstruction (not to be confused with Lock 2 south in Clinton) in the 1980s. This sandstone is characterized by quartz grains fine-to-medium grained and angular to subangular in shape, and it also contains mica grains. The stone used for Lock 2 was quarried by the Briar Hill Company in southwestern Coshocton County. Massillon Sandstone has historically been quarried in Massillon and other places in Stark and southern Summit Counties, so it might have also been used for some original canal locks, but not in Akron, where the Sharon Conglomerate was readily available.

The religious Separatists at Zoar used a beige-to-red-colored local Pennsylvanian sandstone, perhaps the Homewood, for locks. Several layers of suitable sandstone were available in Tuscarawas County. Farther south along the canal, Black Hand Sandstone was quarried at Chestnut Ridge, now a Columbus and Franklin County Metropark just west of Carroll, and at Sugar Grove, along the Hocking Canal. This stone was used for canal repairs and replacement in the central part of the state.[74]

Buena Vista Sandstone, quarried in the Portsmouth area and noted by a number of canal travelers, was used where needed at the southern terminus of the Ohio & Erie Canal.

It is likely that stones in addition to those listed above were used for canal locks and waste weirs, or for riprap to stabilize canal banks and riverbanks adjacent to the canal, since riprap need not be made of the highest quality stone.

Because of stone's weight, its transportation costs were high, though transportation by water has been the least expensive way of transporting stone over long distances since ancient times. Nineteenth-century geological survey reports referring to the area in today's Ohio & Erie National Heritage Canalway are replete with references to canals (and railways) as advantageous for transporting stone. Indeed, stone turned out to be one of the chief items transported by canal.

The Ohio & Erie Canal stimulated the stone trade along its banks, giving impetus to the industries in Independence and elsewhere.[75] Ancillary industries, including those involving cutting and shaping stone, grew along with the quarries. The products of the quarries at Independence—grindstone, block stone, and perch stone—were transported by wagon and canal. One quarrier used a horse-drawn railway to transport stone to the canal.[76] Stone Road, which still exists today and gained its name from the industry it served, was another route used. The Peninsula quarries also used the canal to transport their products. Other stone shipped by canal included brown and yellow freestone (probably Sharon Conglomerate) from Cuyahoga Falls and Massillon. Old maps and advertisements confirm that stone dealers tended to locate along canals.

While the canals were very important in stimulating the use of stone quarried nearby, they also facilitated transport of imported stone, including marble used for gravestones, which eventually replaced local sandstones used for tombstones.[77] At least by the 1830s, imported marble was being used for gravestones in the Cleveland area, and Cleveland became a hub for trans-shipment of marble from the east via the Ohio & Erie Canal.

The stone blocks used for the canal locks were cemented together with mortar made from cement and sand. In fact, the great canal construction projects of the nineteenth century were an important impetus to the development of cement technology in the United States.[78] Hydraulic cement, which can solidify under water, was used, especially for facing stone. According to John Newberry, this cement was made from impure limestones containing some clay material.[79] An eight-inch bed of hydraulic limestone was quarried in the Cuyahoga Valley for use in mortar for the canals.[80] The discovery of a bed of limestone suitable for mortar near the summit of the canal in Akron was particularly important, since a large number of locks and other stone structures needed to be built there. In the 1800s, Jonathan Hale also produced lime from stone found on his farm, now Hale Farm and Village in Cuyahoga Valley National Park.

After construction of the canals, limestone continued to be produced in what is today's Canalway. For example, U.S. Census records for 1880 show that limestone was being quarried in Bethlehem Township in Stark County and shipped, mostly by canal, to the Canal Dover Furnace.

Concrete (a mixture of aggregate, cement, and water) was used for redoing the canal locks in the early 1900s; its use for lock structures had been pioneered in the United States in the 1890s along Illinois's Hennepin Canal. The concrete used along the Ohio & Erie Canal included local materials such as sand, river gravel, pieces of stone removed from the old locks, big pieces of marble and other stone, shells, fragments of ceramic products—and who knows what else. At Deep Lock (Lock 28) in Cuyahoga Valley National Park, a variety of bedrock particles and glacial cobbles, all probably derived from river gravels, can be seen. At Red Lock (Lock 34), also in the park, the concrete includes mussel shells. At Lock 3 in Clinton, broken pieces of redware ceramics, other clay products, and even coal can be seen in the concrete of the lock.

Shales and clays found adjacent to the canal were used in bricks as well as canal linings. Most deposits used for brick were shales found in nearby bedrock outcrops. Bronson's "great brick yards" in Peninsula were one of these.[81] Clay was obtained from the side of the river valley just north of the aqueduct at Lock 29. The Bedford Formation, and perhaps the Chagrin Shale as well, was used along the canal north of Akron. Pennsylvanian-age clays and shales from Ohio's coal measures were used in Stark and Tuscarawas Counties, as well as other counties in the southeastern part of the state.[82]

Coal was expected to be an important export once an Ohio canal was established. After all, its transport had been one of the main reasons for the development of canal routes in England in the late eighteenth century. In the early 1800s, coal was of value only where it could easily be exported. Since roughly half of the Ohio & Erie Canal, and most of the total length of its tributaries, passed through coal-bearing areas, coal did turn out to be one of the most important items, as determined by tolls collected, to be transported down the canal.

The Ohio & Erie Canal is responsible for the start of the coal business so important to Cleveland in the nineteenth and twentieth centuries. The first coal to come to Cleveland was sent in 1828 from Coal Hill (now Chapel Hill) along what is now the Tallmadge-Akron border.[83] One of the coal suppliers, Henry Newberry of Cuyahoga Falls, offered delivery via the canal at Cleveland.[84] Initial acceptance of coal as a fuel in Cleveland, however, was reluctant, but its use grew greatly during the nineteenth century as new coal beds were exploited in Ohio and Pennsylvania and vast amounts were shipped along the Ohio & Erie Canal. In 1838, Ohio geologist Caleb Briggs Jr. noted that large (by standards of that time) amounts of coal were being transported along the canal from the Tuscarawas Valley.[85] Whittlesey observed that the coal mines west of the center of Tallmadge Township were "extensively worked since the construction of the Pennsylvania and Ohio Canal, yielding in 1841, 250,000 bushels."[86] Cleveland received 49,000 bushels of coal in 1833; by 1844, this amount increased to 540,305 barrels.[87] Railways eventually took away much of the canal trade in the second half of the nineteenth century, but transport of heavy raw materials continued. But by 1905, only coal, hay, stone, and lumber were being shipped along the canal.

Gypsum (also then known as crystalline sulfate of lime) from the Sandusky area (Marblehead Peninsula) was another product expected to be among the most important shipped along the canal.[88] It had been one of the key early products transported along the Erie Canal, and, indeed, transport of gypsum is mentioned in a number of accounts of those who traveled along the Ohio & Erie Canal. In 1835, Hildreth reported seeing "crystalline sulphate of lime, white as the driven snow, thrown carelessly on the landing" at Akron.[89]

To summarize, the Ohio & Erie Canal's route was determined by the natural resources and topography of this region. But the canal itself affected the natural areas of Ohio in a number of ways, including the introduction of non-native species and alteration of the hydrogeology of the area. It also opened markets for timber and other natural resources. The canal corridor became a means of dispersing both biological organisms and material culture. The changes in the landscape and in the natural communities of Ohio initiated by the building and use of the Ohio & Erie Canal were accelerated by the next leap in transportation, the railway.

Today, the Ohio & Erie Canal reminds us of a nineteenth-century ethos. It is, as Donald Dean, a Baldwin Wallace College biologist, once put it, evocative of "the unspoiled beauty of a time long past."[90] But that beauty is not at all that of a pristine wilderness, for the canal itself is representative of a time in which its surrounding landscape and the natural habitats along its corridor were vastly transformed.

NOTES

Special thanks are due to Ronald L. Stuckey of Ohio State University, who provided key references on canal biology. Joe Keiper, Robert Bartolotta, and Renee Boronka, the Cleveland Museum of Natural History, also provided information, and Keiper, Bartolotta, and Kathy Farago, Cleveland Heights–University Heights Public Library, commented on earlier versions of the manuscript. Greg Petusky of the museum printed photographs. Thanks are also due to the editors who suggested improvements to the manuscript.

1. W. A. Lloyd, John. L. Falconer, and Charles. E. Thorne, *The Agriculture of Ohio*, Agricultural Experiment Station Bulletin 326 (1918): 76.

2. An 1820 Ohio map drawn by A. Bourne shows the greatest number of lakes in Ohio in Portage and Stark Counties. The map is the frontispiece in Caleb Atwater, "Description of the antiquities discovered in the State of Ohio and other western states," *Archaeologic Americana: Transactions and Collections of the American Antiquarian Society* 1 (1820): 105–267.

3. R. D. Hurt, *The Ohio Frontier: Crucible of the Old Northwest, 1720–1830* (Bloomington: Indiana Univ. Press, 1996), 396.

4. Two good works on the biological effects of the canal are Milton B. Trautman, "Diversions, Canals, and Conduits—Their Role in Introducing Aquatic Organisms into Drainage Basins Where They Did Not Reside Formerly," in *Athens Proceedings of the I.U.C.N. Technical Meeting, Theme 1: National Aquatic Water Conservation* 4 (1960): 175–84; Marvin L. Roberts and Ronald L. Stuckey, "Distribution Patterns of Selected Aquatic and Wetland Vascular Plants in Relation to the Ohio Canal System," *Bartonia* 57 (1992): 50–74.

5. Pioneering works by these two authors were written a century and a half apart. DeWitt Clinton, writing under the pseudonym Hibernicus, published his *Letters on the Natural History and Internal Resources of the State of New-York* (New York: E. Bliss and E. White) in 1822. The work is a compilation of letters he first published in a newspaper in 1820. W. B. Langbein published his insightful 1976 paper, "Hydrology and Environmental Aspects of Erie Canal (1817–99)" as U.S. Geological Survey Water-Supply Paper 2038.

6. William W. Mather, *First Annual Report on the Geological Survey of the State of Ohio* (1838): 1–23.

7. For example, Charles Whittlesey, map of Cleveland, frontispiece, ibid.

8. See A. E. Waller, "Dr. Samuel P. Hildreth, 1783–1863," *Ohio State Archaeological and Historical Quarterly* 53 (1944): 313–38; and Michael C. Hansen and Ralph J. Bernhagen, "Division of Geological Survey," in *A Legacy of Stewardship: the Ohio Department of Natural Resources, 1949–1989*, ed. C. C. King (Columbus: Ohio Department of Natural Resources, 1990), 39–54.

9. For example, John S. Newberry, "Report on the Geology of Cuyahoga County," in *Report of the Geological Survey of Ohio,* vol. 1, part 1, *Geology* (1873): 171–200.

10. John Kilbourne, comp., *Public Documents Concerning the Ohio Canals, Which Are to Connect Lake Erie with the Ohio River, Comprising a Complete Official History of These Great Works of Internal Improvement, from Their Commencement Down to the Close of the Session of the Legislature of 1831–32* (Columbus: Isaac N. Whiting, 1832), 196.

11. John S. Newberry, "Report on the Geology of Stark County," in *Report of the Geological Survey of Ohio* 3 (1878): 151–76.

12. G. W. White, "Glacial Geology of Summit County, Ohio," in *Ohio Division of Geological Survey Report of Investigations* (1984): 123, fig. 4.

13. John S. Newberry, "Report on the Geology of Summit County," in *Report of the Geological Survey of Ohio* 1 (1873): 204.

14. Charles Whittlesey, *Contributions to the Geology of Ohio* (Cleveland: Fairbanks, Benedict & Co., 1869), 11.

15. Canal Society of Ohio, *Ohio & Erie Canal: Akron Cascade to Peninsula: Canal Society of Ohio Fall Tour* (Akron: Canal Society of Ohio, 1996), 46.

16. John S. Newberry, "Report on the Geology of Tuscarawas County," in *Report of the Geological Survey of Ohio* 3 (1878): 69.

17. Kilbourne, *Public Documents,* 28.

18. Edward H. Knight, *Knight's American Mechanical Dictionary,* 3 vols. (New York: Hurd and Houghton, 1876), 1:483.

19. Kilbourne, *Public Documents,* 61.

20. Canal Society of Ohio, *The Ohio and Erie Canal in Cuyahoga County, Ohio* (Akron: Canal Society of Ohio, 1999), 3, 30, 41–42.

21. Terry K. Woods, *The Ohio & Erie Canal: A Glossary of Terms* (Kent: Kent State Univ. Press, 1995), 10–11.

22. C. Gundling, "On the Ohio & Erie Canal in 1908 (as told to Mrs. J. H. McNally)," *Towpaths* 11.2 (1973): 17–18.

23. Woods, *Glossary of Terms,* 38.

24. Langbein, "Hydrology and Environmental Aspects," 68.

25. A. C. Romig, "Growing Up on the Ohio & Erie Canal at Trenton," *Towpaths* 41 (2003): 50.

26. Jared Potter Kirtland, "Report on the Zoology of Ohio," in *First Annual Report on the Geological Survey of the State of Ohio* (1838): 67–68. In 2001–02 the issue of fish versus dam in Kent rose again, but by this time the dam had become a historic structure, although the original lock complex alongside it was no longer functional. In 2004 a compromise between historic preservationists and those wishing to restore the river's natural flow was reached: the historic dam was retained, but the river was directed around it through a bypass created by altering the canal lock.

27. Joseph T. Hannibal, James E. Evans, and Annabelle M. Foos, "Description of Field Stops, Day 2," in *Pennsylvanian Sharon Formation, Past and Present: Sedimentology, Hydrogeology, and Historical and Environmental Significance: A Field Guide to Gorge Metro Park, Virginia Kendall Ledges in the Cuyahoga Val-*

ley National Park, and Other Sites in Northeast Ohio, Ohio, ed. Annabelle M. Foos, Ohio Division of Geological Survey Guidebook no. 18 (2003): 66–67.

28. G. W. White, *Glacial Geology of Northeastern Ohio,* Ohio Division of Geological Survey Bulletin 68 (1982): fig. 9c.

29. Kilbourne, *Public Documents,* 41.

30. Samuel P. Hildreth, "Miscellaneous observations made during a tour in May, 1835, to the Falls of the Cuyahoga, near Lake Erie: extracted from the diary of a naturalist," *American Journal of Science* 31.1 (1837): 54.

31. Stephanie A. Haney, "The Sediment Record of Anthropogenic Impact on the Summit Lake Ecosystem, Akron, Ohio" (master's thesis, Univ. of Akron, 2004).

32. Alfred Dachnowski, *Peat Deposits of Ohio: Their Formation and Uses,* Geological Survey of Ohio, Fourth Series, Bulletin 16 (1912): 86.

33. Woods, *Glossary of Terms,* 19–20.

34. Romig, "Growing Up," 50–51.

35. Based on similar conditions for the Erie Canal, see Langbein, "Hydrology and Environmental Aspects," 58.

36. Ronald L. Stuckey and Douglas P. Salamon, "*Typha angustifolia* in North America: A Foreigner Masquerading as a Native," *Ohio Journal of Science* 87.2 (1987): 4.

37. Roberts and Stuckey, "Distribution Patterns," 50–74.

38. John L. Riddell, "A synopsis of the flora of the Western States," *Western Journal of Medicine and Physical Science* 8 (1835): 329–74, 489–556, republished as *A Synopsis of the Flora of the Western States* (Cincinnati: E. Deming, 1835).

39. F. Higgins, "A catalogue of the shell-bearing species of Mollusca, inhabiting the vicinity of Columbus, Ohio, with some remarks thereon," in *Ohio State Board of Agriculture, with an Abstract of the Proceedings of the County Agricultural Society's 12th Annual Report for 1857* (1858): 548–55.

40. Hildreth, "Miscellaneous observations," 62.

41. Kirtland, "Report on the Zoology of Ohio," 197.

42. Victor Sterki, "A Preliminary Catalogue of the Land and Fresh-water Mollusca of Ohio," in *Proceedings of the Ohio State Academy of Science* 4 (1907): 367–402.

43. According to Sterki, this mussel may have also followed the canal across the continental divide at Akron, but, according to Russell J. Barber, there is evidence for the presence of the unionid mussel *Elliptio complanata* during prehistoric times in the Ohio River basin. See Russell J. Barber, "The Indigenous Distribution of *Elliptio complanata* in Ohio (U.S.A.): Archeological Evidence," *Nautilus* 96 (1982): 130–31.

44. Grace Poh Miller et al., *The Story of Independence* (Independence: Independence Historical Society, 1979), 25.

45. Roger F. Thoma and Raymond F. Jezerinac, *Ohio Crayfish and Shrimp Atlas,* Ohio Biological Survey Miscellaneous Contribution no. 7 (2003); R. F. Thoma, personal communication, January 2003.

46. Kirtland, "Report on the Zoology of Ohio," 190. Kirtland also predicted that the sea lamprey would be allowed into Lake Erie by the construction of

Canada's Welland Canal. This prediction proved correct, but the creature's arrival and the establishment of successful breeding populations took about a century.

47. Jared Potter Kirtland, "Minutes of meetings," in *Proceedings of the Cleveland Academy of Natural Science, 1845 to 1859* (Cleveland: Published by a gentleman of Cleveland, 1874), 113–37.

48. Milton B. Trautman, *The Fishes of Ohio with Illustrated Keys,* rev. ed. (Columbus: Ohio State Univ. Press, in collaboration with Ohio Sea Grant Program, 1981); see also Milton B. Trautman, *The Ohio Country from 1750 to 1977—a Naturalist's View,* Ohio Biological Survey Biological Notes, no. 10 (1977): 1–6.

49. Trautman, "Diversions, Canals, and Conduits."

50. Peg Bobel and Rob Bobel, *The Nature of the Towpath: A Natural History Guide to the Ohio & Erie Canal Towpath Trail* (Akron: Cuyahoga Valley Trails Council, 1998).

51. Kirtland, "Report on the Zoology of Ohio."

52. Cyrus P. Bradley, "Journal of Cyrus P. Bradley," *Ohio Archaeological and Historical Quarterly* 15 (1906): 207–70.

53. Bruce G. Peterjohn, *The Birds of Ohio* (Bloomington: Indiana Univ. Press, 1989), 209.

54. Clinton, *Letters on the Natural History,* 45.

55. Kirtland, "Report on the Zoology of Ohio," 177.

56. Michael J. S. Tevesz, Lewis Rundo, and Robert A. Krebs, "Freshwater Mussels (Bivalvia: Unionidae) of the Ohio & Erie Canal, Cuyahoga Valley National Park, Ohio," *Kirtlandia* 53 (2002): 35–36.

57. Stephen R. Williams and Robert A. Hefner, *The Millipedes and Centipedes of Ohio,* Ohio Biological Survey Bulletin 18 (1928): 106.

58. N. B. Causey, "Studies on the Life History and the Ecology of the Hothouse Millipede, *Orthomorpha gracilis,*" *American Midland Naturalist* 29.3 (1943): 681.

59. Robert B. Gordon, *The Natural Vegetation of Ohio in Pioneer Days,* Ohio Biological Survey Bulletin 3.2 (1969): 37–54.

60. Arthur B. Williams, *The Native Forests of Cuyahoga County, Ohio,* Scientific Publications of the Cleveland Museum of Natural History (1949): 9:56–58; and Bobel and Bobel, *The Nature of the Towpath,* 13.

61. Frank W. Trevorrow, "Early Lock Construction," *Towpaths* 16.4 (1978): 3.

62. Hildreth, "Miscellaneous observations," 63.

63. John Quincy Adams, *Memoirs of John Quincy Adams, Comprising Portions of His Diary from 1795 to 1848,* vol. 11 of 12, ed. C. F. Adams (Philadelphia: J. B. Lippincott, 1876), 420.

64. Lloyd, Falconer, and Thorne, *The Agriculture of Ohio,* 78–79.

65. Clinton, *Letters on the Natural History,* 210–15; Langbein, "Hydrology and Environmental Aspects," 50.

66. Joseph T. Hannibal, *Geology along the Towpath: Stones of the Ohio & Erie and Miami & Erie Canals,* Ohio Division of Geological Survey Guidebook no. 14 (1998): table 1; see also Frank W. Trevorrow, "What Kind of Stone?" *Towpaths* 24.1 (1986): 1–10.

67. "Location of the Canal," *Cleaveland Herald*, May 13, 1825.

68. A July 1825 contract between H. Bronson and W. B. Lawrence (a copy of which is in the Peninsula Library and Historical Society) specifies stone suitable for cutting to be delivered to Lawrence below Bronson's quarry in Boston, but the type of stone is not given. In this particular case, however, it was almost certainly Berea Sandstone.

69. Robert W. Bobel, "The 1991–1992 Restoration of Lock 38 of the Ohio & Erie Canal in the Cuyahoga Valley National Recreation Area by the National Park Service," *Towpaths* 31.4 (1993): 43.

70. Canal Society of Ohio, *Ohio & Erie Canal: Akron Cascade*, 45.

71. Newberry, "Report on the Geology of Summit County," 209.

72. Henry Howe, *Historical Collections of Ohio*, 3 vols. (1888; rpt., Cincinnati: State of Ohio, 1908), 2:588.

73. Joseph T. Hannibal, *Guide to the Building Stones and Cultural Geology of Akron*, Ohio Division of Geological Survey Guidebook no. 19 (2006).

74. D. A. Meyer, *Life along the Ohio Canal-Licking Reservoir to Lockbourne and the Columbus Feeder* (Canal Winchester: Canal Winchester Historical Society, 1998), 2–7.

75. John S. Reese, *Guide Book for the Tourist and Traveler over the Valley Railway: The Short Line between Cleveland, Akron, and Canton, containing a complete description of the scenery and objects of interest along the road, history of each station on the line, biographies of the officers of the road, etc.* (1880; rpt., Kent: Kent State Univ. Press, 2002), 10.

76. Miller et al., *The Story of Independence*, 60.

77. A. Bauer et al., "Distribution in Time, Provenance, and Weathering of Gravestones in Three Northeastern Ohio Cemeteries," *Ohio Journal of Science* 102.4 (2002): 82–96.

78. T. F. Hahn and E. L. Kemp, *Cement Mills along the Potomac River*, Institute for the History of Technology & Industrial Archaeology, Monograph Series, vol. 2, no.1 (1994), chap. 2.

79. John S. Newberry, "Hydraulic cement," in *Geological Survey of Ohio Report of Progress in 1870* (1871), 51. The sons of geologist John Newberry developed an interest in cement and became experts in hydraulic and other cement. Spencer Newberry founded what would become the Medusa Portland Cement Company, until recently headquartered in Cleveland.

80. This bed is noted many times by geologists and those writing about canals. See, for example, Charles Whittlesey, "Mr. Whittlesey's Report," *First Annual Report on the Geological Survey of the State of Ohio* (Columbus: Samuel Redary, 1838), 57. This bed was a silty limestone or calcareous siltstone in the Maxville or Sharpsville Member of the Cuyahoga Formation. Such layers are more common in the Sharpsville Member.

81. *Combination atlas map of Summit County, Ohio, compiled, drawn and published from personal examinations and surveys* (Akron: Tackabury, Mead & Moffett [*sic*], 1874), advertisement, 13.

82. Edward Orton, "The clays of Ohio, their origin, composition, and varieties," in *Report of the Geological Survey of Ohio*, vol. 3, pt. 1 (1838): 61.

83. D. L. Crowell, *History of the Coal-mining Industry in Ohio,* Ohio Division of Geological Survey Bulletin, no. 72 (1995): 123–26.

84. *Cleaveland Herald,* April 11, 1831, advertisement.

85. Caleb Briggs Jr., "Report of Mr. Briggs (on Wood, Crawford, Athens, Hocking, and Tuscarawas Counties)," in *Ohio Geological Survey Second Annual Report* (1838), 149–50.

86. Charles Whittlesey, *A Sketch of the Settlement and Progress of the Township of Tallmadge* (Cleveland: Sanford & Co., 1842), 22.

87. Samuel P. Orth, *A History of Cleveland, Ohio,* 3 vols. (Cleveland: S. J. Clarke, 1910), 1:699.

88. Anonymous, in Kilbourne, *Public Documents,* 38.

89. Hildreth, "Miscellaneous observations."

90. Donald Dean, "An Escape from the Twentieth Century," *Explorer* 20.1 (1978): 13.

Chapter 5

A Traveler's Tale: Along the Ohio & Erie Canal in 1834

Maximilian, Prince of Wied
An Annotated New Translation

JOSEPH T. HANNIBAL, SABINA F. THOMAS, AND MICHAEL G. NOLL

A number of travelers chronicled their trips via canal boat along the Ohio & Erie Canal in the nineteenth century. But the trip of Maximilian, Prince of Wied (1782–1867), stands out among them. This German explorer made important early observations about the canal during June 1834, less than two years after the full length of the canal was opened, in October of 1832. He crossed the entire length of the canal, from the warmer biomes of southern Ohio to the forests of northeastern Ohio. Maximilian's observations stood out for two reasons: he was a highly knowledgeable, experienced naturalist, and he had no personal stake in the settling of the frontier and concomitant suppression of the native peoples of North America.

Maximilian ranks among the greatest of the explorer-naturalists of the first half of the nineteenth century. He was a self-taught naturalist who studied at the University of Göttingen briefly in 1811–12 and was influenced by early anthropologist Johann Friedrich Blumenbach and renowned explorer-naturalist Alexander Von Humboldt. Maximilian, however, lacked Humboldt's resources. The prince could only afford his expeditions by borrowing money from his older brother, the reigning Prince of Wied. Maximilian made two major expeditions, one to South America (1815–17) and another to North America (1832–34). He documented his finds in weighty, detailed volumes that rank among the classics in New World natural history. His detailed account of his South

Maximilian, Prince of Wied, was one of the great explorer-naturalists of the early nineteenth century (Engraving by Heinrich Meyer, circa 1820–25, reproduction by Manfred Bogner, courtesy of Röntgen Museum, Neuwied, Germany).

American expedition, published in German in 1820 and English in 1820 and 1821, established his reputation as a naturalist.

During the latter part of his expedition to North America, Maximilian traversed the Ohio & Erie Canal. He began his trip in 1832, traveling to Boston and New York City, then through New Jersey and Pennsylvania, and down the Ohio River with a major stopover in New Harmony, Indiana, then continuing on the Ohio and Mississippi Rivers, and traveling up the Missouri River as far west as Fort McKenzie. His original plans called for a visit to the Native Americans who lived in the Rocky Mountain area, but warfare prevented it. He returned via the Missouri, Mississippi, and Ohio Rivers as far as New Harmony, Indiana. He then traveled overland to Louisville, then up the Ohio River to Portsmouth, Ohio, where he then headed north on the Ohio & Erie Canal to Cleveland. He took a steamship

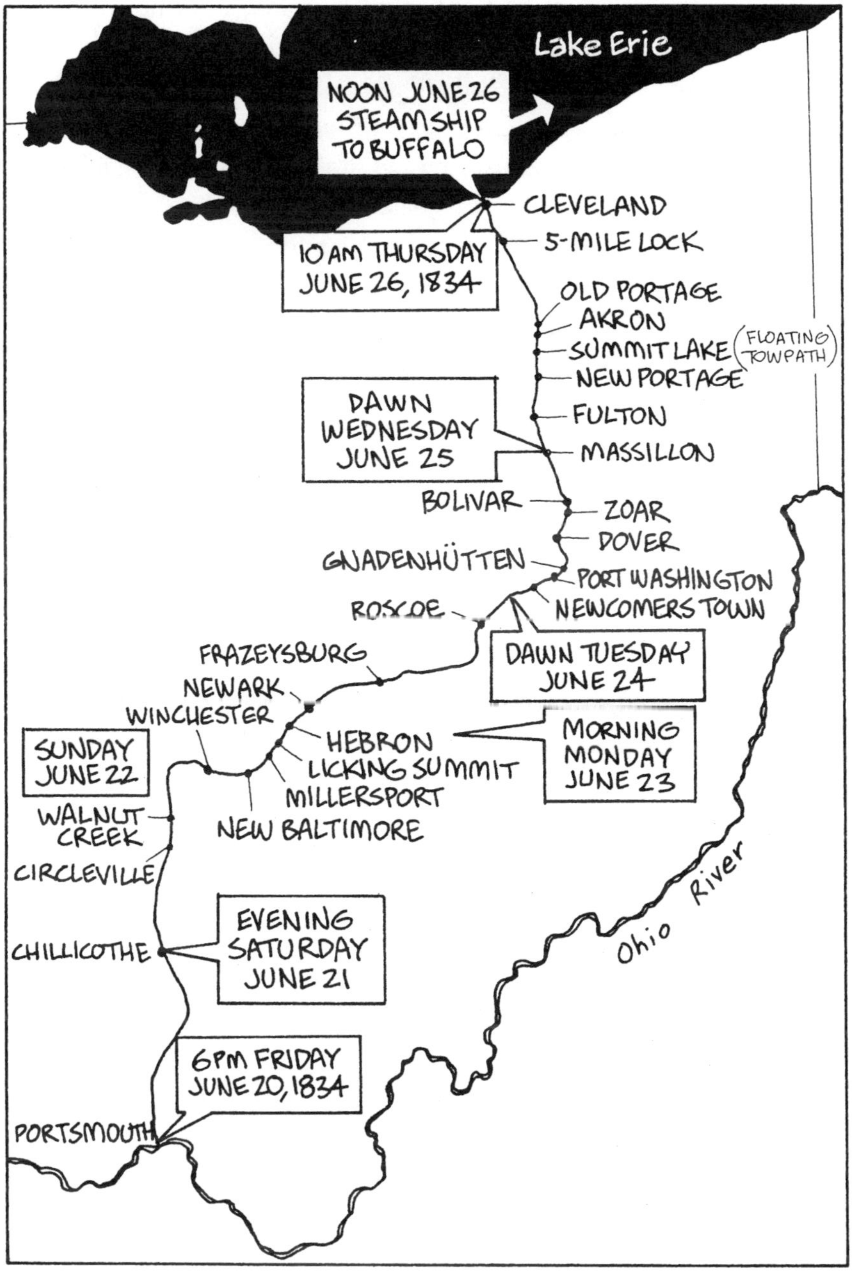

Maximilian traveled the entire route of the Ohio & Erie Canal in June 1834 (map by Chuck Ayers).

from Cleveland to Buffalo and then traveled via the Erie Canal and the Hudson River back to New York City, and then headed home.

Maximilian noted the "well-known Ohio Canal" early on his way out west in 1832, but he was to travel along the canal only on his return from the West. He traversed the entire length of the Ohio & Erie Canal in June 1834. His trip began on the evening of June 20 at Portsmouth, at the southern end of the canal, and ended in Cleveland, at the northern end, at 10 A.M. on June 26, over five and a half days later.

In part, Maximilian traveled the Ohio & Erie Canal to visit Niagara Falls, the outstanding natural tourist attraction of the United States. Such a visit was de rigueur for the traveler in those days. Maximilian had intended to visit the Falls on his way west, but this was derailed by a cholera outbreak in New York. There were other advantages to traveling by canal as well. Roads in Ohio were notoriously bad, and travel by canal was gentle by contrast and provided opportunities to write in a journal. It was also easier to bring larger amounts of material along the canal than in horse-drawn coaches.

The Ohio & Erie Canal portion of Maximilian's account of his American journeys covers pages 383–95 in the original German edition. This new annotated translation, which appears below, was necessitated by the omission of material from earlier translations, including some key observations of the natural history of the canal, and, in some cases, to restore the flavor of Maximilian's German in a way accessible for modern readers. This new translation includes all of the text he wrote about his travels along the Ohio & Erie Canal, including his original notes, which are marked "[Maximilian's note]." To avoid confusion, we have omitted Maximilian's occasional usage of both a German and English term, the latter of which he typically enclosed in parentheses. We have added contemporary spellings or very short annotations in brackets. Longer annotations and comments of our own are in the endnotes. English and Latin terms used in the original German version are usually given as in that original version. Original italicization is also preserved.

. . .

XXXII. Journey along the Ohio Canal, Lake Erie, and the Falls of the Niagara from June 21 to June 30, 1834

Journey along the Ohio Canal—Chillicothe—Licking Summit, highest point of the canal—
Descent of the Canal near Akron—Cleveland—Lake Erie—
Its Navigation—Buffaloe. . . .

Portsmouth is a fairly unsightly place, with short houses and a few broad unpaved roads, built in a corner at the confluence of the Scioto and the Ohio Rivers.[1] The Ohio Canal begins here, connecting the river with Lake Erie. Many boats navigating this beautiful canal are built like Missouri keelboats, yet they are comfortably fitted out with several small rooms. The length of the boats varies between seventy-seven and eighty feet, their width fourteen, and they are pulled by two horses on which the driver, or tower, of the boat rides. These boats traveling the Ohio Canal aren't as well-furnished as the ones of the Erie Canal, where there are two different types of boats for passengers and freight, respectively, which is not the case here; in addition they travel more slowly because fewer horses are harnessed to the boat.[2] In the middle of the boat, one finds a long room for goods—at the front end are two small cabins, and at the back part is the dining room. Along the sides of the cabins one finds upholstered seats on which, like on the floors of the room, the beds are arranged for the night. The second cabin has a sleeping room for the ladies.

In the afternoon just following our arrival [Friday, June 20], we went on board a canal boat, and in said place I found an agreeable, educated companion and observer of nature in Dr. Pitcher, military physician at Fort Gibson at the Arkansa [Arkansas] River, who made this trip along with his family. Our journey started at six o'clock in the evening and the finest weather favored us. The banks of the canal were covered with forests, particularly of sugar maple. Before nightfall we reached some locks and a stonemill where seventy saws were cutting blocks of the local sandstone (freestone) and shaping it for use as building stone, tombstones, etc. On the following day [Saturday, June 21], we proceeded through beautiful forests of sugar maple and beech, where one could see the baltimore [Baltimore oriole] flying about. The land is very fertile here; at one time it used to be forested everywhere, and one catches sight of the individual log cabins of settlers. On many places in the neighboring hills the may apple (*Podophyllum*) grows profusely; others were covered with the undergrowth of the papaw tree; the kingfisher was commonly seen along the canal. We encountered several canal boats, completely occupied with European emigrants. At three connected locks [triple locks] along the canal, so-called feeders were installed that connect it with the Scioto River which is nearby and whose valley one continually follows.[3] A weir is built in the river—in whose depths many soft shell turtles (*Trionix*) allegedly live. About one-and-a-half hours from Chillicothe, after passing Indian Creek, the canal crosses a creek, the so-called Paint Creek. This aqueduct is broad and has three arches and two stone piers, over which the canal water flows, and on each side of that aqueduct there is a plank roadbed, with a railing, for draft horses and pedestrians. In the evening we reached Chillicothe, a small town of two to three thousand inhabitants living in a broad, fertile valley, and evidently growing substantially. About 150 Germans live here; they are usually looked upon favorably. Raising cattle is the main business in this area; cattle and pigs have been exported, as now is some wheat.

When the first settlers arrived, they found two Indian tribes, the Shawnies of the Americans or Chavanons of the French, as well as the Wyandots expelled from the north.[4] Several old Indian mounds used to be located where the city lays now; bones, shards, and beads have been found in one of them, the latter made from hardwood. Another mound was composed of rocks in its upper part, it contained bones and two copper bracelets which have been wrought or hammered, but not cast. A third mound, grown over with trees, is still in existence and lies on a nearby wooded ridge; it contains a mixture of sand and rocks on top, then clay, and underneath ashes with bones that disintegrated rapidly in the air when exposed.[5]

An extraordinarily violent thunderstorm with cloudbursts assaulted us as we left Chillicothe at nine o'clock in the evening, where a helpful German named Baumann had very kindly accommodated us. On the boat we were annoyed by frontiersmen and their pathetic music whose dissonance badly tried our patience. We continued the journey during the night, and we passed several locks on the morning of [Sunday] June 22nd which warmed up early, and then shipped through a low, forested area along the Scioto that was full of small, green, tree-covered islands. Beautiful tall forest trees filled the land, elder bushes bloomed everywhere, and the red-headed woodpecker as well as the kingfisher were plentiful everywhere. We now arrived at the quite handsome town of Circleville, with many brick buildings, whose population must have significantly increased since the visit of Duke Bernhard of Saxony-Weimar.[6] The duke gives a lengthy account of the curious old embankments within which this place was built, but which have already substantially diminished since that time. The courthouse stands in the middle of the circular Indian embankment, and the largest portion of the town lies within it. The circular embankment enclosed a space of 17.75 acres; now most of it is no longer visible. At its western end, outside, lies a hill from which one can gaze over the whole site. The destructive urge of the Americans has left another sad memorial to itself; because instead of protecting these interesting old relics with the greatest care, they have erected buildings at exactly the same place and leveled the old embankments of whose prior nature and opening nothing now is left, but some sketchy superficial accounts by Attwater [Atwater] and some other American writers.[7]

After we left Circleville, a great number of floating mussel shells (*Unio*), greenish with dark stripes and common to this area, became visible on the canal. They were floating mostly without the animal, but some were found dead in the shells.[8] The canal cuts through a countryside pleasantly alternating between woods and meadows, and that previously was covered with an uninterrupted primeval forest. Frequently, along the banks, iris once grew—not in bloom now—and Sagittaria; one could see a low marshland with rushes and reed, with the beautiful red-shouldered troupial (*Psaroc. phoeniceus*) in his most beautiful splendor among the reeds. This beautiful bird prefers to live in marshes and along the water, and there it builds its nest among reeds and water plants. Tringas and totanus bring life to the swampy meadows; in the shrubs one can see the rice bird (*Emb. oryzivora Linn.*).[9] Verbascum, introduced from Europe, bloomed everywhere along the borders of the canal, and Papilio Aiax [*Papilio ajax*] searches for wet spots, something one also notices the butterflies in Brazil do during the hot season, or one saw it flutter among the papaw trees.[10]

After we had traversed a forested area with particularly beautiful sugar maples and walnut trees, we reached Walnut Creek which flows through tall and shady woods. Near the small town of Lockbourn, founded three years ago, eight locks follow one another where the Columbia [Columbus] Feeder leaves the canal. It climbs about one hundred feet here and then continues on at that elevation. Up there the trees are not as tall and the forest has more scraggly wood. It contains many beech trees; gray squirrels appear frequently as do turtles in the canal, and small herons (*Ardea virescens*) are in swampy places. It is by water we cut through the beautiful forests of the state of Ohio, and watched the population in their finery since it was Sunday; it was an entertaining journey during which we comfortably and sociably sat on deck. We had left the Scioto in the area of Lockbourn, now reached Waterloo, Winchester, Havensport, New-Baltimore, and Millersport, and around morning of the following day [Monday, June 23] we reached the highest point that the canal has to ascend. This point is called the Licking Summit because it is located in Licking Township (Muskingum County), which includes the cities of Irville and Nashport. From Portsmouth to the highest point of the canal, one has to go through fifty-one locks.[11]

At sunup we reached Hebron, a town founded in November 1825 in Union Township, along the great so-called National Road between Zanesville and Columbus, that starts at Hegerstown [Hagerstown], coming from Cumberland on the Potomack [Potomac], and passing on through the states of Ohio, Indiana, and Illinois. At that time people were working hard on this road and brought a large number of stones in large, flat, rectangular boats via the canal. Around nine o'clock in the evening, we passed through the first three locks downstream, because the canal now gradually drops in elevation from the so-called Licking Summit to Lake Erie. Here I again noticed the previously mentioned mussels (Unio). We reached the Licking River and shortly after that the small town of Newark in Newark Township, through which the canal passes. In 1830, Newark had 999 souls, but that number has since increased very substantially.[12] This town has broad streets, a large plaza, and several neat churches. Fences, on which one often sees the red-headed woodpecker, surround all crops and fields in the area. Seven miles from Newark, the canal enters the Licking River, a very pretty little river, that flows through a beautiful, rocky, wooded valley, wildly and scenically overgrown with coniferous and deciduous trees. The rocks appear to consist of graywacke and in parts have original bedding, and overhangs or caves where the cattle searched for shade.[13]

The journey of one to one-and-a-half miles through this beautiful wooded chain of hills is romantic. Open areas with settlements then follow as the canal diverges from the Licking, just to come near to the river again soon afterwards. Many high trees grow in the flats between the two bodies of water [the canal and the river], especially plane trees and poplars, partially laden with beautiful vines. From Newark, it is sixteen miles to Nashport, a small place where supposedly a few old Indian mounds remain. The bluffs of the canal are grown over with Verbascum. Ironstone and coal are found in the vicinity. There banks have always been covered with trees, but they have not grown as tall and dense as along and near the Ohio. At times one finds scenic places, locks, and numerous bridges beneath which the boats pass; often the canal continues in a straight line

The canal towpath was carved into the Black Hand Sandstone cliffs near Newark (Louis Baus Canal Photograph Collection, University of Akron Archival Services).

through tall beech forests. About twenty-three miles from Newark, the canal passes fairly high above Tomaka Creek; then one reaches the little village of Frazeysburg in Jackson Township, Muskingum County, with scattered houses, most made of wood. Along the canal, many witch-hazel (*Hamamelis virginiana*) bushes grow on the sides of the canal. The twigs of witch-hazel were used for making dowsing rods, like those of the hazel bush used in Europe; for this superstition crossed the Atlantic Ocean with the emigrants.

During the night we passed the small villages of Webbsport and Roscoe.[14] One mile from the latter, the White-Woman and the Tuscarava [Tuscarawas] rivers join to form the Muskingum. One follows the Tuscarava which pleasantly flows alongside the canal. During the night we reached the village of Newport and at dawn [Tuesday, June 24] Evansburg, and later Newcomerstown, a very dispersed little village in Tuscaravas [Tuscarawas] County, Oxford Township, which did not have more than seven to eight houses. The region is pleasant and diverse. From the canal, one can see meadows, green heights, cliffs, plentiful forests, and beautiful views of the water as the Tuscarava or Tuscaravas flows on the left. Iris and Nymphaea grow in the marshes. In the canal, a yellow-striped snake swam by very fast; we spotted the black snake and the water snake yesterday.[15] The bank of the canal appeared to be covered with Rhus, apparently typhinum [*Rhus typhina*, staghorn sumac]; and the red-headed woodpecker, the Baltimore [oriole], and the blue bird flew there. Near the village of Port-Washington, the valley was broad and wooded; then we reached Gnadenhütten, a small village of about seven houses, originally laid out by the Herrnhuters [Moravians] who have since left, however. Even now the inhabitants are mostly of German origin; the inscriptions at the houses are partly in German, and German was still spoken. In addition, newly arrived German emigrants are present. In this region, near Trenton and Newcastle, there are important coal mines. Immediately at the locks of the canal, the beautiful shrubbery of Rubus odoratus [purple-flowering raspberry] grows scenically among the rocks.

At Lockport, a small village in Tuscaravas [Tuscarawas] County, beautiful views are seen along the river; forests cover its banks; the abandoned channels are completely overgrown with Nymphaea and other water plants; on the floodplain, there are colossal plane trees, and there are dead trunks at places.[16] Near Dover, a nice little town in a pleasant location where the canal is close to the river, a very large covered bridge was built over the river, wasting a lot of wood. Here we found the announcement of a large traveling menagerie that was supposed to include many rare animals. It customarily spends the winter in Philadelphia and travels during summer. In the valley of the Tuscarava, nighthawks, without doubt *Caprimulgus virginianus* [a correct identification to species], were seen flying during bright daylight.

Not far from Dover lies Zoar, a very nice settlement of the Württemberg Separatists, which we reached during pleasant evening temperatures. A certain Bäumler is the head of this colony.[17] He is now advanced in years but, as they say, he is a very capable man. The town is in Tuscaravas County, Lawrence Township, at the eastern bank of the Tuscarava. In 1833, this colony had sixty very neat buildings, each one roofed with new red tiles, which are rare in America and that look very pleasant in the beautiful green valley. From a distance we noticed some handsome buildings and the inn which is shaped like a church. The Ohio-Gazetteer says that this place had originally been built on a plot of land of four thousand acres, which had been purchased by that company in 1810, most of which is now well cultivated. In addition, the Separatists own fifteen hundred to two thousand acres in the region as well as vineyards that supposedly produce very good wine. The location of the village on the broad flat valley floor, at some distance to the river, with rich fields and high trees, is very agreeable. The inhabitants allegedly are very industrious and own various manufactories; unfortunately, I couldn't get better acquainted with this interesting place. A long wooden bridge has been built spanning the canal and river; in whose vicinity an inn is located, built by the community and called the Zoar Canal Hotel. A shepherd drove his large flock over the bridge at this moment, and answered my queries in genuine Swabian German. All of his clothing and equipment were fashioned entirely in the German style, with a shepherd's crook, broad leather bandolier studded with brass figures, a round, flat hat with a broad rim, and a gray overcoat of thick cloth—an unusual costume in America; in addition, his shepherd dogs obediently herded the sheep.

During the night we passed by the villages of Bolivar and Bethlehem, and at dawn [Wednesday, June 25] found ourselves at Massillon, a picturesque town in Stark County that was laid out in 1826. Massillon has about one hundred houses and five hundred inhabitants. Near here, we crossed the Tuscarava [on an aqueduct], which is now flowing to the left of the canal [the river had been on the right before Bolivar]; both have dark-brown water, almost as dark as many Brazilian forest creeks. At eight o'clock, we reached Fulton [Canal Fulton], a village with several pretty houses in Lawrence Township, Stark County. Like everywhere else, there is evidence that this entire area was once covered with uninterrupted primeval forest. Everywhere along the canal, the catbird was frequently seen; we noticed turtles, bullfrogs, tree frogs, and frequently saw snakes swimming quickly across the canal. There were highly inviting forest views along the Tuscarava where a small dwarf rose bloomed along the canal; yet the rose didn't appear to be any different from those that occur in the neighboring woodlands.[18] With its large flowers, it was a most delightful ornamental shrub. Around noon we reached the town of New Portage where the traders used to portage certain goods meant for trade with the Indians, from one river to the other.[19] A swampy area came next, overgrown with a forest of larches (*Larix americana Michx.*) that shed their leaves in winter. Here this type of tree is called tamarack or hackmatack. The trees surround a small lake which the canal passes through. It is covered with grasses, reeds, the yellow flowers of Nuphar, and the beautiful blossoms of the Pontederia. The soil around here is black peatland, in which the beautiful larches grow ubiquitously. A bridge, which horses walk on when they tow the canal boats, has been built across the length of the lake.[20]

Further along, on the other side of a pondlike extension of the canal, the town of Akron appears. It is an important little town in a remarkable location. It was founded in 1825 in Portage County, and already has significant trade, and many nice wooden houses, stores, factories, an iron foundry, and a lathe-work where, with the help of a wheel, beds as well as similar furniture, equipment etc., are being fabricated.[21] Once in the town, the valley already starts to descend steeply; the canal goes through the middle of the town, and about ten to twelve locks have been constructed in a row [a staircase of locks] to get the boats down from the substantial, steep, and rocky heights.[22] The surroundings are complete with scattered buildings, industrious people, much water, shrubs, and beautiful woodlands—a place along the canal really worth seeing! Down at the foot of the heights, one glides on the beautiful dark brown mirror [mirrored surface of the canal] through vigorous greenery where forest and meadows alternate, and where the tall trunks of tulip, walnut, and sassafras trees cast their scenic reflections in the beautifully glistening water. The numerous locks, twenty-one of which could be counted over a range of two and one-half miles, became further apart from each other as we reached the Cayahoga [Cuyahoga] River, which the canal follows down to Lake Erie. The little village of Old-Portage is the first one reaches on this journey.[23] It is located in a green area cleared in the forest, surrounded entirely by beautifully wooded hills. Broad-leafed Asclepias [milkweed] and Phytolacca [pokeweed] now grow strongly skywards but their blossoms have not yet developed. Several miles farther is a stone saw mill where grindstones were manufactured from freestone. Here we find the same rock type as one can observe on the other side of Chillicothe but that displays a coarser grain near the town of Akron.[24]

In the morning of the following day [Thursday, June 26], we were only five miles from Lake Erie, a distance that we covered by ten in the morning, and we approached the little town of Cleveland.[25] The sealike mirrored surface of the great Lake Erie is very surprising as one emerges from the forested valleys, and the view reminded me of the upcoming ocean journey to my homeland. The lake stretches, a dark blue, just like the ocean, towards the horizon. White sails and the smoke of steamships were pleasing to the eye under clear skies in beautiful weather.

Cleveland (Cliveland) is a town of increasing significance, with several thousand citizens, full of life, trade, and commerce. It lies in Cayahoga or Cuyahoga County, is partially situated on top of an elevated ridge, partially built down low, along the river, and its outer part is scattered, yet the main part is laid out in an organized network of streets. Cleveland contains a number of considerable buildings, several churches, a school or academy, a prison, handsome inns, et cetera. Businesses and stores are everywhere, and commerce is very important because of the connection [via the Ohio & Erie Canal] here between the Great Lakes and the Ohio and Mississippi rivers. Here numerous canal boats, as well as the two-mast schooners are gathered. Several large well-furnished steamships, usually filled with passengers, arrive into and depart from the harbor every day. The Cayahóga flows through the lower part of the town. The river's mouth is embraced by wood on both sides; a long pier with a lighthouse at its end is on the right bank; a second lighthouse is built slightly to the right of the pier.[26] To the right, far out, one sees the coast disappear in the hazy distance, and to the left, closer by, it merges into dark forests. In Cleveland, broad-leafed Asclepias [milkweed] grows along the banks of the lake in the sand; in the swampy places along the river, a yellow water lily and some other plants grow. Many blackbirds dwelled in the reeds, and blackish swallows flew over the lake.

We found numerous Germans in Cleveland, in particular very many newly arrived emigrants, and also a young obliging countryman whom I had already seen in Pittsburg, who had found a good position in a business here. Several steamships arrived and departed, headed for Detroit, but finally the *Oliver Newberry* appeared, destined for Buffaloe [Buffalo], and I immediately used the opportunity for us to board heading for that town.[27] Around twelve noon we left Cleveland.

Upon leaving the mouth of the Cayahóga [Cuyahoga], one can easily see the open endless mirror of Lake Erie, with its marvelous blue-green waters, which—like all of these large Canadian lakes—share the exact color of Swiss water bodies. Where the river enters the lake, dark brown waters of the Cayahóga are distinctly and beautifully differentiated from those of the lake. Steering close to the southern shore, the view back towards the town of Cleveland is beautiful. The most splendid weather favored our journey and the large lake looked incredibly beautiful, yet it is known to produce very violent waves during storms and mean much trouble to the shippers, and even is said to be frequently dangerous. The southern, or American, shoreline is not elevated; the northern shoreline is known to form the border to the English territories in North America, that is Canada.[28] The former has no significant heights or hilltops and is covered with deciduous woods in its entirety. The steamship came into Fairport, Achtabula [Ashtabula], and Salem, where a large amount of bats flew around the harbor entry.[29] Continuing our journey, the engine broke during the night, and we reached Dunkerke only on the following morning (June 27), a small place of Dutch design that is not yet mentioned in the *Ohio Gazetteer* of 1833.[30] A lighthouse is built at the land's end nearby. At eleven o'clock, Buffaloe was already in view at the end of the lake, and we witnessed a race between two large steamships. We

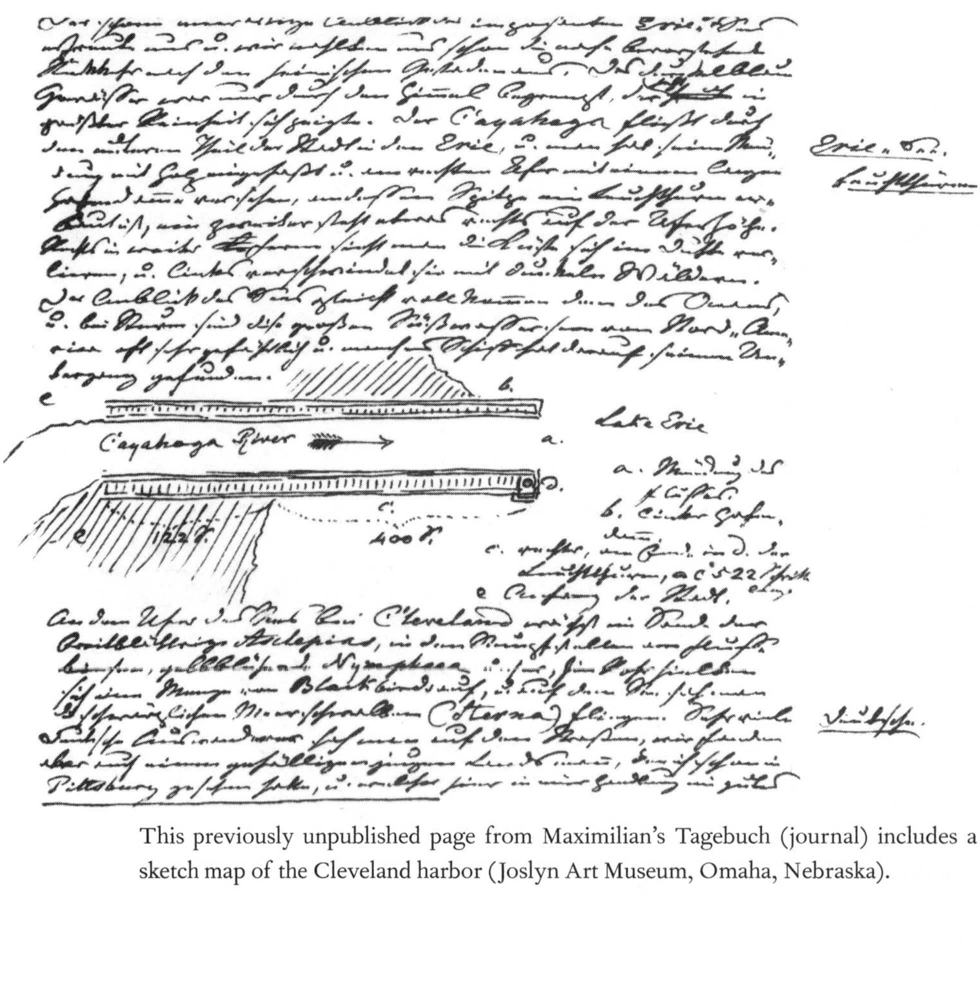

This previously unpublished page from Maximilian's Tagebuch (journal) includes a sketch map of the Cleveland harbor (Joslyn Art Museum, Omaha, Nebraska).

approached Buffaloe where many steamships produced a very lively and attractive view when they filed past us, ornamented with multicolored flags. At twelve we berthed at a landing in Buffaloe.[31]

Although various other travelers made observations similar to those of Maximilian, his account stands out from other accounts because of its very early date; its coverage of the entire length of the canal only one year and eight months after the opening in 1832 of its entire length; and its detailed biological, social, and cultural records and insights. More information on Maximilian's life and work can be found in studies done by Hermann Josef Roth, Paul Schach, and Michael G. Noll.[32]

NOTES

Our more extensively annotated translation of his journey on the Ohio & Erie Canal can be found in the 2009 issue of *Ohio History*. Sabina Thomas was the primary translator of Maximilian's account. The introduction, background, and endnotes were written primarily by Joseph Hannibal and Michael Noll. Bonnie Bowers helped format the manuscript. Timothy Matson and N'omi Greber, Cleveland Museum of Natural History, provided information on vertebrates and archeological sites, respectively. Kathleen Farago, Cleveland Heights–University Heights Library, proofread and critiqued the manuscript.

1. According to Maximilian's previous chapter, he arrived at Portsmouth around noon on Friday, June 20, thus this journey begins on the afternoon of that date, not the twenty-first. The first few paragraphs of this chapter confirm this date. This translation covers Maximilian's chapter 32 up to his arrival at Buffalo, New York.

2. Maximilian rode a lighter, quicker, passenger boat along the Erie Canal on the next leg of his trip, and in his journal he favorably compares Erie Canal packets with the combined passenger boat/freighter. Separate passenger boats, like the packets used along the Erie Canal, would be used in Ohio only at a later date, according to Jack Gieck, *A Photo Album of Ohio's Canal Era, 1825–1913*, rev. ed. (Kent: Kent State Univ. Press, 1992), 36.

3. Feeders are the names of diversion canals that connect the river with the canal in order to draw or release water from the latter if it is too full [Maximilian's note].

4. About the history of the Shawnies or Chavanos, see *Mckenney hist. of the Indian Tribes of N. America*, volume 5, biography of the Catahecassa, and other writings [Maximilian's note].

5. The Chillicothe area is noted for the great number of mounds and other earthworks that were erected by Native Americans. See Ephraim George Squier and Edwin Hamilton Davis, *Ancient Monuments of the Mississippi Valley. Comprising the Results of Extensive Original Surveys and Explorations* (1848; rpt., New York: AMS Press, 1973). In their account, Squier and Davis include

Maximilian in a list of authorities who had published observations on the ancient monuments. The maps of their volume show that the Ohio & Erie Canal passed very close to or through earthworks at several locations.

6. Refer to his *Reise durch Nord-America*, volume 2, page 187, and other works [Maximilian's note].

7. Maximilian here shows his disdain for the lack of respect for archeological remains and the destruction of these remains by the Euroamericans. The destruction of the earthen walls at Circleville that Maximilian describes here was only part of what was to be an orgy of destruction. Maximilian was not the only one to decry the destruction of the ancient monuments in this area; Caleb Atwater, amateur archaeologist from Circleville (1778–1867), whom Maximilian mentions here in passing, also did, lamenting the destruction at Circleville and Chillicothe.

The construction of the canals was part of the noted destruction of ancient earthworks. Squier and Davis noted that at Lockport: "A small truncated pyramid once existed here, but the construction of the Ohio canal, and the subsequent establishment of the village of Lockport at this point, have obliterated this as well as numerous other mounds. Indeed, these causes have resulted in the almost total destruction of the singular maze of embankments" (*Ancient Monuments*, 71).

8. The mussel he mentions is *Pyganodon grandis* (Say), known as the giant floater.

9. The troupial (*Psaroc. phoeniceus*) is the red-winged blackbird. This well-known denizen of Ohio wetlands is now known as *Agelaius phoeniceus.* "Tringas" is the solitary sandpiper (*Tringa*). *Totanus* is a bird genus whose members are known as yellowlegs. The term "rice-bird" has been used for a number of birds, but in the nineteenth century the name, along with the name reedbird, was used for the bobolink. Maximilian's inclusion of a scientific name (*Emberiza oryzivora*) confirms this identification. Supposedly, bobolinks moved into Ohio with the expansion of open lands in the 1800s. Thus, Maximilian has made one of the earliest reports of this bird as it came into the state.

10. Maximilian notes that the banks of the canal here and later at Nashport are covered with introduced *Verbascum*, or common mullein [*Verbascum thapsus* Linneaus]. He was keenly aware of the extremely quick spread of introduced species (aliens) along the canal here as well as the canals of Europe. Maximilian notes the butterfly *Papilio ajax* visiting puddles. This butterfly is the eastern tiger swallowtail, now known as *Papilio glaucus.* Visiting puddles to obtain moisture and especially minerals concentrated in ephemeral ponds is known as puddling, a behavior typically associated with some species of butterflies.

11. Maximilian is correct that Lock 51 is in Portsmouth and Lock 1 of that series is on the south side of the Licking Summit. However, he did not realize that the Licking Summit was only one of two summits along the Ohio & Erie Canal. The other, higher, summit was in Akron.

12. For information about all these places, see the *Ohio-Gazetteer* and other works [Maximilian's note]. John Kilbourne (1787–1833) compiled many editions of this best-selling book, as well as *Public Documents Concerning the Ohio Canals*, published in 1832.

13. At Newark, the canal passed through embankments that formed part of some of the most impressive and complex monuments constructed by Native Americans in Ohio. Then where the Ohio & Erie Canal entered the Licking River it ran along a slackwater, the height of which was regulated by a dam through the Black Hand Gorge. Part of the towpath here was cut into a cliff and built up in part with stone blocks. The famous Black Hand pictograph for which the site is named was destroyed, supposedly by accident, when the canal was being constructed in 1828. Graywacke as used today is a dark gray sandstone containing a fair amount of clay. The rock here at Newark is no longer considered to be a graywacke but rather sandstone. The rock unit exposed along the Black Hand Gorge is the Black Hand Sandstone Member of the Cuyahoga Formation. See Joseph T. Hannibal, *Geology along the Towpath: Stones of the Ohio & Erie and Miami & Erie Canals*, Ohio Division of Geological Survey Guidebook no. 14 (1998): 25–27.

14. Roscoe is now part of Coshocton. Its name lives on in Roscoe Village, a restored canal town within Coshocton (see chapter 14 in this volume).

15. The yellow-striped snake is either the eastern ribbon snake (*Thamnophis sauritus*) or a garter snake (*Thamnophis* spp.). Both can swim, and both can have distinctive longitudinal yellow stripes. *Coluber constrictor* was called the black snake at this time, but today is preferentially called the black racer. However, the black snake Maximilian saw could have been an adult water snake (*Nerodia sipedon*) or another kind of snake. Timothy Matson, personal communication with Joseph Hannibal, 2003

16. Lockport was, as indicated by its name, a canal town. It was originally opposite New Philadelphia and is now part of New Philadelphia.

17. See Dr. Julius l. cit. I page. 198 [Maximilian's note]. Maximilian is referring to one of his footnotes in his chapter 33, in which he discusses the views of Dr. Nicholas Heinrich Julius. The footnote that Maximilian is referring to here deals with the propensity of Americans to name towns after places in Europe, while ignoring more harmonious names of the Native Americans.

18. The dwarf rose found along the Tuscarawas was certainly a member of the genus *Rosa*, possibly *Rosa palustris*, the swamp rose, a native plant.

19. Currently, there aren't any Indians in the state of Ohio; only at the northeastern edge are some rare relic settlements of this unfortunate human tribe. Regarding the injustice that was committed in the United States against the Indians, see also Dr. Julius L. cit. I page 333; and in Georgia where a helpless government (President Jackson) had not been able to protect them, I, page 81 [Maximilian's note]. New Portage was a small town in the early canal days, located at the southern end of the Portage Path, and is now part of the City of Barberton.

20. Maximilian describes Summit Lake, a natural lake and canal reservoir, one of the great natural features along the canal before the decimation of its larch forest. He takes interest in the larch, noting alternative common names for it, including tamarack and hackmatack, the latter an Algonquin name. *Nuphar* is spatterdock, a water lily; *Pontederia* (*P. cordata*), is known as pickerelweed or as pickerel rush. It has distinctive lance-shaped leaves.

21. Akron is now the seat of Summit County, formed in 1840 by combining the western portion of Portage County with smaller parts of Medina and Stark Counties.

22. This well-known staircase section of locks is now preserved in Cascade Locks Park, part of Cascade Valley Metro Park in central Akron. It is located along the steepest section of the Ohio & Erie Canal. The time delay necessitated for locking through all of these locks would have given Maximilian time to investigate the various features he lists.

23. Old Portage was once a well-known village located between locks 21 and 22, now part of Akron.

24. The stone is probably Berea Sandstone, which was the number-one choice for grindstones in the area during the nineteenth century. The location is probably what is now known as Deep Lock Quarry Metro Park.

25. Apparently Maximilian slept through most of what is now Cuyahoga Valley National Park, so we are without his keen observations of an area now enjoyed by park visitors.

26. At the time of Maximilian's trip the harbor and lighthouse would have been seven-tenths of a mile from the end of the canal along the Cuyahoga River in what is now the Flats area of Cleveland, immediately west of downtown. Ahaz Merchant's 1835 *Map of Cleveland and Its Environs* shows the harbor structure and a beacon light located on the east pier at the harbor.

27. The *Oliver Newberry* was a side-wheeled steamer presumably named for Oliver Newberry (1789–1860), a pioneering steamship entrepreneur sometimes called the Admiral of the Lakes.

28. Lake Erie measures 290 miles across its length from the southwest to the northeast; its width is 68 miles at the greatest range; its depth supposedly is nowhere more than 100 to 120 feet [Maximilian's note].

29. Salem was the old name for Conneaut. The bats were probably seen around or just after sunset, as the bats of this area tend to be crepuscular or nocturnal.

30. Dunkirk is in New York State, southwest of Buffalo.

31. In the remaining part of the chapter, which is beyond the scope of this project, Maximilian visits the Seneca and other Native American people in New York, the Niagara River and Niagara Falls area.

32. See Paul Schach, "Maximilian, Prince of Wied (1782–1867) Reconsidered," *Great Plains Quarterly* 14 (1994): 5–20; Hermann Josef Roth, "Maximilian Prinz zu Wied: Leben und Wirken," *Fauna und Flora in Rheinland-Pfalz. Zeitschrift für Naturschutz* Beiheft 17 (1995): 13–26; and Michael G. Noll, "Prince Maximilian's America: The Narrated Landscapes of a German Explorer and Naturalist" (Ph.D. diss., Univ. of Kansas, 2000).

Chapter 6

The Hands of the Diligent

KATHLEEN FERNANDEZ

A contemporary observer of the Society of Separatists of Zoar, P. F. D., in his essay "Harmony Builds a House" (1832), uses a quotation from Proverbs 10:4 to describe the serendipity the building of the Ohio & Erie Canal provided this struggling group of Germans who, driven from their ancestral homeland by religious persecution, came to settle in the Tuscarawas Valley and form a communal society.[1]

> He becomes poor that dealeth with a slack hand, but the hand of the diligent maketh rich.

In just four short years, the Separatists—so called because they separated from the Lutheran state church in Germany—went from desperately scratching out a living from their new land to becoming, in P. F. D.'s words, the "trading center of the region." And it was all because of the Ohio & Erie Canal.[2]

The Separatists so needed the labor of every member—including women of childbearing years—that they made another momentous decision in 1822, just five years after their arrival in the United States, to become celibate. Celibacy, already a tenet of their faith, had been originally optional. It now became mandatory. Men and women who were already married lived in separate households. They all worked together in the fields to survive and earn enough cash to pay off the $16,000 mortgage on their land. They needed a way to get the fruits of their labor to market to obtain funds. The dream of the Ohio & Erie Canal was seen as the means to that end. It was the answer to the religious Separatists' prayers.

After it was determined that the canal would travel seven miles through their lands, the Separatists decided to build this portion themselves. They desired to maximize the $21,000 they would receive from the State of Ohio in return for their land and labor. Because women had no young children to look after, they could work beside the men, carrying the dirt from the excavation in baskets on their heads and in their aprons. They also built a guard lock to regulate the water flow from the Tuscarawas and another for a feeder canal into the nearby village of Zoar. Outside workmen built four stone lift locks along this route. The Separatists obtained additional income by providing nearby canal contractors with food and supplies. In two years of arduous labor, they succeeded; the canal opened to Cleveland, and their mortgage was paid. And in 1829, celibacy ended in Zoar, though it is unknown whether their newfound wealth was the cause.

Evidence of the prosperity brought by the canal can still be seen everywhere in Zoar. Number One House (1835), the Zoar Store (1833), the Zoar Hotel (1833), and many residences date from this time. Travelers on the canal were beginning to discover this little piece of Germany nestled in the Tuscarawas Valley. One, George Washington Heyward, stopped off in 1829 and marveled at the new geometric central garden and its accompanying "hot house."[3]

In 1832, the canny Zoarites, wishing to profit from all aspects of the canal, built the Canal Tavern on its banks; the building still stands as the Inn on the River Restaurant. Overnight packet-boat passengers, boatmen, and their animals were cared for here. Yearly bills to the boat companies totaled as much as $1,000; this trade was so great that the Zoar Hotel was built a year later right in town to cater to the overflow, as well as a burgeoning tourist trade.

Flour, lumber, hides, and other Zoar produce routinely were sent to ports north and south on the canal. Butter, made from the milk of the Zoar dairy herd, was especially prized by the commission merchants in Cleveland and New York. The canal enabled the Separatists to plunge into other business ventures, as well. In 1834, they established Zoar Furnace, just off the canal north of the village, to produce pig iron. A spur was cut into the canal to bring in ore and coal, both mined nearby, and ship out the iron pigs. Finished products were cast in the nearby Zoar Foundry. The community became noted for its cast-iron stoves, which can still be seen in the restored buildings at Zoar. A second facility, Fairfield Furnace, on One-Leg Creek south of town, was purchased from

The canal brought prosperity to Zoar (Ohio Historical Society).

some Canton investors the same year. An entrepreneurial effort, the iron industry employed mainly outsiders. The enterprises contributed great income to the Society and would not have been possible except for the cheap transportation afforded by the canal.

Joseph Bimeler, the Zoar Society's visionary business and religious leader, described the community, including the iron industry, in glowing terms to U.S. postmaster general William T. Barry on June 12, 1834: "The village of Zoar is situated about 9 miles directly north of New

The canal afforded cheap transportation for the Separatists' many enterprises, such as manufacturing iron stoves (Ohio Historical Society).

Philadelphia . . . about ½ mile east of the Ohio Canal and the Tuscarawas River; it is principally inhabited by Germans and contains at present about 300 souls. The improvements consist chiefly in: 1 flouring-mill, 2 saw-mills, 1 oil-mill, 1 woolen and linen manufacturing establishment; 1 warehouse; 1 new and commodious hotel; 1 store and various other places of industry and mechanical business." He goes on to describe the new blast furnace being built, the rolling land and its "products of the soil . . . wheat, rye, corn, barley, oats, flax and hemp. . . . Horses, cattle and sheep are improving." He describes the nearby iron ore "which is daily hauled to the banks of the Ohio Canal, from thence shipped to the several blast furnaces north and south."[4]

But just after this was written, the canal brought an unwelcome gift to the community: cholera. Between August and September 1834, fifty-two of the three hundred souls mentioned by Bimeler perished. This dread disease broke out when the body of Allen Wallace, a canal traveler who had died while staying at the Canal Tavern, was exhumed from the Zoar Cemetery by his wife, who wanted the belongings buried with him. Whether Wallace's body carried the illness or the timing was just coincidental, cholera swiftly cut down many Zoarites of all ages.

The community by now was stable enough financially to rally, and with outside labor it continued its expansion, building a double four-story flouring mill over the canal in 1837. Although not as efficient as its other mills, the section spanning the canal was ideal for storage, as boats were loaded from above without having to dock. Remnants of this huge structure can still be seen north of Lock 10.

The Society kept its own fleet of canal boats, the *Friendship*, the *Industry*, and a flatboat used to haul ore, the *Economy*. In 1837, Zoar figured the cost to operate the *Industry* with member Johannes Petermann (1819–1872) at the helm was $170 per month. In the next year, they hired Captain James Rutter at $218 per month, with Rutter paying his own expenses. His contract was renewed until at least 1843. Jacob Barnhardt of Peninsula custom-built a new boat, perhaps again called *Friendship*, at a cost of $1,100 in 1849.

In 1845, the Society closed the Canal Tavern, having dismissed its proprietor, member Johann Georg Gasely (Goessele), for not following its rules in dealing with the canallers. Gasely sued the Society, and the eventual outcome of this suit, in 1852 in the U.S. Supreme Court established that communal societies have the right to insist that members abide by their signed contracts.[5]

The economy was changing along the canal. Passenger service drifted to the more efficient railroads such as the Cleveland & Pittsburgh, which came to Zoar Station (two miles distant) in the mid-1850s. The Separatists,

Canal boats loaded grain directly from the mill above the canal (Ohio Historical Society).

Traffic declined as more shipping and passenger service shifted to the railroads (Ohio Historical Society).

never ones to miss an economic opportunity, opened a store on land they owned adjacent to the depot.

Canal freight traffic continued, but the local iron industry dwindled with the better Lake Superior ores now being used. The furnaces closed in the 1850s, the foundry in 1875, but local ore still was being shipped to Massillon as late as 1881.

Communal Zoar changed, too. After leader Joseph Bimeler's death in 1853, the Society began slowly to decline. Without this dynamic leader, the old ways continued without much thought. Tourism—brought to the fore in 1882 when the Wheeling & Lake Erie Railroad came right into Zoar—became the leading industry and brought customers, cash, and crisis to Zoar. Church attendance declined without Bimeler's inspiring Sunday Discourses, and many young people left to make their own way in the world. Finally, in March 1898, the remaining Separatists decided to dissolve the Zoar Society.

The Zoar landholdings were divided among the 222 surviving members, and Zoar became just another sleepy Ohio village. A huge clay deposit along the canal and railroad was sold to local interests and became the Zoar Fire Brick Company, an enterprise that thrived into the 1970s. After the 1913 flood ruined the canal for transportation, the State of Ohio's Division of Wildlife constructed State Fish Farm No. 12 in the canal north of Lock 10. This enterprise was never very successful, and the hatchery closed in 1935.

In 1930, the U.S. Army Corps of Engineers proposed moving Zoar to higher ground so it would not be inundated by the impounded waters of its Dover and Bolivar Dams; villagers, both Society descendants and

Zoar Hotel was built in 1833 to serve increased canal and tourist trade. Part of the building remains in the original location (William Bennett Collection of the Massillon Museum).

new residents, persuaded the Corps to construct the Zoar Levee instead. This saved the town but forever separated it from its lifeblood, the Ohio & Erie Canal and the river. That same year, the newly formed Zoar Historical Society opened Number One House as a museum, and Zoar again became a destination for tourists. Number One, the Garden and other acquired buildings, including the 2001-restored Zoar Hotel, were later purchased by the State of Ohio and since 1942 have been administered by the Ohio Historical Society.

In 1965, the canal lands from Zoarville (formerly Zoar Station) northwest to Bolivar were deeded to the Tuscarawas County Commissioners by the State Canal Lands office. Nothing much was done with them until the mid-1970s when the Buckeye Council Boy Scouts developed the Zoar Valley Trail from Fort Laurens in Bolivar to Zoar and then to Zoarville along the towpath. Later, the Ohio Historical Society began giving tours along the towpath, as a way to draw attention to the importance of the canal's history to the village.

With the formation of the Ohio & Erie Canal Corridor Coalition in 1989, the Zoar historic site manager became involved with the creation of the National Heritage Corridor. As part of this effort, the Tuscarawas County Commissioners created the Canal Lands Advisory Committee in 1995. This committee has since been instrumental in improving the towpath, building bridges, and creating a new crushed limestone surface so that hikers, bikers, horsemen and women, and everyone else can again appreciate the canal and how this once-vibrant economic resource, made by the hands of the diligent Zoar Separatists, still touches our lives today.

NOTES

1. P. F. D., "Harmony Builds a House," 1832, trans. by Wolfgang Fleishhauer, 27a. Peter Kaufmann Papers, MSS 136, Ohio Historical Society Library, Columbus.

2. P. F. D. "Harmony Builds a House," 28a.

3. George Washington Heyward, "Journal of a Trip to Ohio," 279, Ohio Historical Society Library.

4. Joseph Bimeler to U.S. Postmaster General William T. Barry, June 12, 1834, quoted in Edgar B. Nixon, "The Society of Separatists of Zoar" (Ph.D. diss., Ohio State Univ., 1933), 37.

5. Zoar Papers, MSS 110, box 3, folder 10, Ohio Historical Society Library.

Chapter 7

Voices on the Canal

PEG BOBEL AND LYNN METZGER

The stories of people who lived on and around the canal when it operated as a transportation system add a rich texture to the description of the actual building and operating of the canal. These are the tales of nineteenth-century settlers and travelers, twentieth-century boatmen, and canal-town residents. The latter are from people who bridged the turn of the century. These appeared in newspapers, magazines, letters, diaries, and in the Canal Society of Ohio journal, *Towpaths*.

In the long scope of history, the canal era was brief. The Ohio & Erie Canal was at times plagued by mismanagement, it was always challenged by the limitations of the seasons, and it was, finally, trod over by the "godless iron horse" of the railroads. However, the canals were and remain an important part of the local and national culture because they were the first thoroughfares to connect the rural Midwest to markets and the world beyond.

The idea for a canal system for Ohio, including the Ohio & Erie Canal, was received with enthusiasm; the farmers of Ohio were desperate for a way to transport their products to markets in the east. The roads in the early 1800s were either muddy and slippery or dusty and rutted, depending on the season. Everyone heard news about the Erie Canal and how it was changing the economy across the midsection of New York State; Ohioans were, understandably, eager for this new transportation system.

The Ohio & Erie Canal was begun in 1825 and completed from Cleveland to Portsmouth by 1832, a total of 309 miles. The canal changed and connected the landscape of Ohio with hard work and intriguing technology, creating what Pearl Nye in song called the "little silver ribbon."

The story of the Ohio & Erie Canal is well documented in history, legal documents, surveys, and plat maps. More difficult to find are the stories of the actual people who built the canal; lived, worked, and traveled on it; and served its community. Probably most did not write very much, if at all. Other stories have been lost in time. But both photographs and stories do exist from the later part of the canal era, when the canal was losing its competitive battle with the railroads.

In the early 1960s, there was a groundswell of interest in the old canal, best noted in the founding of the Canal Society of Ohio and the sustained effort of that group's members to collect stories, journals, diaries, and photographs from the canal era—as well as firsthand recollections from individuals who lived and remembered when the canal was a waterway from Cleveland to Portsmouth. From the Canal Society of Ohio's collection and other sources, we can glimpse what life was like in Ohio when canals dominated the transportation scene. Descriptions of life on and near the canal vary widely, from variations on the "little silver ribbon" theme to comments about a smelly, polluted ditch. Some accounts tell us that life on the canal boats was often a family affair, with the husband/father as captain and the wife/mother as cook, laundress, and general housekeeper. There are many more stories about the men and their activities than about the women and theirs. The men's activities were at the center of the expanding economic development, and, as was the custom, the women provided the support for those activities. And the women did not leave behind many words about their own lives. It is difficult now to comprehend just how they managed the work—living on the boats, cooking for their family and the crew, doing the laundry, and "boat-schooling" their children.

Most important, however, chroniclers talked about the canal as a transportation system that connected places which had never been connected and opened Ohio to immigrants, commerce, and general expansion. Ellis H. Shimp of Newcomerstown, Ohio, collected many canal stories from local elders who remembered the canal days. Writing for the *Newcomers News* in 1975, he reported, "In retrospect, old timers living today say during their youth the Ohio & Erie Canal was truly a sight to behold and without doubt served its purpose well."[1] The following stories shed light on several aspects of the canal-era life, from immigration and travel to canal boat labor.

The canal, as a thoroughfare, served both local travelers and those coming from great distances. When Ohio's economy began to flourish with the movement of goods in and out of the state, there was great opportunity to farm or work in the developing industries. European travelers such as Maximilian, Prince of Wied (see chapter 5), who wrote about their adventures in the new nation of the United States were influential in encouraging people to emigrate; however, even more important were the letters sent home from people who had survived immigration and were settled in this country of abundant land and jobs. We are a nation of children of immigrants, and many of our connections with our past and our identities are found in the stories of immigration to America. Immigration history is rooted in the push-pull factors: the push of the political-social-religious-economic issues of nineteenth-century Europe and the pull of available land, resources, and the need for laborers in America.

The people who immigrated to Ohio came from many economic, national, and religious backgrounds, pulled by the United States' many opportunities. Some came to construct the new canals, while others found work on the canal system or serving it. Other immigrants came to build mills, quarry stone, mine coal, and begin small manufacturing enterprises. Others used the canal for travel to their land holdings in the fertile valleys of eastern Ohio. Clearly the canal system allowed people to travel farther and faster than they ever had before.

In the late 1820s and 1830s, the Irish immigrants were the group most closely connected with building the Ohio & Erie Canal, but German and English immigrants outnumbered the Irish as farmers, owners of businesses, and entrepreneurs. Many immigrants moved several times after coming to the United States, making their way west for richer land and economic opportunity.

Family stories of such immigration are often treasured and handed down through the generations. There is a deep satisfaction in being able to connect with one's ancestors, to say, for instance, "my great-grandmother came from . . . ." or "my grandfather worked at . . . ." The late Frances McGovern, Akron attorney and author, enjoyed describing how her ancestors came from France and traveled to Akron on the Ohio & Erie Canal, remnants of which were just beyond her west Akron backyard. Her family story was featured in the *Louisville (Ohio) Herald* on February 16, 1888. The article, written sixty years after the journey, "A Pioneer Family," describes the family's journey from France to Louisville (near Canton, Ohio). The unnamed author begins by telling readers that Joseph C. Menegay, the second son of Claude Joseph Menegay and "his faithful wife," provided "many anecdotes of the lives and experiences of our early settlers" in what was then the "far west."

The writer continues the story: "Among the good people who helped transform wilderness into a thrifty farming community comprising Nimishillen township [just east of Canton] was Claude Joseph Menegay, his faithful wife and sturdy children, who reached this locality after a journey of over three months—a journey that in this day would take one to the other side of the world and return." Claude Menegay is described as a "sturdy French farmer, in comfortable circumstances," who lived in the Jura Mountains of France, near the border with Switzerland.

> Most glowing letters came to these provinces of the unlimited resources of the glorious land in the new hemisphere. As an example of these inducements Mr. M says his father was assured that if the people here needed eggs they went out and gathered them from the fence corners, and if honey were desired a tree was quickly felled and the want supplied. Of course, this might be true enough, but it was necessary to have the fence corners, the fowls, and the trees. These letters, which did not travel as swiftly or as cheaply as now, were highly treasured and widely circulated. . . . Notwithstanding the too-glowing promises held out to the emigrants, their advantages here were innumerable, judging from the cramped condition of populous Europe.

The story continues with this account of the many segments of the journey:

> On April 7, 1828, the family started across France with their possessions in two wagons. . . . Eight days' travel brought the party to Havre, whence they embarked on a staunch new passenger ship *France* for New York, where they landed after a voyage of forty-two days. Here they continued their journey, going up the Hudson to Albany on a curious steamboat, which towed two barges lashed to her sides. From Albany a two weeks' trip took them across the State to Buffalo. . . . A steamer from Buffalo landed the party in Cleveland. They suffered more from sea sickness on Erie than on the Atlantic. A few days then on the raging canal [the Ohio & Erie] and they were in Akron, where friends from here met them with oxen and brought them to their long-sought home. They brought their two wagons with them, tools, clothes for several years, etc.

There were ten children in the family when the Menegays came and the eleventh was born two years after they settled in Louisville. That child, Simon Menegay, was Frances McGovern's great-grandfather. According to the *Herald* article, the family bought 320 acres for about $8 per acre from the heirs of Ulrich Shevely.

The 1888 author notes:

> People worked hard in those days, and earned all they realized. Laborers were paid but fifty cents per day on the average, the day beginning at four in the morning and lasting until dark, in the summer. Wheat was hauled to the canal at Massillon, and sold for fifty cent per bushel: oats brought a shilling. These with rye, flax, corn, etc. were the staples. In the spring maple sugar was made by the ton, the season often lasting six weeks, and thirty barrels of sap having been gathered in a day. Enough of this sugar for the use of the family was retained; the remainder sold at from three to four cents a pound.[2]

In Akron, the legacy of another immigrant family lives on next to the canal and reconstructed towpath. The Frederick Mustill house and store are prominent features in the Ohio & Erie National Heritage Canalway. The house is an excellent example of the gable-front Greek Revival style of architecture. It has been restored and is being used as a residence. The Mustill store, located next to Lock 15 on the canal, has been refurbished as a museum and is a popular gathering spot for visitors enjoying the Towpath Trail. In the 1830s, this area was called Cascade. Located at the foot of the staircase locks that climbed up to Akron, the little town of Cascade was a busy commercial milling center during the canal era, and the Mustill store was at the heart of the action. The family history of Emma Taylor Mustill, Frederick Mustill's wife, provides another immigration story.

Emma, the daughter of Richard Taylor and Maria Dunham, was one of twelve children. She and three siblings were born in Surrey, England. The family emigrated to the United States in 1831. In an account attributed to a family journal, the journey to America is described as long and difficult.[3] The account reads,

> We emigrated to this country in January 1831 in the packet ship *Columbia*, . . . and landed at Sandy Hook March 20, 1831. . . . Having a very rough voyage, for two days and nights all gangways had to be closed to keep the ship from sinking. Cholera being so bad, that we had to be quarantined three days, then transported to Castle Garden, then came up the river to Cammitas, Onondague County, N.Y., where we lived for eighteen months. One son Richard was

> born there. From there we came to Buffalo and across the lake to Cleveland and from there to Akron on a canal boat. We lived in a plow shop, where Black's drug store now stands.

The Taylor family story continues, recounting the move into a shack that they had built, and describing how the father, Richard, had to be carried there because he was sick for thirteen weeks with a "bilious fever," with "no one to care for him but mother." As soon as he was better, "mother bought this piece of land, it being the 30th day of November, 1833." That autumn, the family built a log house, on what is now West Thornton Street in Akron.

The account continues: "In 1841 we built the house which stands here at the present time. October 2, 1841, five of us were taken ill with typhus fever." Three of Emma Taylor's younger brothers died between October 9 and October 14, and the next year another brother, only five months old, died. Emma's parents, however, lived into old age. Her father died in 1881 at age 82, and her mother died in 1889 at age 84.

Emma Taylor married Frederick Mustill in 1851, and the couple had four children who lived to adulthood: Maria, Frederick W., Edwin, and Frank. Emma very likely played an active part in running the Mustill store. Located adjacent to Lock 15 on the canal and at the base of the staircase locks into Akron, it was in a prime location to serve travelers delayed by the time-consuming process of locking through. Emma lived on the canal during the most active period of the canal era; once she survived immigration and deadly diseases, she lived an active life. She and her family lived in the house next to their store until 1888, when they moved to a house on nearby North Walnut Street. Frederick died in 1900, and several years later Emma moved back to the Mustill house at Lock 15. It was noted in her family history that she had attended the ball in 1847 when the Empire House opened as a hotel. She died March 17, 1911, the day the Empire House went out of business and closed, only two years before the flood of 1913 destroyed much of the canal and severely damaged the Mustill store building.[4]

Some individuals left letters or journals describing their local or regional canal journeys. John Malvin, a leader of Cleveland's African-American community in the late 1800s, included his canal experiences in his autobiography. Malvin's father was a slave, but his mother was free, so he too was considered free, and at the age of 32 he left Virginia and migrated to Ohio. After abandoning a plan to move to Canada, Malvin and his wife settled in Cleveland, where Malvin was employed for a time

The Empire Hotel in Akron in 1847. The Pennsylvania & Ohio Canal runs down Main Street at the far right (Summit County Historical Society Collection, Special Collections Division, Akron Summit County Public Library).

as the captain of the canal boat *Auburn*. Malvin recounts one particular incident which sheds some light on the difficulties he faced as an African American canal boat captain in the mid-1800s.

While traveling south from Cleveland, the *Auburn* stopped in the late evening to take on a passenger. When helped onto the boat, the female passenger saw that some of the crew members were African American and asked to see the captain. As Malvin describes it, "The light shone in my face so that she could easily see my features. The lady, after seeing me, suddenly sprang to her feet, and with great shortness of breath exclaimed, 'Well, I never! well, I never! well, I never.'" Malvin bowed and proceeded to make every effort to assure her comfort, beginning with ordering that the bedding be completely changed on her berth. Nonetheless, the lady sat up all night and refused breakfast the next morning, claiming she was not feeling well. At Massillon she likewise refused dinner but did manage to take "a piece of pie from where she stood."

By the time they reached Bethlehem (Navarre), she had accepted tea and a biscuit. It was a beautiful evening with a full moon. The cook, also African American, came on deck for a stroll and the captain observed that "the lady passenger followed her in a hesitating manner. They promenaded the deck together for a while, and then retired. I suppose the lady took a good night's sleep, for I did not hear anything from her until the next morning."

With the dawn of a new day, the passenger readily came to breakfast, "ate a hearty meal," and seemed at ease with all on board. At Circleville she departed with this thanks: "Captain, when I first came aboard your boat, and not being accustomed to travel in this way, I suppose I must have acted quite awkward. Now, I must return my thanks to you and your crew, for the kind treatment I have received. I never traveled so comfortably in all my life, and I expect to go north soon, and I will defer my journey until you are going north, even if I am obliged to wait two or three days." Malvin, however, never saw the lady again.[5]

A few years later another canal traveler, John B. White, was planning a trip from southeast Ohio to Halsted Hall, in Rochester, New York, to seek medical treatment. The facility, originally named Halsted Medical Institute, was a private "water-cure" facility operated by Hatfield Halsted. Water-cure institutions flourished briefly during the mid-1800s, claiming to cure all manner of illnesses with water—patients ingested large amounts of water, were irrigated with it and immersed in it, and had cold water shot at them. Halsted Hall and other water-cure facilities added rest and outdoor exercise to the regimen, which may have done patients the most good.[6] White's journal of his trip included brief notes about his treatment, including "was magnetized." What the journal also gives us is a great description of the many different types of transportation he used during his trip.

White's journal begins March 18, 1850, and ends on December 31, 1850. The portion describing his trip to and from Halsted Hall, including his stay, goes from March 18 through May 13. He records his trip back from Rochester in detail, along with associated costs. His medical treatment cost $42.89, while his transportation fares included the hack (a horse or carriage for hire) from Halsted Hall, 50¢; the train from Rochester to Buffalo, $2.20 (note that he takes the train even though the Erie Canal also ran from Rochester to Buffalo); passage on the lake boat *Saratoga* from Buffalo to Cleveland, $2.00; and fare on the canal boat *Akron,* from Cleveland to Akron, $1.25. He traveled from Akron to Adams Mills on the canal boat *Coral* for $2.68, took a coach to Dresden for 75¢, and then got on the steamboat *Zanesville,* on the Muskingum River, to Zanesville, for 50¢. At Zanesville, he hired a coach for 12½¢ to convey him to Concord, where he then borrowed a horse from his cousin to ride the four hours home. In total, his transportation cost $10.05. He spent 36¢ for food, and since he traveled on the boats at night and stayed with friends, he did not have lodging costs. White's journal provides insight regarding both the challenges and pleasure of canal travel and confirms the length of time it took to travel between points, whether by boat or other means.

His trip from Buffalo, New York, to home took seven and a half days. He left Buffalo via lake steamer on May 6, 1850, and enjoyed a pleasant trip on Lake Erie, arriving in Cleveland at 1:00 P.M. the next day, from where he sought to reach Dresden via canal. He records that at Cleveland, he "went in search of a canal boat to convey me to Zanesville. Could not find any going this evening. Went to the stage office and ascertained that no stage goes out before tomorrow morning. Finally concluded to go on board a packet bound for Akron. After taking supper at the hotel I was conveyed to the boat which started at eight o'clock."[7]

On May 8, White arrived in Akron midmorning and switched to the canal boat *Coral,* which he would take south toward Dresden. The boat traveled through the night, and White records how he spent part of the next day: "Rose at 5:00 o'clock and found our boat had been laying two or three hours, it having stopped to take in freight. Weather appeared

An 1876 packet boat near Eight Mile Lock south of Cleveland (Louis Baus Photograph Collection, University of Akron Archival Services).

more pleasant than yesterday. As the boat appeared rather slow in starting two of the passengers and myself took the Captain's gun and went ahead in search of game. Had not been long gone when we became alarmed by the appearance of a cloud, and, accordingly made for a house about a mile and a half distant. Rained but little. Boat did not overtake us till 10:00 o'clock. Got as far as Lockport by dark."

White rose early again on the 10th and found himself in the vicinity of Newcomerstown in Tuscarawas County. At 4:30 P.M., he reached Adams Mills, where he hired a coach to take him to Dresden, perhaps because it was quicker. At Dresden a side cut canal connected to the Muskingum River, giving White and other travelers an alternate way to continue south to the Ohio River. At Dresden he stayed all night with a friend, then the next morning boarded the steamboat *Zanesville,* traveling on the Muskingum River. The steamboat took him to Zanesville, where he arrived at 10:00 A.M. So far, his trip from Cleveland to Zanesville by canal boat, coach, and steamer, a distance of about 166 miles, had taken three and a half days. At this point, he was near home, but finding a way to get there became more difficult. He goes on, "Here, after a fruitless search for a conveyance to Chandlersville, I concluded to go to Concord by stage. Left at 3:00 and arrived in Concord a little after five. Spent the evening with cousin Joseph."

White then describes passing the Sabbath, May 12, listening to his cousin Joseph preach at the Crooked Creek Church and spending the night at a friend's house. The last day of his trip was Monday May 13. He completes his narrative of the trip: "Weather pleasant as yesterday. Left Concord after breakfast, having obtained the loan of Joseph's horse and by noon I got to our new home on Salt Creek. Spent the rest of the day in 'chat.' In the evening assisted a little at planting corn."

Years later another traveler kept a more extensive journal of his trip on the Ohio & Erie Canal. S. S. Dustin, an artist as well as an entertaining writer, wrote an article that was published in *Popular Monthly,* "When Garfield Was a Canal-Boy: Notes of a Leisurely Voyage on the Ohio Canal," in 1890. In this he describes his own trip on the canal, during which he reread James H. Earl's account of the future President Garfield's short career as a canal mule driver. It is most notable that he describes places we can see today in the Ohio & Erie National Heritage Canalway. Also, it is interesting that he already refers to the canal as "historic" in the late 1880s, describing the railroads and industrial cities that were flourishing, as well as mines and canal towns that were in decline.

Dustin traveled aboard the *Arthur W. Hall.* He begins his narrative at the weigh lock at Newburg (the northern terminus) and ends at Urichville, where he left the canal and traveled home by train, concluding, "I left at an early hour next morning, well content to get home by steam, and not at all envious of the life of a canal-man."[8] Dustin describes the landscape and towns with an artist's eye and provides the reader with a lively narrative of travel on the canal when it was well past its prime.

He begins by noting that the Town of Boston in the 1830s was the home of the notorious Jim Brown, the leader of a gang of counterfeiters. "After Boston—and dinner—the village of Peninsula was in sight. It is built on the side hill overlooking the valley and some of the prettiest bits of scenery I encountered in my trip. We next came to 'Johnny-cake,' as the boatmen call it, from the fact that years ago they were fed upon that wholesome diet at that port and it was quite a place in those good old days, not alone for corn in the cake but for the 'juice' of the corn. We passed two boats as we came out of Johnny-cake Lock and soon reached Pancake Lock and 'Yellow Creek Basin.'" Dustin continues with a description of Akron in the 1880s. "From Old Portage to Akron, a distance of two miles, there are 21 locks, 16 of them within the corporate limits of Akron. This is a lively city of 40,000 inhabitants. It is a great railroad center and has a number of manufactories of various kinds. Natural water power and the railroad facilities have given Akron a steady and healthy growth. The largest flouring-mills in the State are here. The streets are lighted by electricity, and the street-cars are run by the same power. The city is built on the hills overlooking the Little Cuyahoga Valley, and has many beautiful homes. One hundred years ago this Cuyahoga Valley was the western boundary of the United States" (279).

Dustin was not impressed with the Cascade Locks—they "retarded the progress." But,

> having passed through the south end of Akron, past the paper-mills, the match-factory, rubber-works and numerous lumber-yards, we soon enter Summit Lake, a beautiful sheet of water, surrounded by hills. On its east bank is a summer resort called Lakeside, where throngs of people from Akron and vicinity take their outings. This lake is the highest natural body of water in the State, and one of the feeders of the canal. Its waters flow out in both directions . . . as can plainly be seen from the floating bridge. This bridge, crossing a portion of the lake, is used as a tow-path. Occasionally, while crossing this bridge, the mules are pulled into the lake, and have to be rescued by cutting the tow-line, when they swim ashore. (282)

Part of the experience of a canal trip, at least for the men, seems to have been participation in the process. As John B. White noted, male passengers often rode the mules, went hunting while the boat was locking through, or tried their hand at steering the boat. Of course conversation with the captain was part of the journey. After Summit Lake, Dustin went ashore to walk and talk with a captain who was taking a turn at driving.

> "Well, captain," I said, "you have a fine team of mules." "Yas; that'ere nigh mule is a fine beast. I wouldn't take two hundred dollars fer her, if I could break her of that *hard water step.* You see I am driving for that very purpose. That kid on deck, peeling pertaters, got her into the notion of it." I asked him what he meant by "hard water step," and what caused it. He said: "Don't yer see the mule takes shorter steps with one foot than with the other? They get in the notion when towing very slow, with a measly kid to drive, that don't 'tend to business nohow, and lets the lazy mule loaf, while the other mule tries to get furder and furder ahead all the time, and throws the heft of the load on him." (282)

After this conversation, Dustin asked the captain if he could drive the mules. "It was growing dark as I mounted the saddle-mule and cracked the whip to the leader, who started so suddenly that I nearly lost my seat. Everything went smoothly until I passed another team of mules. It was then quite dark, and as I took the wrong side of the tow-path, the lines became tangled, and nearly precipitated the mules and myself into the canal"(282).

One has to wonder at the canal boat caption's sense of humor, as even after such a mishap he allowed Dustin to continue on the mule.

> It was soon so dark that I could not see the leader. The next few minutes were uneventful; but soon I heard the leader's feet splash into the water. . . . I thought the best thing to do under the circumstances was to dismount and wait for further developments, which soon came, by the captain's asking: "Why in the deuce don't you go ahead? Are you sleepin' straddle that mule? You'll fall off and break yer derned neck." I told him I guessed we had turned around and were about to run into Lake Erie, as I could not see anything but water. He bade me go ahead, as it was only a waste-way; but not knowing what a waste-way was, I declined. Finally he called

> me aboard, where I staid [*sic*] contentedly thereafter, thinking I had earned a promotion, and that if I should ever do further service, it would be as steersman. (282)

Dustin notes that since it was very dark, they stopped for the night and began again at daybreak. Like other travelers, he enjoyed the journey through what we now call the Portage Lakes. He describes the scenes with an artist's eye.

> We were at the edge of a forest, where a beautiful stream ran over a chaotic mass of logs that formed a dam, over which the water rushed, falling on the rocks below with a music that mingled with the songs of the birds. It was enough to make one envy the life of a canaller. . . .
>
> After breakfast we passed through the outlet of the feeder. On our right was Mud Lake; on our left, but hidden by a narrow strip of woods, lay Long Lake, noted for its many summer residences, and a large hotel situated in a pretty grove on a hill. A steam-boat carrying 500 passengers runs between here and Akron along the canal. Just above this lake, and connected with it, are the two Reservoirs. On the banks of one is a summer resort called Cottage Grove; beside the other stands the "Old State Mill," a quaint structure, surrounded by noble elms. (282)

Proceeding toward New Portage, they came to "Robinson's farm, where lies the decaying timbers of the *Ohio*, the first boat ever run on the canal. . . . We soon reached New Portage, which is the head of the Tuscarawas River." Dustin also noted that they passed the end of the Indian Trail, known as the Portage Path. This was the original trail that connected Old Portage to New Portage, connecting Cuyahoga and Tuscarawas Rivers (283).

Wolf Creek Lock is the first lock on the Tuscarawas River, going south over the east-west continental divide. After Wolf Creek proper, he writes of another old out-of-service canal boat, the *G. G. Grady*, which operated for forty years. He is describing rotting canal boats, and the canal is still a transportation system; clearly it was past its most productive years. The Wolf Creek name comes from the numerous wolves killed in the area in the early days. These encounters were the subject of many stories of hairbreadth escapes with wolves long gone from the area.

> Our captain, one of the oldest now running on the canal, told me that, years ago, while lying off Wolf Creek, he had a carcass of veal stored under the stern of the boat, and one night a window was accidentally left open. In the morning a big gray wolf was seen to spring out of the window into the water and swim ashore with a portion of the veal. The boatmen gave chase with gun and ax. The wolf . . . dropped his meat to give them battle; but a well-directed bullet soon laid him low. They thus secured the meat and its purloiner. The wolf was triumphantly exhibited at the stations along the route. At each place the health of the brave captain was drunk, to the ring of overflowing glasses of whisky and apple-jack. (283)

The voyage continued through Locks 2 and 3 into Clinton, once a bustling little mill town, now with little commercial activity, and Dustin, as an artist, was a keen observer of details, noting the Tuscarawas River runs first on one side of the canal and then the other, with lovely trees and flowers everywhere.

> What attracted my attention at Canal Fulton, our next town, was an old wooden hotel, dilapidated but inviting, with a bevy of fresh-looking country lassies at the window. Such a curiosity as an artist in sketching attire, [Dustin,] sitting on the bow-deck of a canal-boat, could not fail to attract a flattering amount of attention.
>
> Here the rain began to pour down. . . . The first outbreak after the storm had gathered was the deep hollow voice of the driver, in the distance, calling to the captain to "steer his old tub to the shore, and get another driver, as *he* would not drive that hide-bound, crippled old biped of a mule another step." He was wet as a drowned rat, and testy as a hornet. However, after much persuasion and a good dinner of raised biscuit, mashed potatoes, ham and eggs, tomatoes, coffee and peach-pie . . . he cheerfully took to the tow-path again, and was soon heard singing, "Wait Till the Clouds Roll By." (283)

Moving along on their journey in spite of the storm, Dustin notes the large deserted old gristmill at "Fulton Lock" (Lock 4), and then Palmers Island (283).

As the canal boat proceeded south it reached the worked out coal areas, passing piles of slag and old coal chutes. They reached Millport, later known as Crystal Springs, a small burg, with large breweries on the banks of the canal. And Dustin wrote of the spot: "A boat was being

S. S. Dustin was impressed with Massillon as a commercial center. This 1896 photo was taken at the Fremont Street Bridge (Louis Baus Photograph Collection, University of Akron Archival Services).

loaded with the barrels. There was water, water everywhere, but not a drop of beer to drink." He was impressed with Massillon; he thought it a thriving manufacturing town that in 1888 had about 12,000 residents. He briefly noted the types of businesses, including the largest threshing-machine and portable engine works in Ohio. The storm continued and Dustin convinced the captain to let him try his hand at the helm and he quickly ran the boat into the bank (284).

"By this time what little sentiment there was in my soul had been drowned out, and I was willing to trust the boat to the care of the captain." It was still raining when they reached Rochester, the next small town, which later merged with Navarre and Bethlehem to become the Town of Navarre. It had been a large grain-shipping hub: "This town, once so prosperous and hopeful, now bears the funereal aspect of so many similar places that depended on the canal for support. . . . The houses looked haunted; the people, as they passed, or grouped themselves under a friendly awning for shelter, seemed discouraged and weary of life. Such, at least, were the weird imaginings inspired by the storm." They tied up in the lock for the night in a place called Savon but were soon forced to move from the lock by another boat, traveling at night. They then did not tie the boat but let it float: "I did not sleep much, having the upper berth. I could hear too plainly the rain on the deck, only six inches above my head. In the middle of the night there was a heavy thud. We had run ashore. With a start, I raised up in my bunk, and received a severe knock on the head. I resolved to lie down again, and risk the terrors of the raging canal. I felt in my little sixteen-inch bed as nearly the sensation of being in a coffin as I cared to experience" (285).

The next day was clear as they passed through "Wild Cat Basin," the site of another canal boat story. "Boatmen tell of a driver who, as he passed this place one moonlight night, whistling and watching the shooting-stars, was startled by a blood-curdling scream. He paused to look back and see what he knew to be a wild cat pursuing him. He sprang into the water, closely followed by the cat. The captain of his boat fortunately saw his danger, and shot the cat just as it was about to fasten upon its somewhat tough prey. The driver thenceforth carried a gun through that dangerous region" (285).

They crossed the aqueduct over the Tuscarawas River, before reaching Bolivar, another shipping point for grain. "Here the old Sandy and Beaver Canal, no longer used, branches from the Ohio Canal, and runs to the Ohio River through a section of the coal and grain country. At the time of its building there were no railroads" (285). The boat then passed through land owned by the Zoar Separatist community (described in chapter 6).

After traveling past the beautiful cattle, river, and fields, all part of the Zoarites' eighteen thousand acres of land, the boat went through four locks near Zoar before reaching the village. "There we run under two immense flour-mills built on the canal, but long since deserted for the new mills near the railroad. Then came Long Basin, leading into the finest stretch of the canal, called Feeder Level. A little below is a waste-way, where mules have to wade belly-deep, after drinking their fill. The saddle-mule lay down to drown the flies that had been bothering him. The driver took a header, coming up much demoralized." Dustin notes the Stone Quarry Lock, and Stone Quarry Level, where there were two salt wells in operation. The next point of interest was Canal Dover, a town of about ten thousand inhabitants. A small island in the river was a summer resort for the local folks: "The river here is wide and deep enough for small steam-boats to navigate. We met one loaded with a jolly crowd of excursionists going to the island" (286).

The boat then arrived at Sugar Creek Basin, with a dam where the creek crossed the canal, followed by New Philadelphia, the county seat of Tuscarawas County, also a great grain region. Then there was Lockport, "a mining and milling town, with Oldtown Basin and its high hills for background, where you can see no less than six coal-banks, some of which have been worked for fifty years. At New Castle Lock, also, the hills are filled with coal, some of the mines delivering immense quantities, while others are exhausted." Dustin left the canal at Trenton and was "well content to get home by steam, and not at all envious of the life of a canal-man" (286). S. S. Dustin appreciated the natural beauty of the canal, but unlike several earlier travelers such as Maximilian, he also saw the economic decline that was due to a poorly maintained canal and competition from the railroads.

Our next two stories are of men who lived during the last years of the canal era and into the post-canal era. Pearl R. Nye, born on a canal boat in 1872, worked on the Ohio & Erie Canal and recorded his experiences in folk songs and journals; James Dillow Robinson (who went by "Dillow"), born thirty-two years later, lived and worked on a canal boat and wrote his memories in poetry and stories. Each provides a personal view of canal life. Nye the balladeer wrote that the "little silver ribbon" was

Pearl Nye, born on a canal boat, devoted his life to writing and preserving canal songs and stories (Summit County Historical Society Collection, Special Collections Division, Akron Summit County Public Library).

"the dearest place of all this earth to me," and penned Dillow Robinson the poet, "If there's canals in that land beyond the great divide, once again an old canal boat I will ride."[9] Both provide nostalgic views of the late canal era that contrast with S. S. Dustin's more critical description.

Nye wrote extensively during his lifetime, and much has been written about him as well. Over the years, facts and fiction have intertwined, creating an almost mythical canal figure. Terry K. Woods of the Canal Society of Ohio has researched Nye extensively, seeking to record a more accurate account of his life.[10]

Of Nye, Woods wrote:

> Pearl Robert Nye, "Captain" Nye, is moderately well known in some circles. Collectors of Folk Songs and fans of that hobby, will recognize his name as that of a fairly successful singer of Ohio's folk songs back in the 1930s and 40s. Canal buffs will recognize the good "Captain" as one of the foremost sources for information about Ohio's long-gone canal system. And to some of the older residents of Akron and Coshocton, Ohio, Nye's name conjures up visions of a crazy old pest. There he is better known as "hermit" or "nutty" Nye. . . . Little is known of his life before the 1930s, and that little is mostly a constant rehashing of information from newspaper stories that Pearl himself instigated in the early 30s. (47)

Pearl Nye was born February 5, 1872, on the canal boat *Reform* while it was tied up in Chillicothe, Ohio. He was the ninth of eighteen children born to William and Mary Nye. William Nye had worked as a boatman on the canal all his life. The family operated their own grain boat and spent most of the season in the southern portion of the canal, between Chillicothe and Columbus. Pearl and his siblings began working on the canal in such jobs as riding the towpath mules. As the family grew older, Nye's older brother Billie had his own boat, the *Tom Marfield,* while William and Mary Nye worked and lived on the *Tom Warren* with their younger children (47–48, 50–51).

Competition from the railroads began to threaten canal business by the 1860s, but the Civil War provided new commerce. When the war was over, however, the railroads quickly absorbed much of the business that benefited from rapid transportation, such as grain shipping. The Nye family had to begin hauling coal, stone, and cordwood. They moved their canal boat into the northern section of the waterway to better deal with the expanding industries. In 1887, when Pearl was fifteen, his father died on his canal boat and was buried in Peninsula (51–52).

There are conflicting stories about what Pearl Nye and his family did after William died. Nye claimed to have run the canal boat for his mother until the flood of 1913, but, as Wood noted, he would have been very young to do so and had an older brother as the more obvious choice to be the captain. No one seems to know exactly, but the account is the basis for Pearl claiming the title "Captain," which he used to promote his position as an old canaller and a songwriter. He was a transitional character, living a childhood on the canal in the years of decline, and in his later years, during the Great Depression, trying to make a living selling his songs and a history of the Ohio & Erie Canal (52–53; see chapter 14 for more on Nye).

James Dillow Robinson, born a generation later than Pearl Nye, is often considered the last canaller. In the 1970s, Robinson, of Independence, Ohio, was perhaps the last living Ohioan who had worked on the Ohio & Erie Canal. Born in 1896, he and his mother and stepfather lived and worked on a state-owned maintenance boat from 1905 until 1917. His experiences and stories connect the end of the canal era to the founding of Cuyahoga Valley National Park.

Although Robinson's childhood ambition to be a canal-boat captain disappeared with the canal's demise, Robinson remained devoted to canal life. He became a local celebrity and expert on the canal and was a founding member of the Canal Society of Ohio.

Robinson was interviewed by several of his fellow Canal Society of Ohio members, including Terry Woods and Edith McNally, and his story provides insight to life on the canal boat at the end of the era. In 1905, when Robinson was nine, he moved aboard a state maintenance boat with his mother and stepfather, Charles Stebbins. He lived on the wooden canal boat twelve years: "There were two cabins on the seventy-eight-foot-long boat, one at the bow where Dillow bunked with the crew of four or five. In the larger cabin, about eighteen-feet long in the stern, were his parents' quarters and the kitchen where Mrs. Stebbins cooked on a coal stove for her family and crew" (53–55).

The open deck in between was used for equipment, a gangplank, and feed for the horses. The horses were stabled ashore wherever the boat was working between Cleveland and Everett, in Summit County. In an interview Robinson noted that depending on where the boat was working, he commuted to school at Brecksville by bike or sometimes the train.

A stereoscopic view of the lock described by Viona E. Findley, located near her home on the canal (University of Akron Archival Services, Louis Baus Photograph Collection).

In the winter the family lived on the moored boat near Stone Road at Valley View.

Clearly Robinson loved his years on the canal. His boyhood was framed by the canal itself and the type of work required of the state maintenance boat; it differed considerably from Pearl Nye's of a quarter-century earlier, which had been in a very large family and uncertain economic times. Robinson's little family of three had a steady job working for the state, keeping the canal repaired between Cleveland and Everett. The waterway provided opportunity for entertainment; there was swimming and fishing in the summer and skating and ice cutting in the winter. Because the maintenance boat covered just a few miles for the work, Robinson not only could go to school more than most canal-boat children, he was able to have friends among the local boys in the towns and farms along the canal. Sometimes the family would spend several weeks in one location.

When Robinson was sixteen, in 1912, he became a paid member of the crew. He worked with Captain Stebbins during the winter, repairing and caring for the boat. Their year-round canal responsibilities included fifteen locks, and three aqueducts, across Mill Creek, Tinkers Creek, and the largest, at Peninsula. Robinson noted that it took a good steersman to get the boat through an aqueduct without bumping sides. The towpath and the canal banks required continual repair. The towpath had to be kept level and mowed for farmers and others who used it as a lane; the canal had to be dredged for silt and stone that washed in from higher banks. They generally worked with hand tools and a wheelbarrow but periodically used a steam dredge.

Although the flood of 1913 devastated the canal in many places, the northern section, where Robinson and his stepfather worked, was not destroyed, and the state boat continued to operate after the flood (see chapter 12 for Robinson's firsthand description of the flood). The state leased the water for several industries in this northern section. Robinson left the canal in 1917 for the army during World War I. In 1921 he returned to work, as a foreman for American Steel & Wire doing canal maintenance work no longer done by the State of Ohio. This included cutting grass, filling muskrat holes, and dredging. He stopped working on the canal in 1924, and he went on to other occupations, but he lived in Independence, not far from the canal.

Viona E. Findley grew up in Lockport, Ohio, first known as Blake's Mills. It was later incorporated into New Philadelphia and it is now the southern terminus of the Ohio & Erie National Heritage Canalway. Like Dillow Robinson, she bridged the late canal era, and remembered well the flood of 1913. She and her husband, Ted, were founding members of the Canal Society of Ohio. Her stories here are taken from her essay written for the October 1967 issue of *Towpaths*.

Findley lived next to the canal; it ran beside her backyard, and as was the case for others who lived in the small canal towns, it was a core feature in the lives of her family members, even after it ceased to operate. Her father had a blacksmith shop near an old swing bridge over the canal. She wrote: "We always watched the big canal boats pass our house, sometimes several in a day, and a favorite pastime of my sister and me, along with all other neighborhood children, was running to the old swing bridge at the corner and trying to hitch a ride. The caretaker would work the crank which turned the bridge to let the boat pass through. If he was in good humor, he would let us sit on the edge of the bridge and ride back and forth. If too many crowded on, all were routed. No trip to the moon ever surpassed that ride for excellence."[11] She also remembered that they "went to sleep to the tune of the frog's song," and "rose early, often to the deep swish of water as an early boat made its way past our house. . . . You could see how life was lived on the old canal boats which were home to many families." She described how they used to boil canal water for washing clothes and how her brother had to haul the buckets of water from the canal before school. They also went fishing in the canal with rather crude poles and homemade lines. When they did catch fish they had to clean them, ready for frying (39).

The canal provided recreation as well: Findley noted that she and her siblings and friends loved to dangle their feet in the water on hot days—swimming was reserved for when the mothers could chaperone. Ice-skating was a fun winter pastime all up and down the canal, and she remembered how the boys would often help the girls with their skates.

The children were warned to be careful around the canal, as the waters were deep and a child could drown.

> I remember a close call of a younger playmate of mine. We went with a group bound for Zoar on a Sunday School picnic. The Latter Day Saint's Church was the third building below us, and the crowd gathered there at nine in the morning with well filled picnic baskets. . . . After reaching Zoar, the men left the boat to go to town. The women and children stayed on the boat. My little friend leaned too far out the side of the boat and toppled over, unnoticed by anyone except my mother, who clutched at her long blond curls which floated on the water. Mother held on tightly against the strong cur-

This canal boat on the Tuscarawas River near Lockport is similar to the type that provided pleasure excursions described by Viona E. Findley (University of Akron Archival Services, Louis Baus Photograph Collection).

> rent which was pulling my friend under the boat until help came and she was pulled back into the boat where she was soon revived and, after dry clothes and a rest, was able to resume her journey. All agreed that my friend's long curls helped to save her. (39)

Findley provides a schoolgirl's description of the 1913 flood, a critical event featured in many canal stories:

> In 1913 came the big flood and the river bridge was washed away. The canal waters came up into our back yard completely covering it. We were entirely cut off from the town, with no gas or electricity. We got out our old oil lamps and candles and did what cooking we could on old cookstoves or any way possible. . . . We stayed off the streets at night as the town was in complete darkness. . . .
>
> The present-day viaduct had not been built and the old sidewalk was a much longer way around. We walked a mile or more to the old Central School building in town. We were in high school at the time of the flood and for several weeks we were unable to get across the river. Finally, when the water receded a little, a home-made raft was built to ferry us across so we would not miss too much school. . . . We had not been sure what might happen. Some men who had tried to cross in a boat were carried down stream by the strong current and drowned. After the flood the canal was no longer used, and an old time era had passed never to return. (40)

Long after the canal ceased to be an economic system, it still remained an important feature in small towns and rural areas. As Nye's "silver ribbon" canal connected towns and people along the way, the canal stories of traveling, fishing, skating, and canoeing have maintained the legacy of the canal through the twentieth century. Its current renaissance as a recreational corridor makes it the new silver ribbon in northeast Ohio.

NOTES

1. Ellis H. Shimp, *Newcomers News,* Sept. 17, 1975.

2. "A Pioneer Family," *Louisville (Ohio) Herald,* Feb. 16, 1888. Clipping from the private papers of the late Frances McGovern.

3. Author unknown, "The Homestead," manuscript, Cascade Locks Park Association, archives, Mustill Store, Akron, Ohio (hereafter cited as CLPA).

4. John Botzum, "Looking Back," unidentified newspaper clipping, CLPA.

5. John Malvin, *Autobiography of John Malvin* (Cleveland: Leader Printing Company, 1879), 24–26.

6. Edward C. Atwater and Lawrence A. Kohn, "Rochester and the Water-Cure, 1844–1854," *Rochester History* 32 (Oct. 1970): 4–10.

7. John B. White, personal journal, transcribed in part by T. H. Findley from the original in possession of Mr. Charles R. Patterson, New Philadelphia, Ohio. Transcribed pages in the Univ. of Akron Archives. Following descriptions of White's journey are taken from this journal.

8. S. S. Dustin, "Where Garfield Was a Canal-Boy: Notes of a Leisurely Voyage on the Ohio Canal," in *Frank Leslie's Popular Monthly* 29 (Jan.–June 1890): 286 (hereafter cited in text).

9. Pearl Nye, "The Old Canal," a collection of verses about canal life, quoted in *The Akron Sunday Times,* Aug. 2, 1931; Edith F. McNally, "The Canaller," *Western Reserve Magazine* 3.7 (Sept.–Oct. 1981): 53–55 (hereafter cited in text).

10. Terry K. Woods, "The Life and Times of Pearl R. Nye," *Canal History and Technology Proceedings* 7 (Mar. 26, 1988): 47–72 (hereafter cited in text).

11. Viona E. Findley, "My Life along the Old Ohio Canal," *Towpaths* 5 (Oct. 1967): 39–40 (hereafter cited in text).

Chapter 8

East versus West

The Industrial Valley

RICHARD SICHA

With the geography of the canal area, could it have been anything but east versus west? A river several hundred feet wide at its mouth at Lake Erie, nestled in the bottom of a valley more than a mile wide and a hundred feet deep, definitely leaves one either "over here" or "over there." The Ohio & Erie Canal, with its north terminus at the Cleveland waterfront, played a significant role in Cleveland's growth into a commercial and industrial powerhouse. The canal also lay in the long valley that separated east from west. For two hundred years, Clevelanders have been devising ways to cross this divide and leveraging the broad valley and its river to shape its economic fortunes.

When Moses Cleaveland and his crew arrived to survey the area in 1796, they already had to cope with the ultimate east-west dividing line. The 1785 Treaty of Fort McIntosh, reinforced by the 1795 Treaty of Greenville, made the Cuyahoga River the western limit of white settlement for the United States. Cleaveland and his crew surveyed only east of the river. Ohio became a state in 1803, and the Native Americans surrendered title to lands west of the Cuyahoga River as part of the 1805 Treaty of Fort Industry.

Once settlement began in earnest on both sides of the Cuyahoga River Valley, two cities on opposite sides began to view themselves as economic rivals: Cleveland on the east bank and the City of Ohio on the west bank. The City of Ohio (population about 1,300) was incorporated as a city on March 3, 1836, two days before Cleveland (population over 5,000).

The two towns vigorously competed for the commercial trade from both the canal and surrounding townships. The intense rivalry culminated in an incident known as the Bridge War. The Columbus Street Bridge was a two-hundred-foot-long covered structure with a center draw to allow passage for sailing vessels. It was built by real estate speculators interested in promoting their development on the east side of the river and given to Cleveland in the spring of 1836. This new southerly access meant travelers and farmers with crops could reach Cleveland establishments and the canal terminus without passing through the commercial area of the City of Ohio farther north and then crossing the only other river bridge, located at Center Street. Tensions rose until a skirmish occurred when Cleveland militiamen attempted to stop a group of City of Ohio residents from destroying the new bridge, which resulted in a number of injuries and arrests. A court ruling declared that more than one river crossing should exist, thus permanently altering commerce and development patterns in favor of Cleveland. The City of Ohio merged into Cleveland in 1854.

One of the prizes won by Cleveland in this community rivalry was more direct overland access to the northern terminus of the canal, which quickly evolved into a center of regional economic activity as a transshipment location. The terminus attracted raw materials and agricultural products from the south on the canal and from well beyond the immediate vicinity of the Cuyahoga River Valley. These could then be processed, manufactured, or loaded as-is on sailing vessels bound for Great Lakes ports, particularly Buffalo, which offered a direct connection via the Erie Canal and the Hudson River to New York City. Conversely, incoming cargo from the Great Lakes could either be reloaded for shipment on canal boats or begin an overland journey to its destination east, west, or south. The basin and terminus, a single location in the bottomlands of the valley, created a successful regional marketplace for more than a generation.

Despite the canal basin's success as a regional hub, Cleveland's population growth during the nineteenth century reinforced residents' east-west orientation. Urban areas concentrated within about four miles of the lakeshore, spreading in an east-west direction and gradually expanding to create neighborhoods farther south on both sides of the river valley. Even at the turn of the twentieth century, as annexations of land into Cleveland slowed and ceased and densely populated first-ring suburbs such as Lakewood, East Cleveland, and Cleveland Heights were taking shape, the southern half of Cuyahoga County remained rural, dominated by small, scattered town centers and farms up to one hundred acres in size.

The confluence of the canal, the Cuyahoga River, and Lake Erie turned Cleveland into a major regional trans-shipment port (Cuyahoga Valley National Park Historic Print Collection, National Park Service).

The only common gathering place was the central business district of Cleveland, the major employment and retail center for the metropolitan area through the mid-twentieth century. Situated on high ground just east of the valley, only West Siders had to cross over the valley. Day-to-day, workers from the heavily populated urban neighborhoods just beyond each valley rim descended into the valley for their jobs, by streetcar and/or on foot. At the end of the day, they returned to their own neighborhoods, where they could find necessary goods and services and a religious community and socialize among their fellow immigrants.

It took a century of engineering advancements, however, to make crossing the river valley a less than laborious task. For decades, wagons, animals, and pedestrians had to navigate the sloping valley walls in all weather conditions. The few small, moveable bridges were situated at riverbank level, rotating on a single pivot point in the middle of the waterway. Delays were frequent due to railroads intersecting streets, poor road conditions, and river traffic, occasionally complicated by the odd ship that would unceremoniously wedge itself between the riverbank and bridge pivot.

A partial solution was the Superior Viaduct, the first bridge across the valley erected above riverbank level. The road surface, seventy-two feet above ground, permitted uninterrupted passage of nearly all ships except tall-masted sailing vessels. Completed in 1878 after six years of planning and construction, the bridge connected Superior and Detroit Streets. The western approach consisted of ten sandstone arches, and the eastern one was built of iron piers and girder spans. Connecting the two sides of the 3,211-foot viaduct was an iron swing span above the river. A similar design, with a swing span above the river, was repeated for the 1888 Central Viaduct.

Additional bridges followed; however, congestion of ships, pedestrians, wagons, streetcars, and, later, automobiles and trucks became more severe. In 1893 there were twenty bridges over the river, ten roadway and ten railroad, each with a swing span. With the increasing size of freighters, in 1913 only 55 percent of ships operating on the Great Lakes could navigate the river, and by 1924 the figure decreased to 32 percent.[1] Swing bridges built on a pier in the center of the river limited the channel width; those constructed on the bank opened parallel to the channel, blocking valuable waterfront space.

The 1918 Detroit-Superior Bridge became the first fixed span bridge of sufficient height to allow ships to pass underneath and the free flow of traffic above. It was followed by the Lorain-Carnegie (1932) and Main Avenue (1939) Bridges. Down at riverbank level, a variety of innovative moving bridges that lifted or pivoted from riverbank locations replaced the earlier spans anchored in the waterway.

The construction of the interstate highway system in the metropolitan area during the 1950s through the 1970s brought another generation of bridges that spanned the valley: the Interstate-71 Innerbelt Bridge connecting downtown Cleveland and the West Side (1959) and the Valley View Bridge carrying Interstate 480 over the Cuyahoga Valley (1978). The freeway network has made it possible to traverse Cuyahoga County in an east-west direction in thirty minutes.

This Main Avenue high level bridge is under construction in 1939. The older river-level bridge with a center pivot can be seen below the newer bridge (Cleveland Photograph Collection, Cleveland Public Library).

Clearly, the physical impediment to travel has been eliminated, but what of the perception of Clevelanders? The Cuyahoga River Valley remains an imposing physical feature, at once complex to navigate, difficult to interpret the overlaid layers of nature and man, and an intense sensory experience, perhaps contributing to a lingering east-west mentality.

The built environment of the valley has conformed itself, for the most part, to physical constraints such as the varying valley width, steep slopes, a meandering river, and a nineteenth-century road network. More significant, the valley evolved as a world of noise, odors, smoke, and fire, blanketed with structures, railroads, and ships of Brobdingnagian proportions. Over generations, hundreds of thousands of Clevelanders became familiar with the valley because they worked in it, but that was the only reason they ventured there. The valley had a singular role in the region—economic engine—and that came with environmental cost. The air pollution peeled paint off traffic signals and turned the surface of downtown buildings black soon after their completion. As for water quality, the Cuyahoga wasn't the only heavily polluted urban river in America, and it wasn't the only one whose oily, debris-laden surface caught fire. It was the one, however, to become an important impetus for the national environmental movement of the 1960s and the passage of the Clean Water Act of 1972.

How does one change the image of a place that has left such an overwhelming impression on generations of residents? After all, Clevelanders made the river and valley what it is, but most people don't know its legacy or feel it necessary to be associated with it. The solutions include telling the valley's stories, weaving more activities amid the existing land uses, and searching for new opportunities for its continuing evolution. Rather than being seen as a gap in both the landscape and our collective memory, the river valley can rightfully be explored, interpreted, and celebrated as a unifying feature.

The stories of the Cuyahoga River of the nineteenth and twentieth centuries focus on commerce and industry. A generation after Moses Cleaveland first surveyed the region, the river and its environs were emerging as a commercial district. By the 1820s, a local economy for the valley's agricultural crops and finished goods existed, supplemented by exchange of some products via lake shipping to cities such as Detroit and Buffalo. The present mouth of the Cuyahoga River to Lake Erie was created in 1827–28, almost one mile east of the natural mouth. This engineering project improved shipping efficiency, bypassing the sandbars that formed at the mouth of the natural channel.

The Ohio & Erie Canal, opened from Lake Erie to Akron in 1827, with its entire length completed in 1832, had an immediate economic impact on the Cuyahoga Valley. The canal provided the expansive interior of Ohio with easy market access, which changed the economy of the state. Cleveland, with its lake shipping access to the Erie Canal at Buffalo, became an exchange point for a wide variety of products headed to and from the East Coast. Outgoing shipments consisted largely of wheat, oats, corn, flour, cheese, and whiskey. Merchandise sent from the east included nails, glass, cloth, salt, coffee, tea, and manufactured goods. Between 1827 and 1834, the annual number of cargo vessels at the port of Cleveland increased twelve-fold, to almost nine hundred.[2]

The economic stimulus of the Ohio & Erie Canal also propelled business and population growth. The canal, located east of the Cuyahoga River, roughly paralleled its course. It joined the river on Merwin Street, just south of Superior, where the Detroit-Superior Bridge now stands. From that point to the mouth of the river, the east bank became a wholesale and warehouse district. Ahaz Merchant's 1835 *Map of Cleveland and Its Environs* showed four slips, as well as a furnace, steam mill, and steam

Across the Flats, by Grace V. Leonard. The industry of the Cuyahoga River Valley was a magnet for artists and was portrayed in the art movement known as the Cleveland School (Departmet of Special Collections, Kelvin Smith Library, Case Western Reserve University).

engine shop. Cleveland's population rose from 1,100 in 1831 to 17,000 in 1850.

The preeminence of the canal, however, lasted only about twenty-five years. Shipments of commodities such as corn, wheat, flour, and coal reached their peak in the early 1850s, for example, totaling over seven million bushels in 1851.[3] By 1860, volume had fallen dramatically and passenger traffic had also declined substantially.

The developing railroad network in Cleveland caused the change. Railroads had advantages over a transportation system that relied on water: they could operate year-round, at faster speeds, and with flexibility as to their locations. In 1850, the first railroad to enter Cleveland—the Cleveland, Columbus, & Cincinnati—began regular operation. By 1853, Cleveland was also connected to Pittsburgh, New York, Chicago, and St. Louis, being situated on the direct route between the East Coast and the developing Midwest.[4] The city became one of the major rail centers in the country by 1860.

The railroads also had a direct physical impact on the canal. In the mid-1870s, the Valley Railroad purchased from the State of Ohio the northernmost several miles and filled them in for a railroad bed. An 1881 Cleveland atlas showed that the basin at the terminus had been converted to railroad sidings and a freight house, and a replacement terminus, with its weigh lock, was created adjacent to the Grasselli Chemical Company.

Railroads and shipping brought the Cuyahoga Valley into the mainstream of the American economy as a commercial center and positioned it as an ideal manufacturing location by virtue of its role as a natural crossroads for raw materials. The abundant coal reserves of eastern Ohio and western Pennsylvania initially reached Cleveland via canal, but by the 1850s the shipments shifted to railroads. By the mid-nineteenth century, the widespread use of the steam engine in shipping, railroads, and industry assured a growing demand for coal. In addition, in 1855 the completion of the canal and lock at Sault Sainte Marie, Michigan, linking Lakes Superior and Huron, opened expansive ranges of iron-ore deposits to the rest of the Great Lakes, benefiting Cleveland's industrial valley.

Over a generation, the Cuyahoga Steam Furnace Company, located on the west bank of the river just south of Center Street, took full advantage of these evolving economic opportunities. Established in 1827, the company had both a blast furnace—to smelt iron ore, charcoal, and limestone brought by the canal and lake—and a foundry to convert the iron into usable products. Originally a maker of mill gearings, the company expanded to produce stationary steam engines (1840), railroad equipment (1842), marine steam engines (1843), and the first locomotive west of the Allegheny Mountains (1849).[5]

By the mid-nineteenth century, immigration had become an important influence on the Cuyahoga Valley, providing labor and creating distinct neighborhoods. Canal construction work attracted Irish laborers, many of whom had worked in New York State on the Erie Canal, while during the same period a number of German farmers settled in the area. Cleveland attracted substantial numbers of Irish, German, and British immigrants from 1830 to 1870, reflecting national trends. The Irish almost exclusively held unskilled or semi-skilled jobs, particularly seasonal work related to the canal, river, and lake. In contrast, about one-quarter of the Germans were skilled craftsmen or worked in the more dependable building trades.[6] Many of the immigrants lived in the valley adjacent to the river and canal or on the nearby slopes, such as the settlement at Irishtown Bend (see chapter 15).

The Civil War also gave development stimulus to the Cuyahoga Valley. Nineteenth-century historian Crisfield Johnson affirmed that "the effect of the war on Cleveland was very greatly to develop its manufactures. The iron business and the oil business in particular sprang forward into immense proportions, and it has been said, with but little exaggeration, that the war found Cleveland a commercial city and left it a manufacturing city."[7] In 1859, at the age of twenty, John D. Rockefeller became a partner in a commission firm dealing in farm produce. He entered the oil business in 1863 as an investor in a refining company. The same year, Andrews, Clark and Company opened the Excelsior Refinery on a large tract of land just east of the canal along Broadway Avenue and surrounding Kingsbury Run, building a group of brick and wooden structures scattered throughout the hilly parcel. Rockefeller entered the oil business full-time in 1865, buying the company and creating the partnership of Rockefeller and Andrews, which became Standard Oil in 1870.[8] The oil industry in Cleveland had expanded to about two dozen refineries by 1865.

The iron industry also grew significantly during the Civil War. For example, the Cuyahoga Steam Furnace Company produced railroad iron for the military. The number of incorporated iron companies increased to twelve, and in addition to large castings and forgings, firms produced diverse items such as nuts, bolts, screws, washers, and rivets. Demand for iron products created a need for more raw materials, to the point that in 1864–65, Cleveland received over half of all iron ore mined in the Lake Superior region. Transporting the ore required additional vessels: in 1863, 22 percent of all ships built for use on the Great Lakes had been constructed in Cleveland; by 1865, the figure had increased to 44 percent.[9] More shipbuilding, in turn, increased iron manufactures' production of items such as fittings, steam engines, and propellers.

From the 1870s through the first half of the twentieth century—with the benefits of geographic location, access to land and water transportation networks, and the emergence of interrelated industries such as oil, chemicals, and paint; sewing machines and clothing; and iron, steel, fasteners, machine tools, automobiles, and shipbuilding—the Cuyahoga Valley emerged as one of the leading manufacturing centers in the nation. By the 1880s, Cleveland's network of railroad connections was the densest of any between New York and Chicago.[10] Every railroad crossed, made connections with, or terminated in the Cuyahoga Valley. With its central location and transportation access, Cleveland became a collection point for raw materials, which facilitated the development of manufacturers, then distributed finished goods to diverse markets. In 1930, industries employing large numbers of Clevelanders included blast furnaces and steel rolling mills (19,000), other iron and steel industries (42,000), and steam railroads (15,000).[11]

The valley became the location of major industrial firms in addition to Rockefeller's Standard Oil empire. These included Rockefeller's chemical supplier, Grasselli Chemical (later merged with DuPont); the White family's sewing-machine companies and their later operations that made pioneering contributions in machine tool and automotive fields; the paint

Cleveland Dock, by Paul Kucharyson. Artists participating in the Federal Art Project depicted views of Cleveland's busy docks (Department of Special Collections, Kelvin Smith Library, Case Western Reserve University).

company formed by Henry A. Sherwin and Edward P. Williams, inventors of ready-mixed paint; the iron-ore houses of Cleveland-Cliffs, M. A. Hanna, and Oglebay Norton; Alexander E. Brown and George M. Hulett, who designed machinery that twice revolutionized the entire process of ore unloading; Globe Iron Works, which launched the first compartmentalized iron- and steel-hull freighters on the Great Lakes; American Ship Building, a major builder of vessels for lake shipping, whose member firms included the Cuyahoga Steam Furnace Company; and fastener manufacturers Ferry Cap and Set Screw, Lamson and Sessions, and Upson Nut.

This transformation also resulted in heavy industry continuing to move farther upstream during the early twentieth century; the large tracts of land available on the valley floor allowed for large facilities and storage yards, along with access to river water for manufacturing processes. The availability of water and construction of railroad yards also permitted receipt of raw materials and methods for shipping finished products. A number of rival steel manufacturers located their facilities along either side of the river, including Corrigan, McKinney and Company (later Republic Steel), Otis Steel (later Jones & Laughlin Steel), and U.S. Steel's American Steel & Wire division. In several places, the river was straightened or relocated to provide sufficient land for their expansive facilities and deepened to allow for navigation by large freighters hauling raw materials. Selected expansion projects even occurred during the Depression, including seventy-two- and ninety-six-inch–wide continuous hot strip mills, the widest in the world. A number of firms that relied on railroad connections rather than waterborne shipping located upstream of the head of navigation, including Alcoa, printing-press maker Harris Automatic Press Company, Harshaw Chemical, and electroplating-chemical specialist McGean-Rohco.

Even though most shipping was done by railroad and freighter by the final third of the nineteenth century, the canal still had economic uses. A number of manufacturers adjacent to the canal utilized it for transportation or as a water source.[12] At the Cleveland Paper facility, located near Grasselli Chemical, the canal included a wharf, along with a spillway to divert water into the plant. The American Steel & Wire Company had a wharf and an intake from the canal, connected to its adjacent pumping station. Just south of the high-level railroad bridge that spans the Cleveland Metroparks Ohio & Erie Canal Reservation, the canal was widened to almost 170 feet, for a length of about 800 feet. Immediately to the south of that bulge, a basin about 700 feet long and 110 to 150 feet wide was constructed adjacent to the canal. On the 1909 canal map there are no descriptions of earlier activities at the site. There is a notation of an "old dock" on the canal in Cuyahoga Heights just north of the Mill Creek Aqueduct, a stream known at the turn of the twentieth century as Sodom Creek. Finally, sandstone blocks from the quarries in Independence Township, concentrated in the higher elevations west of the Cuyahoga River, were customarily transported with canal boats.[13]

The canal was also important to two industrial companies that, because of their manufacturing processes, specifically chose to locate in an isolated, rural section of the Cuyahoga River Valley yet also needed the canal. On the east side of the canal, where today it is crossed by Harvard Avenue in Cleveland, three men started the Cleveland Powder Company in the late 1850s to manufacture black powder.[14] By early 1862 however, the company was experiencing financial problems, and two of the firm's investors, Lorenzo and Linus Austin, bought it at a public auction.[15] They were two of the five Austin brothers—who, along with siblings Alvin, Cyrus, and Daniel—settled in Akron in 1833 and established one of the first powder mills in Ohio, located on the Little Cuyahoga River, where waterpower was available to turn the large milling wheels. The mill also had nearby access to the newly completed Ohio & Erie Canal. It grew into a major regional producer of black powder for Ohio and surrounding states, particularly serving the coal mining industry.

In addition to the Austin powder complex in Akron, the Austin brothers continued to operate their newly acquired powder mill as Cleveland Powder Company from 1862 until March 1868, when the company was sold to Austin Powder. A series of fatal explosions in the early to mid-1860s, culminating with a blast in May 1868, prompted the company to shut its Akron mill and relocate all of its operations to the larger site in Newburgh Township. By 1874 Austin Powder's land holdings totaled almost 90 acres and by 1880 reached about 130 acres, primarily along the canal and the east side of the Cuyahoga River. The company also modified the canal by diverting water through a section of its property and digging out the east wall of the canal to create a large basin, roughly 400 feet long and 150 feet wide. This area would have been suitable for mooring canal boats to handle shipping of raw materials or finished black powder, and the 1909 canal map contained a notation for a coal wharf.[16]

The production of black powder explosives necessitated an isolated location, with its manufacture and storage carried out in multiple small buildings scattered over a wide area to minimize damage from any single explosion. Even those precautions were insufficient, however, to lessen the explosions and fires that occurred on March 16, 1875. A chain reaction of explosions involving an estimated forty to fifty tons of powder in various locations destroyed fifteen to twenty buildings directly or by showering them with burning debris. The only buildings not destroyed were the magazines. Three employees were killed. Other impacts included destruction of the adjacent woods; serious damage to buildings within a half-mile radius of the explosions; and shaken buildings and shattered storefront windows as far away as downtown Cleveland.[17]

As the area became more industrialized and populated, Austin created a new black-powder manufacturing facility and company town beginning in 1892 in Solon Township (later the Village of Glenwillow), an isolated, rural section of southeastern Cuyahoga County. Another major explosion at the Harvard Avenue facility in 1907, along with the increasingly dense industrial and residential development in the area, appears to have marked the phasing-out of large-scale production at the site.

The second firm had direct connections to the early oil and chemical industries of Cleveland. In the 1860s, many small, independent refineries were concentrated along the canal, Cuyahoga River, and Kingsbury Run several miles north of present-day Harvard Avenue. By the mid-1860s John D. Rockefeller was consolidating oil refining in Cleveland under his ownership, and Cleveland emerged as the world's largest oil-refining center during the last third of the nineteenth century. In 1866, adjacent to the canal and next to Rockefeller's property that soon became Standard Oil Company's Cleveland No. 1 Works, Eugene Grasselli opened the Grasselli Chemical Company, which supplied sulfuric acid to Rockefeller and other refineries for petroleum distillation. Grasselli located his firm adjacent to Marsh & Harwood, an existing chemical company situated between the canal and river.

In 1867, Sloane, Anderson & Company opened the Cleveland Acid Rectifying Works in Independence Township about three miles south of present-day Harvard Avenue. Specifically, the site was on the north side of the canal at Lock 40, continuing westward for at least a thousand feet. The Acid Works collected the spent sulfuric acid used in Cleveland's oil refineries, purified it, and returned it for reuse.[18] The canal was used for transport three seasons of the year, with tens of thousands of carboys of acid shipped on canal boats, moving back and forth past the Austin Powder Company. In addition, the Acid Works diverted canal water through a section of their property and had a pipe connection from the canal directly to its facility.[19]

The most prominent feature of the Acid Works was the fire visible for miles, created when the byproducts removed from the acid were burned

This image of the Standard Oil Company's Works appeared in *Cleveland Illustrated* in 1889 (Cleveland Illustrated Collection, Cleveland State University Library).

in a large lake, known as a pitch pond, below the works at its west end. Almost immediately, Cleveland residents living northeast of the plant decried the "intolerable stench," while other residents claimed that the river water had become "unfit for domestic use, being impregnated with the odor and taste of petroleum." The company owner publicly responded, disputing the assertion about the source of the pollution. He further noted, "Our works solve a great difficulty in the very important interest of oil refineries," wherein "8,000 gallons of acid sludge thrown formerly by the oil refineries, daily, into the river, is [now] turned into acid and oil."[20]

R. H. Emerson became the new owner of the Acid Works in 1872, and it appears that another change in ownership led to the company being renamed The Union Acid Company—also known as The Union Acid Restoring Company—in the late 1870s. By 1879, a number of buildings stood on the site, and the plant employed about thirty men, producing six thousand carboys of acid per month. The process to restore the acid required about two thousand tons of coke and about double that amount of coal annually. In terms of equipment, the facility included 160 glass retorts with a capacity of fifty gallons each and five storage tanks with a total holding capacity of six thousand barrels.

The officers of the Union Acid Company were officers of the Grasselli and Marsh & Harwood firms. This ownership relationship continued through the renaming of the company in 1885 as The American Chemical & Manufacturing Company. The company last appeared in the *Cleveland City Directory* in 1888, after which it became part of the Grasselli Chemical Company.[21]

The Acid Works operated through at least 1896, and its demise occurred when the oil industry discovered how to use the byproducts that had previously been sent to the facility to be separated from the acid and burned. The exact date of its closing is not known, although it appears to have been shut before 1909.[22]

The industrialization of the Cuyahoga Valley created tens of thousands of jobs, a substantial portion of which were filled by foreign immigrants. Migration to Cleveland from 1870 until 1914 was similar to that of other Great Lakes cities, with the immigrants mostly southern and eastern Europeans. After 1914 immigration virtually ended, first due to World War I, followed by restrictive federal legislation such as the Literacy Act of 1917 and the 1924 National Origins Act.

Immigrants tended to settle in neighborhoods with others of similar ethnic backgrounds. Sharing similar values, language, and customs quickly created a sense of community. Churches and other social, cultural, and educational organizations frequently established a focal point for the residents. Many communities also established their own newspapers, banks, and insurance funds. In 1920, European immigrants and their American-born children accounted for 75 percent of Cleveland's population.[23] The many ethnic groups settling directly in or along the rim of the Cuyahoga Valley included Bohemians (Little Bohemia and Karlin), Netherlanders (Dutch Hill), Italians (Big Italy), Irish (The Angle), and Poles (Barbarowa and Warszawa).

The industrialization of the river valley and the growth of a major city meant that the river was also at the center of water-quality issues for over a century. By the 1860s, pollution in the Cuyahoga River and its tributaries from sewers as well as manufacturing processes involving oil, chemicals, paper, iron, and lumber became more acute. One result was the repeated moving of the lake-water supply intake farther offshore.[24] The first intake, constructed between 1854 and 1856, was fifty inches in diameter and located 300 feet offshore, just west of the old river channel.

It was soon deemed inadequate due to limited volume and impure water, and therefore was extended during 1869–74, with a five-foot-diameter tunnel, to a point 6,600 feet into Lake Erie. During 1913–17, this intake was extended an additional 16,123 feet, to its present location. In addition, the intake pipes were connected to the Division Avenue Filtration Plant, opened in 1918 just west of the old river channel, which supplied the first filtered water to the city. It was also the most extensive waterworks unit in Cleveland's network, pumping 70 percent of the city's water.

The first two sewage treatment plants for the Greater Cleveland area were both located in the Cuyahoga Valley. The Westerly Wastewater Plant, on the lakeshore adjacent to the Division Avenue Filtration Plant, began operation in 1922. The Southerly Plant opened in 1928, constructed in Cuyahoga Heights on an expanse of bottomland at least partially occupied by the Union Acid Works. Expansions at the Southerly Wastewater Plant have made it the largest wastewater treatment facility in Ohio.

Pollution however, took a severe toll on the river. In 1881, the discharge from factories and oil refineries caused Cleveland mayor Rensselaer Herrick to label the Cuyahoga River an open sewer through the center of the city.[25] On June 22, 1969, a burning oil slick floating on the river caused extensive damage to two railroad trestles at the foot of Campbell Road Hill. Although oil fires on the Cuyahoga were not new, this one received national attention. *Time* magazine, on August 1, 1969, branded the Cuyahoga as one of the most polluted rivers in America. In subsequent congressional hearings, the plight of the Cuyahoga River and other urban, industrial rivers became an impetus for the formation of the U.S. Environmental Protection Agency in 1970 and passage of the Clean Water Act of 1972. Since that time, water quality has significantly improved, because of upgrades in the sewer and wastewater treatment systems and remedial measures taken by industry.

How can people best experience the richness of this unusual landscape, its history coupled with a currently working river, layers of transportation networks, and active industry? The key is to view the entire river valley and its adjacent neighborhoods as one cultural and geographical entity and an educational resource. That effort has been evolving since the mid-1980s; for instance, the *North Cuyahoga Valley Corridor*, published in 1992, approached the Cuyahoga Valley as a major north-south link in a county that has perceived itself as divided into east and west, and it placed emphasis on relationships, rather than physical barriers or manmade designations such as community boundaries. For the first time, it brought together information on the significance of the entire Cuyahoga River Valley and contained strategies to bring it recognition.[26]

East versus west—will the issue ever completely disappear in Cuyahoga County? Probably not. More than two centuries ago, both Benjamin Franklin (1750s) and George Washington (1784) predicted that an economically powerful city could develop at the confluence of the Cuyahoga River and Lake Erie. These men saw the scale of the Cuyahoga as an opportunity, not an obstacle. They envisioned how a city could develop *with it.* Perhaps as we continue to broaden our understanding of our common heritage, with its potential to contribute positively to the economy and quality of life of our region in the future, we may come to realize that much more binds us than divides us.

NOTES

1. Daniel Bluestone, ed., *Cleveland: An Inventory of Historic Engineering and Industrial Sites* (Washington, D.C.: U.S. Department of the Interior, Historic American Engineering Record, 1978), 80.

2. A discussion of the impact of the completion of the canal can be found in Edmund H. Chapman, *Cleveland: Village to Metropolis,* 2d ed. Western Reserve Historical Society Publication, No. 118 (Cleveland: Western Reserve Historical Society, 1981).

3. Robert Wheeler, "Commercial Village to Commercial City: 1825–1860," in *The Encyclopedia of Cleveland History,* ed. David D. Van Tassel and John J. Grabowski (Bloomington: Indiana Univ. Press, 1987), xxx.

4. Ibid.

5. "Cuyahoga Steam Furnace Company," in Van Tassel and Grabowski, *Encyclopedia,* 324–25.

6. Wheeler, "Commercial Village," xxvi.

7. William C. Stark, "Civil War," in Van Tassel and Grabowski, *Encyclopedia,* 189–92.

8. "Samuel Andrews" (34–35), "Maurice B. Clark" (online edition: http://ech.case.edu/ech-cgi/article.pl?id=CMB [accessed Sept. 19, 2008]), "John D. Rockefeller" (837), and "Standard Oil Company (Ohio)" (921–22), all in Van Tassel and Grabowski, *Encyclopedia.*

9. Stark, "Civil War," 189–92.

10. Ronald Weiner, "The New Industrial Metropolis: 1860–1929," in Van Tassel and Grabowski, *Encyclopedia,* xxv.

11. Carol Poh Miller, "Toward the Postindustrial City: 1930–1980," in Van Tassel and Grabowski, *Encyclopedia,* xliv.

12. The source of the items in the following paragraph is G. F. Silliman, *Map of the Ohio Canal* (Columbus: State of Ohio, Bureau of Public Works, 1909), 2, 3.

The date for the Silliman survey in this area was included in a deed between the State of Ohio and Austin Powder Company, recorded December 7, 1916, on file at the Cuyahoga County Recorder's Office.

13. Grace Miller et al., *The Story of Independence* (Independence, Ohio: Independence Historical Society, 1979), 58–65.

14. "Powder Mill Blown Up," *Cleveland Leader,* Sept. 15, 1859, 3.

15. The foreclosure proceedings and public auction were summarized in a deed recorded June 9, 1862, and on file at the Cuyahoga County Recorder's Office.

16. Silliman, *Map of the Ohio Canal.*

17. The March 17, 1875, *Cleveland Leader,* included a lengthy article, "Terrible Explosion—The Austin Powder Mills Entirely Destroyed," beginning on the front page, describing the most damaging industrial accident in Cleveland's history.

18. The method for processing petroleum into its constituent parts in the nineteenth century was different than the current one, developed in the 1910s. Beginning in the 1860s, crude oil was physically separated into its parts by distillation. Heat was applied until the oil changed into a gas. The gas was sent through a long tube (and later up a tower), where each component cooled to its own boiling point, returned to a liquid state, and was collected. Sulfuric acid was one of the chemicals used to purify these distillates, such as kerosene and various lubricants. The lighter fractions, such as gasoline, had little commercial value at that time, and were burned off at facilities such as the Acid Works.

19. Silliman, *Map of the Ohio Canal.*

20. The January 22 and 24, 1868, editions of the *Cleveland Leader* carried a lengthy transcript of correspondence between John Whitelaw, superintendent of the City of Cleveland's Office of Water Works, and W. R. Anderson of Sloane, Anderson & Co., including a detailed description of the process for reclaiming the sulfuric acid.

21. *Sanborn Insurance Maps of Cleveland, Ohio* (New York: Sanborn Map Publishing, 1887) showed Marsh & Harwood, Union Acid, and Grasselli abutting each other. An 1896 *Sanborn* contained no reference to Marsh & Harwood or Union Acid, and the entire area was labeled "Grasselli Chemical Co."

22. Silliman's 1909 *Map of the Ohio Canal* referred to the abutting property occupant as the "old acid works." The word "old" was sometimes used to mean that a facility or business had ceased operation.

23. Weiner, "New Industrial Metropolis," xxxiii.

24. Willis E. Sibley, "Water System," in Van Tassel and Grabowski, *Encyclopedia,* 1029–32.

25. Sam Alewitz, "Sanitation," in Van Tassel and Grabowski, *Encyclopedia,* 867–69.

26. Richard Sicha, *North Cuyahoga Valley Corridor* (Cleveland: Cuyahoga County Planning Commission, 1992).

Part 2

The Long Twilight

Chapter 9

Railroad Fever and Canals in Ohio

H. ROGER GRANT

In the post–Civil War era, railroad fever spread through Ohio, where earlier in the nineteenth century, residents had expressed similar excitement about canals and to a somewhat lesser extent about all-weather post roads, tollways, and turnpikes. But by midcentury the citizenry nearly universally embraced the iron horse. Now Ohioans laugh as they read an old newspaper report from an 1838 meeting of the Lancaster Board of Education: "You are welcome to the use of the schoolhouse to debate all proper questions in, but such things as railroads . . . are impossibilities and rank infidelity. There is no work of God about them. If God had designed that His intelligent creatures should travel at the frightful speed of 15 miles an hour by steam, He would clearly have foretold it through His holy prophets." Concluded the Lancaster Board, "It is a device of Satan to lead immortal souls down to hell."[1]

Although a few Ohioans fussed about passenger trains that operated on the Sabbath, antirailroad sentiment faded. The opposite, in fact, occurred as the post–Civil War decades witnessed an orgy of railroad building. Most citizens defined progress as more miles of iron and steel rails. Some observers might have been surprised at the extent of this construction; after all, on the eve of the Civil War, Ohio already boasted an impressive, integrated rail network of nearly three thousand miles, making it first among the states. Few would likely have guessed that by 1900 the state's railroad mileage would reach 8,951 and would peak eight years later at an astonishing 9,581 miles.[2]

This additional railroad construction was nearly always necessary. In most cases, the iron horse was the only practical method of intercity transport. After all, this was an era when a horse and buggy and animal-powered wagon or cart had a limited range, and these vehicles inevitably encountered roads that were dusty in the summer, rutted in spring, and vulnerable to both heavy rains and snows. Placement of a depot within convenient driving distance became enormously popular and a reasonably sound economic policy.[3]

Moreover, Ohioans learned that railroads were an ideal replacement technology. Not only was the iron horse far superior to horse- and mule-drawn vehicles, but those who had access to the nearly thousand miles of local canals found them hardly ideal. Canals could not always be placed where they were needed; hills of any size stymied their construction, and other geographic features, too, caused problems. The railroads could provide more dependable service since they did not close for cold weather, low water, flooding, and general repairs. And they were much faster: canal boats traveled usually less than six miles per hour, while the iron horse chugged and clanked along even the most primitive rails at speeds that were three or four times greater. As the century progressed, speeds greatly accelerated, and most main-line passenger trains averaged in excess of fifty miles per hour.[4]

As railroad expansion occurred, particularly in the 1870s and 1880s, the transportation map of Ohio revealed four dominant trunk roads. For decades, much of the state's transportation experiences would be intimately tied to the Baltimore & Ohio (B&O), Erie, New York Central, and Pennsylvania systems that through mergers, leases, and construction had become fully interregional carriers. Generally, these companies operated on an east-west axis rather than a north-south one. This occurred largely because of the economic prominence of New York City, Boston, Philadelphia, Baltimore, Chicago, and St. Louis. By 1870, the Windy City, "Nature's Metropolis," had evolved into America's undisputed railroad Mecca.[5]

The development of a heavy east-west flow of commerce differed from traffic patterns established by the state's two principal canal networks, the Ohio & Erie and the Miami & Erie. Because of the early importance of the Great Lakes and the Ohio and Mississippi River systems, enhanced by the advent of steamboats after 1820, it made sense for ditches to link these natural bodies of navigable waters, thus creating a north-south movement of goods and people. When the ultimate destinations were cities along the eastern seaboard, canal routes were hardly ever direct, with

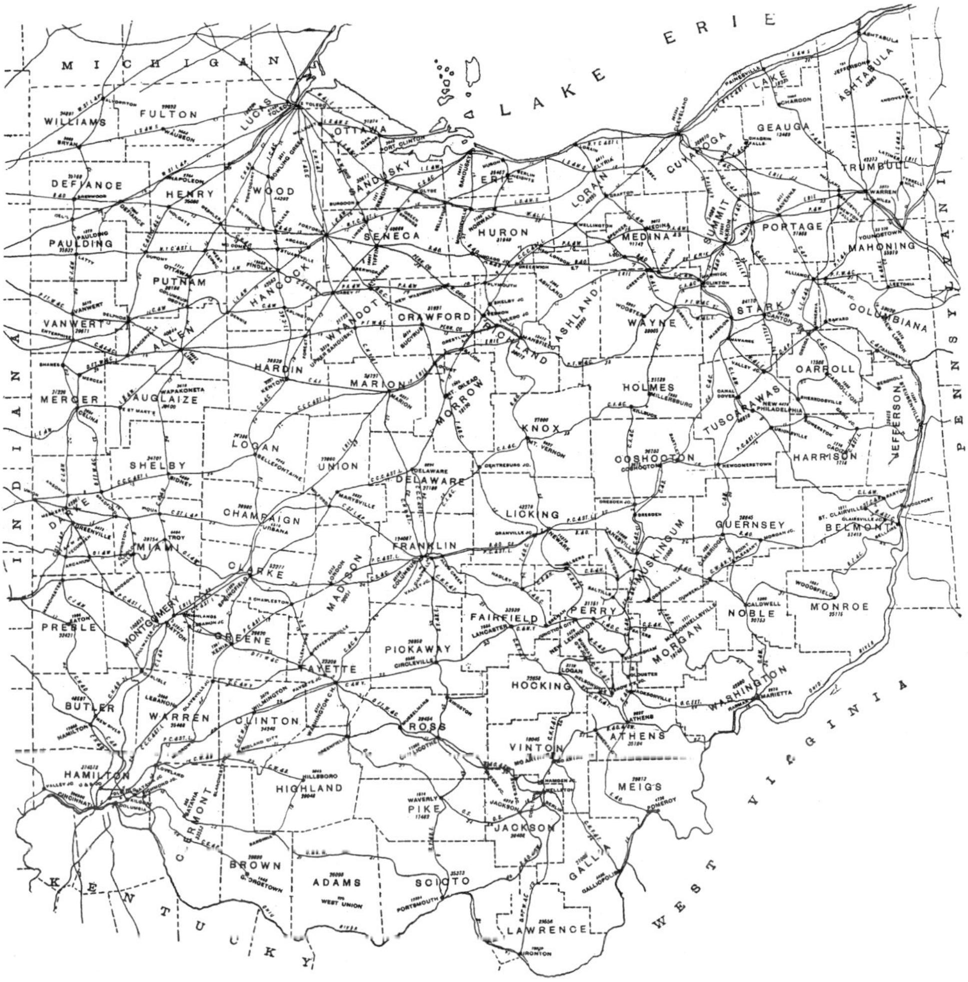

1891 railroad map of ohio (courtesy of H. Roger Grant).

the possible exception of the Lake Erie–Erie Canal–Hudson River water path to New York City.[6]

The canal era spawned considerable economic development. Some scholars have considered these artificial waterways, especially in New York, Pennsylvania, and Ohio, responsible for the nation's economic takeoff. Without doubt, farmers, miners, and manufacturers of all sorts made some canal towns busy and prosperous. Such northeastern Ohio places as Akron, Cleveland, and Massillon boomed because of the Ohio & Erie Canal. It is important to note that with the advent of the Railway Age, promoters, typically local ones, also wished to tie their communities into natural outlets, namely bodies of water, for delivery of their products. The result was commonly rail lines that served canal corridors.

Even as canals or segments of them closed forever, such predominately north-south rail arteries appeared, usually to serve evolving industrial locales spawned or stimulated by these earlier ditches rather than to exploit lake or river connections.[7]

During the latter part of the railroad-building era, many of the new tracks in the Buckeye State were not part of east-west speedways. These lines, often of modest mileage, were frequently designed to bring traffic directly to and from established commercial and manufacturing centers, including the expanding Akron, Canton, Cleveland, and Youngstown area. Some were predominantly tap roads, often hauling principally one product to market, coal especially. Much of this fuel was consumed in the burgeoning factories and mills of these growing metropolises. Unquestionably, coal mining and railroads became inseparable, codependent partners.

Immediately after the Civil War, the expanding communities of northeastern Ohio continued to depend on canals for their shipments of coal. The Ohio & Erie Canal tapped extensive diggings in the vicinity of Canton and farther south. The Pennsylvania & Ohio Canal, the so-called Penn Cross-Cut Canal, or Mahoning Canal, which linked Akron and the Ohio & Erie Canal with the Mahoning Valley and the Ohio River, transported prodigious amounts of coal from mines located along its route and from western Pennsylvania. In fact, it would be this bulk commodity that economically sustained both ditches, although the Pennsylvania & Ohio failed first, largely due to growing railroad competition.[8]

What might broadly be defined as the Cuyahoga Valley witnessed considerable railroad building once the canal era passed its zenith. The first line to penetrate the area immediately south of Cleveland was an important predecessor of the evolving Pennsylvania Railroad system. In 1856, the Cleveland & Pittsburgh Railroad (C&P) joined the cities of its name and served such intermediate communities in the greater Cleveland area as Bedford, Macedonia, and Highland Springs. Even before this pioneer line was completed, a connection linked Hudson, in northeastern Summit County, with Akron, a distance of thirteen miles. Commonly called the Akron Branch Railroad, this appendage reached the City at the Summit in 1852, and Akronites joyfully celebrated its arrival on the greatest of U.S. holidays, the Fourth of July. Soon thereafter, the Akron Branch stretched to Millersburg, via Barberton, Clinton, and Orrville. Financial problems, however, stalled further construction, and the company was reorganized as the Cleveland, Zanesville & Cincinnati Railroad, a name indicating its building ambitions. But more money woes followed, and on

November 3, 1864, the company entered the orbit of the Pittsburgh, Fort Wayne & Chicago Railroad, an affiliate of the ever-expanding Pennsylvania Railroad. Following the Civil War, the self-proclaimed Blue Grass Route pushed through Brink Haven, Mount Vernon, Centerburg, and Sunbury to the Ohio capital city, 144 miles from its northern terminus at Hudson. Although still a separate corporate entity from the Pennsylvania, what officially became the Cleveland, Akron & Columbus Railroad (CA&C) served as an important feeder to the road's east-west main stem, which it crossed at Orrville, and brought large volumes of agricultural and mineral products to Akron and the teeming manufacturing sites in greater Cleveland. And in the process, the CA&C sucked much of the economic life from remaining portions of the Ohio & Erie Canal.[9]

Another carrier that served sections of the Cuyahoga Valley and regions to its south sported a corporate genealogy as complex as the CA&C, the narrow-gauge Connotton Valley Railroad (CVR). In the 1870s and 1880s a cadre of railroad promoters in Ohio and elsewhere considered standard-gauge roads (four feet, eight and a half inches between the rails) impractical for certain transportation needs. Instead, they argued that slimmer pikes (usually three feet wide) had several crucial advantages: they were easier and cheaper to construct, maintain, and operate. A remarkable number of these dreams became reality: between 1871 and 1883, a building boom produced approximately twelve thousand miles of narrow-gauge lines nationally, including about one thousand miles in the Buckeye State.[10]

This "smaller is better" thinking led General E. R. Eckley of Carrollton in the 1870s to spearhead one of the earliest narrow-gauge projects. The general and his associates wished to reach as cheaply as possible the promising coalfields of the Connotton Valley of Carroll County. After a series of battles between Eckley and his supporters over potential routes, a new road, which in 1879 became the Connotton Valley Railroad, emerged. At the beginning of the 1880s, this slim-width pike linked the mines with Canton. More expansion quickly followed, largely made possible by an infusion of funds generated by a syndicate of Boston investors. In 1881, not only did the CVR push south to Sherrodsville, but, on the Fourth of July, it opened from Canton to Bedford, a distance of forty-eight miles. By reaching Bedford, the CVR established a passenger-train connection with the Cleveland & Pittsburgh to Cleveland. Freight bound for that city, however, had to be off-loaded onto standard-gauge equipment at the C&P junction. Yet CVR officials understandably wanted direct rail access to Cleveland for both freight and passengers. Through

Cuyahoga Valley Scenic Railroad—Today

ROBERT W. BOBEL

Since its inception in 1972, Cuyahoga Valley Scenic Railroad (CVSR) has expanded into one of the most successful scenic passenger rail lines in the country. CVSR began through cooperative agreements with the Midwest Railway Preservation Society, which provided a steam locomotive, and the Chessie System (now CSX), which allowed the use of track. These agreements let the scenic railroad initiate passenger service between the Cleveland Zoo, Hale Farm & Village, and the City of Akron. In 1974, what is now called the Cuyahoga Valley National Park was created along the Cuyahoga River between Independence and Akron, encompassing most of the scenic railroad's route. After CSX suspended freight operations on the Cleveland-to-Akron line, it sold the Independence-to-Akron segment to the National Park Service (NPS). In 1989 CVSR entered into a cooperative agreement with NPS and began expanding its excursion passenger service. By the early 1990s, with ridership climbing above twenty thousand passengers a year, the railroad stopped leasing locomotives and passenger cars and began purchasing them. Around the same time, it began hiring full-time staff and using vintage diesel engines instead of its nostalgic, but unreliable, steam locomotive. It also started purchasing streamlined, stainless steel coach cars and expanding its rolling stock, including a restored café car, a concession car, a wheelchair-accessible coach, baggage cars converted to transport bicycles, and a restored round-end observation car. This last, the *Saint Lucie Sound*, was built as a business car for the Florida East Coast Railway, and CVSR uses it for first-class charters.

In 1999, the park service made a major improvement in the railroad's operation when it completed construction of the Fitzwater Maintenance Yard. And in 2003, CVSR began service from Akron to Canton, running on track purchased by Akron's Metro Regional Transit Authority, doubling the length of the excursion line to fifty miles. As of 2008, plans are underway to extend service from Independence north to Tower City in downtown Cleveland, making CVSR the only scenic/recreational rail service to connect three major U.S. cities.

The CVSR season runs from mid-February to the end of December, with trains running over two hundred days a year. Passengers can enjoy traditional scenic rail trips and specialty trains, and they also have the new "Bike Aboard" option; they can bike the Towpath Trail in one direction and take the train in the other. CVSR also maintains an active schedule of educational field trips for area schools. Students learn about the history and nature of the area in which they live and experience firsthand a mode of transportation most have only read about. The railroad's current annual ridership is one hundred thousand. The line's operating budget of over $2 million is supported through ticket sales, government funding, membership dues, fund drives, and general support from foundations, corporations, and individuals.

In 2002, the Kent State University Press published a reprint of John S. Reese's 1880 *Guide Book for the Tourist and Traveler over the Valley Railway*, making this fascinating book accessible to today's tourists and travelers.

much grading and fill work (the four miles between Newburgh and the Flats of the Cuyahoga River involved a drop of approximately 250 feet) and construction of a drawbridge over the navigable waterway, in early 1882 the railroad happily reached its destination.[11]

The CVR, however, became more than a Sherrodsville-to-Cleveland pike. Management took hold of a railroad project that had evolved out of the 1874 incorporation of the Massillon & Coshocton Railroad. In the late 1870s, the successor to this firm, the Cleveland, Canton, Coshocton & Straitsville Railroad, graded about thirty-five miles of proposed standard-gauge line between Barrs Mills, twenty miles from Canton, and Coshocton, with the intended objective of serving coalfields in the New Straitsville area of southern Perry County. Though a subsidiary, the CVR bought the graded right-of-way and in 1882 began laying narrow-gauge track south from Canton, reaching Beach City at the end of the year. A year later, track was extended to Coshocton, fifty-five miles from Canton, and a former key shipping and transfer point on the Ohio & Erie Canal and the feeder Walhonding Canal.[12]

The Cleveland, Akron & Columbus (Pennsylvania) and the Connotton Valley (later widened to standard gauge and part of the Wheeling & Lake Erie Railroad) were not the only railroads that served the greater Cuyahoga River Valley and regions to the south. Another road, the Valley Railway Company (VRC), built its tracks through the heart of the region, closely paralleling the Ohio & Erie Canal between Akron and Cleveland.

The Valley Railway resembled scores of Ohio railroad projects. It was a short line that began as a grassroots project and, like the CA&C and CVR, fell under the control of a larger carrier, in this case the B&O Railroad. The VRC then was a building-block component of that sprawling system, which by the dawn of the twentieth century served thirteen states, with lines reaching Chicago, St. Louis, Philadelphia, and Washington, D.C.

Just as General Eckley fathered the CVR, the VRC owed much to the resources and promotional skills of David L. King. The son of a prominent Warren, Ohio, merchant, King graduated in 1846, at twenty-one, from Harvard College and soon settled in Akron. After reading law and winning admission to the bar, in 1851 he opened a legal practice in Cleveland, but he returned to Akron five years later. King then changed occupations, abandoning law for manufacturing. He believed that his future would be tied to vitrified sewer pipe and became an official with the

Akron Sewer Pipe Company, which grew into one of America's largest producers of this necessity for modern urban living.[13]

Like other manufacturers, King strove to improve railroad outlets for his business. And he, too, was imbued with the spirit of civic boosterism. Although by the immediate post–Civil War period, Akron and Summit County benefited from the broad-gauge (six feet) east-west Atlantic & Great Western Railroad (a future component of the Erie Railroad's New York to Chicago main artery) and the north-south Cleveland & Pittsburgh, shippers and travelers wanted more transportation options. After all, rail competition was thought to mean better service and lower rates. Since neither the Ohio Railroad Commission nor the Interstate Commerce Commission had yet been created, no regulatory body existed to protect the public interest.

In 1869, King, joined by several other Akronites, obtained a state charter for the Akron & Canton Railway. At first, except for acquiring the necessary legal papers, not much happened. A lack of capital stymied the project. Two years later, these backers, joined by several prominent Cleveland businessmen, decided to build a railroad that would do more than connect the two cities. The result was incorporation of the Valley Railway Company, capitalized at $3 million, which, when built, would link Cleveland, Akron, Canton, and communities to the south, including Bowerston, a village in Harrison County, where a connection could be made with the Pennsylvania Railroad's east-west Pittsburgh, Columbus & Cincinnati—or "Panhandle" affiliate. Wheeling, West Virginia, was the final destination.[14]

On January 4, 1872, prospects brightened for a mostly north-south railroad through Akron. Interested representatives from Akron, Canton, Cleveland, Wheeling, and other intermediate communities gathered in Akron's Academy of Music to discuss the project. As at other railroad conventions of the era, optimism reigned. King, for one, argued that the VRC "would develop large quantities of coal and other minerals south of Akron," adding that "a locomotive, after drawing an ordinary train to Akron, could by reason of continuous down grade draw as many loaded cars from Akron to Cleveland, as the same locomotive could draw empty cars back."[15]

This meeting, with its words of encouragement, quickly led to the next step—placing the paper VRC into operation. On January 15, a "vigorous campaign opened all along the line" for public and private subscriptions to the road's common stock. Although Cleveland's response was less than expected, company agents still accomplished much. By the end of

1872, a sizable amount of cash had flowed into company coffers, including $508,250 from Cuyahoga County, $191,700 from Summit County, and $149,750 from Stark County.[16]

The brightening financial picture prompted the VRC to send surveyors into the field. Plymouth Dudley, "Akron's most efficient City Engineer," who served as the road's chief engineer, directed these operations. As with other contemporary railroad projects, multiple lines were surveyed. Crews, for example, staked two routes between Akron and Cleveland. One ran directly down the valley of the Cuyahoga River, and the other extended overland through Bath, Richfield, and Brecksville. Although considerable local support developed for the latter, the VRC opted for the former, likely because grading would be less expensive. By early 1873, the route between Cleveland and Canton had been finalized.[17]

Although 1873, the year of the major Wall Street panic, was hardly an auspicious time to begin construction, the VRC pushed ahead. Not only had the subscription drive generated considerable cash, but the principals had prestige in the business world. The Cleveland backers were wealthy and well connected: Sylvester Everett, Henry Flagler, Henry Payne, John Tod, and Jeptha Wade belonged to the city's financial and power elite, and, of course, these men wanted another railroad to increase service, lower rates, and enhance their city's economic sphere of influence. In August, a mostly satisfied Chief Engineer Dudley reported to the board of directors:

> On the line between Cleveland and Canton, a distance of fifty-seven miles, the grading was commenced last March; but on account of the wet weather in April and May, and other causes, has not proceeded as fast as could be desired. All the bridges are under contract, and part of them up. I am, however, pleased to say that nearly two-thirds of the distance from Cleveland to Canton is graded, and, should the weather continue favorable, I see no reason to prevent the completion of the remainder, ready to commence laying track in October. This would give you the use of the road most of the coming winter, which would be an advantage you no doubt fully appreciate.[18]

The expectation of revenue-producing trains running between Cleveland, Akron, and Canton by late 1873 or 1874 was not met. A dispute between the company and its Akron-based contractors, probably over payments, led to a May 16, 1874, suspension of all construction. And by this time a harsh depression had settled down upon Ohio and the nation. Some stock subscriptions were not being paid, and backers, including the well-heeled Clevelanders, failed to tap pools of either domestic or international investment capital.[19]

Company president King, the board, and its supporters did not abandon hope of completing the initial core of the VRC. In fact, in February 1875, King sailed for England to find investors for the road's stocks and bonds. Although his diligent efforts apparently led to an agreement for bankers to invest, telegraphic news of the unexpected failure of the Toledo, Wabash & Western Railroad, a well-established and strategic regional carrier, caused the deal to fail. A downcast King returned home.[20]

America's centennial year witnessed a rebounding economy, although hard times would continue in many localities until 1878. The VRC took advantage of generally improving financial markets to gain financial support domestically, largely from New York–based investors. With financial backing at hand, the road engaged a replacement contracting firm, and on August 7, 1878, work resumed. At high noon on October 26, King ceremoniously hammered in the first spike at "Old Forge" (Middlebury section of Akron), and track crews immediately began extending rails in both directions. Soon, too, they were joined by another gang, which had started from Cleveland. Then, in January 1879, problems with the contractor again led to a canceled contract and suspension of construction. Fortunately, the VRC found another builder, and work resumed in late spring. But progress was not too rapid, and the road's first inspection train did not travel between the two terminals until January 28, 1880. Shortly thereafter, the company established regular freight and passenger service.[21]

The VRC was a reasonably good railroad for the standards of the post–Civil War era. It lacked major stiff grades and sported cinder and gravel ballast and steel rails that weighed an average of fifty-six pounds per yard. It is not surprising that the initial run over the road was remarkably fast. "Starting from Canton on the return trip at 3 o'clock, P.M. the run from Canton to Akron, twenty-two miles, was made in thirty-eight minutes," noted one observer. "The entire trip from Canton to Cleveland, fifty-seven miles, being made in two hours—a remarkable run, considering the newness of the road, and evincing a very excellent degree of work in the laying of the track and the ballasting of the road-bed."[22]

The long anticipated opening of the Cleveland, Akron & Canton Short Line prompted VRC officialdom to build beyond Canton. Favored by the success of the main core, coupled with a return of prosperity and future prospects for considerable online coal traffic, by July 15, 1882, track layers reached Valley Junction, a rural station twenty-three miles south of Canton and connection with the now-standardized successor to the CVR, the Wheeling & Lake Erie. The extension served the intermediate Stark and Tuscarawas communities of North Industry, Sparta, Sandyville, and Mineral Point.[23]

Although the VRC stalled at Valley Junction, it served its territory well. The coming of the steam-car civilization meant much to the population along the route. Residents in the Cuyahoga River Valley between Akron and Cleveland, for example, now enjoyed access to conveniently placed depots from Akron at Botzum's, Everett, Peninsula, Boston, Brecksville, Independence, and Brooklyn. In the 1880s and 1890s the company customarily dispatched three daily passenger trains and an accommodation, or mixed freight and passenger, train between Canton and Cleveland and one less passenger train between Canton and Valley Junction. These runs stopped at all stations and at the occasional flag stop. Freight trains also traveled when needed; coal, grain, lumber, clay, sand, stone, and an assortment of other goods filled these runs of usually fifteen to twenty cars.[24]

The heavy black smoke and the penetrating blasts of the locomotive steam whistle made a striking difference for valley residents who had grown accustomed to the occasional bellowing of a canal horn, though few likely fussed over these new sights and sounds. Although the Ohio & Erie Canal had boosted property values, the railroad proved to be an even greater financial asset. And the convenience for personal travel and sending goods to and from market was obvious. Old-timers, who had their hopes dashed by an earlier, unsuccessful effort to bring the iron horse to the valley, surely felt more confident about the future. They recalled that in the mid-1850s backers of the Clinton Air Line Extension Rail Road, part of a grandiose scheme to build a rail line from New York to the Mississippi and Missouri Rivers, had graded a few miles of right-of-way in the valley west of Hudson.[25]

It was hardly surprising to area residents that an independent VRC would not survive in a corporate world where consolidations were rampant. Except for the five troubled years sparked by the cataclysmic Panic of 1893, the late nineteenth and early twentieth centuries were times when hundreds of short lines and tap roads entered larger systems, often interregional in scope.

Even before the depression of the 1890s, which struck northeast Ohio especially hard, the VRC failed financially. Excessive construction debt and a slump in freight revenues made court protection necessary, and an Ohio judge granted it on June 15, 1892. By the time of the bankruptcy, however, the VRC was no longer a locally owned property, for on January 9, 1890, the Baltimore & Ohio Railroad had purchased stock control.[26]

The B&O ownership was hardly unforeseen. This nearly seventeen-hundred-mile Baltimore-based company, which traced its roots back to the dawn of American railroading, was in an expansive mood. By 1890, its recently elected president, Charles F. Mayer, a coal magnate, had vigorously extended the B&O, including a new route to Chicago and significant additional mileage in Ohio, Pennsylvania, and West Virginia. Before he left his post in 1896, Mayer had also become responsible for one of the engineering marvels of the nineteenth century, the electrified Howard Street Tunnel under downtown Baltimore, which removed a longtime traffic bottleneck and became a prototype for modern railroad electrification.[27]

Mayer and the B&O board of directors believed that their future rested in building up coal traffic and serving important manufacturing centers. In the early 1890s, the B&O recast its main line by building a seventy-three-mile extension from Akron to Chicago Junction (later Willard), Ohio. It also acquired the Pittsburgh & Western Railroad, which allowed through freight service beginning in August 1891 (and later started passenger service) from Baltimore to Chicago, by way of Pittsburgh instead of central Ohio. In addition, it saw the coal-carrying VRC as a practical means to gain access to Cleveland (via Akron). Without a doubt, the Ohio short line met the B&O's criterion for expansion. And for the VRC, the B&O was a white knight; it would have been difficult otherwise for the VRC to function in an environment of large railroads.[28]

The VRC, which for all practical purposes had entered the sprawling B&O system in 1890, soon changed its name. When the property emerged from court protection on October 3, 1895, the reorganized company, with its reduced debt, became the Cleveland Terminal & Valley (CT&V) Railroad. The B&O retained control and continued to keep it even after its own bankruptcy in 1896.[29]

Although the CT&V had become the official name for the Ohio short line, patrons commonly used the Valley moniker. While they might ignore the name change, even the most casual observer recognized that the property was not the same. Though the B&O remained in bankruptcy for three years, major changes occurred. The parent company modernized the property (for example, laying heavier, seventy-five-pound steel rail) and diverted main-line traffic to and from the Akron-Cleveland segment. In a sense, the Cleveland trackage became more a main line rather than a branch-line appendage. Early on, management dispatched passenger trains 14 and 15 between Chicago and Cleveland with a Canton connec-

Cleveland Terminal & Valley Railroad became the name of the Valley Railway after it was purchased by the Baltimore & Ohio Railroad (author's collection; original source unknown).

tion, bragging that it was "the only line running through Pullman Palace vestibule sleeping cars between Cleveland and Chicago."[30]

This extensive penetration by the B&O brought regional railroad construction mostly to an end. An Akronite of the early years of the twentieth century concluded: "We have no pressing need of further transportation facilities from steam roads."[31] Yet not everyone agreed. In the immediate Akron area, the Barberton-based Akron & Barberton Belt Railroad opened a several-mile extension from Barberton to Fairlawn in 1903 and a year later built to East Akron. Then in 1912, the Akron, Canton & Youngstown

Railroad completed a seven-mile industrial switching road between Akron and Mogadore, a project that had begun in 1907.

The CT&V did not last long as a corporate entity. In a desire to streamline its business structure, the B&O in July 1909 dissolved the Ohio corporation. Still, residents along the old VRC called it the Valley, although after World War I it became for many simply the B&O. The company operated more than coal drags and freight trains; it sent sections of two of its main-line "name trains," the *Chicago-Pittsburgh-New York Express* and *The Ambassador,* over the Akron-Cleveland trackage, making stops at Union and Howard Street stations in Akron and the newly opened Terminal Tower station in Cleveland. Only a poky local that ran between Wheeling and Cleveland via New Philadelphia, Dover, and Canal Fulton (over the former Cleveland, Lorain & Wheeling, which the B&O had taken into its system in 1909) paid calls at intermediate stations including Ira, Peninsula, and Jaite. And by the Great Depression, passenger service had ended south of Akron.[32]

This pattern of operation on the old Valley line mostly continued until the twilight of private intercity passenger service in Ohio. In 1963, eight years before Amtrak made its debut, the B&O ended connecting passenger service to and from Cleveland via Akron, although it operated an east-west train through Akron until 1971. Freight trains, though, continued to rumble over the old VRC, with oil trains originating in Mineral City and slow-moving coke trains from the Pittsburgh area leaving the main line for Cleveland steel mills in the industrial flats.

Just as the VRC had become part of earlier system building, the Baltimore & Ohio, too, participated in the "merger madness" of the 1960s and the later era of mega-mergers. In 1963, a financially struggling B&O joined with the Chesapeake & Ohio Railway to create the C&O-B&O, later becoming part of the expanded Chessie System. Then, in 1980, Chessie joined with Seaboard Coast Line Industries to form one of America's super railroads, CSX.[33]

Mergers led not only to new corporate structures but also to abandonment and sale of duplicate, money-losing, and marginally profitable lines. In 1985, CSX, which could use the former Cleveland, Lorain & Wheeling route to retain Cleveland customers, suspended freight service over the old VRC and subsequently sold the Akron-Independence (Cleveland) segment to the National Park Service. This transaction allowed creation of the Cuyahoga Valley Scenic Railroad, a tourist operation serving the heart of Cuyahoga Valley National Park. In time, the tracks south of

Akron were purchased by Akron Metro Regional Transit Authority to extend the scenic railroad operation twenty-two miles to Canton.

Even though the Valley Railway Company operated less than a hundred miles of line and maintained its corporate independence for only slightly more than a score of years, it holds historical significance. As a type, the VRC represented the widely popular short line of the nineteenth century. Then, when the B&O acquired control, the VRC shared the fate of hundreds of other small, independent roads during the era of system building. As a vital part of the B&O, it eventually became a footnote to the mergers and mega-mergers of the latter part of the twentieth century. Its owner, in this case Chessie System, no longer had need for much of the line, leading to abandonment and sale. Fortunately for the public, a core component remains active as a tourist operation, annually helping thousands enjoy Cuyahoga Valley National Park by rail.

Not to be overlooked is the long-term social and economic impact the VRC trackage had on its service territory. The daily coming and going of passenger trains was once important to residents of all the communities served, especially the smaller ones where it was the only carrier. These trains transported families, friends, and strangers, and they carried the mail and package express. Moreover, the depot agent had direct contact

Railroad bridge near the pumping station in 1900, near the northern end of the canal and in the current Ohio & Erie Canal Reservation (Louis Baus Canal Photograph Collection, University of Akron Archival Services).

The four "highways" between Lock 17 at Port Washington in 1890 (Louis Baus Canal Photograph Collection, University of Akron Archival Services).

with the rest of the world through the magic of the electric telegraph. The local freight trains brought in the necessities of life and carried away farm products, particularly cans of milk. And coal, usually the principal commodity hauled, not only heated homes and businesses but also fired the great smokestack industries of the region. Noted one commentator in 1942: "But the canals had made [the area], giving it an impetus and growth that later attracted the railroads which definitely assured its future." And the VRC made its contribution.[34]

Students of the past occasionally dabble with counterfactual history. That is, what would have happened if some event or movement had never actually happened? Transportation historians, for example, generally agree that if the internal combustion engine had been perfected one or two decades before it was, then electric interurbans, which by 1915 operated on nearly sixteen thousand miles of line, might never had been built, or that mileage would have been limited. A similar argument can be made about canals. If the primitive locomotives that rumbled down the spindly tracks of the Baltimore & Ohio Railroad, Erie & Kalamazoo Rail Road, or South Carolina Canal & Rail Road had done so ten, fifteen, or twenty years earlier and had the technological triumphs of the 1830s and early 1840s occurred in the late 1810s and 1820s, perhaps Ohio and the nation would have seen fewer ditches, including the web of canals that served northeast Ohio. In 1853, an official of the Pennsylvania & Ohio Canal, whose company had felt the sting of railroads drawing away shipments of high-value commodities and a good portion of its bulk items, including coal, admitted that "this Canal was constructed at a time when a railroad of any extent was not known. It is probable if there had been a system of railroads of any considerable extent, this work would never have been completed."[35]

What happened, however, was that only a few canals could compete with the iron horse. The appearance of the Connotton Valley, CA&C, and VRC did not immediately destroy the northern end of the Ohio & Erie Canal. Just as the historic Chesapeake & Ohio Canal hauled coal, sand, and other bulk commodities largely parallel to the main line of the B&O between Cumberland, Maryland, and Washington, D.C., until 1923, the Ohio & Erie did much the same until the Easter week 1913 floods ravaged its locks, banks, and towpaths. Residents of the Cuyahoga River Valley and adjoining areas benefited from alternative forms of freight transport. And just as the remains of the Ohio & Erie Canal carried their last revenue boats, the area's emerging good-roads movement, coupled with the rapidly improving motor truck, expanded transport options. The region is a palimpsest of the transportation heritage of Ohio and the Old Northwest.

NOTES

1. Newspaper clipping, n.d., Norfolk Southern Archives, Atlanta, Ga.

2. John F. Stover, *Iron Road to the West: American Railroads in the 1850's* (New York: Columbia Univ. Press, 1978), 116; H. Roger Grant, *Ohio on the Move: Transportation in the Buckeye State* (Athens: Ohio Univ. Press, 2000), 75.

3. See John F. Stover, *American Railroads*, 2d ed. (Chicago: Univ. of Chicago Press, 1997).

4. Ronald E. Shaw, *Canals for a Nation: The Canal Era in the United States, 1790–1860* (Lexington: Univ. Press of Kentucky, 1990), 153–54; Stover, *American Railroads*, 33; Albro Martin, *Railroads Triumphant: The Growth, Rejection, and Rebirth of a Vital American Force* (New York: Oxford Univ. Press, 1992), 40–52.

5. Grant, *Ohio on the Move*, 18; see also William Cronon, *Nature's Metropolis: Chicago and the Great West* (New York: Norton, 1991).

6. See Jack Gieck, *A Photo Album of Ohio's Canal Era, 1825–1913* (Kent: Kent State Univ. Press, 1988).

7. Harry N. Scheiber, "Public Canal Finance and State Banking in Ohio, 1827–1837," *Indiana Magazine of History* 65 (June 1969): 119–32. See also Harry N. Scheiber, *Ohio Canal Era: A Case Study of Government and the Economy, 1820–1861* (Athens: Ohio Univ. Press, 1969).

8. Harry N. Scheiber, "The Pennsylvania & Ohio Canal: Transport Innovation, Mixed Enterprise, and Urban Commercial Rivalry, 1825–1861," *Old Northwest* 6 (Summer 1980): 107–29.

9. *A Centennial History of Akron, 1825–1925* (Akron: Summit County Historical Society, 1925), 467–68; William Henry Perrin, *History of Summit County, with an Outline Sketch of Ohio* (Chicago: Baskin & Battey, 1881), 289; William B. Doyle, ed., *Centennial History of Summit County, Ohio and Representative Citizens* (Chicago: Biographical Publishing, 1908), 140–41; George H. Burgess and Miles C. Kennedy, *Centennial History of the Pennsylvania Railroad Company, 1846–1946* (Philadelphia: Pennsylvania Railroad, 1949), 182–83, 489, 530.

10. George W. Hilton, *American Narrow Gauge Railroads* (Stanford, Calif.: Stanford Univ. Press, 1990), 75–117, 462–79.

11. John A. Rehor, *The Nickel Plate Story* (Milwaukee: Kalmbach, 1965), 288–97, 312–14; Hilton, *American Narrow Gauge Railroads*, 468–69.

12. Hilton, *American Narrow Gauge Railroads.*

13. Perrin, *History of Summit County*, 725–26; *A Centennial History of Akron*, 306–7; Karl H. Grismer, *Akron and Summit County* (Akron: Summit County Historical Society, 1952), 660.

14. Perrin, *History of Summit County*, 298; *Poor's Manual of Railroads* (New York: Poor's Railroad Manual, 1885), 575.

15. Perrin, *History of Summit County*, 298–99.

16. Ibid.

17. Ibid., 299.

18. Ibid., 300.

19. Ibid.

20. Ibid.; William Henry Perrin, *History of Stark County with an Outline Sketch of Ohio* (Chicago: Baskin & Battey, 1881), 226.

21. Perrin, *History of Summit County*, 300–301.

22. Ibid., 301.

23. *Poor's Manual of Railroads* (1885), 575.

24. Valley Railway Company public timetable, May 18, 1894, possession of the author.

25. Perrin, *History of Summit County*, 293.

26. John F. Stover, *History of the Baltimore and Ohio Railroad* (West Lafayette, Ind.: Purdue Univ. Press, 1987), 171; *Poor's Manual of Railroads* (New York: Poor's Railroad Manual, 1894), 330.

27. Stover, *History of the Baltimore and Ohio Railroad*, 170–80.

28. Ibid.

29. *Poor's Manual of Railroads* (New York: Poor's Railroad Manual, 1897), 306.

30. Ibid.; Cleveland Terminal & Valley Railroad public timetable, January 1897, possession of the author.

31. Doyle, *Centennial History of Summit County, Ohio*, 143.

32. *Poor's Manual of Railroads* (New York: Poor's Railroad Manual Company, 1910), 127; Baltimore & Ohio Railroad public timetable, Aug. 1, 1926.

33. Richard Saunders Jr., *Merging Lines: American Railroads, 1900–1970* (DeKalb: Northern Illinois Univ. Press, 2001), 239–41; Stover, *American Railroads*, 246.

34. Burton P. Porter, *"Old Canal Days"* (Columbus: Heer, 1942), 444.

35. See Grant, *Ohio on the Move*, 66.

Chapter 10

William Bennett's Navarre, the Canal Town

SAM TAMBURRO

Every small town has a historian, the sage of its history and heritage. In the first half of the twentieth century William Loren Bennett served that role for Navarre, Ohio, located along the Tuscarawas River in northeast Stark County. More than that, he captured on film many of Navarre's landscapes and buildings, freezing in time the architecture and appearance of the village. For future generations, Bennett has left visual and written histories of the Village of Navarre and beyond.

Born on November 9, 1869, William, like his father before him, spent his life in Navarre. In fact, his grandfather Oliver F. Bennett was one of the village's earliest residents, arriving in town on the Ohio & Erie Canal. His trip is the stuff of legend.

According to family lore, Oliver was impressed into the British Royal Navy in 1821, at thirteen.[1] Apparently, the ship made several stops; Oliver and two other shipmates went absent without leave during a port call in Quebec, Canada. He and his mates hid for several days with a sympathetic Quebec shopkeeper, and the navy ship left port without them. The shopkeeper secured Oliver a job in a Quebec shipyard, where he apprenticed to be a mechanic. After working in the shipyards of Quebec for several years, Oliver decided he wanted to travel to the United States, particularly Cleveland, Ohio.[2] In 1830, he traveled there by boat to start anew. After working two years on the docks of Cleveland, Oliver planned to travel to New Orleans, journeying by boat on the Ohio & Erie Canal to the Ohio River at Portsmouth. In 1833, he boarded a canal boat to begin his trek south; his first stop was Massillon, Ohio. During an overnight stay in

Massillon, his future was changed. After meeting the daughter of the proprietor (Peter Nave) of the hotel, Sarah Nave, Oliver decided to marry her and stay in the area. After a year's courtship, the couple wed in the summer of 1834.[3] He and his new wife moved to Navarre at a time of tremendous economic boom there.

As one can imagine, the town Oliver Bennett relocated to in 1834 was significantly different than present-day Navarre. In fact, the current Village of Navarre was historically composed of three different villages: Bethlehem, Rochester, and Navarre. After the Ohio & Erie Canal opened, all three towns had the economy of inland port communities, built on grain shipment. In the 1830s, consequently, the towns were experiencing a construction boom, in both business and private sectors.

Oliver Bennett quickly found work as a builder and constructed several of the town's original landmark buildings, like its mill and first hotel. Among his proudest achievements as a builder was the construction of the first steeple on the old St. Clement Catholic Church.

Oliver also was an inventor. In about 1839, he invented an early threshing device, a "knocker," which was used to flail grain. According to a family history, the machine preceded that invented later by Russell and Company of Massillon. The knocker proved effective at separating grain from straw and substantially increased the productivity of farmers, so much so that the overproduction of grain sometimes glutted the market, driving down prices.

Local businessmen searched for a solution to control the supply of grain commodities. Around 1850, they pooled their resources and formed a business alliance, the Farmers' and Mechanics' Association. The association consisted of about fifty businessmen, with the combined capital of $20,000.[4] Although it was not incorporated as a business, it was controlled by a board of directors. It built a large warehouse, a hardware store, and a dry goods store and acquired a number of canal boats to ship products to market and also built twelve wharves along the banks of the canal. The association dealt mostly in grain trade, and during its peak operational years, it purchased nearly 100,000 bushels of wheat and grain from area farmers and shipped it to Cleveland on the Ohio & Erie Canal. During the antebellum period, the Navarre area remained one of the largest trading centers in Stark County.[5]

Since the Ohio & Erie Canal was the transportation artery in Navarre, nearly all the local businessmen had a stake in its day-to-day operation. Oliver Bennett was no exception. In 1847, he completed the construction of a building near Lock 6, which would house his new grocery and provision store, as well as his family. Because of its close proximity to the lock, Oliver's store was a success. Oliver was also closely associated with the canal's day-to-day operation, serving as an assistant to the lockkeeper and often wading into the canal waters to free jammed canal boats from the lock.[6] In spring 1854, after working for hours in the cold canal to repair the mechanisms of the lock gates, he developed a severe cold that worsened into pneumonia. On April 14, 1854, Oliver Bennett died at forty-seven, leaving his widow, Sarah, and son, Henry, to manage the store.[7]

At the time of his father's death, Henry R. Bennett was seventeen years old. After attending Mount Union College in Alliance, Ohio, Henry returned to Navarre to help his mother run the family business. He left for a time, to serve as first lieutenant and captain for the Union army during the Civil War. After returning from the war, Henry and his wife, Amanda Frohman Bennett, had three children: Ivy May (April 9, 1864); Frank (February 4, 1868), who died thirty-five days after his birth; and William (November 9, 1869). Throughout his life, Henry held several elected positions in the village and was the president of the Navarre Deposit Bank. In later years, he also operated, with William's help, a coal mine in North Industry.

After the Civil War, the United States slowly began to transform from an agrarian to an industrial society, and this affected the Village of Navarre. The close proximity of Bethlehem, Navarre, and Rochester—and their similar economies—created an intense rivalry between them. The business communities in the three villages realized that the competition between the communities was injurious to the area as a whole and decided to ask all of the citizens to vote on the issue of incorporation into one village, called Navarre. A majority of the villages' citizens voted to incorporate. By the early 1880s, Navarre received railroad service, which significantly lessened the importance of the Ohio & Erie Canal as a transportation resource. By the 1890s, a number of authors described the decline of the Ohio & Erie Canal and its impact on the economy of Navarre. (See chapter 7 for a complete description of the canal in the late 1880s.) However, the 1889–90 *Massillon Business Directory* view of Navarre is still positive about the town. The directory describes Navarre as "an incorporated village of about 1,200 inhabitants, that at one time was a leading town in Stark County, as numerous large warehouses yet indicate, being the grain market for several counties at the completion of the Ohio Canal. Coal is mined in considerable quantity in the vicinity. . . . Navarre has a graded school, 5 churches, 3 railroads, several well stocked stores, a weekly newspaper and a planing mill. Land [is] gently rolling and very productive. Principle occupation [is] farming and mining. Wheat is raised extensively in this village."[8]

Regardless of the hyperbole, it is evident that the opening of railroads in northeast Ohio adversely affected the Ohio & Erie Canal and consequently the Navarre-Rochester community. Not only was the canal's freight traffic diminished by the railroad, but the advent of the interurban further lessened passenger service on the canal.

In the early twentieth century, the interurban arrived in Navarre to service the community's fifteen hundred residents. In 1901, the Northern Ohio Traction & Light (NOT&L) Company built an electric railway through Navarre, connecting the village to Massillon, New Philadelphia, and points beyond.[9] The NOT&L would operate in Navarre for twenty-eight years, finally closing in 1929 as a result of increased competition from automobiles and buses.

During this period, the State of Ohio did rehabilitate the northern section of the Ohio & Erie Canal, including the Navarre segment. In 1906, the state drained for repairs the canal from Massillon at Lock 5-A to Bolivar, Ohio.[10] On March 25, 1913, a devastating flood inundated Navarre and the Ohio & Erie Canal. Flooding was widespread, with many houses and businesses destroyed. Nearly all of the improvement the state made to the canal in 1906 were washed away. The flood of 1913 effectively ended the operation of the Ohio & Erie Canal in Navarre. A further blow to the community happened on April 25, 1913, when the Bennett warehouse in Rochester Square was destroyed by fire. The first floor of the warehouse was occupied by J. M. Hay and contained flour and farm implements and the offices of the Junior Order of United Americans.[11] During this period of transition in Navarre, William Loren Bennett came of age. And, although by the late nineteenth century the Ohio & Erie Canal had outlived its usefulness, it was a favorite subject for his lens.

William had a typical nineteenth-century childhood in Navarre, delivering newspapers and attending school. During the 1880s, he served as a newspaper agent and the newsboy for Navarre, introducing the sale and circulation of the *Cleveland Herald*, the *Cleveland Plain Dealer*, the *Canton Evening Repository*, and the *Canton News-Democrat*.[12] According to his family history, he worked in the Cleveland, Tuscarawas Valley, & Wheeling Depot, learning how to run the telegraph machine and do railroad bookkeeping. He also carried messages from town to the depot and delivered telegrams to village residents.[13]

It is apparent that Bennett enjoyed writing; he worked as a correspondent for the *Canton Evening Repository* from 1883 to 1886 while a student at Navarre High School. In addition, he eventually published a three-hundred-page history of Navarre that was published in 1936, the centennial anniversary of the founding of the community.

After graduation in 1888, he went into the grain business with his father. The Bennetts maintained a storeroom warehouse and adjoining

In "Mother among the Lilies," Bennett photographed his mother in her garden, June 1912 (William Bennett Collection of the Massillon Museum).

brick warehouse at the southwest corner of Rochester Square, directly adjacent to the Ohio & Erie Canal. They shipped their grain almost entirely on the canal and received their supplies for the shop the same way, which was the most convenient and economical means. They continued to operate the family business until 1905, when Henry died. At that point, William sold the family business and rented the buildings, enabling him to devote more time to his two life passions—gardening and photography.[14] After leaving the grain and warehouse business, he became a property insurance agent, remaining in that profession until his retirement.[15]

After his father's death, William and his mother lived in the family home on the north side of East Canal Street in Navarre. Three years after his mother's death on November 15, 1919, he sold the house to Alfred Nickles, the founder of Nickles Bakery.[16] Eventually, William would move into the residence of Police Chief Sam Dunlap and his wife; he would live with the Dunlaps until his death on November 9, 1951.

William Bennett loved nature and enjoyed hiking in the country. These hobbies led to another one—photography. He purchased his first camera, a Premier, from the Rochester Optical Company at $35.00 around 1896. He owned the only camera in town in the late nineteenth

Alfred Nickles, founder of Nickles Bakery, Inc., in 1909 is pictured here with his family, friends, and decorated trucks, July 4, 1921 (William Bennett Collection of the Massillon Museum).

and early twentieth centuries, and he captured images of the community that augment our current understanding of its history and landscape.

Following his father's death, photography engaged him the remainder of his life. Consequently, he took thousands of photographs, more than two thousand of which he gave to the Massillon Museum. The culmination of his photography "career" was an exhibit of his photographs at the Massillon Museum, which traced the history of photography and the development of the Village of Navarre from 1896 to 1946. His collection forms a pictorial record of the village and its residents.

Bennett's interest in photography coincides with the rise of amateur photography in the late nineteenth century. During this period, many middle-class Americans were enticed by Eastman Kodak's advertisement: "You Push the Button, We Do the Rest."[17] As a result, many Americans purchased inexpensive cameras and captured images of family picnics and summer vacations that filled the pages of Victorian photograph albums.[18] As a result of photography's popularity, it became a well-organized hobby. As historian Thomas A. Denenberg notes in *Wallace Nutting and the Invention of Old America*, "Camera clubs sprang up in major cities in the 1880s, often supported by manufactures of photographic supplies, and specialty journals vied for the attentions (and dollars) of the dabbler."[19]

A 1946 newspaper article by Isabelle McCormick reported that a number of Bennett's photographs were printed as postcard views of the village, produced in Germany by the Excelsior Photograph Company.[20] Two of his more notable postcards are *A Bird's Eye View of Navarre, Ohio U.S.A. from Rose Hill* and *The Building in which President William McKinley Tried His First Law Suit Navarre, Ohio U.S.A.* Nearly all of the photographs he took were signed and dated in distinctive handwriting. There is no evidence that he sold his photographs professionally; however, he did trade them with other photographers, locally, nationally, and internationally.[21]

One of the photographers with whom Bennett corresponded was Belle Johnson, who was known as an eccentric, unorthodox artist whose creativity was uninhibited by conventional photographic techniques. Born in Mendota, Illinois, Johnson operated a portrait studio in Monroe City, Missouri. It is thought that the two were part of a circle of photographers that shared their work by mail. It is clear they exchanged ideas, techniques, and photographs. They would share personal notes on the back of the photographs. Johnson also sent her work to Bennett on holidays and special occasions, adding character to the collection. Although they shared an interest in the art, their subjects were quite different. Many of Johnson's photographs were portraits of adults and children. In contrast,

Lock 6 in the winter (William Bennett Collection of the Massillon Museum).

Bennett focused on landscape photographs, mostly taken in Navarre. Locally, he exchanged photographs with Cleveland's Louis Baus and Akron's Pearl Nye, both prolific photographers of the Ohio & Erie Canal landscape in northeast Ohio.

The subject of William Bennett's photography varied from the Ohio & Erie Canal's Lock 6 to many other historic views of the village. Jack Gieck, in *A Photo Album of Ohio's Canal Era, 1825–1913,* referred to his work: "Another photographer showed up in the 1890s in Navarre, where he couldn't get enough of Lock 6—photographing it both summer and winter."[22] He focused his camera lens on what was closest in his life. Often he would capture on film canal boatmen and their families locking through Lock 6, exposing the drudgery and difficulty of making a living on a canal boat. In fact, Bennett's camera captured several buildings of the village that have long been altered or razed. Within his collection are shots of leafy village streets from the late nineteenth century, replete with interurban tracks and overhead power wires.

He also documented special events in Navarre, including the visits of two different U.S. presidents. He photographed President Theodore Roosevelt on the platform of the rear of a train stopped at the village railroad depot when he was running as William McKinley's vice president.

"The canal was a transportation artery in Navarre. Nearly all the local businessmen have a stake in the day-to-day operation" (William Bennett Collection of the Massillon Museum).

The towpath connected the farms with the town and markets (William Bennett Collection of the Massillon Museum).

Ohio & Erie Canal at Little Italy hillside, July 26, 1886 (William Bennett Collection of the Massillon Museum).

Bennett also took several photographs of McKinley at his home in Canton the day before he was elected president in 1896.

William Bennett made sure his photographs would survive beyond his lifetime when in the late 1930s he donated his entire collection, including his Belle Johnson images, to the Massillon Museum. Out of the many photographs he donated, approximately two hundred were taken by Johnson. Donating his photographs to the Massillon Museum probably was an easy decision for Bennett. Founded in 1933, the museum maintains a substantial collection of Ohio art and local history, including sixty thousand historical photographs. Since the 1940s, Massillon has maintained a vibrant photographic community, and the museum's photograph collection includes the works of such nationally recognized artists as Abel Fletcher, Nell Dorr, and Theodore Teeple.[23] Clearly, by donating his work to the Massillon Museum, he sought to have his collection curated with other significant Massillon photographers and place his work in that historical context.

During the 1930s, he became acquainted with Albert Hise, the first curator of the Massillon Museum. Hise had been involved with the museum since its inception in 1933. Also, as secretary of the Massillon High School Alumni Association, he had collected historical information about Massillon since 1920.[24] It is not clear whether Hise pursued his collection or vice versa. Regardless, the culmination of Bennett's photographic career came in July 1946, when the Massillon Museum ran a month-long exhibit celebrating his photography. The Massillon Museum advertised the exhibit

Canal boats were used for recreation as well as transporting grain and coal. Photo taken in 1896 (William Bennett Collection of the Massillon Museum).

"Bird's Eye View of Navarre, Ohio, USA, 1961 (William Bennett Collection of the Massillon Museum).

Winter clothes-hanging scene along a canal lock. City Hall is in background, Navarre, Ohio, January 14, 1904 (William Bennett Collection of the Massillon Museum).

tracing the history of photography as well as the development of Navarre during the preceding fifty years.[25] Since then, there has not been an exhibit at the museum featuring the Ohio & Erie Canal that did not include some of the Bennett collection.

If every man is his own historian, then every small town and village needs a William Bennett to record and document its history. Although never trained as a historian, he wrote thoughtfully about the heritage of Navarre. Maybe even more telling is the photo-documentation he left. Bennett pointed his camera lens at features to tell the history of his family, the canal, the mill, and Main Street. Using snapshots, he froze Navarre in the twilight of its canal era. Grace Goulder in her *Plain Dealer* article "Ohio Songs and Citizens: A Pleasant Rainy Day in Navarre" summed up Bennett's importance to his town: "There is a kind of unorganized fraternity among people like William Bennett. They gather up the traditions of a place and safeguard them for new generations who are inclined to assume that the world began with them. And word of these interpreters of the past travels about."[26]

NOTES

1. Isabelle McCormick, "Navarre Man Has Recorded Progress in Photographs," *Massillon Independent,* July 17, 1946.

2. William Loren Bennett, "History of the Bennett Family in Navarre, Ohio," William L. Bennett Collection, Navarre-Bethlehem Township Historical Society, 2.

3. Bennett, "History of the Bennett Family in Navarre, Ohio."

4. Marilyn Cook and Don Cooke, *Navarre, Ohio 1806–1981* (Navarre: Navarre Historical Society, 1981), 36.

5. Ibid., 37.

6. Bennett, "History of the Bennett Family in Navarre, Ohio."

7. Bennett, "History of the Bennett Family in Navarre, Ohio."

8. *Massillon City Directory* (Akron: N. H. Birch, 1889–90), 1084.

9. John H. Lehman, *A Standard History of Stark County* (Chicago: Lewis, n.d.), 510.

10. Terry K. Woods, *History of the Ohio & Erie Canal in Stark County* (Massillon: Massillon Museum, 2003), 29.

11. *Massillon American,* Apr. 25, 1913.

12. Bennett, "History of the Bennett Family in Navarre, Ohio."

13. Bennett, "History of the Bennett Family in Navarre, Ohio."

14. McCormick, "Navarre Man."

15. Bennett, "History of the Bennett Family in Navarre, Ohio."

16. Bennett, "History of the Bennett Family in Navarre, Ohio."

17. Thomas A. Denenberg, *Wallace Nutting and the Invention of Old America* (New Haven: Yale Univ. Press, 2003), 27.

18. Ibid.

19. Ibid.

20. McCormick, "Navarre Man."

21. Ibid.

22. Jack Gieck, *A Photo Album of Ohio's Canal Era, 1825–1913* (Kent: Kent State Univ. Press, 1988), x.

23. Vogt, *Towpath to Towpath,* 163.

24. Ibid.

25. McCormick, "Navarre Man."

26. Grace Goulder, "Ohio Songs and Citizens: A Pleasant Rainy Day in Navarre," *Cleveland Plain Dealer,* Jan. 17, 1943.

Chapter 11

Crossing the Cultural Fault Line

The Historic Landscape of the Ohio & Erie Canal

GLENN HARPER

The landscape of the Ohio & Erie Canal encompasses much more than old locks and quaint canal towns. When the canal was built, beginning in the 1820s, it traversed land from Cleveland to Portsmouth, much of which had been surveyed, sold, and occupied by white settlers for over three decades. In northeast and east-central Ohio, white settlers from New England and New York often encountered those from the Middle-Atlantic states of Pennsylvania, New Jersey, Virginia, Maryland, and Delaware, especially along the southern and western boundaries of the Western Reserve, an area encompassing all or part of fourteen northeastern Ohio counties.

Connecticut had retained jurisdictional control over the Reserve in hopes that it would become a New Connecticut. Farther south, in the Congress Lands, initial occupants were primarily from Pennsylvania, Virginia, and Maryland.[1] The canal encouraged migration to Ohio, but in contrast to the traditional east-west settlement patterns, it fostered a north-south flow of immigrants, especially Germans and Irish. They came to Ohio to find work, and they found it building Ohio's canals and later its railroads. Today the story of the lands surrounding the canal can be told through the five federal land divisions, road and field patterns, town plans resulting from the Land Ordinance of 1785, and, to some extent, the cultural imprints of the settlers who made Ohio their home, including many of the domestic and agricultural buildings that still dot the landscape.

Ohio has been called the social laboratory in which Congress developed the basic federal rectangular land system and also where they attempted to

The Ohio & Erie Canal cut across the cultural dividing line between New England and Middle-Atlantic settlers (map by Chuck Ayers).

move a huge portion of the public domain from wilderness to statehood. Because of this, Ohio also was the initial population magnet of the Northwest Territory. Attracted by virtually free land and growing employment opportunities, Ohio's population exploded from just over forty-five thousand in 1800 to nearly two million just fifty years later.[2]

The events that influenced the settlement of Ohio began decades earlier with the Peace of Paris in 1763, ending the Seven Years War between Great Britain and France. The treaty gave the British Crown control of all western lands in America. Because of Indian challenges to their authority, British troops moved into the Ohio country, eventually pacifying the rebellious tribes. As part of a larger effort to reduce hostilities in the West, King George III issued a royal proclamation in 1763, establishing a boundary line along the crest of the Appalachian Mountains in a vain attempt to restrict white settlement west of the Alleghenies. During the Revolutionary War, the British and the Americans vied for Indian loyalty, but in the end the conflict only accelerated the demise of the continent's Native American cultures, secured the United States land claims, and forced the British to recognize the futility of trying to hold onto western lands.[3]

Among the most significant pieces of legislation ever passed by Congress, the Land Ordinance of 1785 established a framework for federal land policy, creating a process for the organized survey, sale, and settlement of public lands. Some decisions had been made prior to the ordinance. The lands were to be disposed of for the common benefit of the United States, and the new states would enjoy "the same rights of sovereignty, freedom, and independence as the other states." Understanding the main provisions of the ordinance is essential to understanding the settlement of much of North America, including the lands crossed by the Ohio & Erie Canal. The ordinance established a pattern for surveying lands from the Alleghenies to the Pacific, well over 70 percent of the land in what are now the forty-eight contiguous states, and is largely responsible for the familiar right-angled grid of much of the American landscape. The ordinance is also thought to be the first example of regional planning legislation by the new federal government.[4]

The ordinance decreed that all land in the Northwest Territory was to be surveyed into townships, six miles square, with north-south boundaries intersecting at right angles with east-west boundaries; however, Congress actually allowed a variety of survey practices. Both the privately surveyed Connecticut Western Reserve and the U.S. Military District of east-central Ohio used the five-mile square instead. The ordinance further specified that each township was to be divided into thirty-six square sections of 640 acres each. Townships were also numbered in north-south ranges from the western borders of the original colonies.

The ordinance facilitated the buying and selling of land. A farmer or other buyer merely told a government land agent he wanted to purchase, for example, Section 12 in Township 3 in Range 4 of the Ohio Territory.[5] Throughout the nineteenth century, the government reduced the section size to as little as forty acres to assist poorer families. The ordinance also had a lasting sociological and cultural impact. The low-cost land (as little as a dollar per acre) reinforced an already established American tradition of land ownership, while the practice of reserving Section 16 in each township for public schools strengthened the concept of education as a national concern.

The ordinance was not without its shortcomings. Some congressmen and settlers, particularly those from New England, worried about the lack of religious communities, neighborhoods, and town centers—with the ever-present meeting house. Locating a school in Section 16 near the center of a township meant unreasonable traveling distances for students living in the corners of the township. The section was sometimes rented or sold to fund school construction across a township, although the funds were often wasted and even stolen by unscrupulous local officials.[6] Locating public roads also proved to be a problem. The earliest roads meandered across the landscape, often along ridge tops or near streams, and were descendents of earlier animal and Indian paths. However, settlers concerned about old roads crossing their newly acquired property insisted that public roads follow the north-south and east-west section lines, requiring township residents to build and maintain hundreds of miles of straight roads and forcing travelers to take the long way around. Because surveyors did not think about avoiding natural obstacles, "roads led deliberately and directly through swamps and over hilltops, tiring horses and infuriating drivers." Worse, some sections were too dry while others were covered by lakes and swamps.[7] Even straight-line tillage, practiced by farmers for generations, was strongly influenced by the rectangular fields resulting from the Land Ordinance. In terms of landscape, one could conclude that the ordinance created only "dullness and mediocrity." However, a rectangular survey was probably the only system that could have provided for such a swift settlement of the continent.[8]

Despite the loss of many small-scale elements—such as fence-rows and hedgerows, small fields, barnyards, and kitchen gardens—one need only follow the straight-line roads to feel the impact of the ordinance and the essential rectangular nature of the landscape. In fact, much of Ohio's landscape could be defined as a vast checkerboard of straight roads and rectangular fields. Though increasing sprawl and suburban development has destroyed or radically redefined much of the rural landscape, one may still find farm houses and barns constructed some distance from each other and in the midst of contiguous fields and near an occasional one-room schoolhouse.

Mahoning County's Western Reserve Road traverses the county in a straight line, east to west, and divides the Western Reserve from the Congress Lands to the south.[9] Here the rectangular landscape of fields and roads dictated by the Land Ordinance begins to disappear, replaced by a landscape that, on maps, appears to be in complete disarray but is really more in harmony with the natural terrain. If you find it easy to orient yourself in the region's towns and villages, it is because the rectangular survey also greatly influenced their platting and development.

In the early nineteenth century, Major Elisha Whittlesey commented on what he saw as the character distinctions between the Yankees and non-Yankees who were rapidly populating northeastern Ohio. He referred to non-Yankees (German, Irish, and Scotch settlers from Pennsylvania, Virginia, and Maryland), then spilling over into the southern part of the Western Reserve, as "such a motley society" that "few or no persons from New England would settle among them." The mixing of cultures was of such concern to some New Englanders that they advised friends and family where to settle. "I fancy your people will be best suited in the north part of the purchase, as a great proportion of the settlers on the south are from Pennsylvania," wrote Calvin Pease to a Vermont acquaintance.[10] The feeling was apparently mutual. Few Pennsylvania settlers chose to settle in the Western Reserve, because of real and perceived cultural contrasts, including religious and agricultural practices. They referred to the New England settlement area as the "cheese district" because New Englanders raised more cattle.[11]

Of course, as the cultural and legal extension of Connecticut, the Reserve was for many New Englanders merely the western equivalent of their ancestral lands. Nevertheless, even those who did not already own land in "New Connecticut" chose to pay almost twice as much (three to four dollars an acre) as they would have for the U.S. Congress Lands to the south of the Reserve. Here they founded churches and schools, built towns, and practiced farming.[12]

Alexander T. Bobersky, David T. Stephens, and Joseph Cencia have explored the idea of a cultural dividing line, or fault line, between New England and Middle-Atlantic settlers across the historic landscape encompassing the Ohio & Erie Canal. One study included sixty northern Ohio townships, half falling within the Western Reserve and the other half in the Congress Lands south of the Reserve. Their findings reinforce the idea of a fault line. The region included several different land surveys that occurred over a period of a quarter of a century. Cultural differences began when the land was purchased. Reserve lands were marketed in New England or by sales agents located in the Reserve, while agents in land offices in Steubenville, Canton, Wooster, and other towns across the state sold Congress Lands. Settlers traveled to Ohio via different routes, with the Genesee Road and the beach ridges of Lake Erie the preferred route of many New Englanders and New Yorkers. Others joined settlers from New Jersey and Pennsylvania along Forbes Road through Pennsylvania, while Maryland and Virginia settlers entered the midsection of the state via Braddocks Road, Zanes Trace, and later the National Road.

The arrangement of settlements also varied: Yankee settlements were initially limited and often located at the center of townships, as they were in New England, while Middle-Atlantic settlers established competing settlements. In general, there were more of these settlements, often along major routes outside the Western Reserve. Place names can sometimes be traced to the initial occupants. Yankees often chose names with New England or English connections—such as Greenwich, Middlefield, New Haven, Northampton, Plymouth, Southington, and West Farmington—or land company proprietors, including Boardman and Elsworth. Along the southern edge of the Reserve and within the Congress Lands, names were more diverse, with natural features and biblical references the inspiration, including Clear Creek, Cranberry, Goshen, and Canaan.

Western Reserve towns, such as Hudson and Mesopotamia, incorporated village greens or commons reminiscent of New England. In fact, central open spaces were prevalent in both the Reserve and Congress Lands. In Ohio, such common lands may be referred to as squares, though these areas in the Reserve tended to be larger than traditional squares and appear to have more in common with typical New England village greens. Even some of the smallest towns in the Western Reserve, whose original building stock has been lost or irretrievably altered, still retain these open spaces.

More modest traditional squares can be found to the south and west of the Reserve. In county seats, courthouses and other public buildings were constructed and continue to occupy this space.[13] A good example can be found in New Philadelphia, where each corner of the intersection is cut away to create the public space.

Religious preference was also an early indicator of a cultural divide. The Congregational Church, a New England institution, dominated the Reserve, while a more diverse group of denominations, including Quakers, German Lutherans, Brethren, and Reformed established churches in the Congress Lands. Probably because of their broader theological appeal, Methodists and Presbyterians were welcomed on both sides of the line.[14]

A single architectural style, Greek Revival, dominated the young nation and with it much of Ohio, including the Ohio & Erie Canal region, during the decades leading up to the Civil War. Many Americans believed the United States, with its democratic ideals, was the spiritual successor of ancient Greece. Recalling its own revolution, the country also empathized with Greece's war for independence from the Ottoman Empire. Contemporary Greek archaeological excavations and measured drawings of Greek temples also inspired the Greek Revival style.[15]

Though the style inspired the nation's first great professional architects, the vast majority of Americans still lived in rural areas and depended on carpenters and mechanics, who relied on builder's guides and later pattern books to design and build residential, commercial, and public buildings. Builder's guides included measured drawings and plates of facades and exterior walls, roof, window and door treatments, and interior details such as mantles and moldings. Ashar Benjamin's *The American Builder's Companion* (1827) and *The Architect or Practical House Carpenter* (1830) and Minard Lefever's *Modern Builder's Guide* (1833) and *Beauties of Modern Architecture* (1835) helped popularize and spread the style across the country. Benjamin's books were most popular in New England and the Western Reserve.[16] Master builder Jonathan Goldsmith designed buildings in the Federal and Greek Revival styles throughout the Western Reserve, drawing on Ashar Benjamin's publications for inspiration.

Identifying features of Greek-inspired buildings include columns and pilasters, or attached columns; bold, simple moldings; heavy cornices; and horizontal transoms and sidelights surrounding primary entrances. Public and religious buildings often included temple-front facades with full pediments and entablatures supported by Doric, Ionic, or Corinthian columns. The Congregational Church in Tallmadge (1822–25) is a high example of the Greek Revival style. Far more common were Greek Revival houses, and in much of the canal region the style is synonymous with two house types that originated in New York and New England, the Upright and Wing and the New England One and a Half.

The Upright and Wing house consists of two parts, a two-story upright and a one-story wing. The overall configuration can be an L or T. The Upright and Wing is said to have originated from the need to enlarge the common gable-front house to accommodate growing families. The wing addition provided additional bedrooms and, most important, a large kitchen.[17]

The New England One and a Half gets its name from the blank or windowless half story under the eaves, though this space is sometimes filled with small rectangular windows. Riding the wave of New England settlers entering northeastern Ohio in the opening decades of the nineteenth century, this modest house appears to have reached its maximum development here.[18] Its facade includes three to five bays or windows. Its floor plans usually have two large front rooms and two small rooms across the rear. As with the Upright and Wing, Greek Revival elements were common. These two house types can be found in small towns and rural areas across the Western Reserve.

The Upright and Wing style of house migrated to Ohio along with the early settlers (photo by Glenn Harper).

Another house type, the I-house, is more prevalent south of the Western Reserve. Though their form varies slightly, all I-houses share several basic characteristics. They all have side-facing gables, are one room deep and at least two rooms wide, and have two full stories. The majority of I-houses were constructed with timber frames and sided with horizontal clapboards, though brick and stone examples can also be found. The facade is usually symmetrical, with a central door and two or four windows on either side.[19] Like the Upright and Wing and New England One and a Half, I-houses may be embellished in Greek Revival details. Gothic and Italianate examples can also be found, but the form is essentially the same. I-houses may be found in hamlets and small villages, where they are often built on small lots with little or no setback from the street, or as part of a farmstead, where they symbolized the nineteenth-century agricultural prosperity of the Midwest. Many people find old houses difficult to care for, which results in many of the region's Greek Revival houses and churches being clad in metal or vinyl siding, concealing and often destroying much of their architectural character.

The arrangement of structures and space commonly known as the American farmstead lies deep in European history. Europeans had long distinguished between temporary, rude habitations and larger, better-built permanent houses. Ultimately, the permanence of the house led to the construction of a rough rectangular complex of buildings, fences, and walls which were called "steads" in English. Later this word was incorporated into the words "homestead" and "farmstead." Though steads varied somewhat across central and western Europe, the basic form was a rectangular enclosure that included the house, perhaps a small stable or cow house, and a granary. Inside the enclosure was the yard, a small garden, and possibly several fruit trees. There is little question that the long tradition of the stead contributed to the evolution of similar complexes in America. However, the freestanding farmstead (house, barn, and outbuildings enclosed in a system of fences to create fields, a barnyard, yard, and kitchen garden) is a distinctly American institution. It evolved in response to seemingly endless land resources, while its location and distribution were strongly influenced by the rectangular grid of the Land Ordinance of 1785. These forces soon established a pattern of farmsteads located some distance from each other and often set in the midst of contiguous fields. This prototype farmstead was reproduced in countless places as the tide of settlement moved west.[20]

By the mid-nineteenth century, Lewis F. Allen's *Rural Architecture* was promoting the farmstead as a "workshop," with every structure designed to "facilitate organized industry." If Allen's description was correct, the barn was the largest and most important machine. Originally designed for grain threshing and winnowing, straw storage, and occasionally animal shelter, the multipurpose barn continued as the industrial center of farm life until well into the twentieth century. Barns found in the canal region can best be understood by again focusing on settlement patterns originating in New England and the Middle-Atlantic states. Two barn types, the English and the Pennsylvania, can help define the cultural fault line.

As the name implies, the antecedents of the English barn can be found in England, where they are often constructed with stone. The English barn is also sometimes called a three-bay, ground, or threshing barn, referring to its interior plan, ground-level construction, and its basic function. The English barn is actually a later version of the double-crib log barn. Like its log predecessor, the mortise-and-tenon, braced-frame English barn is a rectangular structure with a center bay or drive and two flanking bays that provided space for crop storage and stabling. Most English barns have been altered with the additions of sheds, gable roofs, or by one or more flanking bays.[21] Despite its cultural connection, the English barn was probably never very common in the Western Reserve; the Reserve became a major cheese producer as early as the 1820s and this structure, used primarily for threshing and hay storage, was ill-suited for dairying.[22] A later version of the English barn, sometimes referred to as an Erie Shore barn, retains a similar floor plan but is defined by its gambrel roof (which has two flat surfaces on either side of a central ridge). Because development has taken much of the region's rural landscape, barns and other types of agricultural buildings are increasingly difficult to find across northeastern Ohio.

Far more common is the Pennsylvania barn, located across much of Ohio, including the Congress Lands. Pennsylvania barns are also sometimes referred to as forebay, bank, German, Swiss or Switzer, or Pennsylvania-Dutch. The Pennsylvania barn is a two-level, multipurpose structure that housed livestock in the basement, accommodated the threshing of feed grains on the first floor, and stored hay and straw in second-level mows and threshed grains in the bins of granaries, usually located in the forebay. The forebay, the main identifying feature of Pennsylvania barns, is a second-floor extension that projects over the front stable wall. It offered the farmer several advantages, including additional floor space and livestock protection. Granaries were often built into the forebay above the feedlot, and chutes were cut into its floorboards, enabling feed to be dropped to the animals below. In hilly terrain, a Pennsylvania barn was banked into a hill or slope so both the basement and second floor were accessible at grade level. In flatter areas, an earthen bank or ramp was constructed to serve the same purpose. Swiss and German settlers brought the fully developed Pennsylvania barn to America, and it has

Typical Pennsylvania barn (photo by Glenn Harper).

long been associated with Amish and Mennonite communities, symbolizing their superior agricultural practices and agrarian prosperity. It would be a mistake, however, to associate the widespread construction of Pennsylvania barns only with Swiss and German farmers. Nineteenth-century agricultural literature promoted its virtues to the general farm population, making it very popular. In fact, it is not uncommon to find Pennsylvania barns in the Western Reserve.[23]

Though you should be able to distinguish between the English barn and the Pennsylvania barn, be aware that few barns appear as they were originally built. The decades from 1890 to 1930 saw a tremendous increase in farm productivity, increasing the demand for larger interior spaces. Some farmers remodeled and enlarged their barns. Common alterations included shed roof or gable-end additions. Traditional gable-roof Pennsylvania barns were sometimes remodeled by constructing a self-supporting gambrel roof over the lower portion of the earlier timber-frame bents. Even some tradition-bound Amish and Mennonite farmers remodeled their old barns to incorporate the new, lighter-weight roof construction and expanded loft space.

Ironically, the expansion of the Amish community in portions of Trumbull and Geauga Counties has created a different kind of change in the rural landscape. The Amish and their commitment to tend the land with softer, more labor-intensive technologies have contributed much to preserving and conserving the early-settlement character of farmland in various regions of the country. Amish farmers in Ohio, Wayne, Holmes, and portions of Tuscarawas and Stark Counties come to mind. However, their traditionally large families and their desire to keep children close and "on the land" have forced the Amish to continue to look for affordable new areas to settle. As in other parts of the country, this has resulted in clusters of Amish farmsteads, including new farmhouses, barns, and one-room schoolhouses. In a few places, this clustering creates the appearance of a settlement, like one from the nineteenth century. Even historic agricultural practices such as stacked corn stocks can be seen in areas occupied by Amish farmers.

The Ohio & Erie Canal is lined with towns and villages that owe much of their history to the historic waterway. Two towns in particular, Canal Fulton and Roscoe Village, tell us much about how the waterway impacted their growth, development, and eventual decline (see chapter 14).

Canal Fulton was founded in 1826, a year after the state canal commission decided to build the canal on the east side of the Tuscarawas River. Like a watery commercial street, the canal became lined with grain warehouses, their gable peaks and beam winches extending out over the water. Buildings from this era were primarily wood timber-frame construction. A few still stand along Canal Street and the canal and exhibit Greek Revival influences, including entablatures and cornice returns.

By the 1870s, coal mining had usurped the canal as the town's main economic resource. Thirty nearby mines produced high-grade coal, and the village became a coal-mining equipment manufacturing hub. During this period, Canal Fulton made the transition from a canal town to a more traditional commercial center. Brick and stone commercial buildings in the latest Italianate and Queen Anne styles replaced many wooden canal-era structures, while others assumed new uses, such as hotels and an opera house.[24]

The prosperity of the coal-mining era was short-lived. By the early 1900s, the mines were depleted. Canal Fulton was bypassed by the development that affected much of the region during the next three-quarters of a century. However, the lack of growth spared it from the widespread loss of historic buildings that has characterized many rapidly growing communities.[25]

Like that of Canal Fulton, the architecture of Roscoe Village represents two distinct eras, 1830 to 1860 and 1860 to 1900. However, that is where the similarity ends. The village's earliest buildings reflect a degree of prosperity more prevalent in the larger canal towns of Akron, Massillon, Dover, Newark, and Circleville. Large red brick Federal and Greek Revival commercial buildings, some with stepped gables, line the former banks of the canal and Whitewoman Street.[26] Though Roscoe Village retains a sizeable collection of late-nineteenth-century Victorian-era buildings, the earlier architecture makes the village unique.

Canal towns exhibit an evolution of building types and architectural styles directly related to the canal's period of significance and its eventual decline and destruction. A canal town's oldest buildings, many dating from the 1830s to the 1850s, are often found near the canal or its site. Canal Fulton's canal-era buildings consist of both masonry and timber frame construction, while the earliest buildings in Roscoe Village are masonry. The best canal town architecture can be found in communities that failed to develop any long-term alternative-manufacturing base. Further evidence of canal-era economic prosperity can be found in Peninsula, Clinton, Bolivar, Dresden, and Lockbourne. In Cleveland, Akron, and Massillon, many of these earlier buildings were demolished in response to new commercial and industrial enterprises and during the urban-renewal era of the 1950s to the 1970s.

Canal-era building in Roscoe Village (photo by Glenn Harper).

In 1850, Ohio contained approximately 146,000 immigrants. Though only about 7 percent of the population, Ohio's immigrants were overwhelmingly from northern European countries, especially Germany and Ireland. Though it is traditionally believed that Ohio's main attraction was cheap land, immigrants also came to the state to find jobs, often in the rapidly growing urban industrial centers of Cleveland and Cincinnati. They also contributed significantly to the building of Ohio's canals and railroads. Here the north-south orientation of Ohio's canals influenced settlement patterns.[27] A linear pattern of German settlers is apparent in southwest Ohio near the route of the Miami & Erie Canal and all along the route of the Ohio & Erie Canal from Portsmouth to Cleveland. A similar though less apparent north-south Irish settlement pattern is most notable in Perry County, near Somerset, the site of the first Catholic church in Ohio. A comparable pattern is evident near the intersection of the Hocking and Ohio & Erie Canals in Muskingum County, where the Muskingum River was improved for canal traffic before intersecting the Ohio & Erie and along the canal's route from Cleveland through Summit County.

Despite their large numbers, European immigrants left relatively few artifacts on the Ohio landscape. Explanations for this include the increasing presence of standardized construction techniques such as the balloon-frame and mail-order houses, the occupation of areas previously settled by other migrant groups, and the German desire to assimilate.[28] There are major exceptions, including the German propensity to build with brick, in such places as the Over-the-Rhine Historic District in Cincinnati, German

Village in Columbus, and in the small towns and rural areas of Auglaize and Mercer Counties in western Ohio, near the Miami & Erie Canal. West Germans, in particular, brought with them a well-established tradition of masonry construction. Fachwerk, or half-timber, construction is also common in German and Pennsylvania-Dutch settlements in Ohio, including those in Monroe County in southeastern Ohio; Stark, Holmes, and Tuscarawas Counties in eastern Ohio; and Auglaize and Mercer Counties in western Ohio.[29] Many early-nineteenth-century German immigrants first settled in Pennsylvania. Lured by cheap land, they often followed neighbors and relatives to Ohio. Today, the populations of east-central Ohio's Mennonite and Amish communities rival or exceed those of southeast Pennsylvania. This also explains the large number of Pennsylvania barns across the region.

Cultural geographer Allen G. Noble notes that "Irish immigration was born of desperation." Often starving and destitute, many Irish saw little choice but to venture to America. Because of the circumstances under which they emigrated, the Irish arrived in America with almost no possessions or resources. Without money, their mobility was restricted, and at first they concentrated in the large East Coast cities of New York, Boston, and Philadelphia.[30] They were attracted to eastern Ohio to mine coal and later to help build the state's canals and railroads.[31] Because work on New York's Erie Canal ended at the same time as the construction of Ohio's canals began, in the summer of 1825, there may have been as many as three thousand Irishmen ready to begin work. (For more on the Irish, see chapters 3 and 15.)

Like any cultural artifact, the Ohio & Erie Canal and its significance are best understood within the larger context of the historic forces that contributed to the settlement and development of the state. Throughout much of the land crossed by the canal, the cultural imprint left by settlers from New England and the Middle-Atlantic states is still evident. The canal didn't alter existing settlement patterns but instead created new ones, adding European immigrants, particularly Germans and Irish, to the cultural mix. Though its economic lifespan was limited, much of the diverse cultural landscape it contributed to remains today.

NOTES

1. Alexander T. Bobersky and David T. Stephens, "Cultural Faultline? An Examination of Early Settlement Patterns Along the Boundary of the Western Reserve," *Pioneer America Society Transactions* 11 (1988): 89.

2. George W. Knepper, *The Official Ohio Lands Book* (Columbus: Auditor of the State of Ohio, 2002), 1; Hubert G. H. Wilhelm, *The Origin and Distribution of Settlement Groups in Ohio: 1850* (Athens: Cutler Printing, 1982), 2; David T. Stephens and Alexander Bobersky, "The Origins of Land Buyers," *Material Culture* 22.2 (Summer 1990): 43–45; David Stephens and Alexander Bobersky, "Analysis of Land Sales, Steubenville Land Office, 1800–1820," *Pioneer America Society Transactions* 13 (1990): 1–9.

3. George W. Knepper, *Ohio and Its People* (Kent: Kent State Univ. Press, 1989), 32–46.

4. Vernon Carstensen, "Patterns on the American Land," *Survey and Mapping* 36.4 (Dec. 1976): 303; Geoffrey Jellicoe and Susan Jellicoe, *The Landscape of Man* (New York: Van Nostrand Reinhold, 1975), 13; see also Knepper, *Ohio Lands* and Norman J. W. Thrower, *Original Survey and Land Subdivision: A Comparative Study of the Form and Effect of Contrasting Cadastral Surveys* (Chicago: Rand McNally, 1966).

5. Knepper, *Ohio Lands*, 39.

6. Carstensen, "Patterns on the American Land," 308.

7. John R. Stilgoe, *Common Landscape of America, 1580–1845* (New Haven, Conn.: Yale Univ. Press, 1982), 103–4; Knepper, *Ohio Lands*, 9, 57.

8. Carstensen, "Patterns on the American Land," 308–9.

9. Bobersky and Stephens, "Cultural Faultline?" 87.

10. Mary Lou Conlin, *Simon Perkins of the Western Reserve* (Cleveland: Western Reserve Historical Society, 1968), 101.

11. Wilhelm, *Origin and Distribution*, 12; see also Albert B. Faust, *The German Settlement of the United States*, 2 vols. (Boston: Houghton-Mifflin, 1927), reissued as *The American Immigrant Collection* (New York: Arno, 1978).

12. Conlin, *Simon Perkins*, 100.

13. Bobersky and Stephens, "Cultural Faultline?" 87–92; David T. Stephens, Alexander T. Bobersky, and Joseph Cencia, "The Yankee Frontier in Northern Ohio: 1796–1850," *Pioneer America Society Transactions* 17 (1994): 1–10.

14. Stephens, Bobersky, and Cencia, "Yankee Frontier," 7.

15. John C. Poppeliers and S. Allen Chambers Jr., *What Style Is It: A Guide to American Architecture* (Hoboken, N.J.: John Wiley & Sons, 2003), 39–45.

16. Leland M. Roth, *American Architecture: A History* (Boulder, Colo.: Westview, 2001), 98. See also Elizabeth G. Hitchcock, *Jonathan Goldsmith: Pioneer Master Builder in the Western Reserve* (Cleveland: Western Reserve Historical Society, 1980).

17. Allen G. Noble, *Wood, Brick and Stone: The North American Settlement Landscape*, vol. 1: *Houses* (Amherst: Univ. of Massachusetts Press, 1984), 108.

18. Ibid., 104.

19. Ibid., 52.

20. Stilgoe, *Common Landscape of America*, 14.

21. Allen G. Noble and Richard K. Cleek, *The Old Barn Book: A Field Guide to North American Barns and Other Farm Structures* (Brunswick, N.J.: Rutgers Univ. Press, 1996), 77.

22. Correspondence with David T. Stephens, Apr. 4, 2005.

23. For an excellent study of the Pennsylvania barn, see Robert F. Ensminger, *The Pennsylvania Barn: Its Origin, Evolution, and Distribution in North America* (Baltimore: Johns Hopkins Univ. Press, 1992).

24. National Register Nomination, Canal Fulton Historic District, U.S. Department of the Interior, National Park Service.

25. National Register Nomination, Canal Fulton Historic District.

26. National Register Nomination, Roscoe Village Historic District, U.S. Department of the Interior, National Park Service.

26. National Register Nomination, Roscoe Village Historic District.

27. Wilhelm, *Origin and Distribution*, 74.

28. Hubert G. H. Wilhelm, "Germans in Ohio," in *To Build in a New Land: Ethnic Landscapes in North America*, ed. Allen G. Noble (Baltimore: Johns Hopkins Univ. Press, 1992), 65–66.

29. Wilhelm, "Germans in Ohio," 66.

30. Noble, *To Build in a New Land*, 9.

31. Wilhelm, *Origin and Distribution*, 80.

Chapter 12

Rising Water and Waning Support

The Ohio & Erie Canal's Final Years

PEG BOBEL

"Well, it was in late March, and it had been raining for two or three days."[1] So begins James Dillow Robinson's personal account of the 1913 flood that devastated Ohio and neighboring states. Robinson, a young worker on a state canal maintenance boat and later chronicler of canal history, could not have known at the time that what he was witnessing would become what Ohio historian George Knepper terms "Ohio's greatest natural disaster." (For more on Robinson, see chapters 7 and 13.) Nearly every Ohioan would feel the traumatic effects of this monumental flood, but at the time Robinson and his neighbors knew only that the water was rapidly rising and they must act quickly to save themselves and the state maintenance boat tied up at Fourteen Mile Lock (Lock 37 on Canal Road near Alexander Road in Independence). Later they would learn that thousands of individual dramas were unfolding throughout the state. When it was all over, hundreds had lost their lives, and property damages were estimated to be over $300 million. Over sixty-five thousand people were left homeless. The struggling Ohio & Erie Canal was not topmost in people's minds, but along with homes, businesses, and railcars, the great flood of 1913 swept away the canallers' unique way of life and the viability of the canal as a transportation artery.

Dillow Robinson, as he was known, first began working on a state maintenance boat on the Ohio & Erie Canal in 1912. He was picked to be the one worker kept on through the winter to help the boat captain with chores. The rain began on Easter morning, March 23, several days before Robinson and the state boat captain went together, through the

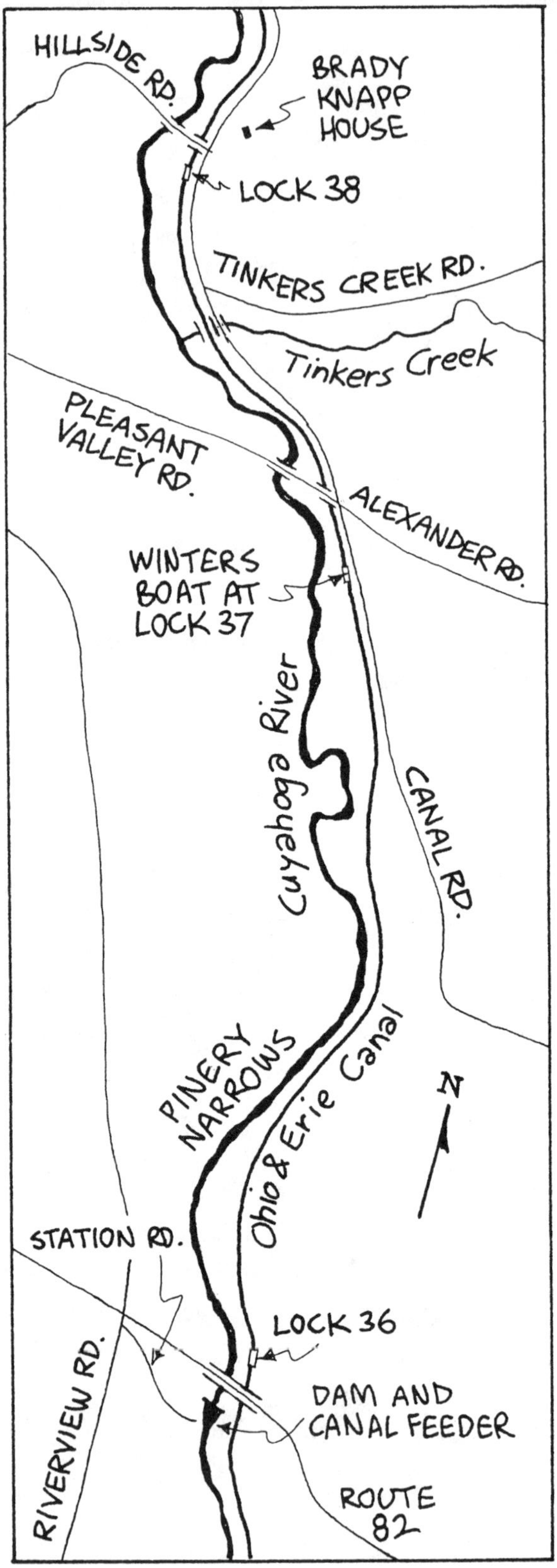

Canal maintenance worker Dillow Robinson experienced the 1913 flood along this part of the canal (drawing by Chuck Ayers).

continuing rain, to inspect conditions at the feeder gate on the Cuyahoga River near Brecksville. The water was rising so fast the captain suggested they harness the team of horses and tow the canal boat from Fourteen Mile Lock, where the boat was wintered, to a bridge where they could secure it better. A man living near Brecksville Station came by and offered to help, so the three men and the horses maneuvered the boat to the bridge, where Robinson proceeded to tie off the bowline onto the bridge's framework. Robinson recalled the episode and the succeeding days in great detail:

> Huey Burns and the Captain unhitched the team and tied the towline to a tree on the towpath side of the canal and secured another line to a tree on the heelpath side. Then they ran still another line from the stern to a tree farther down the towpath.
>
> We next tried to push the boat down into the canal so we could get the bowstem under the iron framework, but the water was too high by then and no matter how hard we tried, we couldn't accomplish it. The water was coming up awfully fast by then so we all moved off the boat to the nearby Brady Napp [*sic*] house. A little while later, a retired Policeman or Fireman from Cleveland came into the house. . . . Then there was another man, . . . went by the name of Peg-Leg John. He mended umbrellas and kitchen utensils and used an old canal boat as his home and place of business. . . . Two of our party waded out to his boat, got him on the back of one of them, and carried him up to the Brady Napp house.
>
> We were all in that house for about two days and two nights. Nobody slept much. . . . Irv' Murphy, the Feeder Tender, went out once and, while he stood at the approach to the bridge, it suddenly lifted under the pressure of the swirling water, took a quarter turn, and sank into the canal. . . . The Captain and I hurried out to see what had happened to the State Boat. Somebody must have been looking out for us: as the bridge made that quarter turn, it sheared the bowline and left the boat riding safe in the choppy water, still secured to the trees. Our big worry then was, where was the bridge? If it was underneath the boat, we would have the devil's own time getting it off when the waters receded. After two days and nights . . . the rising waters forced us to higher ground and we all moved up to the home of a farmer named Carter. . . .
>
> After a time the water began to recede and we went out to look at things. Our fears that our boat would come to rest on top of the

> sunken bridge when the water went down were unfounded. The flood water rushing over the bridge floor had gouged a deep hole into the canal bed below. Then . . . the bridge . . . dropped into this hole and left the boat floating free above it. So we got back on board, loosened the other lines, and floated down stream toward Fourteen Mile Lock . . .—just about where we started from.[2]

But thousands of other Ohioans did not fare so well. On March 25, 1913, the *Cleveland News* headline read, "City Is Flood-Bound—Many Lives Are Lost throughout Ohio." Just a few miles downstream from where Robinson and his neighbors were waiting out the storm, the Cuyahoga River had overflowed its banks and the murky floodwater was carrying bridges, homes, debris, and everything else in its path into Lake Erie. Newspaper accounts reported the rescue of twenty-seven men, women, and children "marooned by the flood under the Denison Harvard bridge." At Lock 42 in Cleveland, William Harry Heidloff, a young boy at the time, was living with his family in the locktender's house. In 1990 he remembered that his father had come by rowboat to rescue him and the rest of the family. They stayed a few days with a family on South Dille Street, then returned to find their home filled with mud and a waterline two feet up the first-floor walls. His home, the weigh lock, and other buildings withstood the flood, however. (For more on Heidloff see chapter 13.)

The 1913 flood inundated railroad tracks and depots located along the Cuyahoga River (Cuyahoga Valley National Park Historic Print Collection, National Park Service).

Akron's North Street was hard-hit by the 1913 flood (Summit County Historical Society Collection, Akron Summit County Public Library).

In Cleveland, the rising flood had halted both streetcar and railroad service and shut down factories, putting thousands temporarily out of work. The *Cleveland Press,* in its March 26 "Flood Extra," printed a "Boil Water" advisory, to avert the threat of a typhoid epidemic. In Akron, about twenty-five miles south of Robinson and his friends, the Little Cuyahoga River was washing through east Akron and filling the Goodyear Tire and Rubber Co. with eight feet of water. By Tuesday evening, March 25, the *Akron Beacon Journal* reported that five lives were lost and five hundred people were left homeless, with millions of dollars of property damage.[3]

Towns downstate were hit even harder. Dayton, at the confluence of three rivers—the Great Miami, the Mad, and the Stillwater—was no stranger to floods and had constructed earthen levees to protect the city. At first, the levees held. In the early hours of March 25, a telegraph operator in Dayton noted that although he had received reports that the Miami River was still rising rapidly both north and south of the city, and was out of its banks at the levees, "certainly no general flood is expected." Less than two hours later the operator wrote: "Water has begun to rise again and much faster than ever . . . at . . . about an inch every five minutes for the past quarter of an hour. . . . Rain is coming down in torrents now."[4] Dayton's populace was now roused by ringing church bells and whistles, warning of the impending danger. Floodwaters roared over the Riverdale levee, and within minutes the Monument levee gave way, releasing a surge of water into downtown Dayton. Homes were tossed and toppled; larger buildings held but were almost immediately swamped under ten to twelve feet of water. The force of the water snapped gas lines, which, in spite of the floodwater, ignited and set upper stories ablaze.

Quite remarkably, a single individual may have saved many lives in Dayton, or at the least brought help and comfort to the frightened, stranded flood victims. John H. Patterson, founder and head of the National Cash Register company, took precautions even at a time when most people believed the city was in no real danger. He ordered the company's whistles to blow as a warning to the town, and on that Tuesday morning he called for a halt in cash register production and had his workforce construct small, flat-bottomed wooden rescue boats. Soon a flotilla of these rescued families throughout the devastated city from the roofs of their houses. Patterson created the Dayton Citizens Relief Association, which collected and distributed food, clothing, and supplies, and cooked thousands of meals for flood refugees. The company's garage served as a temporary morgue for those for whom rescue was too late.[5]

During the 1913 flood, communication throughout the state was nearly at a standstill, leading to rumors and reports of greatly exaggerated death tolls. The *Cleveland Leader,* in its Wednesday, March 26, 1913, edition, began with the headline, "7,000 Dead in Ohio Floods: 5,000 Die in Dayton, 1,000 in Hamilton." The March 29, 1913, issue of the *Cleveland Press* printed a tally of the dead, city by city, totaling an estimated 567 deaths. It ran a detailed account about how the United Press was able to get "the first accurate flood news." The article, bylined "United Press," from New York, lauded reporters for being the ones to give "*approximately correct estimates and figures* while others were announcing *from five to ten thousand were dead.*" The account characterized the reporters' efforts as "a remarkable struggle for accuracy against seemingly hopeless odds." It also explains the difficulties reporters encountered in trying to reach the city and getting reports out of it:

> But they got through and by noon Wednesday, United Press papers from Boston to Frisco gave their readers the first vivid stories of eye witnesses. The transmission was made possible by the co-operation of the American Telephone & Telegraph Co. Out of the wreck left by the storm a single wire had been made good between New York and Chicago, via Canada, but it touched no Ohio point. There was no way to reach the flooded area over the usual route. Wires south of Chicago were down.

> . . . The emergency was met by setting up one of the most unusual circuits in the history of the telegraph press reports. This circuit was routed New York to Buffalo, across Canada to Detroit, thence to Chicago, north to St. Paul, south to Des Moines, to Burlington and to St. Louis and from there to Cincinnati, terminating at Columbus. . . . Later the wire was made good to Phoneton, six miles north of Dayton, and finally it was carried into the offices of the National Cash Register Co.
>
> . . . All week the wire from New York to Cleveland was intact. From Cleveland the wire was made good to Canton and Akron, but no other Ohio city was reached in that way until today.[6]

Once communication was established, there remained the challenge, in the stricken cities, of actually printing the news. The *Akron Beacon Journal* managed to print an edition Tuesday evening, March 25, that included "AN APOLOGY":

> It will hardly be necessary on a day like this, when the industry of the city is paralyzed by the flood horror, for the Beacon Journal to apologize for going to its readers in abbreviated form and a story of the flood that is but a makeshift, when the possibilities of the occasion are considered.
>
> But without electricity Linotype machines cannot run and printing presses are but lifeless machinery. By the aid of motorcycles rigged up as a power plant we were able to run one type setting machine and this small paper has been printed at the plant of the Werner company.[7]

According to Ohio historian George Knepper, the March 1913 flood took 428 lives and destroyed more than twenty thousand houses.[8] It is no wonder that it soon became known as the Great Flood. It took on an almost legendary status—families in towns across the state still share their stories, memories, and photographs with their children and grandchildren, especially in canal towns where the flood also ended a way of life. For instance, when Ann Henman and the Canal Fulton Heritage Society interviewed older residents of the town in the 1980s for the "Tales of the Towpath" oral history project, the interviewees frequently talked about the Great Flood. John Tilton, who would have been eleven years old at the time of the flood, recalled in 1983: "That was the first time I ever saw my mother weep—when we went down there, at the times of the Floods in 1913 and went down to look at the old Miller home and I can still see that terrible slime all over the walls of the downstairs rooms. . . . And Mother looked at that awhile and just started to weep! Dad said 'What's the trouble Julia?' . . . And she said, 'That poor woman trying to clean those walls, scrub them down again.'"[9]

In a 1983 article, Ann Henman recorded the memories of ninety-year-old Helen Bisker Rounds, who was a senior in high school, living with her aunt and uncle in Canal Fulton when the rains began in March 1913.

> In her uncle's house on South Canal Street, rugs were rolled up in preparation for evacuation to the second floor. Water was already in the basement and in the livery to the rear. To the north and south of their home, the waters had crossed Canal Street. . . .
>
> The iron bridge at Cherry Street and the canal began to creak and groan under the pressure of the current and high water. Helen was among the people standing at Blank's grocery waiting to see if the bridge would collapse and be carried downstream, when her aunt called her to dinner. Never one to disobey her aunt, Helen began walking toward home when she heard the bridge go.[10]

Wilbur Bliler was only six years old at the time of the flood, but he remembered one incident vividly. His family lived on Canal Street, and he recalled his mother gathering everyone up to go temporarily to his grandfather's home on higher ground. "And I remember she says, 'Do you want to take anything with you?' And I said, 'Yes. Where's my marbles?' I took a sugar sack and put my nice marbles in there. That's all I had. I carried the marbles in the sack all the way downtown and marched up the hill." His mother, as he recalled, did not take much herself, but he admitted, "she might have had a basket full of things or whatever. I don't remember that, I was more interested in my marbles than anything else, cause they were not commies, they were agates, you know, the good kind, the real pretty kind."[11]

Regarding these delightful oral history interviews, Henman aptly noted that in Canal Fulton "a newcomer . . . soon learns that history is dated from 'before the flood' or 'after the flood.'" The 1913 flood is also usually cited as the event that put an end to the Ohio & Erie Canal. Its trade had been in decline after its 1851 peak, and the canal experienced numerous trials during the last half of the 1800s; some might argue that the flood put a dying canal out of its misery. Parts of the canal continued to work for specific purposes even after the flood, but it was no longer maintained as an intact Cleveland-to-Portsmouth transportation system.

The 1913 flood was the last blow to the canal, but not the only time the canal was damaged by floods. During its life the waterway was repeatedly challenged by major floods and seasonal high water. John Thompson, emeritus professor of geology at Stanford University, notes that heavy rains and "unruly freshets" interrupted navigation on the canals by depositing silt, sand, and gravel, breaking embankments, dislodging fill around the lock structures, and weakening dams and aqueducts.[12] He also writes that while "extraordinary legislative appropriations usually followed major flood damage, routine appropriations and canal revenue generally provided for but nominal dredging of canals, maintenance of towpaths and banks, and repair of locks, aqueducts, and dams."[13]

Floods that damaged the canal were responded to with repairs and sometimes with design improvements. For instance, in January 1828, a major flood ripped through the canal from Akron north. According to the Board of Canal Commissioners report: "This river in many places, rose from one to two feet higher than had ever been previously witnessed by the oldest inhabitants residing near its banks. Such an extraordinary rise of water was not indicated by any water marks which were discoverable at the time of locating the Canal . . . and was not fully provided against by the erection of guard banks, of the requisite height." The canal was repaired and steps were taken to try to prevent future damage. One design improvement made after the 1828 flood was the addition of wasteways, which provided an escape route for high water. In other places, the banks were simply raised. The commissioners noted in their 1829 report that "the locks, aqueducts, culverts and other important structures on the Ohio Canal, so far as they have been tested, prove to have been founded and built in a very permanent and substantial manner, and to answer fully the purposes for which they were designed." None was seriously damaged by the flood, and all were "believed to be as substantial and durable, as any works of the kind in the United States."[14]

Much renovation work was completed on the canal in 1841 and 1842, then in June 1843 the canal was again damaged by floods from the Cuyahoga River. Repairs were made and more waste gates and culverts were added. High water levels on the Cuyahoga in 1858 further eroded the canal embankments, and the commissioners requested money for repairs; however, they were deferred. In 1868 and 1873, ice freshets damaged feeder dams and embankments. Then in February 1883, the highest flood yet on the Cuyahoga River between Akron and Cleveland occurred.

The circumstances were similar to the 1913 event—heavy rain fell on frozen ground. Two dams were entirely destroyed, aqueducts and locks were damaged, and the Pinery Feeder was badly damaged. Yet another flood during the winter of 1883–84 followed, necessitating more repairs (chap. 6).

During these decades, support for the canal waxed and waned. The 1850s saw the tremendous investment in and expansion of railroads in Ohio, and the Ohio legislature as early as 1852 proposed selling the state's canals. (See H. Roger Grant's discussion of railroads vs. the canals in chapter 9.) That did not happen, but in 1855, in response to increasing maintenance expenditures, the Board of Public Works decided to contract with private firms for future repairs and maintenance. Those contracts were declared fraudulent by the General Assembly, and during ensuing lawsuits the canals deteriorated. Governor Salmon P. Chase advocated selling the canals in 1857, and again in 1859 and 1860, but to no avail. The General Assembly would not sell the canals, but in 1861 it did decide to lease their operation and maintenance to private companies. Private operation of the canals continued until 1877, when the state's Board of Public Works again took over operations (chap. 7).

By this time, the Ohio & Erie Canal was suffering from neglect, traffic was declining, and some sections were abandoned or used for railroads, as was the case in Cleveland. Nonetheless, Governor Young, in his January 7, 1878, address, stated that the state could not afford to abandon the canals, and Governor Bishop in 1880 concurred, as did Governor Foraker in 1888. Foraker called for a new canal survey commission "to establish the boundaries and lines of canals, canal basins, reservoirs, etc., by an accurate survey—and to define and protect the ownership and titles of the state in and to all lands belonging to and connected with said canals" (quoted chap. 7, 10). The state legislature, impressed by the survey's results, in April 1902 passed an act stating "that it is hereby declared as the settled policy of this state that the Miami and Erie, together with its water supplies, etc.,—shall be retained and maintained as a public canal; also that the same policy is hereby declared as to the northern division of the Ohio Canal—from Cleveland to Dresden" (chap. 7, 10). As far as the rest of the Ohio & Erie was concerned, the 151 miles from Dresden to Portsmouth, the act stipulated that the canal's condition there would be investigated.

Dillow Robinson recalled: "Actually, there had been very little traffic after about 1906 or 1907 when they rebuilt the locks out of concrete and dredged the channel. Our State Boat made what I think was the last trip down the canal through Canal Fulton [to assist another state maintenance boat]. . . . I left the canal when I was about 23 and I've done a lot of things since, but I've never forgotten my life on the canal."[15] Since the canal had not been thriving, one has to wonder why the State of Ohio decided to embark on a major repair and reconstruction project on the Ohio & Erie Canal in the early 1900s. According to Harlan Unrau and Nick Scrattish, the arguments put forth in favor of continued canal operation were based on one of two assumptions: "that canals offered railroads a modicum of intraregional competition—or that the state was under some sort of moral obligation to preserve the canals, because the canals had done so much for the state" (chap. 7, 15). Such arguments as these prevailed when the state decided to invest in rehabilitation of the Ohio & Erie Canal shortly after the turn of the twentieth century.

In 1902, Chief Engineer Charles W. Perkins detailed the deterioration of the canals and argued for their improvement. In 1904 he further explained the continuing deterioration of the canals and chastised the legislature: "If the Legislature, which in fact directs the affairs and policies of the department, instead of neglecting the public works after their surrender by the lessees, had provided sufficient funds to restore them to a proper state of efficiency, or if it had enforced the fulfillment of the provisions of the lease as to their restoration to the same physical excellence in which they were turned over to the lessees in 1861, the history of the public works would have been one of progression instead of retrogression" (quoted chap. 6, 69).

The state legislature was apparently sufficiently enough convinced that it appropriated $200,000 for the first two years of the reconstruction work, which commenced in 1904. The appropriation act stipulated, however, that the money would not be forthcoming until new water leases were made between the state and the then-current lessees, to ensure an annual income of at least $30,000. This achieved, the work began in 1905. The total cost was estimated at precisely $573,064.33. The work would include rebuilding numerous structures and deepening the canal to five feet to accommodate boats carrying a net weight of 115 tons (chap. 6, 70–71).

Eighty years had passed since the first spade of dirt was removed at the groundbreaking of the Ohio & Erie Canal; during that time, construction techniques and materials and equipment had progressed considerably. In the United States during the 1800s, canals had helped spur advances in materials such as cement and concrete.[16] Similar improvements in cement, concrete, and reinforced concrete were being made in England and France, and those immigrated to the United States. One was Portland cement, which differs from natural cement in that it consists of carefully measured ingredients processed under controlled conditions, resulting in a very strong product. It was patented in 1824 by Joseph Aspdin, a bricklayer in Leeds, England, and imported to the United States by the 1860s.[17] In the first decade of the 1900s, there was a tremendous surge in the production of Portland cement, which coincided with the rehabilitation work on the Ohio & Erie Canal. Indeed, the specifications for the 1905 contract work on the canal included the purchase of Portland cement (appendix S, 49).

Although concrete had been used in previous lock repairs (first noted in 1887), it was now used to a much greater extent, and in a number of places to replace large sections of sandstone block in lock walls, piers, and abutments. The cost of concrete accounted for 25 percent of the total costs of the first phase of work in the first decade of the 1900s, while stone was estimated at only 5 percent. Examples of the concrete used to reface the walls of the locks can be seen today on nearly every lock between Akron and Cleveland, except for Lock 29 in Peninsula, which had been reconstructed using stone and cement in 1882, for $13,385 and did not require major reconstruction in 1905 (chap. 6, 57–58). Lock 29 is the only one in Cuyahoga Valley National Park whose sandstone was not replaced with concrete. Today visitors can examine the fine stonework and the masons' marks by actually walking into the lock chamber itself. For contrast, they can walk through Lock 18 in Akron, also on the Ohio & Erie Canal Towpath Trail, to see what early 1900s concrete looked like.

Another example of some of the major reconstruction begun in 1905 is the work done on spillways around the locks. Spillways, or regulating weirs, as they were first called, were an adaptation, planned just after the first season of navigation of the completed canals. Engineers had observed that in some cases water was backing up behind the locks and causing the water to flow out at wasteways, and reenter the Cuyahoga River. To keep that water in the canal system, they devised spillway structures around the locks, many of which can be seen today. The first spillways were built out of cut stone, and less expensive ones were constructed out of wood placed on rock foundations or on earthen slopes. These spillways also provided waterpower, such as that used at Alexander Mill in Valley View at Lock 37. In 1905 some wood spillways were rebuilt in concrete; two of these are at Locks 38 and 39 in Cuyahoga Valley National Park.

In 1905–06, concrete was also used more in structures associated with some of the feeder dams. The Peninsula feeder dam, located just north of Peninsula, has been washed away over the years; the concrete feeder structures, however, can still be seen, relics rising out of the surrounding forest. The 1906 Board of Public Works report states that contractors built new head gates and a towpath bridge at this feeder and also that the "towing bridge" was "reinforced with steel rails and wire netting" (quoted chap. 6, 76, 88). From the Towpath Trail, which runs alongside the historic towpath at this point, one can see portions of the old towing bridge and the exposed lengths of steel rail that reinforce the concrete.

The invention of reinforced concrete—that is, concrete placed around iron, steel, or even wood to increase the tensile strength of the concrete—is usually attributed to a French gardener by the name of Joseph Monier, who patented his procedure in 1867.[18] Although reinforcing rods were not in the specifications for the work done on the canal locks in 1905–06, the work report describes that such rods, or rails and wire netting, were indeed used.

Another 1905 concrete specification called for it to be mixed in a machine. This was probably a small batch mixer, since concrete plants would not be developed for a decade or more (appendix S, 50–52). The specifications also note that cement "shall meet any tests heretofore made or prescribed by the American Society of Civil Engineers." As Jack Gieck explained in chapter 2, engineering was not yet recognized as a profession when construction on the canal began. Engineering schools and societies began emerging in the mid-1800s, ushering in a century of rapid advances in a wide range of engineering technologies, including testing materials and setting standards for them.

During the major rebuild period of 1905–09, state maintenance crews also performed routine maintenance and new construction. Visitors using the Towpath Trail in Cuyahoga Valley National Park can easily see one more concrete structure from this period. In the Pinery Narrows, just north of the Station Road Bridge, is a bulkhead wall across Galley Run on the east side of the canal (north of Lock 36, which was buried when the State Route 82 bridge was built). The bulkhead was built to slow or prevent the deposition of gravel into the canal from the side stream and came to be called Mudcatcher.

Dredging and deepening the canal was a major part of the work prescribed in 1905 and was estimated to account for more than 16 percent of the total cost of rehabilitating the Northern Division.[19] A memoir from 1908 describes one dredging project that was completed between Everett and Akron. The writer, Mrs. Carl Gundling of Parma, Ohio, had intimate knowledge of the dredging business—she served as a cook on a dredge boat—and describes dredging that was not always drudgery. More than sixty years later, she recalled that in 1908 her husband, having

Much of the work in the later years of the canal focused on dredging and deepening the waterway in the struggle to keep it in business (Louis Baus Canal Photograph Collection, University of Akron Archival Services)

been laid off from his job in the local quarry, found employment with the canal, operating a dredge for $30 a month, and she was hired to cook for $50 a month.

The Gundlings boarded the boat at Bolanz Road in Everett and began their new employment, living aboard the boat from spring into fall. When the weather began to turn colder, they sent their two-and-a-half-year-old son to stay with Mrs. Gundling's parents on their farm. Quarters on the dredge were tight, with only one small bed; Mr. Gundling slept on the floor. Mrs. Gundling's description of life aboard the boat gives us a glimpse into both its challenges and pleasures.

> The back section of the boat was open and the coal for the cookstove was stored there. My washtubs and clothesline were also back there. I washed for my family, but the men took care of their own washing or had it done by people who lived along the canal.
>
> As the dredge worked down the canal, the roust-a-bout would move our boat along the bank. A plank was laid from the boat to the towpath and, many times in the nice weather, I would do my mending on the stern while my little boy played back and forth between the boat and the bank with his dog Tippy. . . . [O]ne day, . . . all of a sudden, there was little Edward splashing in the canal and

> Tippy—looking down at him. Somehow I reached down from the plank and pulled him out. When he was safe on board, all he could say was, "Tippy did it, he pushed me." But he wasn't hurt and it was a warm day, so he soon dried out. That was the only time he fell in the canal. . . .
>
> We bought some of our food from farms along the canal—fresh vegetables, eggs, apples, berries, milk and butter. I baked bread, pie, and cake every day on that old coal stove. I had to cook breakfast and supper twice each day, once for each shift. But I only had to cook dinner once a day. There was a midnight lunch to set out for the men, too, before I went to bed.
>
> It was hard work for all of us, but there were farms and towns along the way and we met lots of nice people. Sometimes, if there was someone to play the fiddle, the farm people would have a square dance in the yards, and we would go. When we were tied up at Old Portage, we would walk up the B & O railroad tracks to the Old Grand Theater in Akron for the show. We had our good times, too.[20]

It took the crew eight months to dredge the canal from Everett to Akron, about ten miles. Mrs. Gundling summed up the typically mixed feelings about the canal: "They were busy days for us and I would not want to live on that boat again, but I will never forget those days on the canal."[21]

In spite of the extensive repairs and improvements made on the Northern Division of the Ohio & Erie Canal, the canal's chief engineer, John I. Miller, noted in his 1912 report that public sentiment had not much changed: "I have discovered a tendency which is crystallized into public opinion in many parts of the State, to further the process of decadence of the state's valuable canal properties by encroachment, and by a strong spirit of opposition to any movement that seeks to rehabilitate these water-ways and rather desires their absolute abandonment" (quoted chap. 7, 11). Miller noted that the Ohio & Erie had been rebuilt for most of the way from Cleveland to Dresden but dredging was stopped due to lack of funds, and because there was no aqueduct at Roscoe, boats could not travel the entire length of the canal. He accused the state of a policy of "indecision and disintegration" toward the canals, noting how one legislative session would appropriate money to repair the canals and the next would refuse to. Work begun would end, and the canal would again need repair before the next appropriation. Engineer Miller begged the state to "either take the necessary steps to restore the canals in the minimum time that it would require, or abandon them outright" (chap. 7, 12).

Canal Maintenance in the Twenty-first Century

PEG BOBEL

In recent years, communities have come to view the old canal not as a nuisance but as a resource—for understanding the past, for recreation, and for wildlife. Along the 101-mile-long Ohio & Erie Canal Towpath Trail, cities, counties, and park districts are maintaining the towpath, and sometimes the canal basin itself, for recreational use. In the century since the major rehabilitation effort of 1905, construction techniques and materials have changed considerably; however, the challenges posed by floods, muskrats, and the wear and tear of time remain much the same for those maintaining the recreational trail alongside the canal.

About twenty miles of historic canal lie within Cuyahoga Valley National Park (CVNP). Only six miles of it are kept watered. Cleveland Metroparks manages another four miles of watered canal north of the park, while Stark Metroparks and the Ohio Department of Natural Resources maintain other sections of watered canal south of it. Today's park managers keep water in the canal for lock demonstrations in CVNP, for fishing and wildlife habitat in Cleveland Metroparks, and for the excursion boat, the *St. Helena III,* in Canal Fulton.

Heavy rains and occasional floods still erode the towpath, canal banks, and riverbanks, but the parks deal with this differently today than they would have in the past. Engineers design bank-stabilization projects that both maintain the integrity of and enhance the natural values of the river or the canal. Often a softer engineering approach is recommended, such as using soil bioengineering methods. Such methods use a combination of man-made and natural materials, including geosynthetics and rocks, along with soil and plant cuttings, which, when mature, stabilize the banks and promote improved water quality.

Dredging is now done only to maintain a constant reliable source of water in the canal where needed, and, if necessary, to protect the towpath. Another change is that such work in and along the canal and rivers is now regulated through a permit process spelled out in the Clean Water Act, to protect the water from adverse impacts. Provisions in the National Environmental Protection Act and the National Historic Preservation Act also guide and regulate work affecting the historic canal.

The structures requiring maintenance in the watered sections of canal include those necessary to keep an appropriate water level, such as the river gates under the State Route 82 bridge in Cuyahoga County and some locks and aqueducts. The Tinkers Creek Aqueduct carries the Ohio & Erie Canal over a major tributary of the Cuyahoga River in CVNP. The aqueduct that the National Park Service acquired was the latest of several generations of aqueducts at that site and was in badly deteriorated condition. The original structure was built between 1825 and 1827 and consisted of a wooden trunk with timber framing supported by a central pier and stone abutments. In 1845, a completely new aqueduct was built a couple of hundred feet north of the original one. This also had two spans and was supported on a central pier, but the pier was built using cut stones. In 1905, the King Bridge Company of Cleveland built a steel superstructure for it. In 2007, the National Park Service removed most of the deteriorated Tinkers Creek Aqueduct and began a re-

Miller was promoted the next year to superintendent of the Board of Public Works, but public sentiment toward the canals remained unchanged. The canals that had shone so brightly and served the state well were fading, while new possibilities in transportation, even beyond the competing railroads, were beginning to glow. The good-roads movement was underway, actively lobbying Congress for money to improve and expand roads, and pioneering pilots were demonstrating that airplanes might be used to transport mail and commercial materials. So Miller put his effort into two tasks: continuing the surveying and platting of canal lands that was begun in 1906 and dealing with lawsuits that resulted from the state's attempt to recover its property.

According to the 1906 Board of Public Works report, in some cases the state had simply taken the property needed for the canal, and no deeds, maps, or plans existed to show what was taken (or given, as in the case of Simon Perkins, who donated land in return for the state routing the canal

---

placement project. The first phase was completed in the summer of 2007 and includes a new Towpath Trail bridge.

Today's park managers also have opportunities to restore or rehabilitate parts of the canal or canal structures. True restoration, in the National Park Service's definition, "is the process of accurately recovering the form and details of a property and its setting as it appeared at a particular period of time by the means of removal of later work or the replacement of missing earlier work." In 1991, the National Park Service at Cuyahoga Valley National Park began restoring Lock 38, in front of the park's Canal Visitor Center, so that visitors could see how a lock operates. The restoration was completed between 1991 and 1992 and is well documented in two issues of the Canal Society of Ohio's *Towpaths* (31, no. 4 and 32, no. 1).

The restoration process revealed valuable information abut the lock's original materials, design, and construction. Where appropriate, as in the concrete mix, modern techniques and materials were used, but blended to match the historic appearance of the structure. In some instances, traditional techniques and modern methods were both used. For instance, workers secured new floorboards using traditional treenails, octagonal wooden spikes. For the lock gates, the restorationists created mortise-and-tenon joints, as in the original gates, but had an easier job of it, using a chain-mortise machine. They did, however, finish the gates using hand tools.

Maintaining today's recreational canal, with the available mechanized equipment and new materials, reveals just how challenging it must have been to keep the old canal in working condition. Inspections are now completed in a fraction of the time they would have been in the past; phone calls can be made from the field, and reports e-mailed instantaneously. But when a sinkhole appears on the towpath, or a flood washes out the canal banks, or the lock gates begin to leak, for a moment, today's canal tenders share a common experience with the pioneering canal-era engineers.

through Akron, his new town). To compound the problem, early records were missing, and there were few actual titles to the lands the canal occupied. Therefore, in 1888, the Board of Public Works created a canal survey commission. According to Ernest L. Bogart, it was to establish "the boundaries and lines of canals, canal basins, reservoirs, etc., by an accurate survey—and to define and protect the ownership and titles of the state in and to all lands belonging to and connected with said canals" (chap. 7, 10). When the commission found many early records missing, it began gathering second-hand information—such as records of awards of damages and testimony of engineers and contractors.

Surveys and maps were made where the canal was still obvious, but it was more difficult to recoup lands that appeared to be in possession of other parties. Some disputes were settled by the courts; perhaps the best-known of these was in Cleveland, where the state was attempting to recover the last three miles of canal abandoned between Locks 42 and 44. The Cleveland Terminal & Valley Railroad filled in part of the canal right-of-way in Cleveland for its new railroad line, paying the state nothing. In 1912, the Ohio Supreme Court ruled in favor of the railroad, handing the public works what Miller considered the "most humiliating defeat."[22]

So in 1913, as Superintendent Miller was overseeing these matters, the rain began to fall and, in effect, made the decision the state had been reluctant to. The Ohio & Erie Canal was now just one of many parts of the state's infrastructure washed away. When all was over and the slow process of rebuilding had begun, the canal commission examined what was left of the canal and made its recommendations. Dillow Robinson just happened to be on the least damaged, most salvageable part of the canal. South of him, however, the sixteen-mile stretch of it between Brecksville and Akron was largely destroyed. In Akron, locks were dynamited to release the built-up water, sending the tremendous flood downstream.[23]

Elsewhere, the force of the floodwaters simply washed away banks and filled the canal with debris and sediment. The canal commission entertained the possibility of making part of Ohio's canal system into a barge canal, but this was not thought possible. The Board of Public Works' 1914 report concluded: "The rehabilitation of the canals of the State on the original basis or standard of construction is impracticable and highly inadvisable" (quoted chap. 7, 14). The commission did advise that the state retain ownership of the rights-of-way of the Ohio & Erie and other canals "producing revenues in the way of water rentals," for waterpower and other industrial uses. Visitors to the Ohio & Erie Canalway today can ap-

Toward the end of the canal era, Ohioans began enjoying the recreational aspects of the Ohio & Erie Canal (Louis Baus Canal Photograph Collection, University of Akron Archival Services).

preciate this recommendation, for had not the state retained these water interests, the entire canal right-of-way might have disappeared from the public domain, and thus from public access.

As for the rest of the Ohio & Erie Canal? The commission wrote this epitaph: "The Commission recommends . . . that the canals be drained at such points where the revenues do not justify the cost of maintenance, and placed in such condition as to prevent their becoming nuisances to the communities through which they pass" (chap. 7, 14). It was like pulling the plug from a tub; the once-vital canal slowly drained away.

The last years of the working Ohio & Erie Canal saw pleasure boating, limited commercial traffic, major rehabilitation, and monumental flood damage, the last sending the canal into a deep slumber. Nostalgic out-of-work canallers and history buffs kept the stories and lore alive here and there along the banks, while wildflowers and wildlife reclaimed the narrow piece of state real estate. The original purpose of the waterway was no longer viable, but a new one was dormant in the mud, awaiting the right time and the right minds to bring it to life.

NOTES

1. James Dillow Robinson, "The 1913 Flood," *Towpaths* 11.1 (1973): 5.

2. Ibid., 5–7.

3. The authors are grateful to Fred Shuld of Independence, Ohio, for loaning them his collection of newspaper headlines and other flood-related accounts.

4. The Montgomery County Historical Society, "Research & Resources: History at a Glance," http://www.daytonhistory.org/glance_flood.htm (accessed Oct. 5, 2004).

5. Ibid. After the flood of 1913, the National Cash Register company and other Daytonians began to investigate how to protect the city in the future. Their efforts resulted in the 1914 Ohio Conservancy Law permitting the formation of watershed conservancy districts. Today's Ohio & Erie National Heritage Canalway's southernmost section passes through the Muskingum Conservancy District, created in 1933 under that same law.

6. "Here's How the United Press Got the First Accurate Flood News," *Cleveland Press*, Mar. 29, 1913 (emphasis in original).

7. "An Apology," *Akron Beacon Journal*, Mar. 25, 1913.

8. George W. Knepper, *Ohio and Its People* (Kent: Kent State Univ. Press, 1989), 340.

9. John Tilton, "Tales of the Towpath," oral history project interview transcript, 1983, Canal Fulton Heritage Society, Canal Fulton, Ohio.

10. Ann McLaughlin (now Henman), "Octogenarian Recalls History of Canal Fulton," Feb. 9, 1983, newspaper clipping, in "Tales of the Towpath" project file on Helen Bisker Rounds.

11. Wilbur Bliler, "Tales of the Towpath," oral history project interview transcript, 1983.

12. John Thompson, "Addressing the Elemental Challenges to Navigation on Ohio's Towpath Canals," *Canal History and Technology Proceedings* 23 (Mar. 20, 2004): 132.

13. Ibid., 131.

14. Harlan Unrau and Nick Scrattish, *Historic Structure Report, Ohio and Erie Canal, Cuyahoga Valley National Recreation Area, Ohio* (Denver: U.S. Department of the Interior, National Park Service, Denver Service Center Branch of Historic Preservation Midwest/Rocky Mountain Team, 1981), chap. 6, 6–7 (hereafter cited in text).

15. Robinson, "The 1913 Flood, 8.

16. Howard Newlon Jr., "Introduction," *A Selection of Historic American Papers in Concrete: 1876–1926*, ed. Howard Newlon Jr. (Detroit: American Concrete Institute, 1976), 44.

17. Historical Timeline of Concrete, http://www.auburn.edu/academic/architecture/bsc/classes/bsc314/timeline/timeline.htm (accessed Oct. 19, 2004). Aspdin named his product Portland, because he felt it resembled stone found on the Isle of Portland off the British coast.

18. Jasper O. Draffin, "A Brief History of Lime, Cement, Concrete and Reinforced Concrete," 1943, in Newlon, *A Selection of Historic American Papers*, 29–30.

19. Thompson, "Addressing the Elemental Challenges," 138–49.

20. Mrs. Carl Gundling, as told to Mrs. J. H. McNally, "On the Ohio & Erie Canal in 1908," *Towpaths* 11.2 (1973): 17–18.

21. Ibid., 18.

22. The surveys and maps from the later years of the canal have been helpful to today's preservationists, historians, and Towpath Trail designers, especially since they show the location and description of structures throughout the canal, including drawings of bridges, culverts, and aqueducts.

23. See especially Ted Dettling, "The Day They Blew Up Lock #8," *Towpaths* 11.2 (1973): 21–22.

Chapter 13

The Ditch and the Path in the Backyard

PEG BOBEL AND LYNN METZGER

In the collective memories of the elders in the cities and small towns along the Ohio & Erie Canalway, canal history is divided into two parts: life before and after the 1913 flood. Although the heyday of the canal was long past before the extensive canal rehabilitation of 1905–09, this work had created some optimism that the old transportation system would survive, if on a limited basis. However, the State of Ohio did not appropriate funds to continue the necessary repairs to make it navigable south of Roscoe. If the 1913 flood killed the canal as a transportation system, the railroads and roads had already made it obsolete. The canal and towpath, however, were integral parts of the towns and villages along the route, and they did not just disappear. In a number of areas, industry already leased canal water; the canal was also used for recreational boating and fishing, and the towpath, long used as a connection between the towns, was still a connecting thread. But for several generations of nearby residents and the historic record, the old transportation system was merely a ditch and a path in the backyard, to be ignored, drained, filled, farmed, and forgotten.

After the 1913 flood, people turned their backs on the canal. Some fondly remembered the way of life, but most Ohioans were looking ahead as technology rapidly expanded. Wildflowers and tree saplings were poised to take over much of the canal route. But the ditch that took seven years to dig was not about to disappear completely. As they did in the memories of the elders, the canal and towpath remained a physical presence on the landscape.

"Quite a few of the boatmen pulled their craft up on a convenient shore, roofed them over with lath and tarpaper to make homes" (Louis Baus Canal Photograph Collection, University of Akron Archival Services).

Even before the flood, canal life was ebbing, and canal boats were disappearing or appearing in different venues. The poor condition of the canal made it difficult to use effectively for a trip of any length. Terry K. Woods of the Canal Society of Ohio interviewed old boatmen in the late 1960s and early 1970s and noted, regarding the last days of the working canal, "Many of the remaining boatmen gave up. Basins and wide-waters all over the northern section of the canal were soon studded with rotting boats."[1] Old photographs depicting rotting, sinking boats conjure up the sadness that must have settled in some boatmen's hearts.

Since many boats were owner operated and entire families lived on them, some boatmen merely parked their boats and converted them into stationary homes, either on shore or in the water: "Quite a few of the boatmen pulled their craft up on a convenient shore, roofed them over with lath and tarpaper to make homes."[2] Here canal families kept scraps of their former lifestyle and lived among other canallers. The houseboat residence *Cozy Corner* was permanently moored in Akron's Upper Basin in 1910. Don Cooke, lifelong resident of Navarre, remembers another canal-boat house in Navarre. In their later lives, some of the boats were disguised more than others. Take, for instance, a pleasure boat operated by a Mrs. Watts that had carried groups on Sunday afternoon excursions on the canal from Navarre to Zoar when the canal was still in operation. Later, as Cooke described, "the boat was then taken apart and became a long, narrow house on Ohio Street," the home of a schoolmate.[3]

The more locally famous of the canallers, Pearl Nye, who was first introduced in chapter 7, lived on a canal boat turned permanent residence. "The Nyes, Pearl, Ma, and one or more of the younger Nyes lived in the converted canal boat 'IQUICKE' as late as the 1920s. That home sat on the bank of the lower basin near Exchange Street in Akron."[4]

Near the end of his life, Pearl Nye again lived in a converted canal boat, or at least part of one. In 1939, Nye built a one-room log cabin in Roscoe, across the river from Coshocton "against the double lock that once lowered canal boats 12 feet from the mouth of the Walhonding Aqueduct to the Roscoe level."[5] Later he added to his cabin by attaching the hulk of State Boat #2, which had been rotting away nearby, and connected the cabin to the double locks with catwalks. Although he called his home "Camp Charming," neither he nor the camp were popular with the local residents.[6]

To some extent, how people related to the canal after its demise was determined by whether or not a particular section still held water, and this was mostly determined by whether or not there were water leases on it. When the canal was in operation, canal water served more purposes than just floating the boats. Early on, entrepreneurs recognized the value of the running water as a source of power. For instance, a wasteway that carried excess water around a lock had enough drop to power a mill wheel, such as the one that powered Alexander's Mill (now Wilson's Mill), still visible today in Valley View. After 1913, when the state deserted the canal as a transportation system, it recognized the potential value of leasing canal water to neighboring industries. For example, in 1922 it negotiated a lease with American Steel & Wire of Cleveland, allowing the manufacturer to use canal water for cooling purposes. The lease stipulated that the company was responsible for maintaining a sufficient head, or vertical drop, of water for its own lease and other lessees.[7] The company's responsibilities further included maintenance of the feeder dam at Brecksville, the canal prism itself, the towpath, and the water-control gates in several locations along the eleven miles or so between the dam and the steelworks in Cuyahoga Heights. In subsequent years, the lease was extended, amended, and renegotiated.

A 1970s version of the lease agreement is between the State of Ohio (represented by the superintendent of Public Works) and U.S. Steel Corporation, which by then owned the American Steel & Wire operation. That lease refers to allowing the following uses: "hydraulic, condensing, manufacturing and railway right-of-way" as well as "for filling purposes."[8] Similar hydraulic agreements were made between the state and industries in Barberton and Akron, including both B. F. Goodrich and Firestone Tire and Rubber. Goodrich was located directly adjacent to the canal in Akron, whereas Firestone, south of Goodrich and east of the canal, drew its state-leased water from Summit Lake, a natural lake that was lowered in the 1800s and used as a feeder reservoir for the canal.

Where unmaintained, the canal did not hold water for very long, but where it had been taken care of, such as in the northernmost section, it attracted more than industrial uses. Anglers, swimmers, ice-skaters, and picnickers were drawn to the grassy slopes and still, shimmering waters. Toward the end of the canal era, pleasure boating and excursions had already become popular; these continued in some places after shipping ceased. As a child William Harry Heidloff lived with his family in the locktender's house at Lock 42 in Cleveland from 1910 to 1915. Seventy-five years later, he described how pleasure boats used the lock to move from canal to river and back during their excursions. On weekends and holidays, these boats took groups to picnic areas south of Cleveland, undoubtedly to areas now used by national park visitors. Heidloff specifically recalled one of these as a canal boat owned and operated by William Kelly, a teamster who lived on South Dille Street near the terminus of the canal. Kelly carried groups to picnic spots in the country south of the city, to places such as Zimmerman's near Lock 39.[9] Grasselli Chemical Company was also situated near Heidloff's home, and he noted that the company's employees owned and used many of the pleasure boats for their weekend recreation.[10]

Another pleasure boat, the *Sophia,* was often docked at Lock 42. According to Heidloff, it was built by Joe Verbsky and his brother Lol, who moved it to the canal with help of friends from Grasselli. Heidloff's father's daybook recorded the dockage fees paid by owners of pleasure boats, canoes, and other types of crafts docked near Lock 42.[11]

Heidloff's recollections are especially interesting because not only did he live in the locktender's house at the end of the canal, both in place and time, he also lived with the contrasts of his father's life as a fisherman and the growing industries that surrounded their home. His father and his fishing partner left the house at 6 A.M. to set nets on Lake Erie and

Excursion boats took groups to picnic areas south of Cleveland. This picture is of people and boats arriving at Zimmerman Tavern near Lock 39 (Louis Baus Canal Photograph Collection, University of Akron Archival Services).

then returned in the afternoon to serve the customers lined up for fresh fish. His father made his own fishing nets and spent a good deal of the winter months working on them. But this life sat like a bubble in the sea of industry. As Heidloff described it, "The dirty red iron ore dust from the Corrigan-McKinney Steel Co. on the west side of the River blew our way day and night. When the wind was from the east we could smell fumes from the Grasselli sulfuric acid and zinc chloride manufacturing departments. When the wind was from the north, the power plant gave us its share of black smoke. Even though the air was heavily polluted, our family remained fairly healthy. All the companies around us operated day and night, year round and there was never a time of peace and quiet."[12]

Heidloff and his brothers played in the canal and river and fished for minnows. They also skated, as did other children up and down the canal, and "the skating was fair. The ice was usually four to six inches thick and safe, but was usually covered with power plant soot and cinders."[13] His family moved from the locktender's house in 1915, but Heidloff's life remained close to the canal, as he eventually went on to work at Grasselli, retiring after it consolidated with E. I. duPont de Nemours and Company.

Because of water leases south of downtown Akron and into Barberton, the Ohio & Erie Canal was filled for another ten-mile stretch. This part of it was fed by the Portage Lakes, a series of lakes already popular for boating in the late 1800s. Today these are seven lakes connected by navigable channels. Prior to construction of the Ohio & Erie Canal, the glacially formed kettle lakes were surrounded by extensive swamps. Designers of the canal system took advantage of the lakes and altered them to form reservoirs capable of feeding water into the canal going north and south. Similar reservoirs served the canal system in other parts of Ohio.

Both the reservoirs and canal channels could continue to be exploited as water sources for industry and municipalities, but, for the lakes especially, it was easy to move from serving the canal to serving weekend pleasure seekers. Toward the end of the canal era in Ohio, the state began to see these reservoirs as potentially having other public benefits, recognizing that they were already serving as water supplies and recreational places. In 1894, the General Assembly of Ohio set a policy establishing the feeder lakes as public parks.[14] In Akron, commercial excursion boats took advantage of the continuous state-owned navigable waters and offered rides from the heart of the industrial city out into the fresher air of the lake-studded countryside. For instance, excursion boats in the late 1880s carried passengers from Lock 1 in downtown Akron to picnic grounds on Summit and Long Lakes by navigating the canal, then locking through to a channel that connected it to Long Lake (then called Long Pond).[15] The first stop was Lakeside Park, a popular picnic place. Summit Beach Park, an amusement park complete with a dance hall, a skating rink, a swimming beach, a roller coaster, and vaudeville shows, which took over Lakeside Park in the 1900s, was the weekend destination of many city dwellers.

The pleasure boats took picnickers on rides around Summit Lake and also had scheduled service south into Long Lake where there were more picnic grounds and another amusement park. According to Karl H. Grismer, city folk were attracted not only to the picnic grounds and amusements but also the "inns which were famed for their fish and chicken dinners."[16] A 1908 ad promotes a fourteen-mile round-trip excursion on the Crescent Launch Line, from Lock 1 to Long Lake and back, for twenty-five cents.[17] State maintenance boat worker James Dillow Robinson recalled that when the state boat reached Lock 1 in downtown Akron, a launch from the Crescent Line would take over and tow the state boat along the canal and across Summit Lake, the floating wooden towpath being in too poor a condition for teams to use.[18]

Anyone owning their own canoe or rowboat could likewise navigate from canal to lake and back. Canoeing was especially popular from around 1910 through the 1920s; one canoe livery, built by Melvin F. "Pop" Cooper, was soon joined by many others lining the Ohio & Erie Canal near where it merged with Summit Lake. "Each livery had its own canoe club. The clubs sported colorful Indian names such as the Mohawk Canoe Club and the Tippicanoe Club. The main purpose of the clubs was to promote the enjoyment of leisurely cruises on the lake. As the popularity of the clubs grew, the canoes became ornate showpieces."[19]

The various clubs and paddlers tried to outdo each other in decoration and equipment. "A typical club canoe was gaily decorated with colored Japanese lanterns, electric lights, pillow, blankets, and in some cases, a victrola!"[20] Canoe clubs also participated in races, using especially large "war" canoes and racing crews. The Depression, World War II, and increasing pollution in Summit Lake all contributed to the eventual decline of the canoe clubs.[21] A few canoeists continued to enjoy using the canal and lakes, nonetheless. For instance, E. J. Bissler of Alliance traveled by canoe from Cleveland to Akron in the 1930s via river and canal. There was a brief resurgence in canoeing on Summit Lake around 1945, but the clubs and liveries were mostly gone. Pop Cooper's livery, the first to appear on the canal near Summit Lake, was the last to go. The boathouse was razed in 1959 to make way for an expressway.[22]

Muscle power, steam engines, and gasoline engines have all powered various watercrafts on the canal and reservoirs. Boats using the lakes were not restricted by size or draft, but those using the canal were confined by the narrowness and shallowness of the channel. Steam-powered boats plied the lakes until gasoline engines came into use, but steam excursions were more rare on the canal itself, although even as early as 1858 the Ohio Board of Public Works recommended that steam-powered boats replace mule-drawn boats for greater speed and tonnage.[23] Some entrepreneurs did experiment with steam power on the canals, and there are written reports of a paddlewheel steamboat, the *Arvine*, that traveled the canal during the later years of the canal's operation. It was used chiefly as an excursion boat, making trips to picnic spots along the canal outside Massillon and as far south as Newark. The *Newcomerstown Visitor* stated that "it was rather a new and novel sight to see a steamboat make its appearance on the canal in this port last Saturday evening," so apparently steam-powered boats were few and far between on the Ohio & Erie Canal in the late 1800s.[24]

Wherever the canal held water it became the local swimming hole. Historic photographs show swimmers jumping off the wooden floating towpath in Summit Lake while others used the towpath as a convenient fishing platform, poor water quality notwithstanding. Canal Fulton residents, interviewed in 1984 for the "Tales of the Towpath" project,

Where the canal was maintained for water leases its shimmering water attracted local folks for recreation, especially swimming. At the Wolf Creek Lock the boys are enjoying some skinny-dipping (Louis Baus Canal Photograph Collection, University of Akron Archival Services).

mentioned swimming and fishing in the canal as favorite activities. In a 2004 interview, Don Cooke of Navarre recalled that his swimming hole on the canal was demarcated by two large wooden spools placed in the canal like buoys.

Another popular pastime both during and after the end of the canal era was ice-skating. Charles Rhoades recalled: "I'd get up in the morning and look out my bedroom window and if there wasn't any snow on the ice, I'd go down skating. And I'd skate downtown until it was time to go to school and take my skates off and leave them up at the restaurant and go to school and come back and put my skates on and skate back up to the house. And then on Saturdays . . . we'd skate to Massillon. That was nine miles. And once you were down there, you had to come back. That was a long trip."[25] Vera Finefrock, another who had loved to skate on the canal, recalled: "I could hardly wait until it froze over so I could go skating. . . . We didn't pay much attention to it until it was frozen over because I did love to skate."[26]

Canal Fulton resident Ted Edwards, born in 1917, after the canal was no longer used commercially, noted that it was a recreational attraction no matter what the day. "Having fun along the canal was not reserved for a Sunday afternoon. I spent more time than I like to remember skating, swimming, and trapping, hunting, along the Canal—it was a way of life."[27]

From around the 1920s on, various uses of the canal and towpath were made possible by the state policy that permitted and encouraged leases, easements, and even the sale of canal lands. Possible uses included "drainage courses, roads and highways, or other projects of public nature."[28] In effect, much of the canal system in Ohio was cut up and recycled. The old Ohio & Erie Canal carried pleasure boats or sewer lines, depending on what entity held a lease, easement, or ownership. Many people used the towpath of the canal, and in many different ways. Its use as a road and trail connecting villages along the canal continued after the demise of the canal—the towpath was often the shortest route between neighboring villages. Its condition varied from region to region, partly dependent on whether the canal was still being used. Where maintained for a hydraulic

Ice-skating was a favorite winter sport all along the canal (Louis Baus Canal Photograph Collection, University of Akron Archival Services).

What Is in a Name?

SAM TAMBURRO

The correct name of the Ohio & Erie Canal was the subject of local debate for some years. Most old maps refer to it as the "Ohio Canal" or sometimes as the "Ohio and Erie Canal." This is not unusual: for most transportation systems, there is an official name and a common one, for everyday use. There are numerous examples of common names for nineteenth-century railroads, such as the "Nickel Plate Road" for the New York, Chicago & St. Louis Railroad or the "Big Four Railroad" for the Cleveland, Cincinnati, Chicago & St. Louis. This pattern is also apparent for the Ohio & Erie Canal. During all of the nineteenth century and most of the twentieth, the Ohio and Erie Canal was known simply as the "Ohio Canal" in advertisements, maps, personal correspondence, and even official state documents. The people who built, traveled on, and made a living off of the canal called it the "Ohio Canal." Only recently have we begun using again the official "Ohio & Erie Canal," now with an ampersand instead of "and." Although the ampersand was commonly used during the canal era, it was not part of the official name.

The official, incorporated name for the canal that connects Lake Erie at Cleveland with the Ohio River at Portsmouth is the Ohio and Erie Canal, which appears on the 1825 Canal Bill, passed February 4 of that year. After much survey work of potential canal routes, the Board of Canal Commissioners endorsed two canal projects: the Ohio and Erie Canal and the Miami Canal. Historians have speculated that the inclusion of the Miami Canal in the bill was designed to gain support for the Ohio and Erie Canal from the heavily populated southwestern region of Ohio, especially Cincinnati. Other measures were included to guarantee the canal bill's passage, namely road appropriations for districts to be bypassed by the canals and a progressive tax feature that tied real estate assessments to property values.

Although the 1825 canal bill named the southwestern canal the "Miami Canal," the Ohio Board of Public Works officially changed its name to "Miami & Erie Canal" in 1845 after the completion of a connection with the Wabash & Erie Canal, which stretched from Toledo, Ohio, to Fort Wayne, Indiana. The Miami & Erie was finally connected with Lake Erie via that junction with the Wabash & Erie at Junction, Ohio. In the previous twenty-two years, the Ohio and Erie Canal served as the only trans-state canal and became Ohio's only canal with statewide and national recognition. Hence, in the collective consciousness of nineteenth-century Ohioans,

Survey maps of the late 1800s refer to the "Ohio Canal" (1892 Canal Commission of Ohio map, National Park Service).

lease, the towpath was often as good as a one-lane road. It was used as a driveway, hiking path, or access road in some places, and in others it was obliterated and overgrown.

North of the Village of Boston in Summit County, Jaite and Boston residents and Jaite Mill workers used the towpath as a road for about seventy-five years; some even referred to it as "Towpath Road." The Jaite Mill produced paper bags and related material from 1906 to 1984, when it was purchased by the National Park Service. Although the mill used several small parts of the old canal as holding ponds for the manufacturing process, it was the towpath that was an integral part of the Jaite employees' lives. Even before the 1913 flood, the employees who lived south of the mill, especially in Boston, used it as a road. The towpath was the shortest route between Jaite and Boston and was maintained by the mill.

---

the system became known by the common, shortened name, the "Ohio Canal."

The change in the name from "Ohio Canal" to the legal "Ohio and Erie Canal" or "Ohio & Erie Canal" appears to have been driven by research conducted by the National Park Service (NPS). With the organization of the Cuyahoga Valley National Recreation Area in 1974 (now Cuyahoga Valley National Park), the NPS began exhaustive research on the canal, a primary cultural resource of the newly formed park unit. One of its first reports was the *Proposed Ohio and Erie Canal Suitability/Feasibility Study* (1975), which identified canal resources from Cleveland to Portsmouth. Throughout the report, the legal name "Ohio and Erie Canal" is used, and the cover of the report uses the ampersand between "Ohio" and "Erie." In 1984, Harlan Unrau and Nick Scrattish prepared a detailed research report on the canal in the Cuyahoga Valley, *Historic Structure Report: Ohio and Erie Canal, Cuyahoga Valley National Recreation Area, Ohio.* They used the legal name throughout the report. The real change came in 1993, when NPS staff wrote a feasibility study for the creation of a canal heritage corridor between Cleveland and Zoar, Ohio, entitled *A Route to Prosperity: A Study by the National Park Service of the Ohio & Erie Canal Corridor.* The NPS study consistently used the ampersand instead of "and," in essence changing both the official and common names to "Ohio & Erie Canal."

The "Ohio & Erie Canal" name was codified by Public Law 104–333, which established the Ohio & Erie Canal National Heritage Corridor in 1996. This name appears on all documents, maps, and interpretive material created since the 1970s. In 2003, for marketing purposes, the Ohio & Erie Canal Association, the management entity of the Ohio & Erie Canal National Heritage Corridor, produced a new name for the heritage area: the Ohio & Erie Canalway.

The late John Lahoski, son of Ben Lahoski, the manager of the Jaite Mill before it was purchased by the National Park Service, knew the scene well—he and his brother were responsible for cutting, with a scythe, the weeds along the towpath-road during the summers. The mill burned coal for energy, so there would have been a lot of cinders available for paving and filling in holes.[29] Lahoski described an old road grader that was pulled behind a dump truck and used to grade the towpath smooth and to plow snow in the winter.[30]

The towpath near Jaite was a one-way street that changed with the work shifts: folks came north to work, and then those leaving could head south. But there was an unwritten code. "Say after ten after three you never left Boston to go to Jaite . . . because everybody knew that 3:30 everybody's coming home . . . from work."[31] The late Nina Stanford, longtime Boston resident and granddaughter of canal engineer Richard Howe, also described her experiences with the towpath when she worked at the Jaite Mill. "We rode down the towpath. Everybody did, and there were only a couple of places you could pass somebody. . . . There was this one place where there was a tree sitting out by the edge of the road, you had a road around it. That is where you could pass, but most of it was just trees and . . . the old canal bed."[32]

In a 2003 interview, Betty Puchalsky, ninety-plus years old, who had worked at Jaite until she was seventy-three, remembered one adventure that occurred while driving her Model T Ford to work. "I drove off it. I was late, you know and somebody was coming." Betty's son John Puchalsky, provided more details. "The story goes she tried to pass because she was already late, and she turned over in the canal, but thank goodness it was the part that was . . . dry and [she] didn't end up in the water . . . but they said it was sort of funny because she pulled over and it was like slow motion. It was cinders, that's all, and it sort of gave away. She was stopped and . . . just rolled over. So in those days three or four guys stopped, and they just rolled it, pushed it back over." And Betty continued on to work, unharmed.[33]

In other locations along the historic canal route, the towpath was a road or driveway, often dead-ending at an isolated house. In what is now Cuyahoga Valley National Park, a section of the towpath going south from Station Road formerly served as a road to reach a gravel pit, a home, and utility lines. Another such towpath road led south out of Clinton to a watering hole known as the Blue Goose Saloon, and yet another section of towpath became Ferndale Street in Akron. North of Akron, Riverview Road was partially laid in the canal itself, eliminating the towpath there.

And a couple of miles south, the canal bed was a convenient place to locate the main trunk sewer line running from Akron to the treatment plant.

After the end of the canal era, in many areas the ribbon of canal and adjacent lands turned wild again and began to harbor wildlife. Beavers moved in on territory formerly monopolized by muskrats. Birds found shelter and food in the thickets crowding the towpath. Hikers, anglers, hunters, and trappers made narrow towpath passageways to reach favorites spots.

Where the canal wasn't being clearly used by industries, some of its neighbors began to appropriate its real estate. Small docks for private rowboats and canoes appeared. Sandstone blocks from locks and other structures began to vanish as neighboring farmers and others found them useful. Outbuildings spilled onto the towpath and even into the canal basin itself. A photograph of the canal in Chillicothe, taken around World War I, shows a stranded canal boat that housed the owner until he died. A number of other buildings were built in the canal right-of-way after 1911, including a movie theater.[34]

In some cases, the canal was a convenient dumping ground. After Cuyahoga Valley National Park was established in 1974, volunteers from the local Sierra Club group began trash cleanups at sites that had been used locally for dumping prior to landfill regulations. These volunteers discovered that canal locks—at least the ones near roads—especially seemed to attract illegal dumping. At Red Lock near Jaite, for example, volunteers removed mounds of household refuse and dragged out dozens of tires.

A 1952 engineering report prepared for the City of Akron notes that north of Lock 1 in the downtown area, the canal "has become, so to speak, its back yard. Within the narrow right-of-way are small plots that the State has leased for approved occupancy and use, but in the main, the old canal now serves for random use and abuse, being a storm water channel, a dump, and parking area. Down its main axis is laid one of the principal sanitary intercepting sewers for the city, and over and around this conduit the old channel receives not only the storm flows from the summit reach upstream, but also the storm sewage from over ten square miles of the more populous and industrial portions of the city."[35] Perhaps the ultimate affront to the historic canal came later, in the 1960s, when Akron decided to bury portions of it under urban renewal development. But the canal could still be heard, running behind the Civic Theater and under a department-store parking garage, a sound out of darkness, incorporated as part of a scary Halloween walk held at the "haunted theater" during the late 1960s. Of course, Akron would later change its opinion of the old canal and begin to reintegrate it and its history into the fabric of the city.

The canal in downtown Massillon was regarded similarly to the one in Akron—a source of industrial water, sometimes a health and safety menace, and, eventually, available land for new development. In general, city people regarded the canal as representing old-fashioned ways and looked for "modern" ways to either use it or eliminate it. In more rural settings, the tendency was to let it be or use it for recreation. During the Depression, Massillon received funding for a storm sewer through the downtown canal land, while during the same decade Works Progress Administration workers were making a park out of the Lock 4 area south of Canal Fulton, including building a small replica of a locktender's house alongside the towpath.[36] In 1950, Massillon purchased the canal lands from the state, paving the way for later major redevelopment projects.[37] Downtown street names had been changed a couple of decades earlier, eliminating clues to the location of the historic canal.[38]

The canal in memory and myth is best captured by Pearl Nye and James Dillow Robinson. While most people ignored the old transportation system or used the canal and towpath in new ways, these two sages kept the canal memories alive and created a folk-legend past for the canal era by recounting stories and recording their perspectives on canal life.

Nye was immersed in the canal life at least until the time of his father's death in 1887. After the canal was no longer used for its original purposes, Nye attempted to adapt to the rapidly changing times. He was occasionally employed as a carpenter, spent some time in Chicago where he received a patent for his easy-cleaning window, moved to California to seek financial backers for this invention, and eventually returned to Akron to ride out the Great Depression and World War II. He recalled that it was only late in life, when he stood in Columbus where his father's canal boat had rested one winter, locked in the ice, that memories and strong feelings began to wash over him. Clearly, Pearl Nye remembered his life on the canal with his parents and their large family as a wonderful, fun-filled time, full of security and adventure.[39]

Nye wanted to preserve his memories and be remembered as a canaller. He turned his energy to recording those canal stories for posterity. Nye's mother loved music and songs, and as a boy he helped her memorize songs they heard along the canal. When he was over sixty years old and living in Akron rooming houses, Nye wrote his memoirs, gathered photographs of the canal era, and corresponded with anyone he could interest in its history. He found transcribers for his canal songs and made acquaintance with newspaper reporters and history buffs. Finally, his efforts and national circumstances came together. In 1933, John Avery

Lomax and his son Alan Lomax began collecting folk songs for the Library of Congress. In the late 1930s, an Akron reporter, Helen Waterhouse, contacted Alan Lomax to tell him about her acquaintance Pearl Nye, and his vast collection of canal songs. He responded, came to Akron, and recorded about one hundred of Nye's seven hundred songs.[40]

Nye's songs illustrate his lifelong love of the canal. To him it was the dearest friend in his entire life (drawn by Chuck Ayers).

Clearly, the canal was the love of his life, and his songs helped record his way of life for posterity. His love can be seen in the first lines of his masterwork, "The Old Canal":

There's a little "silver ribbon" runs across the Buckeye State,
'Tis the dearest place of all this earth to me,
For upon its placid surface I was born some years ago
And its beauty, grandeur always do I see.[41]

Nye's encounter with Alan Lomax led to an invitation to perform at the National Folk Festival in Washington, D.C., in 1938. Apparently, he was well received, as he was invited four more times to perform at the national festival, though he may not have been able to attend all four. According to canal historian Terry Woods, Nye definitely appeared at the festival in New York in 1942 and in Cleveland in 1946.[42] A 1942 newspaper clipping reported: "Akron's oldest canal boat captain, P. R. Nye, sang his canal ballads before a vast throng of people at Madison Square Garden . . . as a feature of the national folk festival. . . . The rotund and jolly 'boatman,' who was one of 18 children born on the canal boat 'Warren' as it plied its way between the Ohio River and Lake Erie, has been living for more than a year in Coshocton County. He built his own home there out of materials from an old lock on his beloved canal."[43] Nye's 1946 performance in Cleveland was his last public one. In his later years, he became increasingly isolated, bitter, and suspicious, believing that, since his songs and histories brought him no money, he had not proven the value of his life.[44]

Dillow Robinson, who was first introduced in chapter 7 and was a less eccentric man than Pearl Nye, also wrote poems commemorating the canal. Both men span the time between the end of the working canal and the beginning of interest in understanding, respecting, and preserving its history. At least one canal historian, Ted Findley, knew both men. Terry Woods reported that Findley accompanied Nye on excursions along the canal and helped type up many of Nye's songs.[45] In 1961, Findley cofounded the Canal Society of Ohio. He and other canal buffs did history a great service by collecting firsthand knowledge and recollections of life during the canal era from individuals such as Nye and many others. Robinson channeled his canal interest into practical efforts to preserve the physical canal and its history, joining the board of the Canal Society of Ohio in 1965. He showed his slides, gave numerous talks about and tours of the canal, and in 1977 participated in the 150th anniversary of the Akron-Cleveland section of the canal. In an interesting coincidence, Pearl Nye died in 1950 in Hawthornden Psychiatric Hospital, located just up the hill from the section of canal that Robinson worked on and knew so well. Robinson continued to contribute to the efforts to preserve canal history and lived to see his favorite section of the canal preserved as part of Cuyahoga Valley National Park. Robinson died in 1980 at age eighty-two. Both of these men carried the muddy, buoyant, mule-drawn canal life into the annals of history.

NOTES

1. Terry K. Woods, "The Life and Times of Pearl R. Nye," *Canal History and Technology Proceedings* 7 (Mar. 26, 1988): 53.
2. Ibid.
3. Don Cooke, interview by Peg Bobel and Lynn Metzger, Nov. 19, 2004.
4. Woods, "Life and Times," 53.
5. Ibid., 61.
6. Ibid.
7. Lease between the State of Ohio and American Steel & Wire dated December 22, 1931, Canal Society of Ohio Collection, Univ. of Akron Archives, Akron, Ohio. This lease covers the period 1932–47 and refers to the original lease beginning January 17, 1922.
8. Lease between the State of Ohio, superintendent of Public Works, as director of Public Works, and United States Steel Corporation of Delaware, Dec. 8, 1970, Canal Society of Ohio Collection.
9. W. Harry Heidloff, "Ohio & Erie Canal in Cleveland, 1910–1915, Part 2, Lock 42, The Weigh Lock and the 1913 Flood," marked "Draft," 1991, Canal Society of Ohio Collection.
10. W. Harry Heidloff, "Ohio & Erie Canal in Cleveland, 1910–1915, Part 1, Lock 42, The Second Terminus and the Locktender's House," marked "Final Draft, 10-4-90," Canal Society of Ohio Collection.
11. Heidloff, "Ohio & Erie Canal in Cleveland, Part 1," 5–6.
12. Heidloff, "Ohio & Erie Canal in Cleveland, Part 1," 3.
13. Heidloff, "Ohio & Erie Canal in Cleveland, Part 1," 7.
14. The Department of Public Works managed the canal-related lake lands for recreation until 1949, at which time the Ohio Department of Natural Resources was created and took over responsibility for the lake recreation areas.
15. For more information on how the lake, river, feeder channel, canal system worked, see "The Portage Summit Water Supply," by Larry Turner and Brad Bond, *Towpaths* 42.1 (2004): 1–6. Turner and Bond note that the junction between the canal and Long Pond, including the lock and a brick road, was destroyed by the construction of Manchester Road in 1955.
16. Karl H. Grismer, *Akron and Summit County* (Akron: Summit County Historical Society, 1952), 284.

17. Jack Gieck, *A Photo Album of Ohio's Canal Era, 1825–1913* (Kent: Kent State Univ. Press, 1988), 51.

18. James Dillow Robinson, "Canal Maintenance and Recollections," *Towpaths* 17.1 (1979): 8.

19. Diane DeMali Francis and David W. Francis, *Summit Beach Park: Akron's Coney Island* (Akron: Summit County Historical Society, 1993), 54.

20. Ibid.

21. The Firestone Tire and Rubber plant that formerly used Summit Lake water for cooling is no longer operating. Although improvements are still needed in the lake's water quality, migratory waterfowl frequent the lake in the spring and fall and apparently find sufficient food. Also, some canoeists are once again using the canal, paddling from Nesmith Lake, through Summit Lake, and on to Lock 1 in downtown Akron.

22. Francis and Francis, *Summit Beach Park*, 109, 67.

23. Harlan Unrau and Nick Scrattish, *Historic Structure Report, Ohio and Erie Canal, Cuyahoga Valley National Recreation Area, Ohio* (Denver: United States Department of the Interior, National Park Service, Denver Service Center Branch of Historic Preservation Midwest/Rocky Mountain Team, Mar., 1981), chapter 6, 26–27. See also the photo of a self-propelled steamboat operating on the Miami & Erie Canal in Jack Gieck's *A Photo Album of Ohio's Canal Era*. Also the article by Fred W. Bishop, "Boat Building at Peninsula," in *Towpaths* 19.2 (1981): 13–23, relates that five or six steam-propelled canal boats were built in the Peninsula boat yards but "gained no great popularity."

24. Al Simpson, *Along the Towpath: A Journalist Rediscovers the Ohio & Erie Canal* (Akron: Univ. of Akron Libraries, 2003), 34–35.

25. Charles Rhoades, interview for "Tales of the Towpath" project, 1984, transcript.

26. Vera Finefrock, interview for "Tales of the Towpath" project, 1984, transcript.

27. Ted Edwards, interview for "Tales of the Towpath" project, 1984, transcript.

28. *Ohio Revised Code*, title 1, chap. 123, Department of Administrative Services. Section 123.681, repealed.

29. John Lahoski, interview, Jaite Ethnography Project, Univ. of Akron Anthropology Class, Spring 2003, transcript, Jaite Collection, Univ. of Akron Archives, Akron; also in Peninsula Historical Society Archives.

30. Lahoski interview.

31. Betty Puchalsky and her son John Puchalsky, interview, Jaite Ethnography Project.

32. Nina Stanford, interview, Jaite Ethnography Project.

33. Puchalsky interview.

34. Jim Henry, "After the Canal Closed," internal Canal Society of Ohio information sheet, Canal Society of Ohio Collection.

35. George E. Barnes, consulting engineer, "Study and Report on Improvements to the Ohio and Erie Canal at Akron," consultant's report to the City of Akron, 1952, 2, photocopy in author's personal collection.

36. Margy Vogt, *Towpath to Towpath: A History of Massillon, Ohio* (Massillon: Bates, 2002), 165; Canal Society of Ohio, Spring Tour 2000, 14, Canal Society of Ohio Collection.

37. Vogt, *Towpath to Towpath*, 196.

38. Ibid., 161.

39. Woods, "Life and Times," 57.

40. Ibid., 60.

41. P. R. Nye, "The Old Canal," Canal Society of Ohio Collection.

42. Nye, "The Old Canal," 62–66.

43. *Akron Beacon Journal*, clipping with handwritten date of 5–1942, Canal Society of Ohio Collection.

44. Woods, "Life and Times," 63.

45. Ibid., 59.

Part 3

Cultural Preservation to Canal Renaissance

Chapter 14

Saving the "Little Silver Ribbon"

BOB DOWNING AND RUSS MUSARRA

For a generation or two after the devastating floods of 1913, conversations about the Ohio & Erie Canal were mostly nostalgic. People who were present when the packets and freighters floated along the waterway reminisced among themselves and to those who came along later about how great things used to be. Following in their footsteps were the individuals who began the preservation movement, the precursor to the drive to create the Ohio & Erie Canalway. The second half of the twentieth century inspired these preservation pioneers to think beyond nostalgia; they began calling for a rebirth of activity along the towpath. They called for saving stories of the canal, canal-era buildings, photographs, and records, as well as the canal and towpath.

Foremost among these preservationists in the 1960s were Edward and Frances Montgomery of Coshocton's Roscoe Village; Ted H. Findley of New Philadelphia; Clyde E. Gainey of Canal Fulton; journalist Al Simpson of Canton; U.S. Congressman Ralph Regula of Navarre; and Lily Fleder and Robert L. Hunker of Peninsula. Jack E. Gieck of Akron preserved photographs of the canal era throughout the state. There were others, of course, but the efforts of these individuals were symbolic of the grassroots movement that stimulated interest in the Canalway many take for granted today.

The impetus for beginning preservation efforts differed in each location, but all led to saving a piece of the past. In Coshocton a painting of three canal boats in the 1850s along the Ohio & Erie Canal in booming Roscoe Village led to canal preservation. Zoar Village in northern

Tuscarawas County was saved largely because of the influence of the Ohio Historical Society and the Zoar Community Association, and the significance of the German Separatist communal society that had lived there. In Canal Fulton in northern Stark County, the Canal Fulton Heritage Society spearheaded the grassroots effort to take advantage of the canal. In Summit County, the Village of Peninsula sparked a new interest in its history in the 1960s when it became involved in saving the historic Bronson church. Grassroots support for the community's past grew. Certainly other communities along the Ohio & Erie Canal tout their canal ties, but these four stand out as communities that recognized the importance and possibilities surrounding their local histories and worked to develop them to attract and educate visitors and to offer something special to residents.

The history of Roscoe is similar to those of other canal towns, once bustling economic centers, flourishing in the 1830s and then languishing after the railroads shifted population and industry away from the canal. Roscoe, located where the Tuscarawas and Walhonding Rivers form the Muskingum River, was started in 1816 when James Calder moved across the river from Coshocton, built some log cabins, and started the new Village of Caldersburg. The canal came through from 1827 to 1830 and was built between the two towns. That benefited Caldersburg with its 81 inhabitants more than it did Coshocton, population 333. The canal boat *Monticello* was the first to arrive, on August 21, 1830.

Industries blossomed along the canal at what became Roscoe in 1831. This included saw- and flour mills, canal-boat manufacturers, and barrel makers. Roscoe became the fourth-largest wheat-shipping port along the canal from Cleveland to Portsmouth. And by 1841, the boomtown had sixty dwellings, five or six stores, two apothecaries, a boatyard, an iron foundry, and mechanics' shops. The town had four hundred residents plus seasonal employees. But all that changed in 1866, when the Steubenville & Indiana Rail Road was built between Coshocton and the Ohio River and the canal became less of a transportation route. After the 1913 flood, it no longer operated; it became the ditch with a path, used by local folks. But in the 1960s it was rediscovered and the area became the historic Roscoe Village, a tourist destination spot.

In Coshocton, the canal ran north of Whitewoman Street, where state Route 16 now lies. In 1960 the Coshocton National Bank commissioned New York artist Dean Cornwell to paint a scene to mark the county's 1961 sesquicentennial. He painted the canal, much to the surprise of community leaders. Cornwell's work, on specially woven fabric, was twenty-four feet long and eight feet wide. It was unveiled on May 14, 1961. When people in Coshocton for the ceremonies asked to see the inspiration for the work, they were driven to Whitewoman Street to view the aging brick buildings next to the canal. The painting led Edward and Frances Montgomery to look anew at their hometown, and their vision, dedication, and financial resources helped re-create historic Roscoe Village.[1] It is estimated the village attracts about twenty-five thousand visitors a year. Cornwell's Roscoe painting now hangs in Bank One of Coshocton, and a smaller reproduction hangs in the lobby of the Roscoe Village Visitor Center.

Community visionaries Edward and Frances Montgomery led the movement to preserve the canal port in Coshocton. Edward Montgomery had founded the Edmont Glove Business in Coshocton in 1934, and in 1952 he created the Montgomery Foundation. In 1966, millionaire Montgomery sold Edmont to Becton-Dickerson, a surgical supplies company. But he and Frances continued to live in Coshocton. The following year, Frances suggested to her husband that they restore an old canal tollhouse that was in disrepair. They purchased the 1840 house for $1,200 and spent $41,000 to restore it.[2] Other purchases followed, and soon the Montgomerys were restoring the old canal port. The couple, whose favorite vacation destination was Virginia's Colonial Williamsburg, also studied then-developing German Village in Columbus. Historical preservation was just emerging in the United States and was still largely a do-it-yourself operation. In late 1967, the Montgomery Foundation announced creation of Roscoe Restoration, with Earl Shurtz as manager.

The Montgomerys had actually started quietly buying land along Whitewoman Street earlier that year, in an effort to keep the prices from becoming overly inflated in the rural economically depressed community. By late 1969, Roscoe Restoration had acquired 70 percent of the property along Whitewoman Street.[3] The Montgomerys wanted the project to be a working museum so that visitors could enjoy a visit to the nineteenth century in restored Roscoe Village.[4]

At that same time, the Coshocton Chamber of Commerce was beginning to develop a new recreational facility along the canal. Edward Montgomery was a key committee member in the chamber and helped raise the money to purchase 228 acres for a water park near Roscoe Village. There, one can take a two and a half mile round-trip on a canal boat, the horse-drawn *Monticello III* operated by the Coshocton City and County Park District.[5]

Edward and Frances Montgomery, along with Jay Shaw and Seward Schooler, restored the Old Warehouse and turned it into a restaurant, which opened in 1969, and later gave it to the Roscoe Village Foundation. The master plan for what had historically been called West Coshocton centered on the square with the tollhouse, an old warehouse, and the Roscoe Building. The late architect-designer Robert Gaede of Cleveland noted that Edward Montgomery had "caught the bug." Friend Seward Schooler said, "Ed Montgomery is a single-track fellow . . . something he wants to get done, he gets the right people around him and he gets it done."[6]

Edward noted his wife's enthusiasm: "My Frances was so much interested in the beauty of the village. I could tell in the morning she could hardly wait for what she had planned for the day." She was equally involved in the project, especially in the gardens and the landscaping. Frances Montgomery also pushed for perfection and was a stickler for details. The Montgomerys came to rely heavily on consultants and learned what some called "the delicate process of restoration."[7]

Edward Montgomery served as the unpaid chairman of the Roscoe Village Foundation, the nonprofit group that owns many of the old buildings, which was funded by grants from the Montgomery Foundation and other sources. Gaede said the restoration succeeded because "one magnificent couple without international prestige and incalculable wealth undertook to start something they did entirely at their own risk."[8] Both spent eight hours a day every weekday and some weekends on the village restoration. "All we talk about at home is Roscoe Village," Montgomery said in a 1974 newspaper interview. He described how they had often driven the village streets and had seen how the buildings had fallen into disrepair, but it was Cornwell's painting that really jump-started the restoration. "By 1969, we were under way. I decided that the Roscoe Village restoration was a fine project for the family foundation I started back in 1952. I really thought it would be good for the community."[9]

At first, only a few buildings were purchased, but the scope of the project grew, in large part because "there were so many ugly buildings between the ones I wanted to keep. Soon the village rose like a phoenix out of the ashes," he said. "Those who came for the dedication of the mural in 1961 saw the ashes. Those who came in 1968 saw my dream of the restoration at its beginning."[10] In 1968, the local community created a grassroots support group, the Roscoe Village Society.

Early efforts were costly; the Montgomerys learned that it would have been easier to tear down many of the old buildings than to rehabilitate them. But they believed authenticity was worth the extra work and cost.[11] In early 1968, Edward Montgomery outlined their plan at a public meeting, where there was little opposition. Later there was minor disagreement with creating such a historical district, and some local resentment against the Montgomerys' dream continued to smolder, but the restoration continued.[12] In 1973, Roscoe Village was placed on the National Register of Historic Places.

By 2005, Roscoe Village consisted of more than thirty-five buildings including thirteen specialty shops, a fifty-one-room inn, and four restaurants. It featured living history tours of the canal-era buildings with costumed interpreters and craft demonstrations. However, according to Executive Director Joel Hampton, due to rising costs the Roscoe Village Foundation started selling off buildings—the hotel, three restaurants, and seven shops—and it leased shops to private business interests. However, the foundation continues its educational programs, plus festivals and other special events.

About forty miles north of Roscoe is an even older historic community, Zoar. A German communal society, it was founded along the Tuscarawas River in 1817. It was primarily a religious community, but the German Separatists introduced a communal living system to help pay their land debts and provide a living for the people. They came from the Württemberg region, near Stuttgart in what is today southwest Germany, and had broken with the established Lutheran Church.[13]

The village grew and prospered as it built seven miles of canal on its land and provided supplies to other canal workers. The society also operated at least four boats on the canal. (See chapter 6 for a complete discussion of the historic community and the role of the canal in Zoar's development.) Picturesque Zoar was an attraction for curious tourists almost from its beginnings. It was known for its simplicity and charm and its buildings' color and symmetry. It reached the height of its prosperity just before the Civil War, with its assets valued at $1 million and a membership of nearly five hundred.[14] One of the most distinctive symbols of Zoar was its large community garden, a sign of New Jerusalem as outlined in the Book of Revelation. A Norway spruce stands at the center, surrounded by a hedge and twelve juniper trees. Twelve walks, representing the twelve tribes of Israel, lead away from the central area.[15]

Zoar suffered economically in the late 1800s because of the failure to modernize its operations. As a result, the community's idealism and morale waned, young members left, outsiders were hired, and church attendance declined. Tourists also had an impact on Zoar and its economics. Then the railroad came to Zoar in 1882, and canal traffic waned. In 1898, the 222 Zoarites voted to dissolve their community. Each family received its own house in the village, about fifty acres of land and $200. Each member retained clothing and personal effects and kept the household furniture. Farm animals and tools were auctioned off. The dissolution left the town hall, schoolhouse, and meeting house as corporate property belonging to the village that had been established in 1884.[16] Since 1898, there have been many changes in Zoar; some Separatists moved away, but some remained, especially those who received businesses in the dissolution. Outsiders have moved in, buildings have been razed, and some have been converted into homes.

In the mid-1920s, the federal government proposed moving Zoar away from the Tuscarawas River to higher ground as protection from devastating floods, such as the one in 1913. There was resistance to that plan, and instead the U.S. Army Corps of Engineers decided in 1927 to build a flood-control levee around the village. The levee wiped out many of the village's industrial buildings that had fallen into disrepair. It also cut off Zoar's view of the river and canal, and it limited the village's ability to spread outward. However, it also led villagers in 1929 to re-create Zoar's community garden, resulting in the formation of the Zoar Historical Society in 1930 and its successor, the Zoar Foundation, in 1936. This group worked closely with the state to arrange for the purchase of buildings by the state. Former Zoar members found enough furniture and other Zoar-made items to create a museum in Number One House. Those things became the core of today's collection at the Zoar State Memorial. Zoar descendant Paul Riecker, the last child born before the dissolution, restored four of the original log cabins in 1930.[17]

The Great Depression had a strong impact on the village. During it, few tourists came to the hotel. Zoar became a community of older descendants and younger outsiders who bought the homes of Zoarites who died. The State of Ohio purchased its first Zoar properties in 1941, including the Zoar Garden, the gardener's house, and Number One House. The following year, the state bought the tinsmith shop, and in 1943 the Bimeler-Sturm House was acquired under a behest. Although the state bought other buildings, Zoar remained a sleepy and somewhat isolated village.[18] Ohio voters in 1965 and 1968 approved state bond issues that enabled the Ohio General Assembly to appropriate $300,000 for Zoar improvements, which resulted in the purchase of additional buildings and improvements to those already acquired.

The state began to use costumed interpreters in the early 1970s in the Tin Shop, Wagon Shop, and Blacksmith Shop; the Zoar Store was acquired in 1970 and restored by 1980. Next the state restored the Dairy and the Kitchen-Magazine complex; both opened in April 1995. The 1830 Sewing House now accommodates offices but is slated to be restored to show Zoar's textile history. The state bought the Zoar Hotel in 1996 with the goal of turning it into the main visitor center.

The state's restoration efforts at Zoar have been augmented through the years by grassroots groups and local citizens. For instance, in 1953, Zoar celebrated the centennial of the meeting house with a play written by descendant Hilda Morhart (1899–1978), which later became the basis of a book, *The Zoar Story*, published in 1967 for Zoar's sesquicentennial. That month-long celebration led to the creation of the Zoar Community Association that same year.[19]

In 1971, the Community Association leased the Zoar Schoolhouse, empty since 1953, and completed the restoration in 1985. It also restored the Zoar Town Hall by 2001. The association stages the Zoar Harvest Festival, complete with a reenactment of bringing the final wagonload of grain into town. That ceremony is accompanied by a band, a thanksgiving service, and a celebration. The association also sponsors Christmas in Zoar, a Descendants Days reception every June, and other public events.[20]

In the Village of Zoar, there are ten state-owned buildings open to the public, and they are surrounded by privately owned buildings, many of which have been turned into in-home shops and bed and breakfasts. The mixture of publicly and privately owned historical structures in the twelve-square-block historic district makes Zoar unique among Ohio historical sites. In all, the state historical society owns 10 percent of the land in the historic district, including eighteen historical structures. Zoar, with its seventy-five resident families, remains an important site because it housed one of the longest-lived communal societies in the United States, and it also memorializes a story of an oppressed group coming to America to find religious freedom.[21]

Stark County was home for many leaders in the canal preservation movement. It had an unusually high level of community memory and interest in the canal era. U.S. Congressman Ralph Regula, who represented Ohio's 16th Congressional District from 1972 through 2008, was Navarre's village solicitor when the State of Ohio in 1964 decided to divest itself of the canal lands. Local governments were given first call. If they passed on the opportunity, the lands would be sold to private entities. Regula didn't want that to happen so he urged the Stark County commissioners to take control of the county's canal land. He also met

In 1964, Ralph Regula and Al Simpson's sixteen-mile towpath walk fostered the canal preservation movement in Stark County (Canal Photograph Collection, University of Akron Archival Services).

with the managing editor of the *Canton Repository* in 1964 and suggested a reporter join him on a sixteen-mile hike from Canal Fulton to Navarre to explore the land's potential for public use.

Al Simpson was the reporter assigned to take that rainy-day hike. The resulting article, published on May 10, helped lay the groundwork for the column "Along the Towpath," which continued in the *Repository* through early 1970 and chronicled, among other things, establishment of the Stark County Park District and community efforts to build the *St. Helena II*, a wooden replica of a canal boat. Simpson began that first article: "Sixteen miles and 16 million raindrops. Of these ingredients—and more—this tale is woven. It is a story of a man and an idea to save the Ohio & Erie Canal." Regula was the man of whom Simpson wrote, and the two would become friends and associates as Regula's political career took him to the Ohio House of Representatives (1964–66), Ohio State Senate (1966–72), and to the U.S. Congress. After he retired from the paper, Simpson was Regula's press aide for ten years.[22]

From the beginning, Simpson drew parallels between what Regula was proposing and efforts led by U.S. Supreme Court justice William O. Douglas a decade earlier to save and restore the Chesapeake & Ohio Canal. "In 1954, Justice Douglas focused the nation's attention on the C & O Canal when he led 36 conservationists and newsmen on an eight-day hike along it," Simpson wrote in his inaugural article. "The waterway's scenic and historic values were threatened with destruction as the result of a proposal to construct a motor parkway along the towpath and, in some places, the bed of the canal. In protest, the towpath march was made and the resulting publicity helped defeat the highway proposal. Shortly afterward, the National Park Service recommended that the canal property be preserved as a national park. Today the vestiges of the Ohio & Erie Canal are in danger of eradication. To avoid that eventuality, Ralph Regula and other interested persons have initiated action to save the canal lands."[23]

In June 1964, Simpson wrote of traveling with Regula to explore the 185-mile Chesapeake & Ohio Canal and to meet with Justice Douglas and National Park Service officials in Washington to learn how the restoration was accomplished. Simpson concluded his article with a vignette about canal fever: "The Navarre solicitor says there are three kinds of canal fever: the malaria type, which affects the men who build the canals; the get-rich-quick fever, which struck investors who were lured into financing uneconomic canals; and the modern-day canal fever, which infects people with the idea of preserving the big ditches as combination historic-recreational parks. Ralph has a good case of the latter fever and I'm running a high temperature myself. Actually, we hope it's catching."[24]

Simpson's collected columns were published as *Along the Towpath: A Journalist Rediscovers the Ohio & Erie Canal* by the University of Akron Press in 2003. The book presented the chapter and verse of the grassroots effort, with stories about Boy Scouts earning merit badges by clearing and cleaning sections of the towpath, garden clubs building and installing bluebird boxes along the trail, and, of course, the painstaking efforts to finance and build the *St. Helena II,* first launched in June 1970, retired in 1988, and replaced by a ferro-concrete replica, the *St. Helena III.*

In 2003, Congressman Regula credited Simpson with doing a good job of capturing his dream for the canal: "Al's articles were a key element. He told the story that got the public interested."[25] Regula's own efforts were recognized in October 2003 when the Stark County Park District renamed that county's portion of the Ohio & Erie Canal Towpath Trail in his honor. Each of eight trailheads along the Congressman Ralph Regula Towpath Trail is marked with a bronze plaque, including one in his hometown, Navarre, bearing an inscription acknowledging his forty years of work on behalf of "the preservation and development of this valuable natural, historical and recreational resource for the citizens of Stark County and future generations."

While the Montgomerys focused on their hometown of Coshocton, and Regula and Simpson rallied canal supporters in Stark County, Ted H. Findley was rekindling passion for canal history throughout the state. His work earned him a place in the American Canal Society's Canal Buffs Hall of Fame. In its biography of Findley, the American Canal Society credits him, Lew Richardson of Cleveland, and Ted Dettling of Akron with spearheading formation of the Canal Society of Ohio in October 1961. Findley served as its first president until fall 1968, and was the group's historian until his death in 1969.

Summing up the Canal Society of Ohio's objective of preserving and maintaining artifacts of Ohio's canal systems, Findley told members at the 1965 annual meeting, "Our job is to bring the canal history to the front. We hope someday to have a museum where we can store and exhibit the tremendous amount of material we are accumulating. We just got started 20 years too late." In his memorial tribute to Findley, "The Passing of a 'Canawler,'" Simpson wrote, "His interest in everything associated with Ohio's canals led him to assemble possibly the largest private collection of canal memorabilia of any citizen of the state. . . . All who knew Ted, including this writer, will miss him and his willingness to share his vast knowledge of the canals."[26]

Looking back in 2005, David Lieberth of Akron suggested Findley and other canal enthusiasts came along just in time. Lieberth was barely out of his teens when his family doctor, Ernest L. Hackney, an early member of the Canal Society of Ohio, took him hiking on the towpath in the New Philadelphia area in the 1960s. Lieberth, then a University of Akron sophomore, met Findley through Hackney and got the idea of creating an oral history on the canal by bringing the canal buffs into a radio studio and just letting them talk about their experiences while the tape recorder was running.

On hand for the initial session, Lieberth recalled, were Findley, Hackney, Frank Trevorrow of Oberlin, and James Dillow Robinson of Independence. The result was five hours of memories that became the basis of a fifteen-part radio series titled *Along the Ohio Canals*, which aired on the university's station WAUP-FM during the summer of 1966. "Walking the canals was their thing," Lieberth said of the canal enthusiasts, who, he was pleased to discover, were eager to tell their stories.[27]

Lieberth noted how important were the canal-era memorabilia they unearthed and preserved, many of which would have otherwise wound up on the trash heap. The archival libraries of the University of Akron and Wright State University are home to many of these artifacts, including the Canal Society of Ohio's newsletter and *Towpaths*, an illustrated quarterly of historical canal information, as well as canal history collections of books, maps, photographs, and other memorabilia.

Clyde E. Gainey provided the spark that rekindled interest in the canal in Canal Fulton. Gainey, who died in 1987 at age ninety-two, established and operated the village's Old Canal Days Museum, played a key role in getting the *St. Helena II* canal boat completed in 1969, and was a charter member of the Canal Fulton Heritage Society. Some called him "Mr. Canal Fulton." When he opened the tiny museum in 1966, it was an outgrowth of canal memorabilia he had collected and displayed two years earlier during Canal Fulton's sesquicentennial. For thirteen years, the museum sat behind Gainey's 1842 house off Canal Street in a two-story summer kitchen/coach house and typically attracted seven to ten thousand visitors a summer. In 1979, the twelve-foot-by-sixteen-foot building was moved next to what is now the Heritage House Museum off Erie Street and Route 93 at the entrance to Canal Fulton Community Park along the canal. Gainey called the museum his "Memories of Yesterday House." He had strong ties to Canal Fulton. He was the village clerk from 1929 to 1956, was clerk-treasurer of the school board, worked twenty-five years as an engineer for Stark County, and served as a radio dispatcher for the Canal Fulton Fire Department for fifty years. He was also involved in the Akron-Canton Airport, which he served briefly as interim director.[28]

At about the same time Gainey was running his one-man museum, others were calling for building a canal boat. The *St. Helena II* was the nation's first historically accurate canal-boat replica. Construction of this symbol of renewed interest in the canal took nearly four years and was accomplished mostly by volunteers, many from the Louisville Sportsman's Club, and a few professionals who were paid with funds donated for the project.[29]

IBM retiree Jim Guest, vice president of the Louisville Sportsman's Club when "Simpson and Regula came in to pitch the project" in 1967, had no previous interest in the canal. Guest savors memories of working Tuesday evenings and Saturdays, fueled by beer and sandwiches, with "men of unbelievable skill and knowledge" whom he called godfathers of the sixty-five-foot boat. He included among them the designer, Carroll Gantz, now of Seabrook, South Carolina, and Richard Mohler of North Canton. Guest later became an active early member of the Ohio & Erie Canal Corridor Coalition.[30]

The Sportsman's Club began construction of the *St. Helena II* in May 1967 with a crew supervised by Ray Preece. Gantz, a Hoover Company engineer, drew plans from a model at the Stark County Historical Society. The following spring, Maryland-based consultant James B. Richardson came to Canal Fulton and offered technical advice on building the boat with white oak, like the original canal boats. In late 1968, the Louisville Sportsman's Club turned the project over to the Stark County Historical

Carroll Gantz instructs the volunteers building the *St. Helena II* as the boat takes shape (photo by Clyde Gainey, courtesy of Jim Guest).

Society. In early 1969, work continued on the boat, with caulking it and treating it with linseed oil. The boat, built upside down, was righted with two sixty-ton cranes. It then needed decking and cabins before it could be launched in June 1970.

Money for Canal Fulton's boatbuilding came from the Stark County Historical Society, the Timken Company Charitable Trust, the Hoover Foundation, the Stark County Foundation, and countless volunteer donations. The boat was sixty-five feet long and thirteen feet wide; it weighed twenty-two tons and drew eighteen inches of water and was pulled by two Percheron horses. It could carry sixty passengers per trip and carried about twelve hundred passengers a season on the two- and one-half-mile trips. Improvements were also made to the canal from Canal Fulton south to Lock Four Park in Lawrence Township. The wooden *St. Helena II*, suffering from dry rot, was replaced in 1989 by the ferro-concrete-hulled *St. Helena III*.

In 1968, during the *St. Helena II* construction, the Canal Fulton Heritage Society was formed. It has organized community canal festivals, offered house-museum tours, published a historic newsletter, and compiled oral histories. This work helped spawn additional community interest in the canal. In 1982, the Canal Fulton Heritage Society, then headed by Ann McLaughlin (now Henman), pushed to get a turn-of-the-twentieth-century flavor to downtown Canal Fulton.

"Our buildings weren't torn down, and our canal wasn't paved over," said McLaughin, who also served as chair of the village's Historic Zoning Commission. "We'd like to promote Canal Fulton as a working canal town, not a fake. We'd like to show our visitors what a working nineteenth-century town is like. We're not re-creating history or trying to make it look prettier. We think it is a good idea economically for the village." About 25 percent of the village's downtown structures are on the National Register of Historic Places. "Nothing was ever torn down," said McLaughlin. She noted that Canal Fulton had seventeen saloons that once served boaters on the canal and nearby miners.[31]

Thirty-two miles north of Canal Fulton, in the heart of the Cuyahoga River Valley, another village had begun also to preserve its heritage. The historic Village of Peninsula, surrounded now by Cuyahoga Valley National Park, prospered with the 1827 opening of the Ohio & Erie Canal. It retains much of its nineteenth-century charm with its well-preserved buildings of different architectural styles. Peninsula once boomed as a shipping center and a town of boatbuilding, saloons, mills, railroads, and quarries. It once had fourteen saloons and five hotels to serve boisterous canal workers and travelers. As with many canal towns, much of its commercial activity disappeared after the 1913 flood. Many families lived in the area for generations. Roads improved, and just as the train had replaced the canal, the automobile replaced the train. Peninsula, between Cleveland and Akron, was far enough from both to be protected from rampant development, and there were citizens of the village interested in keeping it from significant change.

A significant threat to the area occurred in the late 1930s when state and federal officials were exploring the concept of developing a lake in the Cuyahoga Valley. Robert Bordner, a reporter for the *Cleveland Press,* took up the cause. Ron Cockrell, National Park Service senior research historian, credits Bordner's leadership in pointing out "the havoc the project would wreak on the valley." Specifically, the lake would have inundated all of Jaite and Boston Mills and two-thirds of Peninsula and eradicated many of the valley's farms, he contended in February 1937. "Although economics, not Bordner's efforts, killed the grandiose lake project, a preservation ethic flickered to life and was espoused through Bordner's columns."[32]

In 1940, Bordner founded a small preservation group, the Cuyahoga Valley Association, which functioned for about a year. In 1962, he was among the founders of the Peninsula Valley Heritage Association, which by the end of 1971 would change its name to Cuyahoga Valley Association.[33]

Another major preservation fight swirled around Peninsula's historic Bronson Memorial Church, a white-framed structure measuring thirty-six by twenty-four feet and the village's first church. Built in 1839, it was at the center of a public battle in 1961–64 and spawned grassroots groups that later played key roles in pushing for creation of a federal park in the Cuyahoga Valley. One such group, the Bronson Restoration Committee, grew from the efforts to keep the church in Peninsula. The committee started raising funds locally in 1958 to fix up the church.

The church, built in the Greek Revival style favored by Western Reserve early settlers from Connecticut, was founded as the Bethel Protestant Episcopal Church. The congregation was formed in 1835 and chartered by the Ohio Legislature in 1837, the same year Peninsula became a village. The church, which would also serve as the village's first library, was built at a cost of $1,000. Hermon (also spelled Herman) Bronson, a veteran of the War of 1812, who had moved to northern Summit County in 1824, spearheaded the effort. (Before the church's construction, religious services were held in the family's log cabin.)

Bronson was credited with trying to introduce moral and religious tactics among the unruly canal boatmen. Hermon Bronson's brother, Abra-

The efforts by this group to save the Bronson church from being moved helped to forge a dynamic preservation group in Peninsula (Peninsula Library and Historical Society Photo Collection).

ham, was the first minister in Peninsula. The church had thirty members in 1842. It was remodeled in the Carpenter Gothic style in 1889 by Ruth Ranney Bronson, the widow of Hermon's son, Hiram. It was renamed from the Bethel Episcopal Church that year to honor founder Hermon Bronson.[34]

In 1939, the congregation numbered two and had only grown to eleven by the end of World War II. Regular church services were discontinued in 1954. However, the church, off State Route 303 east of Riverview Road, was open for special occasions, including weddings. Because the church required so much repair, the Episcopal Diocese of Ohio and the Cleveland-based Western Reserve Historical Society advanced a proposal to move the tiny church to nearby Hale Farm and Village in Bath Township, where it would be restored and preserved. The thought of losing the historic church crystallized strong community opposition. People wanted it to remain where it was.

Led by Lily and Franklin Fleder, who moved to Peninsula in 1957, the community rallied to keep the church in Peninsula. "Peninsula itself was a pioneer village," Lily Fleder said in a 1961 letter to church officials. "The building is not threatened by highway, housing developments, community

Magnolia and the Sandy & Beaver Canal

RUSS MUSARRA

Just as Akron was created because of the Ohio & Erie Canal, Magnolia, a village of slightly less than a thousand residents at the southeast corner of Stark County, owes its origins to the Sandy & Beaver Canal, which linked the Ohio & Erie Canal at Bolivar with Glasgow, Pennsylvania, more than seventy-three miles away on the Ohio River.

Magnolia, which occupies less than one square mile, mostly in Stark County but spilling over into Carroll County, was platted in 1834 by Richard Elson, John Smith, and John Whitacre, the same year Elson built a mill that is still in operation and the same year construction began on the Sandy & Beaver. Elson, who came to Ohio from Brooke County, Virginia (now West Virginia), knew the canal was coming when in 1830 he bought and homesteaded large tracts of land in what would become Magnolia. Elson's Mill produced twenty-five barrels of flour a day at its start. Elson also raised merino sheep, operated a woolen mill, manufactured barrels, and was an abolitionist who sheltered runaway slaves on their journeys to freedom in Canada.[1]

To be sure, Magnolia is more than the Elson mill and the Sandy & Beaver Canal. It was the birthplace of labor leader I. W. Abel (1908–1987), who headed the United Steelworkers of America from 1965 to 1977 and served a term as a vice president of the AFL-CIO.

But it is the mill people see when they come to Magnolia, and it is the canal they have never stopped talking and caring about, even though it operated only four years. Although Elson's Mill prospered, the Sandy & Beaver was a disaster. Economic problems delayed its completion until 1848, and the canal's middle section fell into disrepair, making travel along the entire length impossible. Operations ceased after the Cold Run Reservoir Dam broke in the spring of 1852, damaging property around New Lisbon, destroying a large section of the canal, and putting Sandy & Beaver Canal Company out of business.

The mill began operating in 1834 (*Stark County Atlas*, 1875).

Nearly a century after the canal closed, writer Grace Goulder Izant observed, "The real reason the Sandy-Beaver lives is the romance and legend that flourish along its banks. A magic spell has been thrown over the old canal. No boat has passed over its water since 1852. Yet the canal is still a very real part of the Ohio scene. Many . . . have devoted their days to collecting data about it, tramping the length of it, fascinated with the story of its building, a heartbreak tale of setbacks, disappointments and ultimate failure."[2] That was in 1948. Today the memory of the canal is alive and well with its own advocacy organization, the Sandy & Beaver Canal Association, that preserves the memory and provides information on its own Web site.

The Elson mill is now owned by Stark County Park District and continues to operate as a mill and feed store (photo by Ed Metzger).

The Elson mill continued as a family business for four generations. A. R. (Augustus), Richard's only son, took over the mill in 1847 "after working for his father one year" and set out "to make this mill the best producer of flour in the country." He began a series of milling equipment upgrades that continued into the twentieth century. Over the years, the mill has been powered by water, steam (which proved unsatisfactory), water again, and electricity. At one time, the mill provided enough electricity for the whole town. One of A. R. Elson's customers, a wholesale baker in Fenton, New Jersey, purchased four to five train cars of flour each month. Using Elson flour, the baker won gold medals at the 1876 Centennial Exposition in Philadelphia and the 1900 Paris Exposition. A. R. Elson "bought the right of way and gave it to the (Chicago & Pittsburgh Railroad) company for the valley railroad branch to Magnolia. A train track ran to the back of the mill." He also gave land for the village park and moved the train station from its original location to a spot at the back of the mill.[3]

In 1904, A. R. Elson's three sons, Frank, Richard, and John, took over the business, which had been incorporated as the A. R. Elson Company in 1898. The company produced flour made from the surrounding area's soft red winter wheat and milled lumber used to build the majority of the early homes within twenty-five miles of Magnolia. A Christmas specialty was Magnolia Buckwheat, and Richard "Mack" Elson developed a grass seed recipe for sandy soil that became another specialty of the mill. Other products included feed for goats, deer, lambs, llama, alpaca, swine, and pigeons; corn meal; and cattle feed.

Mack Elson's son, Augustus "Gus" R. II, represents the fourth generation to head the business. He and his wife, JoLane née Brothers, also own the Elson Inn, a bed and breakfast they opened in 1999 in the eleven-room Victorian Italianate home built in 1879 by his grandfather.

In October 2004, the Elsons sold the mill, the section of the canal behind it, and Lock 24 to the Stark County Park District.[4] The district's goals are to keep the mill running and expand interpretive programming to showcase the role of the mill and the canal in the development of Stark County. Park officials say they enjoy a cordial relationship with the Elsons, who have given the park district the right of first refusal should they decide to sell the inn.[5]

indifference nor wrecking ball. There have been at least a half dozen attempts to restore this legally fettered building."[35] The church's deed was held by the Episcopal Diocese of Ohio after the church was abandoned. Lily Fleder contacted Helen Duprey Bullock of the National Trust for Historic Preservation in Washington, D.C., for help. Bullock came to Peninsula and Hudson in 1962 and recommended that Peninsula work to preserve its remaining features along the Ohio & Erie Canal and Hudson work to save its New England–village look. She suggested each community form a grassroots preservation group.

Fleder received additional help when Robert L. Hunker, an architectural and interior designer, moved his offices from Akron to Peninsula. Hunker hosted a dinner party in Bullock's honor for preservationists from Peninsula and from Hudson, where residents were fighting to save a historic bank building. That led to the formation of both the Peninsula Valley Heritage Association and the Hudson Historical Association, spawning new interest in historical preservation in northern Summit County. The Peninsula Library and Historical Society supported the effort and praised Fleder's efforts. Of her, its board said, "Where all others despaired, Lily lit fires, fed them, and kept them burning."[36]

In 1963, the community embarked on a campaign to raise $20,000 for the project. The Summit County commissioners and the Summit County Historical Society also supported the effort. According to Fleder, the bishop of the Episcopal Church in Ohio, Nelson M. Burroughs, granted the local committee more time for fund-raising. But the community knew that the church could still be moved if the local effort failed. More than five hundred individuals contributed to the campaign, directed by Peninsula's Robert P. Bishop. Peninsula Valley Heritage Association also sup-

"We are happy to put the Historic Elson Mill in their hands," Gus Elson said, at a public gathering when the agreement was announced. "It has been listed on the National Register [of Historic Places] since 1999 and will become a learning tool for the young and old, as well as a source of recreation. Tourists visiting us by the busload for years will continue to be able to view the workings of a mill in a canal town."

NOTES

1. JoLane Brothers Elson, interview, Sept. 14, 2004.

2. Grace Goulder Izant, "Ohio Scenes and Citizens," *Cleveland Plain Dealer*, May 2, 1948.

3. Elson interview.

4. Connie Rubin, Stark County Park District, interview, Aug. 25, 2005.

5. Rubin and Elson interviews.

ported the effort to keep the church in Peninsula.[37] Among its founders was the late John Seiberling, a longtime congressman and the man behind what became Cuyahoga Valley National Park.

Work on the church began in 1964 and was completed in 1968. This included a new foundation, roof, and belfry; numerous repairs; and the addition of central heat and electricity. In 1965, the Summit County Historical Society acquired the church from the diocese. Fleder recalled, "It was an important project and something that had to be done." To keep the building managed locally and better cared for, the Summit County Historical Society deeded it to the Peninsula-based Robert L. Hunker Historic Preservation Foundation in 2003. The village "has and always has had a good group of people aware of Peninsula's history and our canal history," Fleder also noted. The village had old-timers who recalled the canal and its history and there was still evidence of the canal, mills, and quarries in Peninsula.

The battle over the Bronson Memorial Church came at a time when sleepy Peninsula was starting to change. Ronald Clark, in a 1966 *Akron Beacon Journal* article, said that the new Peninsula with "its rural, nostalgic character" was "dedicated to preserving the best of the past for the future." Some changes occurred in the 1960s when an influx of artists, writers, and musicians arrived in Peninsula.[38]

Although Peninsula has attracted writers and artists since 1910, according to Randy Bergdorf, director of the Peninsula Library and Historical Society, it is also a community with strong family histories.[39] The Bronson Church preservation was only one of several issues that galvanized the Peninsula residents in the 1960s. They also organized strongly in opposition to the Ohio Department of Transportation plans to route Interstate 271 through the village, to building the Coliseum in nearby Richfield Township, and to the routing of electric lines through Peninsula and the Cuyahoga Valley.

Some Peninsula historical features were open to the public in 1963, when the Akron Metropolitan Park District opened the seventy-five-acre Deep Lock Quarry Metro Park. The park, off Riverview Road, includes the deepest lock on the Ohio & Erie Canal and a sandstone quarry dating to the nineteenth century. Peninsula's second quarry, on Route 303, opened as a community swimming site in 1956.

Robert Hunker played a key role in Peninsula's rediscovery of its past; he purchased an old barn at State Route 303 and Riverview Road for his offices. He also bought the Grand Army of the Republic Hall when he learned it was to be demolished and has restored it. He then renovated the

Wood Store and other Peninsula buildings, including the rail depot that was moved to Peninsula from Boston.

In 1974, Peninsula became the fourth Ohio village to be added to the National Register of Historic Places by the U.S. Department of the Interior. The designation was largely derived from the two years of work by Hunker and Eric Johannesen of Cleveland's Western Reserve Historical Society. That preservation effort was driven, in part, by advice from then–U.S. Rep. John Seiberling to block the Ohio Department of Transportation's plans to widen State Route 303 in the village. The village, with its seven hundred residents, was designated because it was a key canal and mercantile town in northern Ohio in the mid-nineteenth century.[40]

Grassroots efforts in the early 1960s also started to look beyond Peninsula to the Cuyahoga Valley. In 1962, the Peninsula Heritage Association became the Peninsula Valley Heritage Association. Its focus was largely to preserve the scenic and historical beauty in the Cuyahoga Valley; within a year, it had 130 members. Its success in keeping the Bronson church in Peninsula convinced members to tackle other preservation issues in the Cuyahoga Valley. In 1972, the Peninsula Valley Heritage Association was renamed Cuyahoga Valley Association (CVA).

Henry Saalfield, the organization president in 1971, supported the move to transform the group into the Cuyahoga Valley Association "to include memberships of many diversified and interested groups."[41] This came at a time when Congress was first considering legislation to create a national park in the Cuyahoga Valley, and support of the proposal was among the new association's goals, in line with its stated purpose of protecting and preserving the valley's open landscape and fighting encroachments.

Saalfield asked fellow board member James S. Jackson, who had only recently retired from the *Akron Beacon Journal*, to lead the Cuyahoga Valley Association. National Park Service historian Ron Cockrell noted that "it proved to be an ideal choice. . . . Jackson used his considerable journalistic talent to produce a newsletter . . . *The Voice of the Cuyahoga Valley Association*. Through *The Voice*, which enjoyed a wide distribution, Jackson effectively communicated the issue of preserving the valley by establishing a park. It was a useful tool for enlisting support and new CVA members. Jackson used his extensive professional contacts to spread CVA's cause throughout Ohio and to the national media as well. In his efforts, Jackson had the indefatigable assistance of his wife, Margot."[42]

Margot Jackson, a librarian who worked briefly for the *Beacon Journal* in the mid-1930s, was coauthor with her husband of two books on the history of the canal and the valley. They wrote *The Colorful Era of the*

Ohio Canal: Cleveland to Akron, 1827–1913 for the canal's sesquicentennial commission in 1977, and they revised it for reprinting by the Summit County Historical Society four years later. The booklet is filled with details, maps, drawings, and photos. The Jacksons' *Cuyahoga Valley Tales* is an anecdotal short course about places and some of the people who have populated them since prehistoric times, including two chapters about the canal.

In 1974, the Cuyahoga Valley Association helped create the Cuyahoga Valley Park Federation. It was designed to bring together eighty-plus local groups pushing for a federal park. Cuyahoga Valley National Recreation Area (now Cuyahoga Valley National Park) was born in the final days of the 93d Congress, with President Gerald Ford's signature, on December 27, 1974. Footnotes to its creation include the fact that the initial legislation, introduced in April 1971, included the canal in its name. The bill, H.R. 7673, was to establish the "Ohio Canal and Cuyahoga Valley National Historical Park and Recreation Area." That bill, sponsored by the late John Seiberling (D-Akron), Frank Bow (R-Canton), Charles A. Vanik (D-Cleveland), and sixteen other congressmen, failed. Seiberling, Vanik, and Ralph Regula (R-Navarre), elected in 1972 to replace Bow, who had died, tried again in 1973, reintroducing the bill, H.R. 7077, to establish Cuyahoga Valley National Historical Park and Recreation Area. It was hailed as the "first major national urban park in the Middle West."[43] The canal wasn't part of the park's name, but it figured prominently in the minds of those who would mold and shape its future.

Vanik's support was no surprise. He had proposed establishing a national park along the canal from Cleveland's outskirts to Akron. Al Simpson wrote in his May 1, 1966, column: "Readers may recall that two years ago this month Ralph Regula of Navarre and I . . . proposed substantially what is being sought now except that we suggested the possibility of a state-long parkway, similar to the Chesapeake & Ohio Park, which would serve people in communities all along the old canal route from Cleveland to Portsmouth."[44]

Once the park was authorized by Congress, Regula and Seiberling turned their attention to the canal corridor, Seiberling recalled in 2003. "Ralph became the leading person in that," said Seiberling, who retired from Congress in 1986. "If anybody deserves credit, it's Ralph Regula. His support was crucial, obviously, since [part of] it was in his district."[45]

Another force for preserving canal history came in the form of the many films and publications of independent filmmaker Jack E. Gieck of Akron. Gieck became interested in the canal when he first came to Akron in 1947 as an engineer for Firestone and discovered the waterway's remnants. In 1950, he followed the canal from Cleveland to Portsmouth and produced a 16-mm film titled *The Ohio Canal.* That was just the beginning of an interest that continues to occupy his time. In 1951, he produced a slide show that a number of groups used for years to stimulate interest in canal preservation.[46]

In 1978, Gieck, the former Canal Society of Ohio president, traveled more than thirty-three hundred miles researching Ohio's canal system and taking photos for *Ohio's Canal Era,* which earned him the silver medal in that year's International Film and Television Festival in New York City. Gieck used new images along with vintage photos, engravings, and paintings to tell his story. "Some of the photographs are almost as old as photography itself, going back into the 1840s! I tried whenever possible to locate the spot where the photographer had stood so that I could shoot exactly the same scene as it appears today."[47] Gieck reproduced many vintage photos, especially those collected by two amateur photographers, Akron's Ted Dettling, of the Canal Society of Ohio, and Carl Pockrandt, who headed the Summit County Historical Society for more than twenty years. Gieck's labors also resulted in the popular book *A Photo Album of Ohio's Canal Era, 1825–1913.*[48] Gieck's 2008 book, *Early Akron's Industrial Valley: A History of the Cascade Locks,* contributes to the understanding of that short but complex section of canal.

Local history and historical preservation are important and can make a big difference in our communities, as proven in Coshocton, Zoar, Canal Fulton, and Peninsula. Historic preservation is generally seen as a means to improve or maintain a community's quality of life. It provides cultural and aesthetic value to communities. But it is not an end in itself. It reminds us of where we have come from and how we got where we are today. It promotes an identity and celebrates our rich historical heritage, our roots.

Historic buildings are an important element in our flow of culture. They provide a link to the past and a sense of our place in time. They represent the tangible roots of our communal memories. Preserving historical buildings keeps alive the connections between the past, present, and future. Preservation encourages neighborhood revitalization, which improves the look and the conditions in a neighborhood. It can create jobs and help develop tourism.

However, historic preservation must be done with a solid economic plan to back it up. Communities cannot invest time and money into saving a building or an old canal without having a strategy in place to later manage the resource. Preservation needs to focus on what makes a community different, interesting, or special. It is important that we preserve a broad range of resources so our full history can be told through what we save. Preservation of our history enables us to know where we have been and also where we want to go as a community or a region.

NOTES

1. Lorle Porter, *Roscoe Generations—Regeneration* (Coshocton: Roscoe Village Foundation, 1991), 276–77.

2. Ibid., 278–80.

3. Ibid., 302.

4. Mary Strassmeyer, "Millionaire Puts Town Back on Map," *Cleveland Plain Dealer,* May 19, 1974.

5. Roscoe Village media kit.

6. Porter, *Roscoe Generations,* 301, 287.

7. Ibid., 290–92.

8. Ibid., 400.

9. Strassmeyer, "Millionaire Puts Town Back on Map."

10. Ibid.

11. Porter, *Roscoe Generations,* 297.

12. Ibid., 299.

13. Ohio Historical Society, *Zoar: An Ohio Experiment in Communalism* (Columbus: Ohio Historical Society, 1997), 7, 11.

14. Kathleen M. Fernandez, *A Singular People: Images of Zoar* (Kent: Kent State Univ. Press, 2003), 11.

15. Ohio Historical Society, *Zoar,* 37–38.

16. Fernandez, *A Singular People,* 13–15.

17. Ibid., 16–17.

18. Ibid.

19. Ibid., 18.

20. Ibid.

21. Kathleen M. Fernandez, interview by Bob Downing, May 2004.

22. Al Simpson, *Along the Towpath: A Journalist Rediscovers the Ohio & Erie Canal* (Akron: University of Akron Libraries, 2003), 1, vii.

23. Ibid., 1.

24. Ibid., 6.

25. Ralph Regula, interview by Russ Musarra, Sept. 10, 2003.

26. Simpson, *Along the Towpath,* 210.

27. David Lieberth, interview by Russ Musarra, Oct. 20, 2005.

28. Obituary of Clyde E. Gainey, "Clyde E. Gainey, 92, 'Mr. Canal Fulton,'" *Akron Beacon Journal,* Sept. 18, 1987.

29. Simpson, *Along the Towpath,* 183, 207.

30. Jim Guest, interview by Russ Musarra, May 6, 2005.

31. Ann Henman, interview by Bob Downing, Aug. 2004.

32. Ronald Cockrell, *A Green Shrouded Miracle: The Administrative History of Cuyahoga Valley National Park* (Omaha, National Park Service, United States Department of the Interior, 1992), 34–35.

33. Ibid.

34. Bronson Memorial Church, 1839 and 1889, pamphlet, Bronson file, Peninsula Library and Historical Society (Peninsula).

35. "Debate Fate of Old Church," *Akron Beacon Journal*, Nov. 10, 1961.

36. Grace Goulder, "Belfry Battle in Peninsula," *Cleveland Plain Dealer*, May 27, 1962, Sunday magazine, 4.

37. Lily Fleder, interview by Bob Downing, July 2004.

38. Ronald Clark, "Peninsula Preserves the Past for the Future," *Akron Beacon Journal*, Oct. 9, 1966, Sunday magazine, 14–15.

39. Randy Bergdorf, interview by Bob Downing, July 2004.

40. David Hess and Bob von Sternberg, "U.S. Tags Peninsula as Historic Village," *Akron Beacon Journal*, Aug. 29, 1974.

41. Cockrell, *Green Shrouded Miracle*, 36.

42. Ibid.

43. Ibid, 96.

44. Simpson, *Along the Towpath*, 94.

45. John Seiberling, interview by Peg Bobel and Lynn Metzger, Apr. 23, 2003. Seiberling passed away August 2, 2008.

46. Jack Gieck, interview by Russ Musarra, Aug. 24, 2005.

47. Jack Gieck, marketing information for "Ohio's Canal Era" film strip. Cinemark Productions, Akron, Gieck's personal files, Dec. 12, 1978.

48. Jack Gieck interview.

Chapter 15

Reading the Past

LYNN METZGER

The concept of a cultural landscape proposes a unifying theme to suggest that people do not passively inhabit a place, but that their imprint survives in the archaeological record, in oral histories, and in place names as well as in the economies and social systems of present day groups.[1] To read the cultural landscape of the past is to draw on the research and skills of different disciplines. For the Ohio & Erie Canal, there are many written records about the construction, economic contribution, and demise of the canal system. There is far less written about the people who lived the canal life, traveled, worked, or lived in the canal towns. Another way to read the past and better understand the lives of its people is to study the materials they used and made. Often these materials are artifacts, remnants, pieces of objects used in everyday life. Whether broken and battered pottery, old bricks, broken pipes, or pieces of imported china, they all provide clues to the life stories of those who used them. Research using archaeological methods studies these clues to the past and combines them with the written record to travel back in time, make the remnants whole, and provide many details of everyday life. Although this tour of the past focuses on the canal era, it is important to remember this region was home to native peoples long before European settlers displaced them; these new settlers often obliterated their imprint on the cultural landscape.

Archaeology is often connected with an excavation, in which the cultural materials are found by digging. Artifacts from the prehistoric time include such things as arrowheads, tools, and campsites. In northeast Ohio, the historic archaeological period begins in about 1650. Artifacts from this period include materials left by explorers, missionaries, soldiers, and settlers; these chronicle the progression of settlements, economies, and peoples. Many clues to the past can be clearly read in historic structures, or features, and artifacts scattered across the landscape, but other signs are discovered through systematic archaeological excavation. Along the old Ohio & Erie Canal and towpath, now the National Heritage Canalway, many features and artifacts provide evidence of the life during the canal era. Remnants of canal lift locks, wasteways, aqueducts, and bridges all help to tell the story. These remains, made and modified by humans, now form the core of the Canalway, just as in 1827 they were the core of a new transportation system that opened Ohio to the wider world.

Canal area archaeology is best considered at two levels: the actual canal structures and foundations that dot the landscape along the prism of the old canal and towpath and the everyday-life artifacts found in excavation. The people who lived and worked on or near the canal left behind many traces of their lives and activities in the structures they built and the objects they discarded. By comparing the archaeological evidence with the historic written record, much can be learned about canal life.

This is an armchair journey into the past along the Towpath Trail. The areas that provide the most archaeological and historical evidence are the locations along the canal where there were concentrations of human activity, places such as lift locks, mills, canal basins, and boat-repair sites or drydocks. Because it took ninety minutes to go through a lock, folks frequently got off the boats to shop for supplies, eat, drink, and visit. Most canal towns became hubs of commercial activity because of the locks. Cleveland, at the mouth of the Cuyahoga River and on Lake Erie, developed as a major shipping port during the heyday of the Ohio & Erie Canal.

Most significant for historic archeology are the many artifacts people left behind, and their placements. For example, are they found around an old house site? Are they from the household dump? What is known about the period the artifacts were made, used, tossed aside? Along the Ohio & Erie Canal there are some common features among the artifacts that help show how the canal worked as an integrated transportation system, from Cleveland to Portsmouth. There are also clear differences in sites along the way. Akron was a major grain-shipping port, as were Canal Fulton and Massillon, but later, Clinton, Canal Fulton, and Massillon began to ship coal from the many small mines in the hills bordering the Tuscarawas River Valley. Many sites along the canal south of Summit Lake still have evidence of that old coal trade.

View of Cuyahoga River bank area know as Irishtown Bend, circa 1885 (Cleveland Public Library Photograph Collection).

Most household sites contain remnants of broken clay pipes, evidence that the men often smoked small clay pipes, imported first from England, and later made locally. The immigrants often brought with them a few treasured pieces from their homelands, objects such as silver spoons, special pitchers, china cups and saucers, pieces that when broken or severely damaged were tossed aside, leaving clues about their lives for future researchers. Prosperous folk imported china from England, and there is later evidence that local pottery became popular.[2]

This journey begins along the towpath/canal in Cleveland, at the mouth of the Cuyahoga River, where some of the early immigrant Irish laborers settled, likely only a few of whom were canal builders. Most of those construction crews moved south as canal construction progressed, but on their heels were the laborers who worked the port and the canal shipping industry. They built their houses on land near the river, which was cheap because no one of means wanted to live near the river with its prevalence of disease. Irishtown Bend, added to the National Register of Historic Places in 1986, was such a living area. Since the structures no longer exist, much of our picture of the community comes from several archaeological excavations.

This distinct neighborhood began in the 1840s when unskilled Irish laborers built their houses on the banks overlooking a large bend in the Cuyahoga River, often called The Angle. The neighborhood remained largely first-generation Irish through the 1880s, then, for the next twenty years, as the Irish moved out they were replaced by immigrants from eastern Europe, mainly from Hungary. By 1900, many houses were gradually abandoned, and by 1910 over one-third of the residences had been demolished or were vacant. By 1952, only five vacant houses remained. Only a concrete construction garage, built on four lots in about 1954, disturbed what was later to become a historic archaeological district. The Cleveland Metropolitan Housing Authority purchased the properties by 1960 but did not use them for construction.[3]

Although the Irish community spilled over the borders of the historic archaeological district, the nineteenth-century boundaries were Riverbed Road (formerly West River Road), the Cuyahoga River, Erie Railroad coal docks to the east, Columbus Road to the south, and Franklin Avenue on the west. It is not clear whether the community west of Franklin Avenue was as dominated by Irish residents, as was Irishtown Bend, or if it was ever considered part of Irishtown Bend.[4]

The neighborhood was probably abandoned for several reasons. It was never considered healthy to live near the river because of the prevalence of malaria and cholera; this was compounded by a lack of safe drinking water and good sanitation. As the Irish and eastern European immigrants gained better paying jobs, they moved to better housing sites. Immigration from Europe virtually stopped during World War I, and the strict immigration and literacy laws that followed closed the nation's doors almost entirely. There was no longer a need for the Irishtown Bend minimal housing, so the area was abandoned, and nature took over.

When the Cleveland Museum of Natural History's archaeological research team began work at Irishtown Bend in the late 1980s, they found this important part of Cleveland's history largely intact, having been undisturbed for seventy years. This was unusual for an urban historic site because these are often buried under many layers of successive construction or filled in with material from another area.

The Cuyahoga River with bridge and the overgrown hillside of Irishtown Bend in the distance. There are no longer any houses on the Bend hillside (photo by Ed Metzger).

It is difficult to picture a neighborhood of small houses clinging to the steep hillside overlooking the Cuyahoga River and early industrial Cleveland. Today it is a bramble-covered bank, with considerable history covered with honeysuckle gone wild. However, using systematic, scientific excavation methods, the museum archaeological team folded back the layers of vegetation and provided a sketch of life in the second half of the nineteenth century.

The archaeological work was carried out between June 1987 and May 1989. Although many sites were tested, three households were excavated extensively: the John Conners property in 1987 and the Connley and Quinn properties in 1988. "Taken together, these three households reflect some degree of the variation in economic status and social position among mid- to late-nineteenth-century ethnic Irish residents. They range from a widow with no children (Connley) of working age to a relatively well paid Cleveland policeman (Quinn). John Conners stands in between these two extremes and was selected for investigation as being in many ways typical of a large number of Irish dock workers who lived in the neighborhood."[5]

The archaeological research provides a picture of small but substantial dwellings for the time. Quinn's was a frame house with a sandstone foundation, and the Conners site had a twenty-six-by-twenty-six-feet two-story frame house with a brick foundation. The artifacts retrieved in the excavation revealed some distinctions in both quantity and quality that note a variation in economic levels among the households. The archaeologists note these differences in both household artifacts and in the types and quantity of animal bones found on the properties.

> The relative wealth of the Quinn household, as compared to the Conners and Connley households, is especially apparent. The Quinn family, in the period 1880 to 1900, owned at least one complete *set* of dishes, whereas table ware from the other two households are all of differing patterns indicating that they were purchased as individual pieces from open stock (and probably as discontinued patterns). The Quinn assemblage also contains a wider variety of what at the time were more expensive decorated table wares, including one serving piece of imported English porcelain. There is both greater quantity and variety of modest luxury items in the Quinn property assemblage, including a silver plated tankard, glass "crystal" lamp prisms, and woman's semi-precious jewelry. Refuse from all three households includes a few items that predate the documented immigration of the family from Ireland. The quantity and cost of those items brought from the old country parallels the relative economic status of the three households soon after their arrival in Cleveland.[6]

Bowls and soup plates are also important artifacts at the Connley site, indicating that the family most often ate soups and stews, whereas there were more plates of different sizes at the Conners and Quinn sites. The Quinn site also had more cups and saucers, an important economic status indicator because tea and coffee were luxury items. Animal-bone remains are important indicators of economic status as well: "The Connley assemblage is clearly dominated by very inexpensive cuts of pork and beef, mainly shank roasts, shin cuts and stew meat." However, bone analysis on the Conners site indicates he was raising and butchering his own pigs. The Quinn site contained more bones that indicate expensive cuts of pork and beef. Chicken bones were also found there; chickens were used more for egg production than eating in the 1800s.[7]

The three sites all indicated there had been children living there, leaving behind marbles, ceramic doll parts, and cast lead soldiers. Inexpensive

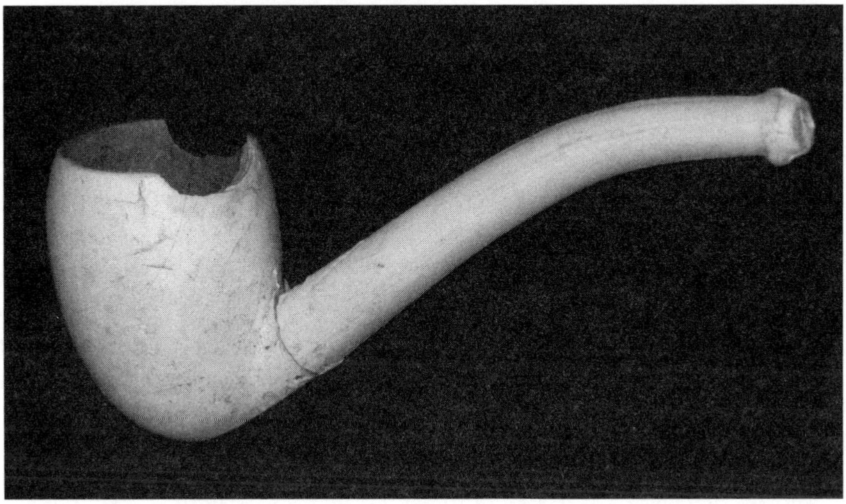

Clay pipes such as this were found in archaeological excavations all along the Ohio & Erie Canal (artifact in the collection of the Community Archaeology Program, University of Akron; photo by Ed Metzger).

ceramic tobacco pipes were found at all the home sites but on the widow Connley's property, where numerous pipes were found in the two small storage outbuildings.[8]

In contrast to excavated evidence at Irishtown Bend, two short watered sections of the old canal across the river can be seen. These will be preserved as part of Canal Basin Park, the northern terminus of the Ohio & Erie Canal Towpath Trail. When completed, the trail will connect at Harvard Road. The Harvard Road Trailhead begins the Cleveland Metroparks Ohio & Erie Canal Reservation, where trailside interpretation explains the industrial heritage of the Cuyahoga Valley through stations that illustrate the various systems, environmental, industrial, and transportation, that coexisted in the valley since the early 1800s. The interpretive stations explain the industrial history of the valley even as great blue herons fly by and folks fish in the canal. The peacefulness of the river and trail is broken by the sound of a train crossing on a bridge high above the valley. Here a side trail heads up the hill to the Leonard B. Krieger Canalway Center, on Whittlesey Way in Cuyahoga Heights. The interpretative format of the Krieger Center explains the varied historic uses and misuses of the Cuyahoga River and Valley. Easily reached by car, it merits repeated visits.

Continuing south, there are many remnant features of the canal system, such as wasteways and an aqueduct tucked under bridges and along the path of the old canal. The towpath follows sections of watered canal as it winds its way south, often along or near Canal Road. Across Rockside

Road is the northern edge of Cuyahoga Valley National Park, and about a mile south are the Cuyahoga Valley National Park's Canal Visitor Center and Lock 38. This center provides interpretation of the canal era with a model of a working lock and numerous historic photographs. In front of the center, the towpath passes Lock 38, a restored working lock, where national park staff present lock demonstrations.

The Canal Visitor Center at Lock 38 is an example of preservation and adaptive reuse of a historic canal-era structure. The National Park Service restored it in the late 1980s as part of the development of Cuyahoga Valley National Park. They brought its exterior back to its 1855–1900 appearance, and they refurbished its interior, making it a visitor facility with a small museum and offices. Interpretation of the building is based on preparatory archaeological and historic structure research the Park Service conducted in 1983 and 1984 to identify and substantiate the structure's 170-year history.[9]

Although local lore, oral histories, and written accounts often refer to the building at Lock 38 as a lockkeeper's house, there is no documented evidence that lockkeepers ever occupied the structure. The lock did not require a lockkeeper, as the boat's crews worked the locks themselves. Even though some ambiguity exists about the very early life of the structure, there is considerable information about it from the late 1820s. The owners are identified, and they left substantial amounts of material culture behind. The research suggests the structure was built sometime between 1818 and 1825 as a house (HS 125). The early occupants would have been among the first European Americans settling the valley. Jeffery J. Richner, the National Park Service archaeologist responsible for the excavation at the house, notes, "They would have faced economic isolation, lack of manufactured goods, and rudimentary transportation systems in a frontier setting. By 1825 they would have seen a huge influx of workers as canal construction began. They would have known the horrors of the malaria and smallpox contracted by many canal workers in 1826 and would have begun to participate in an economic awakening of the valley."[10]

The archaeological evidence indicates they participated in the new economy that brought new people, trade goods, and services to the area.[11] This is evident in the substantial assemblage of artifacts, such as china, pottery, pipes, and bottles. Excavations such as were conducted here and at Irishtown Bend fold back the past inch by inch, exposing different time periods as reflected in the artifacts that can be identified and dated. Even in the 1820s, china, pottery, bottles, and pipes were usually marked with the manufacturing company's name or logo or had stylistic characteristics that provide evidence for identification.

Of the assemblage excavated at the center, Richner notes, "The late 1820s occupants of the house ate their meals from dark blue transfer printed Staffordshire whiteware vessels which depicted actual scenes of the Eastern United States, France, and England. Many of the designs on these vessels were copies of carefully crafted works of art. . . . The residents probably attempted to ameliorate their health problems with patent medicines such as 'Turlington's Balsom of Life.'"[12]

The canal-side residence, also a tavern, was, like the canal, always affected by the larger national boom-or-bust economic cycles. By 1835, John Rowan had lived in the structure and operated a store and tavern for about two years, when he lost it in a sheriff's sale. By 1840, Moses Gleason had purchased the property, and the Gleason family owned it for sixty-eight years, through the canal's success and decline. While continuing to operate the tavern and live in the structure, Gleason invested money in repairs and additions; then he sold it to his son Edmond in 1843. The discarded ceramic assemblage of the time included patterns with names like "Moral Maxims," "Clyde Scenery," and "Picturesque Views."[13]

The record shows that Edmond operated the tavern business into the early 1850s and probably served travelers from both the canal and nearby Canal Road. "Good meals of steaks and hams would have been served along with the requisite drinks of the day. Evidence from the waste bones scattered throughout the site indicates that some cows and other animals were butchered on-site for use as food for the tavern." The archaeological remains also indicate that the customers ate from similar-looking blue printed dishes, featuring romantic patterns named "Siam," "Lucerne," and "Ontario Lake Scenery." The guests might have smoked tobacco from small clay pipes, long in fashion, as well as the newer large-bowl varieties.[14]

By 1850, the building had been expanded. The archaeological evidence included an expertly crafted foundation and new building techniques. Family economic stability, tied to the canal, began to slip in the 1860s, and in 1867 Edmond sold the tavern and residence to his brother Sardis, but he continued to live there until he died. The ceramics that were broken during his ownership changed as well, with plain and mold-decorated white surfaceware replacing the more colorful transfer wares of twenty years earlier. The archaeologists found more glass bottles and stoneware pottery pieces, indicating the introduction of new items during the Civil War.[15]

Sardis Gleason, a farmer, occupied the structure in the early 1870s, probably ending its days as a tavern. By 1875, he had died, and Harriett Gleason, widow of Edmond, occupied the building, marking the beginning of a long decline that included renters. "Discarded artifacts continued to accumulate around the structure, but at a lower rate than in previous years. Technological advances continued to appear, such as oil-burning lamps with fancy scalloped glass chimneys."[16] By 1908, the Gleason family no longer owned the building, and several twentieth-century owners later modified it, adding porches and heating and plumbing, contributing yet another layer of more modern archaeological evidence in and around the structure. The restored structure, now the Canal Visitor Center, is one of the few Cuyahoga Valley–area buildings to see both the initial Euroamerican settlement and the current Canalway. Directly in front of the Canal Visitor Center is Lock 38, which was restored in 1992 as a working demonstration lock.

South of the Canal Visitor Center, the towpath and watered canal curve through the area called the Pinery Narrows, a very narrow part of the valley and one of the most peaceful sections of the trail. One soon comes to the beautifully arched State Route 82 bridge that crosses above the valley. Here is the Brecksville feeder dam and the water control system that directs water into the canal. Below the dam is a favorite fishing spot along the river. A short connecter trail links to the historic Station Road Bridge, refurbished in 1992. The floor is made of wooden brick, wood laid cut-end up in a brick-type pattern. The bridge, built in 1881, was an important connector between both sides of the valley until the State Route 82 bridge was built. Now a footbridge only, it leads to the Station Road Bridge Trailhead and a train station for the Cuyahoga Valley Scenic Railroad.

Red Lock, or Lock 34, is located near Vaughn Road. Red Lock is easy to see from both the road and the adjacent parking lot. Hardy goldfish manage to live in the lock from year to year. Although the lock is the only canal structure in view here, this is the northern edge of a unique area, with an important past, both visible and hidden.

Across Vaughn Road is a ghost town, home of the former Jaite Paper Mill and company town. Jaite is now within the boundary of Cuyahoga Valley National Park and has quite a different past from both Irishtown Bend and the Canal Visitor Center. Jaite was a thriving company town, centered on the paper mill that operated there from 1906 until 1984. The company town's ghosts have been replaced by national park staff, now that the uniformly light yellow buildings on both Vaughn and Riverview Roads are the hub of Cuyahoga Valley National Park.

One hundred years ago, however, the houses and Jaite Paper Mill were the center of an economic and social community unique to the valley. The history of the mill and town are well documented, and the site of the old mill and the company houses provide visual evidence of the past. However, the most intriguing stories came from people who lived and worked in Jaite over a seventy-year period. In 2002 a University of Akron anthropology class interviewed about thirty former residents of the company town and mill employees, and they shared their memories of growing up in the five company duplexes on Riverview Road or the managers' houses on Vaughn Road. A number of interviewees and their families lived in the duplexes, which at times contained ten families with about thirty-five children. They described the large gardens in the backyards, the duplex outhouses, dances in the streets, and community turtle hunting with turtle soup feasts to follow. Movies were shown on Saturdays in the second story of the store (now the park administration offices). Shows were ten cents, with each person bringing a chair and food. Interviewees remembered that as children they delivered lunches to their parents at the mill, collected wild ramps and berries, and worked for local farmers. Many called the valley their playground, and even though times were often hard and money scarce, they loved their community. The voices of the people who lived in the community add a rich, authentic texture to the interpretation of the old company town.[17]

Founded by Charles Jaite in 1906, the mill used the canal for a few brief years before the 1913 flood destroyed it. Afterward, it still used small sections of the canal, for settling ponds rather than transportation. However, the canal's towpath was used extensively as a road, especially between Jaite and Boston. It was surfaced with cinders from the mill's furnaces and otherwise maintained as a one-lane road, used largely by employees.

The Jaite Paper Mill was the center of life in what was then a relatively isolated area of the valley. The mill's steam whistle framed daily activities; in an era when few had watches, it was their timepiece. The National Park Service restored company houses as offices; this stands in sharp contrast to the old mill. The Park Service purchased the mill in 1984, and it remained idle until it was demolished in 2006. In 1984, remaining mill operations were transferred to the Tecumseh Corrugated Box Company in Twinsburg, Ohio. In its most productive period, the 1920s and 1930s, the mill had 268 employees, a third of whom were women. A shortage of raw materials during World War II caused the mill to shift production and products. National Container purchased the mill in 1951 and merged with Owens-Corning in 1956. Tecumseh purchased it in 1967; by then the mill manufactured boxes from scrap materials. Ben Lahoski, who started working there in 1937, managed the mill through a highly productive post–World War II period, when it produced about twenty thousand tons of paper products a year.[18] However, the equipment was antiquated, the working conditions hard compared to modern plants, and by 1975 the mill's twenty-three acres were surrounded by the Cuyahoga Valley National Park. Lahoski represented the company and organized the closing of the plant in 1984, when it was sold to the National Park Service. Later the mill building was partially destroyed by fire and too unstable to be reused by the national park. Even after its subsequent demolition, there are still mill remnants providing the basis for interpretation.

Another national park visitor center, not far from the mill, is in Boston. The little village is a historic site in itself. The Boston Store Visitor Center is the most prominent of a cluster of historic buildings that have been preserved and carefully adapted for reuse as an information center and museum. Next door to the store is the restored 1950s M. D. Garage, used for special exhibits.

As with other areas in Cuyahoga Valley National Park, archaeological research combined with historic information provides a picture of a busy town in the mid-1800s, with mills, stores, a hotel, and more houses. The Cleveland Museum of Natural History conducted archaeological excavations in 1985 at the store and outbuildings; then in 1991 and 1993 the National Park Service's Midwest Archaeological Research Center continued work at different points on the site.

The Boston Store Visitor Center contains a unique interpretative display of canal-boat building. The exhibit features part of a canal boat, tools, and other artifacts related to boatbuilding. It explains that the store was not really a store but a warehouse, perched on the edge of the canal for loading and unloading goods.

Proceeding south from the Boston Store Visitor Center trailhead, the Towpath Trail follows the river closely, passing under both the long bridges of Interstate 271 and the Ohio Turnpike before coming to Stumpy Basin. It is now a wetland, bordered on the east side by the high banks that support the Ohio Turnpike and on the west by the Cuyahoga River. The Towpath Trail cuts through it on a boardwalk, designed to have the least impact on the wetland below.

There are many tales about the area; it was much larger than it looks today because the Cuyahoga River has moved into the basin. The basin was an important holding spot for boats waiting to unload cargo in either

Boston or to the south in Peninsula, or for stopping overnight, before proceeding through the next lift lock. The basin was also a good source for ice in the winter, and two icehouses were located here. Ice was packed in sawdust and stored for use during the warmer months by restaurants, grocers, and wealthier residents who had ice boxes. Ice from Stumpy Basin was hauled to Cleveland and Akron. The basin was also a popular place to fish and ice-skate.

Some of the basin's past still lingers since it was also a place where many canal boats were abandoned after the 1913 flood. Time, erosion, and flooding helped to fill it in, but bits of wood occasionally emerge along the Cuyahoga River's banks as reminders of the skeletons of another era buried under all the cattails. These bits could be piers, remnants of the old dam at the Peninsula Feeder at Lock 31, or old canal boats. This eroding and the exposed pieces are carefully monitored by the National Park Service archaeological teams. Although some canal-boat devotees occasionally argue for excavating such remnants, they are better preserved where buried. When old wooden structures that have been buried or submerged underwater are exposed to air, they decay very rapidly without expensive preservation methods.

South of Stumpy Basin, the river and Towpath Trail lead to one of two well-known Peninsula locks and remains of the aqueduct in which canal boats floated high across the Cuyahoga River. Lock 29 is easy to walk into to observe the cut sandstone typical of lock construction as well as to note some of the mason's marks chiseled by the men cutting the stones. Since they were paid per stone, each mark was an individual mason's timesheet. This lock did not require rehabilitation in 1906.

The Towpath Trail skirts the top of Lock 29 and crosses the river on a bridge positioned in the same spot as the historic towpath bridge. The landscape, viewed from the bridge, provides a great opportunity to read the past. The geological past is displayed in the stratigraphy of the high riverbanks to the west of the bridge. The historic canal past is apparent not only in the lock but also in the foundations of the aqueduct that still cling to the banks on both sides of the river. The commercial heritage of Peninsula is apparent in the remains of the foundation of the Thomas Moody Mill. The river still runs through the channel where the waterwheel once provided power for the mill. The adjacent national park parking lot is also a good place from which to see the old dam and the mill remains.

The second Peninsula lock is Deep Lock, the deepest lock in the Ohio & Erie Canal system; it raised and lowered boats fourteen feet. This lock is south of the Village of Peninsula in Deep Lock Quarry Metro Park; it is accessible from Riverview Road. This lock is located below a steep bank, at the top of which is Deep Lock Quarry. Remnants of the quarrying enterprise abound along the trails in the park. This lively commercial operation not only provided stone for canal locks but, after the canal was built, shipped building stones to Akron and points south for use in public buildings such as the courthouse. The quarry also manufactured grinding stones for use in the paper and automotive industries in the early 1900s. Deep Lock Quarry is the southernmost of an important string of Berea Sandstone quarries. Large artifacts from its operations are visible along the trails above the lock and are the basis of interpretation for the Metroparks.

The trail south from Deep Lock passes through farmland and wetlands with numerous beaver dams. The most interesting spot is the boardwalk area over what is locally called the Beaver Marsh. The spot is a testament to the canal builders as well as the beavers; vestiges of the canal bank still peak through the water lilies and cattails along the boardwalk. The wooden structure allows minimum impact on the environment. It is a prime bird-watching area and, at dusk, a great place to spot beavers.

Parts of Locks 25 and 24 can be seen along the side of Riverview Road, which in places is located in the old canal bed. When the trail crosses from west to east of Riverview Road, south of Bath Road, it follows the river along the main trunk sewer line of the City of Akron's Water Pollution Control facility. The smells remind the travelers of the alternative uses of the historic canal. The large sewer pipe that resides in the canal bed was first built in 1916 and extended to the sewer plant in 1928. The trail proceeds through the commercial area of the Merriman Valley and soon is in young woods, where it reaches Big Bend, a trailhead of Sand Run Metro Park.

Although this tour of the past is focused on the historic canal era, the region has a rich prehistoric past as well. Native peoples traveled through and lived in the river valleys since about 1000 B.C.E. The Towpath Trail traverses a seasonal campsite in the Merriman Valley, where the trail was built a short distance from the historic route because the Cuyahoga River had changed its path. The camp location, on a flat terrace above the river, and protected from the west by a high hill, was ideal, with water nearby and a small wetland to the north.

The wayside information panel along the Towpath Trail features a concept drawing of a small camp. Archaeological research and excavation conducted during the summers of 1998 and 1999 by faculty and students from the University of Akron uncovered evidence of seasonal occupation over a period of years dating from about 1000 C.E. to around 1400 C.E. Some of the evidence includes flint points, fragments of animal bones, berries, seeds and nuts, as well as marks in the soil left by decaying shelter posts. This site seems to have many characteristics of other sites labeled Whittlesey, named for Charles Whittlesey, a historian and early archaeologist who recorded numerous archaeological sites in northern Ohio. The Whittlesey point or arrowhead, characteristic of the small points found during this period, is also named for him.[19] Fortunately, this terrace was barely disturbed by canal-building efforts and displaced soil, so it maintained much of the prehistoric archaeological integrity. The results of the archaeological testing provide a picture of a small, seasonal prehistoric living site consistent with others found in the Cuyahoga Valley.

In the journey south from Big Bend, one can again see Akron's large trunk sewer line in the canal bed; the new Towpath Trail is west of the canal, and then crosses it and the trunk line on a bridge at the edge of the Valley View Golf Course. Then there are a viewing station and interpretative panel at the point where the Little Cuyahoga River joins the Cuyahoga, which curves to flow north. The trail follows the Little Cuyahoga upstream into Akron.

The next prominent location is a hub of historic sites almost in downtown Akron, which includes the restored historic Mustill Store and Mustill house, and across North Street, the stairstep Cascade Locks and Schumacher's Cascade Mill site. These all testify to the vibrant commercial canal era, and the three sites combined teem with stories, artifacts, and structures. The area was a center of commercial activity for two reasons: first, people got off the boats to conduct business, shop, and socialize while they waited for boats to move through the locks. Second, a powerful stream of water came down the hill, providing waterpower for a whole line of commercial enterprises. This commercial development began a city. At Lock 18, the wayside "Anatomy of a Lock" explains how the lock works, and the walls of the lock display mason's marks. The bramble-covered banks on the west side of the Towpath Trail at Locks 17 and 16 were once a busy neighborhood, home to millworkers and others who worked in the area.

South of Lock 16, the Little Cuyahoga River swings east, and the canal depends on water that comes from the Portage Lakes, entering the canal opposite Young's Tavern on Manchester Road. However, the important waterpower for many commercial operations located along the Cascade Locks came from a waterway called Crosby's Ditch. Water from the Little

Cuyahoga River was dammed upstream in Middlebury, near the current Goodyear Tire and Rubber Company headquarters, and was fed into a mill race that ran for nearly two miles along the Little Cuyahoga Valley. It turned south at Main Street and west at Mill Street to power Crosby's Old Stone Mill (1832) at Lock 5. After being used by the mill, the water flowed north along the east side of the canal and proceeded down along the Cascade Locks, powering mills and factories along the way, including Schumacher's Cascade Mill. The water returned to the river north of Lock 15. Later, when the Pennsylvania & Ohio Canal was built, it used some of Crosby's Ditch before it merged to join the Ohio & Erie Canal.[20]

The canal-era Mustill Store and house, dating from the 1840s, were both restored in 2000, the store as a museum and the house as a private residence. The Cascade Locks Park Association manages them both. The museum is perched on the west bank of Lock 15, the most intact of the Cascade Locks. The Mustill Store museum provides another way to read the past, with its interpretation of a canal-era store complete with barrels and a potbelly stove. It features historic photos as well as more contemporary scenes of archaeological excavations and building restoration. The highlight view of the past is the wall-size mural by local artist Don Getz that depicts the Mustill and Cascade Locks and Schumacher Mill in 1842.

Over a number of years, extensive archaeological research was conducted on the area around the Mustill Store. Although the city had filled in much of the area and the old towpath was now called Fern Street, the archaeological investigators discovered the route of Walnut Street as it came down the hill from the west, as well as that of the wasteway water channel that ran under the porch. Most significant, the archaeological excavation determined the position of the long-lost meat-market addition on the north side of the store, so it could be replicated in the restoration. All the information obtained in the excavations was compiled to help create the museum exhibits.[21]

Across North Street is the channel of old locks and basins. The Towpath Trail makes its way up the hill on the west side of the locks, then crosses to the east at Lock 11, following the historic route to the top of the hill to Martin Luther King Boulevard.

An important remnant of past industrial history is the site of Ferdinand Schumacher's Cascade Mill. The Mustill and Cascade Locks and Schumacher's Cascade Mill site combine to create a hub of a growing urban redevelopment area, and the site of the Cascade Mill is in the center of that hub. The mill was built in 1840 by Leicester King and William Mitchell and purchased by Ferdinand Schumacher in 1868. Schumacher, a German, immigrated to America in 1850, and his first industrial efforts centered on making the type of rolled oats popular in his home country. Although not especially popular in the Akron area, he sold large quantities of rolled oats to the Union army in 1861, allowing him enough capital to purchase several mills before buying the Cascade Mill. Schumacher became a major owner and operator of mills in Akron and managed to remain so through fires and consolidation. His last consolidation resulted in losing control of the company, then American Cereal Company, which was renamed Quaker Oats, in 1903. Schumacher is an important figure in Akron's early industrial history, and the site of his Cascade Mill offers physical evidence of some of that history.

Although there were many other mills in the area, most were demolished and other structures built on their sites. The Schumacher site remained unused; trees and grasses filled the void. However, in contrast to the Irishtown Bend site, which was totally undisturbed, the Cascade Mill site was covered with urban fill dirt, creating a rather flat and parklike area that successfully hides its past life. The monumental First Energy electric tower now on the site reminds one of the present even as water still cascades down the old canal channel.

At a site such as the Cascade Mill, it is impractical to excavate with the small grids and hand tools used at Irishtown Bend or Big Bend. The nearly five feet of different materials dumped to fill in the old basins and mill cavity are not connected with the mill or the canal era. In addition, the ground was disturbed extensively in the 1930s by the construction of the first electrical tower, which was replaced in the 1960s by the transmission tower that dominates the site today. Hidden under brushy overgrowth up the hill from the tower, the round iron plate of a manhole aligning with what looks like a concrete beam crossing the canal is the only visible sign of the underground conduit that carries high-voltage cables. The date of its construction is not known, but its location, crossing the southern portion of the site between Locks 13 and 14, is likely to have disturbed any remnants of the entryway of the original Cascade Mill building.

Despite all of the disturbances to the site, there were still two major questions archaeologists could address: first, was the thirty-seven ton waterwheel still left buried on the site, and second, what if any, remnants of the rest of the mill were under all that fill dirt? The Cascade Locks Park Association and the University of Akron's Community Archaeology Program conducted archaeological investigations in 2002 and 2003.[22] The work began with historical research, including a deed search, using nineteenth- and early-twentieth-century maps, and interviews with local canal and history experts, then using new noninvasive ground-penetrating testing and traditional excavation methods, except with the aid of a backhoe.

The buried wheel was a cherished urban myth that had prevailed for years; supposedly the thirty-seven-ton wheel was buried on the site. No one had any memory of what happened to it, and no official record of its scrap reclamation was ever found, so there was still some hope of finding it. During the search for clues preceding any excavation, the archaeology team found a photograph in the July 21, 1925, issue of the *Akron Beacon Journal*, which showed the fire-scorched remnants of the brick wall of the wheelhouse, with the entire waterwheel in place. The accompanying article explained that the photo was "taken in the summer of 1923, just before the wheel was torn out." Another photograph, dating around 1925, showed the same brick remnants, with only the center hub of the wheel remaining.[23]

There are no records to indicate what was done with the center of the wheel; however, research continued, focused on finding remains of the mill walls. When features such as these are buried so deep, geophysical testing can be used. At this site the research team used electric resistivity, a noninvasive technique that can determine what is under the fill dirt. Where images indicated a change in material underground, they were laid over historic maps using a mapping software to evaluate the alignment between them. Where the geophysical maps indicated a possible feature that lined up with the walls in the historical map, that area was identified as a good place to excavate.

Several trenches were excavated by backhoe, supervised by archaeologists from the university team. The fill was removed slowly, in small increments, to expose features and the layering of the soils. If features were present, they were excavated manually, photographed, and recorded. All soils associated with the features were screened for artifacts, most of which dated from the 1930s. The largest and first of these trenches uncovered the sandstone base of the 125-foot chimney at the north end of the building. From the chimney, excavators followed the northern wall of the powerhouse foundation, which jogged and continued along the barrelhouse foundation. The investigation provided enough physical evidence to help Schumacher's Cascade Mill tell its own story of its significant role in Akron's history, providing a framework for interpreting the mill site within the context of early Akron.

The site is a reminder of grain, mills, and canal shipping and also of the evolving energy sources. Initially, the mill used power from the thirty-six-foot overshot waterwheel powered by water from Crosby's Ditch. Then, to increase power, Schumacher added the tall chimney stack built for the coal furnaces. The First Energy electric tower, a sign of the next stage in power technology, stands next to where the waterwheel originally turned.

There are many canal features along this section of the trail: for example, the wasteway to the east of Lock 14, which channeled water out around the lock to prevent it from flowing over the gates. Two historic structures cross the canal as it proceeds up the hill: a trestle built for the Valley Railway (now the Cuyahoga Valley Scenic Railroad), and over Lock 11, the nine-hundred-foot–long railroad trestle built by the American Bridge Company. Under that bridge are the massive stone pillars of the first trestle, built in 1890.[24] The various locks and basins contain pieces of the concrete used to rehabilitate the canal in 1906. As the Towpath Trail climbs the hill along the Cascade Locks, the wayside interpretive stations draw visitors back in time and encourage them to picture boats being raised or lowered through the locks, boats parked in the adjacent basins, and a flurry of people and commerce.

As was the case with other commercial centers, such as Cleveland and Massillon, in Akron the historic integrity of the canal and towpath was often buried under roads, bridges, and buildings. Here, the canal runs through concrete culverts under many buildings along Main Street, currently resurfacing south of the Civic Theater. When buildings were demolished in the 1990s, this area was uncovered and made into the Lock 3 Park. As at Schumacher's Cascade Mill site, there was considerable commercial activity along the canal and two basins nearby. A great deal of information was lost when the structures were demolished and bulldozers shaped the park. Local history buffs collected some interesting artifacts, such as marbles and miniature toys, but without any systematic context, the larger historic archaeological picture was lost.

Moving south, the towpath had once crossed Summit Lake on a floating bridge that was destroyed in the early 1900s. In this section, the canal is fed by the Portage Lakes and Tuscarawas River as it flows south from the continental divide. The Tuscarawas River Valley is fairly wide and flat compared to the Cuyahoga, and canal engineers did not have the same challenges as they did from Cleveland to Akron. Lock 1, south of Akron, is in Barberton at Wolf Creek and is buried. The distance between locks stretches; the next two are in Clinton.

The Village of Clinton lies on the southern border of Summit County. It acquired 2.2 miles of the canal right-of-way in the 1960s and in 1999 entered into a partnership with Metro Parks to restore the towpath. Now the Towpath Trail extends south to join with the Stark County section of the trail. The Clinton Historical Society and the Clinton Canal Corridor Committee assisted the University of Akron archaeology team in conducting research in the village from 1997 through 2001.

About a half-mile north of the village is an isolated and intriguing historical site. Here, Locks 2 and 3 are located a few yards apart; in the canal era they were at two ends of a large canal basin. The village filled the old canal bed over time, a house and pond were built in the 1940s, and some of the area was used as a dump. The locks, however, remained intact, providing evidence of the commercial past.

The high lands bordering the Tuscarawas River had once contained many coal deposits, some close to the surface. Local farmers mined their own coal, and small mining companies shipped coal on the canal, north to Lake Erie and south to the Ohio River. This occurred all along the Tuscarawas Valley. On the west side of the canal basin was the Messenger Coal Canal, built in 1847. It was actually just an extension of the basin, and it connected to a small rail tram that brought coal down from the upland.

A small spur from the current Towpath Trail ends on top of Lock 2 at a viewing spot over the old basin area, Lock 3, and the wasteway. The trail crosses the wasteway before coming to Lock 3 and the interpretive station overlooking the remnants of the lockkeeper's house. Archaeological tests and excavations conducted by the University of Akron team over a four-year period provided information about canal-related activity around the locks. However, as at Schumacher's Cascade Mill, excavation does not always substantiate local lore. Excavation on the east side of Lock 2 did not reveal any evidence to support the long-held idea that the building on the east side was once a tavern. Although there were some household artifacts, tavern-related artifacts, such as parts of barrels, stays, or mugs, were not found. The remains of the building's foundation are visible through the vegetation on the east side of Lock 2, along the trail.[25]

In contrast, the excavation at the Lock 3 lockkeeper's house uncovered many household items, a probable cold cellar, a well pipe, a brick walk, and a substantial foundation. Information gleaned from the artifacts, paired with the written record, help tell the story of this dwelling. Records note the lockkeeper was Nichols Smith and that his wife sold milk and eggs to the canallers. There is also a bit of a mystery here. During the excavation, two burials were found lying side by side, one a large dog, the

Excavation at the lockkeeper's house, Lock 3. This was a busy commercial center, with two locks close together, repair facilities, and a small coal canal joining from the west (Collection of the Community Archaeology Program, University of Akron).

other a wolf, and the wolf skull had a bullet hole through it. Archaeology can only tell so much; the real story has long since disappeared, leaving visitors with the mystery and, of course, their imaginations.[26]

Just north of Clinton the route of the historic towpath crosses the Tuscarawas River on a bridge. Historically, the canal emptied into the river, where boats then crossed the river on ponded water created by a slackwater dam. From here, the boats went into the Clinton Guard Lock, one of two in the Ohio & Erie system, designed to allow boats to reenter the canal from a section of the river. The lock also protected the village from flooding from the junction of the area behind the slackwater dam and the canal. Boats do not change elevation when they pass through the guard lock. The lock has earthen sides, and its stone ends are still intact, but the gates are no longer there. The hydraulic system used butterfly valves or wickets to control the water flow, and two such valves, made of bronze, were found in the excavations, weighing about five hundred pounds each.

The wayside sign on the Towpath Trail where it crosses Main Street says that Clinton had been a "Busy Inland Port" in the heyday of the canal. It had been a forwarding area for grain and coal and the center of commercial activity that supported shipping. From blacksmith shops and grocery stores to hotels and mills, the village provided services for both packet boats and freight traffic. The town grew with the construction of the Cleveland, Zanesville & Cincinnati Railroad in 1852. By the beginning of the twentieth century, however, commercial activity declined along with the canal. A 1909 fire destroyed many commercial buildings along Water Street, and they were never rebuilt. Scattered about the village are canal lock stones, now ornamental features in many yards; most of them are old capstones that were discarded when the canal was rehabilitated in 1906.

The Town of Canal Fulton, four miles south of Clinton, offers more chances to read the history and life along the Ohio & Erie Canal. In Stark County and managed by Stark Parks, the canal lands have been under the control of the county since the mid-1960s. Here, many wonderful historic homes and structures are still well cared for. The trailhead off Cherry Street begins with a small museum run by the Canal Fulton Heritage Society, while beside it is the reconstructed *St. Helena II*, built in the late 1960s and replaced in 1989 by the *St. Helena III*.

Canal Fulton was a hub of activity during the canal era. Canal Society of Ohio member Jim Guest describes it as the center of a wheel, with roads radiating out into the adjacent farm lands, enabling farmers to bring the grain to the mills from which it was shipped both north and south on the canal. Coal was mined in the adjacent hills and brought to town to be shipped as well. Interviewees in the "Towpath Tales" oral history project done in the late 1970s described their memories of a bustling canal town, with hotels, an opera house, restaurants, and bars until the 1913 flood destroyed many buildings.[27]

Just south of town along the towpath is the McLaughlin Dry Dock, restored and adapted in 1976 to house the *St. Helena III*. The dry dock was not covered originally. Two cradles, called stanchions, that held the boats were in the dock, and the water came in from the canal but was drained out on the west side to the Tuscarawas River. The original dock was built in 1830 and E. J. McLaughlin acquired it in 1860; boats were built and repaired here until the 1913 flood. Coal was also loaded here, from a small tram that connected to mines west of the Tuscarawas River. Dry docks were important for efficient operation of the boats, which were subjected to considerable wear when going through the locks. Most canal villages had a dry dock; however, this is one of the few remaining and probably the only one still in use.

About a mile south is Lock 4. From 1937 to 1939, the Works Progress Administration (WPA) repaired this section of the canal and created a small park. There is a watered canal basin on the site and a small red

As of 2007, the only dry dock still in use in the Canalway; historically it did not have walls or a roof. It was an active manufacturing and repair facility (photo by Ed Metzger).

brick building, unrelated to the canal era, constructed by the WPA, using bricks from old State Route 21. The section of the canal and towpath south of Lock 4 is heavily wooded, but in the canal era there were commercial enterprises along the banks that included mills, tramways bringing coal, saloons, and at least one brewery. Although there are some remnants of canal-era structures here, there is no archaeological data for this section of the trail comparable to that in the northern counties. Most of our information comes from the extensive research of the members of the Canal Society of Ohio and the National Park Historic Structure survey done in 2002.

After Lock 4, the Towpath Trail to Crystal Springs is wooded, shady in the summer and full of wildflowers in the spring. In the fall and winter, when there is less vegetation, one can see some remnants of canal-era structures. According to the Canal Society of Ohio, "the next six miles or so were a beehive of activity. Tramways brought coal from the mines on the west side of the river in the loading points on the canal. . . . The Crawford Slip had a basin on the towpath side large enough to hold two waiting boats while the third loaded."[28] At Crystal Springs, the Schuster Brewery sent two boatloads of beer a week down the canal to a bottling company in Massillon. The brewery burned sometime before 1925, and the Smith grist and cider mill was built on the same site. A 1914 iron bridge spans the Tuscarawas River between High Mill and Forty Corners Street Northwest. The Jackson Township Historical Society saved it from demolition; today it is restricted to walking and bicycle traffic.

The current Towpath Trail stays close to the river, ducking under Route 21 at the north edge of Massillon, with access at the Lake Avenue Trailhead. The trail skirts the parking lot before climbing up the levee, built in the 1930s by the Army Corps of Engineers on the east side of the Tuscarawas River. The canal originally went through Massillon but suffered the same fate as it did in Akron, being covered by streets and buildings.

Much of the towpath south of Massillon is completed and follows the river valley. The canal town of Navarre once contained many canal-era business structures. Today, however, a few canal features remain intact; these include a small sluice next to the Navarre waterworks at the north edge of town, a big sluice opposite the village park south of town, and a portion of Lock 6 that is now incorporated into a loading dock at the Nickles Bakery.[29] The little town is an interesting place to take a stroll and look at the canal-era houses. The Navarre-Bethlehem Township Historical Society operates the 1836 Mathew House, now a museum, and the Heritage Education Center, located behind it.

Near the Tuscarawas County line, the canal and towpath are more difficult to find, although plans are in place for connecting the trail there, but that requires a bridge over the Tuscarawas River. However, from the State Route 21 bridge over the river, one can look north and see the remnants of the stone pillars of the old wooden Tuscarawas aqueduct, marking the route of the former canal. Vestiges of the canal can be seen along the road going into Bolivar. In the town, Interstate 77 obliterated the canal and towpath, leaving few visual clues to the past. Nonetheless, Bolivar is working hard to bring the public as close to the old route as possible.[30]

Just south of town is Fort Laurens, a Revolutionary War site, park, and museum. Originally built in 1779 as one of a series of forts that General George Washington planned to construct between Fort Pitt and Detroit, it fell into disuse after one disastrous year. The Ohio Historical Society has owned the eighty-one-acre site since 1917, and it constructed a small museum there in 1971. The Ohio Historical Society carried out extensive archaeological research in the 1970s and 1980s. Archaeologists found the remains of the unknown defenders of Fort Laurens in a mass grave; these are reburied in a crypt in one of the museum's walls. The Fort Laurens Park and museum is a good example of historic preservation and interpretation, with much of the presented information coming from archaeological excavations and historic documents. There is some historic irony at this fort site; in the 1830s, the canal destroyed some remains of the fort, and nearly a hundred and forty years later the interstate wiped out the canal.

A trail bridge over Interstate 77 connects Bolivar, Fort Laurens, and the Towpath Trail south of the fort. The trail continues south and passes remnants of Locks 7, 8, and 9 and a turning basin. The German Separatist Zoarites built seven miles of this section of the canal, completed in 1828. They also constructed a slackwater dam and guard lock in 1835 to better connect the village with the canal. Although a few features remain along the river, most of the Zoar industrial buildings were buried by the Zoar flood-control levee, built in 1935, which divided the historic Zoar Village site from the remains of the canal and towpath. Both Zoar Village and the Canal Society of Ohio have documented the many ways the Zoar community used the canal for shipping. The Zoar Iron Bridge is an exciting restoration project that connects the Towpath Trail to the Zoar Village State Memorial; on it one can cross the river and then climb up over the levee and down into the village. This three-span Pratt truss was built in 1884 by the Wrought Iron Bridge Company of Canton and is 265 feet long.

An important feature along the Towpath Trail are the remains of the State Fish Farm Number 12. The Ohio Division of Wildlife built the ponds in 1921 within the prism of the canal, using stones harvested from Lock 10. The ponds were placed there because there was a good source of spring water to supply the proper conditions for the fish. The enterprise was never successful, and in the fourteen years of operation spring floods washed out the ponds, then they lacked water during dry spells. Pollution from road and farm runoff also contributed to the hatchery's 1935 closing. The remnants of the ponds are next to the trail a few yards south of Lock 10.[31]

The last stop on this armchair journey is the Dover Dam. While not a canal-era structure, it is an integral part of the modern landscape and a feature of the Towpath Trail. It is also the reason for the levee between the Tuscarawas River and Zoar. Built in 1935, it is one of a series of flood-control dams built by the Army Corps of Engineers as part of the Muskingum Watershed Conservancy District. When the floodgates are closed, Zoar Village might possibly be under water; the levee was built to protect from such flooding.

This Canalway journey is based on archaeological and historical research conducted along the Ohio & Erie Canal for the development of the National Heritage Canalway. The topography, concentrations of populations, commercial development, and ownership along the 110 miles are so varied that there are vastly different levels of archaeological and historical research; clearly, Cleveland is different than Stark County and Zoar. The National Historic Preservation Act of 1966 authorized policies and procedures to preserve rapidly disappearing prehistoric and historical resources from the persistent threat of bulldozers, but they only can protect those areas controlled by the federal government or that use federal government funds. This has led to more archaeological research in areas such as highway construction and is significant in some parts of the Canalway where many different organizations receive federal funds for construction. In southern Summit County and much of Stark County, for example, where the towpath in rural areas was still somewhat intact and restoration did not include disturbing the landscape, archaeology was not considered necessary. In other locations, such as Clinton, it was important to gather information to support the fragmented historical record. The work the Cleveland Museum of Natural History did at Irishtown Bend and the University of Akron did in Clinton and at the Schumacher mill site contributes to the historic archaeological records and to future planning for preservation and interpretation.

The concept of a cultural landscape proposes that humans do not passively inhabit a space; they alter, create, and discard parts of material culture, and those features, structures, and artifacts help future generations understand the past. This is not just an old canal and towpath; it is an economic and transportation system that connected people and brought in new residents, tradespeople, and travelers, as well as goods, plants, and animals. To understand how extensively it altered the cultural landscape, we have to combine the stories of ethnic groups, travelers, and floods with the information provided by these material features. This integrated, coherent whole tells the story of the past.

Standing at the Dover Dam, one can look northward for nearly 110 miles and grasp the development of a material culture begun in the 1820s with the canal that changed a wilderness into a national and global cultural landscape. This new cultural landscape of the Canalway and its Towpath Trail also pulls viewers to a better understanding of both the wilderness and the canal era.

NOTES

1. Veletta Canouts, *Common Ground,* National Park Service, Park Service Initiatives (Summer–Fall, 1998).

2. Anthropology and Archaeology Laboratory Records, Community Archaeology Program, Univ. of Akron.

3. Alfred M. Lee, Nomination Form for Irishtown Bend Archaeological District, National Register of Historic Places, July 1989, Cleveland, Ohio, Cuyahoga County, Cleveland Museum of Natural History, Cleveland.

4. Lee, Nomination Form.

5. Lee, Nomination Form, section 7, 2.

6. Lee, Nomination Form.

7. Lee, Nomination Form, 4.

8. Lee, Nomination Form, 2.

9. Ronald W. Johnson and Paul Newman, *Historic Structure Report, Adaptive Restoration, Historic Structure 125, Lock 38, Ohio & Erie Canal, Cuyahoga Valley National Recreation Area, Valley View, Ohio* (Denver, Colo.: U.S. Department of the Interior, National Park Service, 1993), 8.

10. Jeffery J. Richner, *Archaeological Excavation at Site 33-Cu-314: A Mid-Nineteenth Century Structure on the Ohio & Erie Canal.* Midwest Archaeological Center Technical Report No. 14 (U.S. Department of the Interior, National Park Service, 1992), 121.

11. Ibid., 122.

12. Ibid.

13. Ibid.

14. Ibid., 123.

15. Ibid.

16. Ibid.

17. Jaite Ethnography Project, Univ. of Akron Anthropology Class, Spring 2003, transcript, Jaite Collection, Univ. of Akron Archives, Akron; also in Peninsula Historical Society Archives.

18. Ben Lahoski material, Jaite Ethnography Project.

19. Paul J. Pacheco, "Interim Report, 1998 Phase I & II Archaeological Investigation at Big Bend," unpublished, Archaeological Laboratory Records, Community Archaeology Program, Univ. of Akron, 12–13.

20. Pacheco, "Interim Report," 1–3.

21. Cascade Locks Park archives, Cascade Locks Park Association, Mustill Store, Akron.

22. This archaeological work is documented in Jack Gieck's *Dig: An Archaeological Investigation in Akron's Cascade Locks Park,* DVD (Akron: Cinemark, Inc., 2005), made for the Cascade Locks Park Association.

23. "Lost Wheel," *Akron Beacon Journal,* July 21, 1925, Canal Society of Ohio Collection, Univ. of Akron Archives.

24. Jack Gieck, "Akron's Cascade Locks Guide for Tours," Cascade Locks Park Association, Mustill Store, 5.

25. Nigel Brush, "Interim Report, Clinton Locks," 2000, Archaeological Laboratory Records, Community Archaeology Program, Univ. of Akron.

26. Nigel Brush, "Interim Report, Clinton Locks," 2000, Archaeological Laboratory Records, Community Archaeology Program, Univ. of Akron.

27. Canal Fulton Heritage Society archives, Heritage Society Museum, Canal Fulton.

28. "Canal Society of Ohio Spring 2000 Tour," unpublished manuscript, Canal Society of Ohio Collection, Univ. of Akron Archives.

29. "Canal Society of Ohio Spring 2000 Tour."

30. Richard Lebold, interview by Peg Bobel and Lynn Metzger, Oct. 24, 2005.

31. "Ohio & Erie Canal Towpath Trail Interpretive Guide: Zoarville to Fort Laurens," Tuscarawas County Canal Lands Development Committee and Canal Society of Ohio Tour, 1996.

Chapter 16

Grassroots and Connections

PEG BOBEL AND LYNN METZGER

The Ohio & Erie National Heritage Canalway, or simply the Canalway, builds on a long northeast Ohio tradition of recognizing the value of green space. This Canalway is a designation of a lineal swath of land containing historic, natural, and recreational resources along the northern section of the historic Ohio & Erie Canal, from Cleveland to New Philadelphia. The Canalway is a product of many regional partnerships between communities, governments, and nonprofits, all sharing a common vision.

Advocating for saving the Cuyahoga Valley and the canal lands began in 1925 when the Akron Metropolitan Park District Board (now Metro Parks, Serving Summit County) hired Olmsted Brothers, a firm established by the son and stepson of famous landscape architect Frederick Law Olmsted, to identify potential park areas. Their report raved about the "richness of opportunity," especially in the impressive Cuyahoga Valley north of Akron. They wanted to preserve it all, "brink to brink."[1] Their plan, which included canal lands, did not address the valley north of the Summit County line. The northernmost part of the valley was already the heart of a vital industrial area in Cleveland, and in 1915, Frederick Law Olmsted Jr. began consulting with William Stinchcomb, first director of the Cleveland Metropolitan Park District, on a design for a series of suburban parks known today as Cleveland's Emerald Necklace, which rings the City of Cleveland, providing green space and connecting trails for residents of Cuyahoga County.[2] That park system did not include the northern Cuyahoga Valley; for most residents of the area, the valley was but an ugly expanse whose floor contained major industrial and manufacturing companies.

The idea of preserving the scenic parts of the river and the old canal between Akron and Cleveland slumbered for many years; progress in the early twentieth century was defined as the development of large-scale industry and business enterprises, which needed land and water. Between Cleveland and Akron and south of Akron, in southern Summit, Stark, and Tuscarawas Counties, the areas surrounding the old canal were still rural, and there were long stretches where the canal and towpath were intact. Indeed, the canal and towpath were frequently used for recreation, while other sections of the canal were maintained for industrial use.

The preservation ideas finally developed as a movement in 1960, when individuals and communities began advocating for preserving what remained of the old transportation system and canal history. In the 1960s, members of the Canal Society of Ohio, many from Stark and Summit Counties, began identifying and calling for preservation of canal resources. Then the future congressman Ralph Regula of Navarre and *Canton Repository* writer Al Simpson began their campaign to save canal lands in Stark County.[3]

Building on the many voices from the past featured already, the following chapters use contemporary voices, feasibility studies, reports, and photographs to tell the new canal fever story.[4] All of this material facilitated the spread of the new fever to engage people and communities along the towpath route from the Cleveland waterfront 110 miles south to New Philadelphia. By the end of 2008, 85 miles of towpath had been restored and made into a multiuse path; the remaining stretches were either under construction or in the planning stage. The Cuyahoga Valley Scenic Railroad now connects Canton with Independence, and the Ohio & Erie Canalway's scenic byway, part of the America's Byways program, provides for interesting tours of the Canalway.

The story of the transformation of the "old ditch and path" into the Canalway is multilayered, with Cuyahoga Valley National Park and two grassroots movements at its center. The core of the movement begins with the founding of Cuyahoga Valley National Recreation Area in 1974, which was renamed Cuyahoga Valley National Park in 2000 (CVNP).

The park also geographically separated the north and south grassroots movements. Two important organizations became major advocacy groups. First the Cleveland-based North Cuyahoga Valley Corridor, Incorporated (NCVCI), was founded in 1984, then in 1989 the Ohio & Erie Canal Corridor Coalition (OECCC), based south of the park in Sum-

OHIO CANAL CORRIDOR

Ohio & Erie Canalway Coalition

Left: This first, Cleveland-based, advocacy group began in 1984 as the North Cuyahoga Valley Corridor, Inc., with the goal of connecting the national park to Cleveland. It changed its name to Ohio Canal Corridor in 1992 (Ohio Canal Corridor). *Right:* This advocacy group for the Canalway was founded in 1989 as the Ohio & Erie Canal Corridor Coalition. The name was changed when Canalway became the official name for the corridor (Ohio & Erie Canalway Coalition).

mit, Stark, and Tuscarawas Counties, was organized. They provided critical avenues for volunteers who wanted to support the effort to develop a heritage corridor. Both organizations, NCVCI (north of the park) and OECCC (south of the park), are nonprofit groups that work with local communities to raise funds for the development of the Ohio & Erie Canal National Heritage Corridor (Canalway), educate the public about its benefits, and advocate on its behalf at the state and federal level. Both of these organizations had name changes as their focuses changed.[5] Here we will refer to these organizations by their original names. Both organizations operate in cooperation with the national park, and during the formation of the heritage corridor there was often a great deal of grassroots work going on simultaneously both north and south of the national park.

This story really begins with the national park, which has been critical to preservation efforts in the region. Since its founding, Cuyahoga Valley National Park has both divided and united two different regions and constituencies. The geography, history, industry, and demography of the Cuyahoga Valley and canal differ in the thirteen miles north of the park (Rockside Road to Lake Erie), from that of the Cuyahoga and Tuscarawas Valleys south of it. The north Cuyahoga River Valley was largely industrialized in the early twentieth century, with high population concentrations on either side of the valley, comprising different political units, including Cuyahoga County and the City of Cleveland. The southern region, comprising Summit, Stark, and Tuscarawas Counties, is still more rural with less industrial area, and its primary population concentrations are in Akron, Canton, Massillon, Dover, New Philadelphia, and several small canal towns. So, as the terrain is different, the stories of the grassroots movements are also reflecting the populations, industry, and urban/rural differences in the region.

John Debo became the third superintendent of the park in 1988. His interest and vision led the park to reconstruct twenty miles of the canal towpath as its core trail and to help neighboring communities and local organizations extend the trail. The National Park Service both facilitated that outreach and was prodded into it by organizations that recognized the park as a regional asset that needed to be connected to the communities around it. The people in these groups all contributed to the vision, leadership, and energy necessary to reconnect the canal communities in ways that were severed by the 1913 flood.

When Debo became superintendent, the park newsletter was called *Where the Sidewalk Ends.* Actually, this new park was not yet connected to any sidewalks or any urban area. The park had little infrastructure, and years of land acquisition had caused considerable negative feelings among neighbors. The canal and towpath were as yet largely undeveloped for recreation.[6] However, local advocates already had ideas for connections to the park. Debo remembers that by July 1988, he had been given a tour by boat of the Cuyahoga River in Cleveland, guided by NCVCI leaders committed to connecting the park to Cleveland, and treated to a tour of the neglected and overgrown Mustill Store section of the canal in downtown Akron by preservationists intent on saving this remnant of canal history. Debo soon reached the conclusion that "for this park to achieve its full potential, it really needed to be connected. It needed to be physically connected and it needed to be programmatically connected."[7]

The idea of using the canal's towpath as a core trail was not new. Ron Thoman, chief of interpretation until 1990, described how the idea of the towpath as a spine trail had been discussed with the first two park administrations, even to the extent of developing a proposal to rewater the canal. There had been discussion of extending a trail into Cleveland and to Akron, but they did not envision it extending farther south. Undoubtedly, public opinion hindered the new park in some outreach efforts. As Thoman said, "People didn't understand the park. . . . They could not get their arms around it." Then the staff came up with ideas about the towpath. "It's the linear theme; it links almost all the other historic features and could link communities. It could also link east to west as well."[8]

Even though park planners in 1985 recommended making the canal trail a spine of the trail system in the park, park administration did not take any action regarding towpath restoration until John Debo became superintendent. A major hurdle for the park was to acquire title to the canal right-of-way, which was owned by the State of Ohio and encumbered by several leases and use agreements. Since the national park could not buy state land outright, it had to get the state to agree to give it title. Once the park owned the canal lands, it constructed twenty miles of the towpath as a multiuse trail in CVNP; this became the spark that ignited the movement. This trail provided the example, prototype, and stimulus for the expanding excitement, dedication, and federal support for the longer Ohio & Erie Canal Towpath Trail in areas both north and south of the park.

John Debo had extensive experience with and interest in parks with canals that led to his Canalway leadership. He was stationed at Lowell, Massachusetts, where he worked for the Massachusetts Department of Natural Resources and helped foster the preservation of Lowell's canal system. Later, after he joined the National Park Service, he was assigned back to Lowell. On his own, he also toured and studied the canal system in Great Britain. He said:

> The opportunity to come to Cuyahoga Valley National Park emerged in the late winter of 1987–88. It would have become apparent to me at some point that there was this old relic canal in the park. And immediately I recall being excited . . . maybe there's something we can do with this thing.
>
> The General Management Plan for the park did talk about the Ohio and Erie Canal towpath serving as a trail. I don't think in that planning document it was clear to anyone what the significance of the towpath would be when it was developed. . . . It struck me that the canal towpath could serve as kind of the unifying element for this park, something that would draw the park together, connect all these scattered land parcels; by no means was it the only resource in the park, but it had the potential to be the icon resource in Cuyahoga. . . . It is the kind of focal point in what can allow the public to attach an image to the park.

By the time the park began developing the canal and towpath, NCVCI had already been advocating for some type of park-urban connection for five years. Tom Yablonsky, the first president of NCVCI, told us the story of the founding of the group. He, Jeff Lennartz, and Mike Giangrande were its founding trustees, and its beginning is a prime example of grassroots volunteers in action. Their challenge was to promote saving an old, beat-up river valley and connect it to the national park and neighboring communities. To do so, they had to create a broad-based advocacy organization and secure volunteer, political, and economic investment. Giangrande soon moved from the area, but Yablonsky and Lennartz became an effective team, devoting countless hours to educating the public about the valley and the unique opportunity to reclaim it for public use.

Yablonsky, a native of Parma, had a master's degree in environmental planning and was drawn to the park and the potential it offered urban Cleveland: "The idea of the corridor linking Cleveland to the park really grew out of my moving back here and seeing the Flats [the lower Cuyahoga Valley] starting to bubble up. And the park was a vast no-mans-land. So my focus initially was really the north Cuyahoga Valley corridor. I had no sense . . . it just wasn't in my vision, to assume that other people would work on linking the park the other way."[9]

Yablonsky volunteered at Cuyahoga Valley National Park and there met Ron Thoman, chief of interpretation. As a volunteer, he conducted a survey research project for Thoman on the demographics of the area outside the boundaries of the park and in doing so became even more intrigued with the idea of connecting the park with Cleveland. He and Ron Thoman had long conversations about how that might happen.

The incident Yablonsky believes sparked the beginning of their organization and the connecting moment in Cuyahoga County occurred when he attended a CVNP volunteer-appreciation dinner at Thanksgiving in 1983. At that event Thoman said to him, "I've got to introduce you to this other person because you both have similar ideas." Then he met Jeff Lennartz, a park volunteer from the local hiking clubs. Lennartz described with bemusement the scene as Ron Thoman introduced them, saying, "Now you two talk." Lennartz commented that it took a few minutes before they figured out what they were to talk about. Thoman knew that they were both committed to saving the natural and historic resources in the valley by making them accessible to the public and connecting the northern valley to the national park. Lennartz recalled: "Before the evening was out, I understood what was being proposed and . . . I was all for it. After that I don't know how often we met, but we had a formal coming-out party in January. Within two months, we had an idea of what we wanted to do."[10] This was the beginning of many years of conversations, planning, organization, and generally creating the mission and goal for the NCVCI. The organization received its nonprofit designation in March 1984, which provided official status and launched the beginning of public activism on behalf of the river, valley, and the effort to connect it to the national park.

Yablonsky and Lennartz complemented each other. As Yablonsky's background and political and corporate contacts were critical to the early organization efforts, Lennartz's experience as a hiker, environmentalist, and naturalist determined his contributions to the NCVCI and its goals. He grew up hiking the Cuyahoga Valley with his father, and, as an adult, he became an active member of both the Sierra Club and the Cleveland Hiking Club. He knew what the valley had to offer. Lennartz described his volunteer contributions as that of a fieldworker; he wrote and mailed newsletters, constructed photographic slide shows, and led hiking trips. "I knew better than Tom what was physically down there."

Lennartz and Yablonsky's plan was to make contacts with the national park, define the resources at the north end of the river valley, and lay out concepts for potential connections. Their goal was to change the way the local communities viewed the Cuyahoga River Valley as a dividing line and have them think about it as a place of history and natural resources. Lennartz noted, "You have this river valley connecting them [the east side and west side neighborhoods], which was basically neglected, overlooked, and abused." Together this visionary team began to spread the word about the resources and value of the Cuyahoga River Valley. They solicited other people's ideas as to what they might see happening. "But . . . it was understood, at least by Tom and me and those we spoke to . . . that this would be a networking, a connecting of all kinds of resources up and down this valley to revitalize, and it was considered also a way to connect the national park to Cleveland." Their vision included a trail that would link two hubs—the Cleveland Flats and Cuyahoga Valley National Park.

They used slide shows and hikes to gain public support and raise awareness. Lennartz led tours and walks. "And twenty or thirty people would show up sometimes that had no idea what was there and were interested in finding out, and they would walk in these beautiful areas . . . and ooh and ahh and love it." The pair's message of preservation and reuse was reinforced in 1987 when Cleveland Metroparks reclaimed Garfield Park, which thousands of people used the first year it reopened. This restoration showed what could also happen in the valley.

Lennartz and Yablonsky were convinced that there was enough support to change the uses of the valley, but they were never sure just when it would come to be. After five years of their volunteer leadership, hundreds of slide presentations, tours, meetings, and more meetings, their organization's treasury was down to $11, and the membership was stable but small. They both recall a conversation in which they agreed that something had to happen soon or the organization would fold. But their work had already begun to bear fruit, and many things began to happen at the same time, in both the organization and local and regional organizations and communities around the northern Cuyahoga Valley. By 1988, the NCVCI had moved from worrying about its own end to becoming the major coordinator of the connecting process.

The story of the organization includes four important decisions that facilitated its growth and influence. First, it held a benefit event to expand the treasury; second, it hired Tim Donovan as executive director; third, it created an advisory board and expanded its operating board; and fourth, it formed a partnership with the Cuyahoga County Planning Commission to sponsor the *North Cuyahoga Valley Corridor* plan.

To address the low treasury balance, the NCVCI held its first benefit event on Father's Day 1989, on the old closed Superior Avenue viaduct in Cleveland. This event was the creation of Tim Donovan, who had organized fund-raisers for Yablonsky's Warehouse District and had helped the NCVCI for several years with public relations work. He produced a successful event around the theme "When I Grow Up I Want To Be Just Like Dad" in fifty-two days, with twenty-five people helping and without any money. A restaurant created a giant sandwich, the "Cuya-hogie," for the event. People were excited to be up on the viaduct, which overlooked the city and the valley. Yablonsky described a surprise that occurred near the end of the event as it got dark. "All of a sudden, fireworks started shooting off at the end of the bridge." No one knew who set them off, but the event planners did not admit that—people were too impressed, and it looked spectacular.[11]

This event not only raised $10,000, it also drew people who were new to the idea of connecting with the valley, and, from the viaduct, they could see it stretching out before them. People had fun, and the committee deemed the event a great success. The benefit was well supported by the national park and other advocacy groups as well as the media. Other successful benefits followed, and Tim Donovan became an employee of the NCVCI in 1991.

The creation of a twenty-person advisory board that met four times a year was very significant for the future of the organization. The board included representatives from business, industry, and the communities abutting the valley. They were an interested and influential board who raised the expectations for progress each season. Donovan, Yablonsky, and the expanded operating board continued to network with organizations and communities to create a larger advocacy base and further the idea of connecting community to park.

Nonetheless, to really promote the concept of connecting Cleveland to the national park, the leaders had to have a concrete plan of what could be done with the valley. Thanks to Jim Kastelic, the planning document called *North Cuyahoga Valley Corridor* was developed. In 1988, Kastelic was the acting director of what would become the Cuyahoga County Planning Commission and was shepherding the organization through structural changes and a renaming process. He read an article about the NCVCI in the *Cleveland Plain Dealer* and then met with Yablonsky. They talked about the Cuyahoga as a hidden valley, one that had so many stories to tell about the industrial history of the region and of the natural environment. But they also understood that to convince the public that the valley was an important cultural resource in need of preservation they needed a well-designed plan of action.[12]

Kastelic developed a work plan, but the two men initially were not successful in raising grant funds. So they decided to approach the county with the idea that public seed money should be made available to get the project started and provide a base for other donors. It worked—the county commissioners provided the funds, and, together with other donors like the Cleveland Foundation, The George Gund Foundation, and the BP America Charitable Trust, about $70,000 was raised.

Kastelic remembered assigning this study in 1989 to Richard Sicha, a young, new employee of the planning commission. Sicha, with degrees in history and historic preservation, had grown up on what he calls the south side of the Cuyahoga Valley, in Independence. As a junior high school student there in the late 1960s, he worked on a volunteer history project and had the opportunity to meet and spend time with Dillow Robinson, one of the last canallers. (For more on Robinson, see chapter 7.) Sicha's canal-buff social studies teacher Fred Schuld, Schuld's son, and Sicha spent time with Robinson, touring important canal sites in northeast Ohio and interviewing him about his days on the canal. It was serendipity that his first project for the Cuyahoga County Planning Commission was to manage writing the *North Cuyahoga Valley Corridor* plan.[13]

After some days of fieldwork, Sicha called Kastelic to report his findings. "I can't believe what I saw. I was down there behind some industries, walking around . . . there are like hundreds of acres down there that are just totally wild." He added, "I saw blue heron, I saw a fox, I saw all kinds of birds and animals . . . and you know, you're only a few miles from downtown, but you're like in a wilderness." The land Sicha was describing had been zoned industrial, the back property of seven major corporations, all of whom would be stakeholders in and gatekeepers to any plan that would follow the river and canal northward.

Of the corridor plan, Sicha noted, "We focused on six main topics: economic development, heritage education, transportation, recreation, open space, and environmental policy statements." The planning commission also worked with a technical committee composed of local and CVNP consultants. The plan was printed in 1992 and provided a blueprint for a different future for the valley. It encompassed many of the visions of the NCVCI and partner organizations, offering a professional assessment that supported and advocated the preservation and connecting mission of the organization. Sicha had developed a comprehensive plan that not only outlined the various components and possibilities but did so against the backdrop of the history of the valley's industrial portion. According to Kastelic most of the plan's recommendations have subsequently been or are being accomplished, as is evident along the Towpath Trail from Rockside to Harvard Roads.

Many community groups were waiting anxiously for the findings of the report to become public. Jim Kastelic believes that the study was very influential; it received considerable attention from public officials in Cuyahoga County, in Cleveland and in adjacent cities. Suddenly, people began to think that it was important to be part of the effort to revitalize the valley. "When the study was completed, we not only published sixty copies of the original document, but I think we did almost five or seven hundred of the executive summaries, and we ran out of them." Part of the significance of the *North Cuyahoga Valley Corridor* plan was that it included recognition of the industrial history, of immigration patterns in the labor force, and the relevance of the communities bordering the Cuyahoga Valley.

Kastelic credits the Clean Water Act (1965) and other environmental laws for beginning to change the paradigm of how we view the river and valley. Kastelic gave Yablonsky and the NCVCI credit for understanding the valley's resources, promoting the *North Cuyahoga Valley Corridor* plan, and doing a terrific job of promoting a new view. He also said, "But I really think that our views changed because . . . no local government can do anything by itself. It has to rely on partnerships with county, with state, and with federal governments, and I think that was what we realized was the challenge; the way we look at the valley now is quite different than . . . twenty years ago." This change in perspective challenged groups to think regionally.

Others were also discovering the beauty, wilderness, and potential of the industrial valley. Much of the land along the river was owned by seven businesses; most important, the canal was watered and maintained as an industrial water source for American Steel & Wire, part of the U.S. Steel Corporation. The company began to retool to reopen under the leadership of Tom Tyrrell in 1986. Tyrrell had lived in a number of areas before coming to Cleveland, and, coincidentally, he had worked near and used all three of the existing national canal heritage corridors.[14] He described himself as a person who liked to be active outdoors, especially as a runner, so exploring the company's back acreage was important to him.

American Steel & Wire owned 230 acres, of which 40 were under roof. In the back acreage there was a settling pond, then the canal and the river, with a berm in between. "We had the responsibility for the maintenance of the canal at that point and time for . . . about twenty miles. . . . It was our emergency water source. So if something happened to city water and our settling pond did not have enough water in it, we could go down and use water out of the canal." Occasionally during storms, the canal would break through the berm and into the river, and then the company was responsible for the repairs. Maintenance of the canal and towpath was a condition of the water lease.

Tyrrell was very excited about the acreage with the canal and towpath, on which he regularly ran and encouraged his employees to use as well. He was surprised at the quiet, the deer, fox, and great blue heron. "And the more I rode it, ran it, the more I was just totally impressed with it." As leader of American Steel & Wire, Tyrrell was in a unique position to lead the valley's industrial community into a partnership with corridor development.

In 1986–87, Tim Donovan of NCVCI and Vern Hartenburg, director of Cleveland Metroparks, explained the canal's story to Tyrell and enlisted him to help extend the range of Metroparks through the industrial valley. Tyrrell became a member of the NCVCI and began to work on planning concepts. After careful consideration of the liability issues, he agreed to give some of the company's land to Metroparks. Once he committed American Steel & Wire as a participant, other businesses followed his example. This enabled Metroparks, with the help of the NCVCI and Tyrrell, to gain assess to privately owned canal lands that stretched from Independence to Harvard Road. Cleveland Metroparks then moved forward to explore the feasibility of developing what later became the Ohio & Erie Canal Reservation.

Of course, all the work and planning going on north of the national park was not happening in a vacuum. While the Cuyahoga County Planning Commission worked on the northern valley, the national park had construction crews busy on its twenty miles of the Towpath Trail. The 1993 completion of this work heightened the interest in the corridor project and spread canal fever as people began to experience the trail. So in the middle of the grassroots efforts to create a heritage corridor and connect to the national park, the park created a model for how the larger region could preserve resources and reconstruct them for recreational use.

The geography, history, and demographics south of the national park presented a different kind of challenge than that of the regions north of it. When Superintendent John Debo arrived in 1988, he found NCVCI advocating for connecting the park to Cleveland. South of the park, there was no single group pushing for connecting the park to Akron or to any other point south. There was, nonetheless, some talk of connecting it at least to Akron. Akron's *Cascade Valley Park Master Plan* had been amended to show the possibility of preserving a narrow green corridor about two and a half miles long, along the Cuyahoga River from the north edge of the proposed city park to the south edge of Cuyahoga Valley National Park.[15] The park's trail plan mentions the potential of a restored towpath "to become a recreational link to both Cleveland and Akron."[16]

The Cuyahoga River south of the park was lined with apartments, commercial buildings, and light industry, as well as the city's sewage treatment plant and sludge composting plant, but some wooded green space remained. The only established recreational space was the Buckeye Trail (for hikers only), which used a short section of the riverside corridor as part of its statewide trail system. Akron bicyclists trying to reach the national park's scenic roads had to first negotiate the narrow, busy Merriman Road at the edge of the city limits. Debo recognized that there needed to be a grassroots movement south of the park similar to what was occurring north of the park. Just after NCVCI gave him the tour north of the national park, he was invited to tour a piece of Akron's canal remnants.

Debo's hostess for the Akron visit was Virginia Wojno Forney. He recalls, "[I began] to hear from people about this broader concept that there is something beyond the boundaries of Cuyahoga Valley National Park that just might be worthy of some attention and focus. Virginia, with the Mustill Store [was one], and I remember meeting her for lunch at the Cascade Club and then she took me down to this overgrown, dilapidated

Preserving the Mustill Store, shown here in 1989 in its pre-restoration condition, became the focus of a multiple partnership (photo by Rob Bobel).

site and introduced me to Pete Ramnytz. Virginia made it clear she was asking for help . . . well, I had no ability to help whatsoever; there was no basis for a park service to go out there, other than providing moral support, and I recall making a call to city hall in Akron . . . because, at that point, the issue was the demolition of the Mustill Store."

Wojno Forney persisted, and later, when asked why her project was so successful, she replied, "Five fanatics, and any project will succeed." But, in truth, her enthusiasm, vision, and quiet tenacity were just what the Mustill Store needed. In 1988, she formed the Cascade Locks Park Association to focus on the preservation and development of a small section of historic canal land, canal buildings, and associated canal structures. She has since been the consistent leader in the project that has culminated in the successful Cascade Locks Park, part of Cascade Valley Metro Park and a gem in the Canalway.[17]

Besides Yablonsky and Wojno Forney, John Debo was also hearing from other people, one a persistent voice from Stark County, Ann McLaughlin (now Ann Henman). At that time, Henman was living in Canal Fulton. When she moved there in 1977, she found that, in general, "people were not proud of the canal, were not proud of their ancestors." Nonetheless, there was by then a replica canal boat, the *St. Helena II*, that made excursions from the town to a small park around Lock 4 (see chapter 14). Henman restored a historic house in town and soon found her interest in historic preservation expanding into the community, leading her to becoming president of both the Canal Fulton Heritage Society and the Stark Preservation Alliance. In the late 1980s, she enrolled as a communications student at the University of Akron. Her argumentation course required an outline of an argument, and, as she explained, "I thought, well, I'll just argue for the canal. . . . There should be an Ohio & Erie Canal National Heritage Corridor in northeastern Ohio."[18]

And argue well she did, armed with extensive research, including "Tales of the Towpath," an oral history project she had completed for the Canal Fulton Heritage Society; visits to canals in the United States, Ireland, Belgium, and the Netherlands; and attendance at a conference at the Illinois and Michigan Canal National Heritage Corridor, where she met Debo, and they exchanged ideas about preserving canal history and connecting the park to the cities along the canal. Henman began to distribute her argument, which still stands as a blueprint for what has become the Ohio & Erie National Heritage Canalway. Henman had already thought through the entire idea, and she succinctly spelled it out, documenting the significance of the canal's history, preservation efforts to date, widespread interest in the canal, the idea's timeliness, and the canal's "parallel resources and needs to those listed for the existing corridors."[19] Now the concept expanded beyond an interest in connecting the national park to Cleveland and Akron to one that envisioned the preservation of the heritage of the region centered on the history of the canal.

Debo would be the catalyst for acting on these ideas, but meanwhile, he was dividing his attention between the work inside and outside Cuyahoga Valley National Park. Within it, he focused on turning the Ohio & Erie Canal remnants into a developed asset, including turning the towpath into a trail, planning for access and parking, and restoring associated historic structures. The focus of the work outside the park was crystallized at a meeting in the park's conference room. By Debo's account, "the purpose of the meeting was to talk about the 'corridor,' and it was essentially at that moment where we went from talking about the canal towpath in the park to a project. . . . That is where it obtained the name 'Ohio and Erie Canal Heritage Corridor.' At that point it wasn't 'national,' because we weren't at all thinking about any kind of federal designation, but rather this idea of an Ohio and Erie Canal corridor."

He recalled that he and other staff rolled out maps and discussed at length the boundaries of such a corridor. Although no one was very familiar with the resources north of the park, they were clear in their desire to take the towpath all the way to downtown Cleveland and its lakefront. He explained, "This was for connectivity, this was so that people in Cleveland would have *access* to the towpath *in* Cleveland, and be able to work south." He was fully aware that at the same time the Cuyahoga Valley Scenic Railroad was also exploring a rail connection between the national park and Cleveland. Most vivid in his recollection of the meeting, however, was that although the goal for the north was clear, "it was not so easy to talk about the canal corridor heading south." Some people suggested Akron be the terminus, while others pointed out that there was a lot of "nice canal land" south of Akron and in Stark County. Various end points were suggested, including Canal Fulton, with its already established excursion canal boat. Then someone suggested Zoar as an appropriate destination: it was a historical canal village where the Ohio Historical Society had a presence, and it was where the North Country Trail, a national scenic trail, would intersect the historic canal towpath. The idea that the proposed corridor would connect to a planned national scenic trail sold Zoar as the southern endpoint.[20]

Now the superintendent was faced with the question of how to proceed with the corridor idea south of the park. As he explained, "We have to have some sort of interest group. . . . It was very clear to me from the beginning, it wasn't going to be a top-down National Park Service leads the charge to develop the Ohio & Erie Canal from Cleveland to Zoar [process]—this was going to have to be a community-based kind of thing in order for it to work. And that's when we began to talk to Rob and Peg Bobel and Christine Freitag and others about the idea of a new organization to the south, and that's when Ann Henman's name surfaced." Debo turned to those who seemed logical allies in this new enterprise—leaders of the Cuyahoga Valley Association (CVA) and trail advocates from the Buckeye Trail Association and the Cuyahoga Valley Trails Council. The CVA had led the grassroots support for creating a national park in the Cuyahoga Valley, and by 1988, Christine Freitag, president of the association, was pressing the group to reorganize itself as a friends group, hire a staff person, and open an office. The Bobels had long been supporters of the park and were two of the founding trustees of the Cuyahoga Valley Trails Council, formed to help the park build and maintain a trail system. In 1989, Peg Bobel was hired as the new executive director for the CVA. Debo made a few phone calls, and things "south of the border" began to roll.

Now with contacts being made both north and south of the park, Debo was strategizing as to how the park service could assist the effort, since his job was clearly to stay inside the boundaries of the national park, where there was plenty of work to do. He needed a way and a person to focus just on the corridor idea. Less than a month after a spring car tour of the potential corridor, he attended a meeting in Harrisburg, Pennsylvania. As Debo recalled, "at that conference I met a guy named Paul Labovitz. We met . . . in the morning at about 8:00, and, from my perspective, by 5:00 he had been hired."

Labovitz was already working for the National Park Service in the Rivers, Trails, and Conservation Assistance Program, a branch of the park service that gives technical assistance to communities that are trying to conserve land such as river corridors and trail greenways. He had the perfect combination of skills and experience for the project back in Ohio. He would be duty-stationed at Cuyahoga Valley National Park but would work exclusively outside the park on the Ohio & Erie Canal Corridor project. Meanwhile, Christine Freitag and Peg Bobel arranged a meeting of individuals who had been identified as potential leaders for the grassroots corridor effort south of the national park. In July, ten people met in the conference room at the administrative offices of Metro Parks, Serving Summit County. Included at the table were John R. Daily, then secretary-director of Metro Parks and host of the meeting; Superintendent John Debo; former congressman John F. Seiberling; Ann Henman; Virginia Wojno Forney; Peg Bobel; and representatives from Kent State University; Barberton's parks and recreation department; and Akron's planning department. By the end of the meeting, it had been decided that Henman, Wojno Forney, and Bobel would draft a letter of invitation to a larger list of people—mostly names gathered by Debo and Henman—inviting all to a meeting on September 14, 1989, at the Canal Fulton Village Hall.[21]

John Seiberling, the former congressman for Ohio's 14th District and founder of Cuyahoga Valley National Park, was invited to moderate the meeting, but various community leaders, including Canal Fulton's mayor, would present parts of the agenda, a conscious effort to keep the emphasis on a community-driven process. No one knew what to expect or who would show up, but that night a standing-room-only crowd filled the village hall meeting room. By the end of the evening, a twelve-member steering committee had been selected and the next meeting date set. Many participants came forward with ideas, support, information, and offers to help.[22] Henman's argument and Debo's vision had found a receptive audience. Henman recalled: "It was fantastic. . . . I mean when you send out a letter you think, who will come? . . . but I think there were seventy people there. . . . [There] may have only been five people [from the invitation list] missing." As she further reflected, "It was just an idea that was right. All the elements were there. We needed it to be done before this urban sprawl just ruined everything. And people needed to understand connection, that we were all part of the same story, rather than this piece, this piece, this piece."

The group began to use the name Ohio & Erie Canal Corridor Coalition (OECCC) immediately after the September 1989 gathering, and the steering committee started meeting monthly, in the basement of the Old Canal Days Museum in Canal Fulton at first. In the beginning, the committee worked swiftly to draft a statement of purpose, create an organizational structure, select officers, assign work to committees, and plan regularly scheduled public meetings at different locations in the corridor. The public meetings gave the steering committee a chance to report back to its grassroots supporters and offered the public opportunities to engage in the planning process. By January 1990, the fledgling group had $55 in its treasury, and by the end of February founding trustees Ann Henman, Don Cooke, and Lawrence Turner had incorporated it.[23] Its purposes included stimulating interest and support for "the protection, preservation, development, and enhancement of the historical, cultural, natural, industrial, commercial, and recreational resources along the route of the historic Ohio & Erie Canal," to encourage recognition of the Ohio & Erie Canal Corridor, and "to work toward establishing a continuous physical linkage along or near the planned canal corridor and work with businesses and industry along the planned corridor to incorporate their needs into a canal corridor plan."

Meanwhile, in Akron Virginia Wojno Forney was devoting attention to developing Cascade Locks Park and serving as OECCC board secretary. Henman became chair of the OECCC, and Bobel later became membership chair. In May 1990, Henman completed her University of Akron degree and decided to leave Ohio, but, before leaving, she encouraged Don Cooke to accept nomination as president of the coalition. He began his presidency in January 1991 with $1,250.77 in the group's accounts; one of the first items on the agenda was fund-raising.

With just over a year of operation under its belt, the OECCC was already well organized, with 149 members, several working committees, and a newsletter edited by Kathy Fernandez, then site manager for the Zoar Village State Memorial. She chose the name for the newsletter, *The Silver Ribbon*, from one of caller Pearl Nye's songs. She edited the newsletter from its inception and also came up with the idea for the group's first fundraiser, held in Zoar, called "Cavorting on the Canal," an annual event.[24]

The level of enthusiasm in the young organization was high, with clear goals and good leadership. Labovitz provided the planning expertise, official guidance, and coordination of the corridor project. Debo, meanwhile, was never far offstage, keeping an eye on developments and using his official influence and his planning background to facilitate the project. He also kept in close touch with the local congressional delegation.

Grassroots activities and official planning proceeded side by side. For instance, the OECCC inventory committee, under the leadership of canal buff Larry Turner, hosted a Canal Corridor Inventory Day on April 28, 1990. Teams up and down the canal, from the Southerly Sewage Treatment Plant in Cleveland to Tuscarawas County, walked assigned portions with clipboards and cameras, noting on inventory forms the condition of the canal and towpath; available access points; ownership, if known; problem areas; and any interesting discoveries, such as special natural areas or current uses of the canal lands.[25]

Two months later, the steering committee held an all-day planning retreat, and, by the end of July, U.S. Representative Ralph Regula, one of the canal's biggest champions, had requested federal funds for a formal study of the Ohio & Erie Canal corridor. In November 1990, $175,000 was approved in the federal budget for the study.[26] Now Labovitz could assemble a team and formally begin the study process.

While the study got underway, the two grassroots groups continued to spread the word about the project, explaining to the public the relatively new concept of a "national heritage corridor." At the time, only three such corridors existed. These, the Illinois and Michigan Canal National Heritage Corridor in Illinois, the Blackstone River Valley National Heritage Corridor in Massachusetts and Rhode Island, and the Delaware and Lehigh National Heritage Corridor in Pennsylvania, provided models for the Ohio & Erie supporters. Debo and Labovitz were familiar with these and with ways other countries protected their heritage areas and special landscapes, short of creating government-owned and -operated parks. Debo in particular saw the concept as a vehicle for combating the homogenization of place in the United States, the creation of an undifferentiated landscape of fast-food restaurants and box stores.

One helpful tool in spreading the word about the potential Ohio & Erie Canal heritage corridor was the old stand-by—taking slide-show talks on the road. And while the concept initially took some explaining, it was also widely inclusive and therefore appealed to a variety of interest groups, including nature enthusiasts, bicyclists, civic leaders, business leaders, historic preservationists, and parents looking for a safe place for their youngsters to ride their bikes. For many the idea was appealing because it lifted their image of northeast Ohio from a depressed rustbelt to an area rich with national significance, with historic and interesting places to visit and to be understood, valued, and enjoyed. Debo said, "We all spent huge amounts of time out there talking to everybody and anybody that would listen . . . you name them, we would talk to them. . . . And what was so interesting was to see how quickly people coalesced around this concept. There was tremendous latent interest in preserving the Ohio & Erie Canal."

By the time the OECCC organized, NCVCI had already been presenting slide shows and taking groups on hikes to introduce people to the attributes of the north valley. During the early years of grassroots activism, both groups were feeling their way through turf issues; while both clearly saw the vision for a united, continuously linked heritage corridor, each knew best its piece of the geography and its social and political climate. NCVCI had its roots in Cleveland, and the OECCC, south of the national park in Akron and Canal Fulton. While there were always cooperation and specific opportunities for collaboration, the two groups tended to stay separate when educating the public about the corridor. When the National Park Service study got underway, the study team acted as ambassadors in keeping the north-south elements connected.

Along with the talks, slide shows, and public meetings, two particular events helped advance the heritage corridor idea both north and south of the national park. The first was the groundbreaking for the Towpath Trail in Cuyahoga Valley National Park mentioned earlier, with Debo noting the twentieth anniversary of Earth Day. Representatives from all the major partners in the heritage corridor project handled the shovels that day.[27] Debo has often commented that the construction of the Towpath Trail should be understood in terms of the effect it had on the efforts and vision of others; once other officials and civic leaders could actually see the towpath being developed and the tremendous response it was receiving, they could more easily grasp their own plans to extend the trail and the corridor concept beyond the boundaries of the park.

The second event was the Second International Conference on Historic Canals held in Akron in autumn 1991, hosted by the OECCC, the National Park Service, the Cuyahoga Valley Association, the Cascade Locks Park Association, the Canal Society of Ohio, the Summit County Historical Society, the NCVCI, the City of Akron, and the Akron Convention Bureau. Dan Rice, then the society's curator, represented the

Left to right are Steve Coles, John Daily, John Debo, Ann McLaughlin Henman, Tom Sawyer, John Seiberling, and Tom Yablonsky lifting shovels for groundbreaking of the Towpath Trail in Cuyahoga Valley National Park (photo by Rob Bobel).

Summit County Historical Society. While working on the conference planning committee, he caught a serious case of canal fever and began volunteering for the OECCC. Later, he became the group's first paid executive director, a position he still holds. During this conference, the Ohio & Erie Canal heritage corridor project was spotlighted. Tours introduced locals and visitors to various sites and attractions, from downtown Cleveland to Zoar, highlighting the benefits of preserving and federally designating the corridor. It was an opportunity for the northern and southern groups to work together and the first planned event that presented the corridor as a linked, continuous landscape.

Meanwhile, Labovitz and two new park service associates, Rory Robinson and Barbara Nelson Jameson, were working on the official suitability/feasibility study, funded in the 1991 federal budget. Over the next two and one-half years, the three would complete exhaustive research while hosting public meetings, consulting with officials, and participating in numerous meetings with grassroots groups and local leaders.[28] The intent of the study was "to provide information to Congress to guide decisions concerning the future of the Ohio & Erie Canal Corridor," and to conduct "an analysis of the corridor's national significance and its suitability and feasibility for inclusion as an affiliated area of the National Park Service or as a unit of the potential National Heritage Partnership system."[29] According to Robinson, two leadership meetings—one held in Canton and one in Cleveland—were key to preparing the study. The planners invited two to three hundred leaders to each meeting, presented the slide show, and introduced the heritage corridor concept. As Robinson explained, "You could just see people, as we tried to explain the idea, saying, yeah, this is pretty neat, and pretty non-threatening." As he also said, it was important for people to understand that this "was not a federal land grab" and that the challenge of thinking and planning must be faced regionally. "But it was a challenge that was relatively easily overcome, because I think the corridor concept is . . . a concept that people could embrace as being relatively non-threatening."[30]

Robinson had also learned an especially interesting lesson while working with the Blackstone River Valley National Heritage Corridor staff in 1991. "In the Blackstone, you have mill towns where they'd have a public meeting and somebody would come from one mill town, from the next mill town . . . telling folks that 'this is the first time I've been in this town.' These mill towns historically were competing against each other, and the heritage corridor concept really worked to break down the barriers that developed over two hundred years of history." Back in Ohio, "we felt the best way to do this, the feasibility study, was to do it in a very, very public format so that not only would we have a traditional park service say 'yes this is feasible, yes this is suitable,' but we would have a very, very, very strong basis of support for the idea, whether or not legislation passed." Robinson believes this process ultimately was critical to the success of the Canalway.

As the National Park Service planners embarked on their work in 1991, they were well aware of the study underway in Cuyahoga County to the north of the national park. The park service planners worked closely with Cuyahoga County planners and grassroots advocates, finding the inventory material and well-articulated concepts in the *North Cuyahoga Valley Corridor* study especially valuable. The report was released in February 1992, and it acknowledged that the federal study was underway by including an explanation of how the North Cuyahoga project could relate to a larger national heritage corridor.[31]

The National Park Service's study, *A Route to Prosperity: A Study by the National Park Service of the Ohio & Erie Canal Corridor*, also referenced earlier studies: "Protection and enhancement of the diverse resources of the Ohio & Erie Canal Corridor are not new ideas." Appendix A of the study, "Not a New Idea," describes at least eight other studies and plans, beginning with the 1925 Olmsted Brothers plan for the Akron Metropolitan Park District Board of Summit County, which included a parkway south to Clinton, with connections north to Cleveland Metroparks. A 1970 Ohio Department of Natural Resources publication, *Tuscarawas River and Ohio & Erie Canal Recreation and Development Study*, concluded that sections of the canal in Summit, Stark, and Tuscarawas Counties could be developed as a recreational parkway, a "lengthy river corridor with activity nodes at selected locations," but the plan was not carried through.[32] The first legislation proposing creation of a national park in the Cuyahoga Valley also included the canal lands south of Akron and into Stark County.[33] A 1975 National Park Service study (immediately following enactment of Cuyahoga Valley National Recreation Area) looked at the entire length of the historic canal and concluded that it had national significance, but that what remained of the physical structures themselves "lacked integrity." Nonetheless, it described the canal as "an open corridor of substantial recreation potential." Stark County had long been working to maximize the recreational potential of its portion of the canal corridor and had already preserved canal lands in the county and created the Stark County Park District to manage them. *A Route to Prosperity*, building on those ideas, described four possible alternatives for protecting and managing corridor resources, from "No Action" to a federal initiative. The grassroots groups and Congressman Regula were successful in gaining federal authorization (see chapter 17).[34]

The context in which the work took place might have helped make this effort successful. Certainly the earlier studies provided evidence of the public interest in preserving the canal corridor, and they documented both the condition of the resource and its potential, but for the most part action did not follow. The creation of Cuyahoga Valley National Park was a major accomplishment, and although it did not preserve as much of the canal lands as was first proposed, it did focus significant resources on twenty miles of canal. But it was not feasible to protect more within the context of a national park; the national political climate was changing and would lead to a different kind of preservation movement. The national park was created during President Lyndon B. Johnson and Secretary of the Interior Steward Udall's "new conservation" movement, which was designed to bring parks to the people. Cuyahoga followed such parks as Indiana Dunes National Seashore just east of Chicago, Golden Gate National Park in San Francisco, and Gateway in New York City.[35] This burst of urban park energy, however, was challenged during the Reagan administration, from both within the administration and without, by private property–rights advocates. Nonetheless, at the beginning of President Reagan's second term, conservation and recreation leaders urged him to create an advisory commission to review the state of the nation's outdoor recreation. The commission's work resulted in a published report, *The Report of the President's Commission: Americans Outdoors, The Legacy, the Challenge*.[36] The commission called for "a prairie fire of concern and investment, community by community," and by including case studies, it gave communities real-life examples of how to provide more recreation for their citizens. One chapter in *Americans Outdoors* deals entirely with the concept of "greenways." The recommendation was clear: that "communities establish Greenways, corridors of private and public recreation lands and waters, to provide people with access to open spaces close to where they live, and to link together the rural and urban spaces in the American landscape."

Americans Outdoors also emphasized the importance of partnerships among private for-profit organizations and nonprofits and public agencies. "The key to successful partnerships is to match resources to achieve mutual goals." The report discussed balancing conservation and economic needs and recognized how partnerships for recreation could also revitalize urban areas, especially waterfronts and downtowns. It also suggested sources of funding beyond traditional ones, to include the Highway Trust Fund, which has since made a significant contribution to the construction of parts of the Ohio & Erie Canal Towpath Trail. The report's emphasis on the needs of urban citizens made it especially relevant to the work that was to take place in northeast Ohio in the 1990s.[37]

Although most Americans may have never been aware of the "prairie fire" called for in the report, and a local "Prairie Fire Forum" in Summit County was lightly attended, a fire was lit nonetheless. Good timing added more fuel; in spring 1991, the same year the International Conference on Historic Canals was held in Akron, another meeting in Ohio creatively put forth the notion of combining historic preservation with natural resource protection and recreational development. A Toledo group, which later became the Maumee Valley Heritage Corridor, Incorporated, advocated for a heritage corridor along the Maumee River. Partnering with the National Trust for Historic Preservation, in April they presented a conference: "Common Ground: Managing Cultural and Natural Corridors."[38] The keynote speaker was Charles E. Little, who inspired the conferees with his talk based on his recently released book, *Greenways for America*, which followed up on the *Americans Outdoors* report and provided more inspiring examples and helpful references. Among the people he interviewed for it was Gerald W. Adelmann, the leader of the effort to create the Illinois and Michigan Canal National Heritage Corridor. Just after the Toledo conference, Adelmann spoke at the Cuyahoga Valley Association's annual meeting in Peninsula. He became a tremendous help and inspiration to Ohio & Erie project advocates.

It was in this context that Labovitz, Robinson, and Nelson Jameson studied their way from Cleveland to Zoar, and, on September 16, 1993, *A Route to Prosperity* was officially released. With the study in hand, advocates could now point to the conclusion "that the Ohio & Erie Canal Corridor is both suitable and feasible for designation as a component of the potential National Heritage Partnership system." And the National Park Service sponsored "Thinking Corridor," a workshop "to explore some of the strategies for implementation of the corridor way of thinking in Northeast Ohio."[39] It was held the same day as and just prior to the ribbon cutting for the Ohio & Erie Canal Towpath Trail in Cuyahoga Valley National Park, which officially opened the trail to waves of visitors, many of whom had already been enjoying the trail.

Typical of meetings and discussions and events that would follow, the workshop had many cosponsors, including two relative newcomers, the Cascade Locks Park Association and the NAVBETH Corridor Development Corporation (NAVBETH refers to Stark County's Navarre–Bethlehem Township area). These groups are two more examples of what was already happening in communities along the proposed corridor when the official study was released. The corridor way of thinking was already well rooted and bearing fruit and was destined to continue whether or not national heritage corridor designation was achieved. The Cascade Locks Park Association and the NAVBETH Corridor Development Corporation were dealing with very different sections of the corridor but were using similar skills and relationships developed from earlier work on the corridor.

The Cascade Locks group had taken on a neglected, abused, and overgrown urban section of the historic canal area in downtown Akron, while the NAVBETH group was working with thirteen miles of rural, green corridor, some of which was already being used by hikers, anglers, and bird-watchers. While very different, these projects shared some common ground: each was led by a strong, dedicated, visionary individual surrounded by a small group of volunteers; each had learned how to garner the support of local officials, public agencies, and the media; and each was forging partnerships to achieve goals. Both locations would become hubs of activity in the emerging corridor, and while the NAVBETH group dissolved after achieving its goal, the Cascade Locks Park Association at this writing is engaged in further development and enhancement of its small section of Canalway.

What makes the Cascade Locks story especially impressive is the contrast between the area before 1989 and in 2008. Just north of downtown Akron is one of the most historically significant and interesting sections of canal landscape, including a staircase of locks and canal-era buildings, but by the late 1980s it was unknown to all but a few individuals. One of those was Walter Sheppe, who had moved to Akron in 1968 to teach biology at the University of Akron. He began to explore around the city in the 1970s and became intrigued with the surprisingly wild land in the Little Cuyahoga and Cuyahoga River Valleys. His explorations led to his founding of the Portage Trail Group of the Sierra Club, which advocated creating a park along the rivers, largely out of land already owned by the city, an area that would eventually become the Cascade Valley Metro Park.

While documenting the potential of the proposed park area, Sheppe became acquainted with Pete Ramnytz, who, with his wife, Julia, lived next to Lock 15. The Ramnytzes owned and cherished one of the oldest houses in Akron and the building next door, the Mustill Store (both circa 1840–50). The two buildings were among the very few structures from the early canal era still surviving in the city. The house was historic in appearance, but the store looked more like a garage and was chock full of artifacts and finds Ramnytz had collected. He realized the historic significance of the buildings and had tried to preserve them as far as his resources allowed.[40]

Sheppe, in the Sierra Club's 1976 proposal, *Akron's Cascade Valley Park*, advocated for preserving the house and store. The city's *Cascade Valley Park Master Plan* of 1979 also noted the historic significance of the Mustill Store, but funding for developing the new park was focused on the larger natural areas farther north that were already owned by the city.[41] Around 1988, Sheppe again visited the Ramnytzes and saw that the property was for sale—Mr. Ramnytz could no longer care for it—and the city was not interested in buying it. Sheppe's concern for this piece of Akron history led him to Virginia Wojno Forney.

Wojno Forney was president of Progress through Preservation, a new historic preservation group in Akron. Sheppe invited Wojno Forney to visit the Mustill house and store, "in perfect innocence, not expecting anything to come of it." But before he knew what was happening, she had organized a "Save the Mustill Store" committee to try to find a buyer for the historic property. The committee met for a year or so, when one of its members declared, "I'm getting tired of this . . . we're getting nowhere. Why don't all of us chip in $5,000, and we'll buy it and mothball it until . . . we can find a buyer." Wojno Forney agreed that was the only thing that made any sense. At that point, committee member Jim Alkire, then planning director of Akron, realized that they were serious, went to city council, and convinced the city that this property was of value to Akron and that it should be preserved.

That, however, was just the beginning. Alkire then came back to Wojno Forney and challenged her: "Well, I bought your house and store, what are you going to do with it?" She formed the Cascade Locks Park Association and used her knowledge and influence throughout Akron to involve anyone she thought would be helpful to the cause. Tom Long, of the City of Akron's Planning Department, recalled in 2003, "If I had to describe significant moments or milestones in an effort to preserve the canal corridor, I would go all the way back to when I initially started working with the Cascade Locks Park Association. Literally, the Cascade Locks area was a forgotten urban geography, a jungle. There were locks in there somewhere, but the area was so overcome by vegetation that you couldn't see a thing or get to them." Cascade Locks requested help from the city to clear a foot trail, and Long turned that appeal into an Ohio Civilian Conservation Corps project in the summer of 1992. Now that visitors could see and get close to the historic set of canal locks near the Mustill Store, interest in the area grew even more.[42]

Wojno Forney sought out John Debo to help save the Mustill Store. Her request for federal help and his inability to provide anything but moral support strengthened his interest in finding a way for the National Park Service to assist on worthy projects outside the park boundary, a goal eventually met when the legislation created the Ohio & Erie Canal National Heritage Corridor. But Wojno Forney and her group were committed to preserving this small but significant piece of the canal whether or not it became part of a national heritage corridor, and they had things well underway in 1993 when the corridor study was released. Just as the volunteers north of the national park were forging partnerships to advance their plans, Wojno Forney and her group were partnering with the City of Akron and Metro Parks, Serving Summit County, among others, to achieve their goals.

The NAVBETH Corridor Development Corporation gives us another example of how communities and grassroots groups were already preserving parts of the canal corridor when the NPS study was released. Don Cooke, one of the founders of the Ohio & Erie Canal Corridor Coalition, formed a group in Navarre in 1990 specifically to establish the corridor in that village and in surrounding Bethlehem Township and to open the thirteen-mile section of Towpath Trail within the township and village. Cooke made a formal request to Paul Labovitz and the National Park Service's Rivers, Trails, and Conservation Assistance Program for help in planning the corridor in Navarre, just as the corridor study was being completed and long before there was federal designation and the funds that came with it. The National Park Service planners working with Cooke's group produced a short but detailed plan for all elements of developing the "canal greenway" in Bethlehem Township and Navarre, getting that section of Canalway underway just after release of *A Route to Prosperity*. Besides finding help with planning, groups such as the NAV-BETH Community Development Corporation were practicing partnering and were exchanging ideas and information throughout the proposed corridor. As Cooke explained, "This Canalway has brought both ends together, and it's really helped the national park."[43]

North and south of Cuyahoga Valley National Park in the early 1990s, grassroots groups were laying the foundations for the creation of a national heritage corridor. Certainly, when NCVCI was first founded, its focus was to simply link Cleveland to the national park along the Cuyahoga River corridor. The Ohio & Erie Canal Corridor Coalition from its beginning saw that the heritage corridor would encompass a swath of land from the Cleveland lakefront to Zoar. The 1993 *A Route to Prosperity*, both in process and on paper, began to give the grassroots groups one clear focus: achieving national designation and acquiring federal funds to make their dreams come true. However, in 1993, it was clear that much work was already underway, partnerships were working, and money was flowing. These successes and the strong grassroots support they represented would make the federal legislation succeed and would truly create the Canalway. As Congressman Regula stated when the study was released, "It is not funding from the federal government that will make this corridor project a reality, but rather strong grassroots support from the local communities, the people and business interests along the corridor. I am confident we have the makings of a very successful partnership in northeast Ohio and it is the people in the communities along the corridor that must transform this vision into reality."[44]

NOTES

1. Frances McGovern, *Written on the Hills: The Making of the Akron Landscape* (Akron: Univ. of Akron Press, 1996), 185–86.

2. Carol Poh Miller, *Cleveland Metroparks, Past and Present: Celebrating Seventy-five Years of Conservation, Education, and Recreation, 1917–1992* (Cleveland: Cleveland Metroparks, 1992), 4.

3. See Al Simpson, *Along the Towpath, A Journalist Rediscovers the Ohio & Erie Canal* (Akron: Univ. of Akron Libraries, 2003), a collection of Simpson's newspaper columns, also entitled "Along the Towpath."

4. From 2003 to 2005, the authors interviewed thirty-seven individuals involved in developing the Ohio & Erie National Heritage Canalway.

5. The North Cuyahoga Valley Corridor, Inc., began in 1984 and changed its name in 1994 to Ohio Canal Corridor. The Ohio & Erie Canal Corridor Coalition began in 1989 and changed its name in 2004 to Ohio & Erie Canalway Coalition.

6. A three-mile section of trail existed in the north end of the park and was managed by Cleveland Metroparks in cooperation with the U.S. Steel Corporation; similarly, Metro Parks, Serving Summit County, maintained a short section of trail on the towpath south of Peninsula.

7. John Debo, interview by Peg Bobel and Lynn Metzger, July 15, 2003. (Further Debo remarks are from this interview.)

8. Ron Thoman, interview by Peg Bobel, Feb. 22, 2005. (Further Thoman remarks are from this interview.)

9. Tom Yablonsky, interview by Peg Bobel and Lynn Metzger, Aug. 25, 2003. (Further Yablonsky remarks are from this interview.)

10. Jeff Lennartz, interview by Peg Bobel, Oct. 9, 2003. (Further Lennartz remarks are from this interview.)

11. Tim Donovan, interview by Peg Bobel and Lynn Metzger, Oct. 1, 2003.

12. Jim Kastelic, interview by Peg Bobel, Oct. 8, 2003. (Further Kastelic remarks are from this interview.)

13. Richard Sicha, interview by Peg Bobel and Lynn Metzger, Oct., 20, 2003. (Further Sicha remarks are from this interview.)

14. Tom Tyrrell, interview by Peg Bobel and Lynn Metzger, Feb. 3, 2004. (Further Tyrrell remarks are from this interview.)

15. City of Akron, Ohio, *Cascade Valley Park Master Plan* (Akron: City of Akron, 1979), prepared by Wallace McHarg Roberts & Todd, Architects, Landscape Architects, Urban and Ecological Planners.

16. U.S. Department of the Interior, National Park Service, *Trail Plan and Environmental Assessment, Cuyahoga Valley National Recreation Area* (Brecksville, Ohio: U.S. Department of the Interior, 1985), 20.

17. Virginia Wojno Forney, interview by Lynn Metzger and Peg Bobel, Oct. 8, 2003.

18. Ann Henman, interview by Lynn Metzger and Peg Bobel, Mar. 12, 2004. (Further Henman remarks are from this interview.)

19. Henman outline proposing an Ohio & Erie Canal National Heritage Corridor, personal papers of Peg Bobel.

20. That meeting did not end the discussion of the southern terminus of the heritage corridor, however. Roscoe Village was also discussed, and there even remains interest today in extending the corridor the entire length of the historic canal. The *Ohio & Erie Canal National Heritage Corridor Management Plan* of 2000 set the official southern boundary at New Philadelphia, Ohio, about twelve miles south of Zoar.

21. Meeting sign-in sheet; Cuyahoga Valley Association letter to Rob Bobel, Aug. 14, 1989, both in Peg Bobel's personal papers.

22. "Canal Corridor," *Voice* (Nov.–Dec. 1989): 5.

23. Ohio & Erie Canal Corridor Coalition minutes, Jan. 31, 1990.

24. Kathy Fernandez, interview by Lynn Metzger and Peg Bobel, Feb. 2, 2004.

25. Inventory Day invitation, personal papers of Peg Bobel.

26. Ohio & Erie Canal Corridor Coalition minutes, Nov. 19, 1990.

27. "First Shovels," captioned photo, *Silver Ribbon* 1 (July 1990): 1.

28. Rory Robinson left his position of supervisory park ranger in Cuyahoga Valley National Park to join the study team. One of his last duties with the park was to oversee the development of the Canal Visitor Center, located in a historic house on the canal at Lock 38. Barbara Nelson Jameson joined the team when she and her husband, Lee, came to Cuyahoga Valley National Park for Lee to begin his position as chief of maintenance, in which he oversaw construction of the Towpath Trail in CVNP.

29. *A Route to Prosperity: A Study by the National Park Service of the Ohio & Erie Canal Corridor* (Omaha, Neb.: U.S. Department of Interior, National Park Service, 1993), 7.

30. Rory Robinson, interview by Lynn Metzger and Peg Bobel, Mar. 3, 2004. (Further Robinson remarks are from this interview.)

31. Cuyahoga County Planning Commission, *North Cuyahoga Valley Corridor* Executive Summary (Cleveland: Cuyahoga County Planning Commission, 1992), 9.

32. *A Route to Prosperity,* 15, 67–68.

33. John F. Seiberling, interview by Lynn Metzger and Peg Bobel, Apr. 23, 2003.

34. *A Route to Prosperity,* 14–15, 67, 63–66.

35. Dyan Zaslowsky and the Wilderness Society, *These American Lands: Parks, Wilderness, and the Public Lands* (New York: Henry Holt, 1986), 37. See also Representative Ralph Regula's statement in House Committee on Interior and Insular Affairs, *Proposed Cuyahoga Valley National Historical Park and Recreation Area, Part II, Hearing before the Subcommittee on National Parks and Recreation of the Committee on Interior and Insular Affairs, House of Representatives* (93d Congress, 1974), 6–7.

36. The President's Commission on Americans Outdoors, *The Report of the President's Commission: Americans Outdoors: The Legacy, the Challenge* (Washington, D.C.: Island Press, 1987), ix–x.

37. Ibid., 189–91, 258.

38. Glenn Harper, conversation with Peg Bobel, Oct. 29, 2005.

39. "Thinking Corridor" workshop flyer, personal papers of Rory Robinson.

40. Walter Sheppe, interview by Lynn Metzger and Peg Bobel, Feb. 25, 2004.

41. Sierra Club Portage Trail Group, *Akron's Cascade Valley Park* (Cuyahoga Falls: Sierra Club Portage Trail Group, 1976), 24–26; *Cascade Valley Park Master Plan*, 10, 33.

42. Tom Long, interview by Lynn Metzger and Peg Bobel, Apr. 2, 2003.

43. Don Cooke, interview by Lynn Metzger and Peg Bobel, Nov. 19, 2004.

44. U.S. Representative Ralph Regula, press release, Sept. 16, 1993.

Chapter 17

Journey to Canalway

PEG BOBEL AND LYNN METZGER

This chapter continues the story of the old Ohio & Erie Canal, as the effort to preserve it changed from a grassroots, local initiative to a well-coordinated drive toward national recognition. Canal fever was intense, and the advocates were focused and determined to both develop the corridor and achieve the national designation. Success was in the air. When Congressman Ralph Regula (R-Ohio) announced in 1993 that he was drafting legislation "to have the 87-mile corridor from Cleveland to Zoar dedicated as the nation's fourth National Heritage Corridor, making it an affiliated area of the National Park System," the grassroots organizations throughout the proposed heritage corridor sharpened their focus toward one goal: passage of federal legislation to create a national heritage corridor.[1] *A Route to Prosperity*, the suitability/feasibility study that evaluated the resources in the Ohio & Erie Canal corridor for possible national designation, was released in 1993, and by 1994 both major nonprofit organizations, the Ohio & Erie Canalway Coalition (OECC) and the Ohio Canal Corridor (OCC), had hired executive directors, set up offices, and were evolving toward more professional organizations.[2] Working alongside National Park Service (NPS) employees and Ralph Regula and his staff, they rallied support for national designation.

In 1993, only three other areas in the United States had been designated as national heritage corridors: the Illinois and Michigan Canal National Heritage Corridor (1984) in Illinois, the Blackstone River Valley National Heritage Corridor (1986) in Massachusetts and Rhode Island, and the Delaware and Lehigh National Heritage Corridor (1988) in

Pennsylvania. This type of affiliated area was new to the National Park Service, and its attitudes and opinions about such areas varied widely. When the planners in the National Park Service's Rivers, Trails, and Conservation Assistance Program were researching and drafting the Ohio & Erie study, they decided to convene a roundtable discussion in Cleveland, among people who had experience with heritage corridors. The National Park Service had been studying "heritage areas" and had reached the point of proposing legislation to create a national program, giving such places a definite position in the National Park System, rather than treating each one individually, under separate legislation. As Rory Robinson, one of the National Park Service planners, explained, in the process of that study, groups across the nation wanted to learn more about heritage areas and how to have their region recognized as one.[3]

This roundtable discussion marked perhaps the first time that such a diverse group of individuals with different heritage-area interests sat down together for a frank discussion about what was working, what was not, and what should be done. Two distinct opinions from within the park service were expressed and are still debated today. The first claimed adding heritage areas to the National Park System was a "thinning of the blood," diluting attention and funding from already stretched-to-the-limit budgets. The second, shared by proponents of the Ohio & Erie Canal project, argued that an official program would be an efficient way "for the park service to extend its philosophy and mission without taking over direct management and having to find the resources to do it."[4]

Reflecting this uncertainty within the National Park Service, *The Route to Prosperity* found that "the Ohio & Erie Canal Corridor is eligible as a National Heritage Corridor, an affiliated area of the National Park System." Then, referring to draft legislation under consideration in Congress at that time to create a defined program for heritage areas, it also concluded "the Ohio & Erie Canal Corridor is both suitable and feasible for designation as a component of the potential National Heritage Partnership system."[5] (To date, there is still no legislated heritage areas system within the National Park Service, and heritage areas continue to be created by separate laws.)[6]

In November 1993, Congressman Regula introduced the first bill (H.R. 3593) to create the Ohio & Erie Canal National Heritage Corridor. John Debo, superintendent of Cuyahoga Valley National Park, recalled intense meetings during the lead-up to that bill. Key players were Regula and his aide Barbara Wainman; Rory Robinson from the Rivers, Trails, and Conservation Assistance Program; Dan Rice, executive director of the OECC; Tim Donovan, executive director of the OCC; and Debo from Cuyahoga Valley National Park. It was a period of significant collaboration, with drafts of the bill flowing back and forth between the team in Ohio and the subcommittee in Congress. According to Debo, "finally Mr. Regula got to the point where he was comfortable, and he introduced that bill."[7]

Regula's bill proposed to designate the eighty-seven miles of the historic Ohio & Erie Canal as a national heritage corridor managed by a twenty-one-member commission, following the model set by the existing national heritage corridors. The commission would include representatives from the National Park Service, the Ohio Department of Natural Resources, the four county governments, and the local business community, and its first job would be to prepare a management plan for the heritage area. Regula also included in the bill specific language limiting the commission's powers—the commission would have no regulatory authority, nor could it condemn private property. Finally, the bill proposed "a modest federal investment" that would require a dollar-for-dollar match. The modest investment was limited to no more than $250,000 per year for the acquisition of land, $400,000 per year for commission operations, and $1.5 million per year for development.[8]

Included in Regula's announcement were two important points. First, like the other corridors, this Ohio & Erie heritage corridor would depend on partnerships for its success. As he explained, "In this age of declining budgets these partnerships, which require state and local matching funds, are the wave of the future if we are to continue to protect and preserve our natural heritage." Second, an advantage not shared with the other heritage areas was that this corridor had an established national park in the center. The press release referred to the national park as "an asset none of the existing corridors can claim."[9]

The announcement of this bill was embraced warmly by the supporters in northeast Ohio and by the local media. The *Akron Beacon Journal* ran a supporting editorial, which concluded: "The entire northern Ohio region will be the better for it."[10] The editorial also surmised that the progress on the bill would be slow, and it did take several months for anything to be done, but in April 1994, a House of Representatives subcommittee scheduled hearings on it. Rory Robinson, who had assisted with drafting the legislation, was invited to sit in on the committee hearing. He recalled, "It was neat to see Congressman Regula walk in the door and have on the table and refer to frequently a pile of support documents, and I'm not exaggerating to say, a foot high."

Newspaper coverage and grassroots support continued, and in September 1994, legislation headed to the full House. By this time, however, the bill had been folded into a new one, sponsored by Representative Bruce Vento, D-Minnesota, which included nine other heritage corridors and set up generic rules for new corridors. The bill also extended the lives of the three existing ones. For the Ohio & Erie corridor, it specified that there be a commission; it provided for funding the commission and for development of the corridor, but it dropped the earlier provision for funding land acquisition.[11]

Hopes were high for passage, but Regula cautioned that there might not be time for the Senate to pass similar legislation in the 103d session of Congress, and he pledged to reintroduce the bill in the 104th Congress. In October, a Cleveland-based magazine, *Northeast Ohio Avenues*, ran a sixteen-page special insert on the proposed corridor, including a schedule for the third annual "Towpath T's," a public event touting "Eight Days and Twelve Ways to Enjoy the Developing Ohio & Erie Canal Towpath Trail."[12] Approaching the celebration, supporters were following the status of federal legislation: the House passed its bill on October 5, 1994, but the Senate bill was blocked from coming to the floor for a vote.[13] Interestingly, the senator who blocked the bill did so in support of House opponents who believed it would infringe on the rights of private property owners. Representative Bob Smith, R-Oregon, was quoted at the time, saying, "This bill is benign coverage for a land-use taking plan by the federal government," even though the bills explicitly protected private property rights and had no funds for land acquisition.[14]

The news of the legislation's failure came the same week of the Towpath T's events. Nonetheless, another *Akron Beacon Journal* editorial noted that Representatives Ralph Regula and Tom Sawyer were already at work on legislation for the 104th Congress, confident of its passage: "One source of their confidence comes from the many communities that have rediscovered the 167-year-old waterway and whose residents are busy creating a new canal era."[15]

During this time of uncertainty regarding the prospects for federal designation, it became clear to some that, legislation or not, the corridor was happening. Superintendent Debo remembered "thinking and discussing with this now large group of interested parties that we weren't sure about whether in fact we could get a piece of legislation through Congress, but at some point it became clear that in one sense it didn't matter because the corridor was now beginning to take shape—municipalities had gotten interested. . . . The city of Akron was looking towards a commitment to develop the canal towpath into downtown Akron before the federal legislation even passed. . . . It seemed to us, at some point, 'well, it will be a great thing if we can get the federal designation, but even if we don't, we will have an Ohio & Erie Canal Heritage Corridor.'"

Two especially significant examples that show the corridor was indeed going to happen were Akron's plan to extend the Towpath Trail from the national park to the city and Cleveland Metroparks' plan to create a new reservation along the Cuyahoga River, with an extension of the towpath from the north boundary of the national park to the new reservation. Already the overriding goal that had been talked about in the 1980s and was still being vigorously pursued by Debo—physically connecting Cuyahoga Valley National Park to the nearby urban centers—was being accomplished.

Akron's plan to connect to the national park via the towpath was discussed as early as 1992, spurred on by Debo's request that the city add a bike lane to an already planned resurfacing of Riverview Road between the city and the national park.[16] In October 1994, Akron City Council approved the plan to extend the popular Towpath Trail from the south boundary of the national park to downtown Akron, thereby providing a safer route for bicyclists.[17] The passage of the Intermodal Surface Transportation Efficiency Act of 1991 (ISTEA), a small percentage of which provided a source of funds for "transportation enhancements," helped advance plans such as this one, since "enhancements" included facilities for bicycles and pedestrians and for historic preservation projects.[18]

The extension of the Towpath Trail fit nicely into the already existing Cascade Valley Park plan. Cascade Valley Park, in the works since 1979, signaled a new direction for the City of Akron and Metro Parks, Serving Summit County. Until that time, the two entities had worked separately, with Metro Parks managing its mostly rural parks and the city, small recreation parks. In the case of Cascade Valley, the city already owned hundreds of suitable acres within the city limits, adjacent to Metro Park land. The two groups forged an agreement whereby the city would develop the park and Metro Parks would manage it; it could also be used to help implement the emerging heritage corridor.[19]

Tom Long, design administrator for the City of Akron's Department of Planning and Urban Development, made the point that the city's early 1990s central business district concept recognized the centrality of the historic canal, and the Cascade Valley Park plan likewise acknowledged its importance, but both plans were essentially local. Not until Paul Labovitz, National Park Service coordinator for the corridor project, approached the city did city planners began to partner and plan regionally. In the case of the Cascade Locks area of the park, the City of Akron, Metro Parks, the nonprofit Cascade Locks Park Association, the National Park Service, and the OECC all joined forces because, according to Long, "We all believed in the partnership."

Around the same time these developments were unfolding in Akron, Cleveland Metroparks began to reexamine its mission. To do so, it polled forty-five hundred individuals who used the parks, interviewed fifteen hundred who said they did not use the parks, and held about twenty public meetings to gather more public input. They learned that the park system was underserving minorities, lower income groups, and the elderly.[20] This correlated directly with the location of the existing parks. Steve Coles, former Cleveland Metroparks chief of planning, said that the park system had a hole in the middle of its service area: "Those people who lived closest to the center had to travel the farthest of anyone using the parks."[21] This wonderful system of parks, the Emerald Necklace, ringed the city and served the suburban population well. But it did not provide for those "who grew up basically around asphalt."

So the strategy in the mid-1990s was to sustain the infrastructure, expand the Emerald Necklace, and create an urban presence relevant to those living in the core of Cuyahoga County. Metroparks took over management and did major improvements on Garfield Park, Brookside Reservation, Washington Reservation, and a one-and-one-half-mile Mill Creek corridor link to the Mill Creek waterfall, all urban projects. And they created the Ohio & Erie Canal Reservation, which, as Director Vern Hartenburg of Cleveland Metroparks noted, serves as an anchor to the others.

The concept, planning, and design for the Ohio & Erie Canal Reservation was complex and challenging and grew out of the OCC's idea for connecting Cleveland to the national park.[22] The driving forces came from Cleveland Metroparks, Cuyahoga Valley National Park, the OCC, and the Cuyahoga County Planning Commission with their *North Cuyahoga Valley Corridor* study, published in 1992. Partnerships developed among these groups and representatives of businesses along the canal right-of-way in regard to connecting and using the canal lands, with the on-the-ground leadership coming from Cleveland Metroparks.

Of the factors that came together to create the Ohio & Erie Canal Reservation, three are especially pertinent. First, as Steve Coles explained, Cleveland Metroparks, like the City of Akron, could apply for ISTEA funds for designing and building the trail.

Second, Cleveland Metroparks was already expanding its service to the local communities. But creating the Ohio & Erie Canal Reservation required a shift in thinking about green space and preservation. Coles described a meeting with the park commissioners in August 1993 as a critical turning point. They met at the Canal Visitor Center in Cuyahoga Valley National Park, then had lunch and listened to a presentation by John Debo, who explained how important it was for the park to be connected by the Towpath Trail to both Akron and Cleveland. The group rode golf carts on the towpath to Rockside Road, rode buses to an area north of Interstate 480, then got into canoes. They canoed about a mile and got out on the bank, where they were met by the then-president of American Steel & Wire, Walt Robinson. Robinson welcomed them and invited them to accept the land that the company was prepared to donate for a park. (Other companies were also willing to donate some of their canalside lands.) By the end of the day, the commissioners understood the concept and were committed to making it all happen.

The third factor was the need to sell the public on the value of turning the remnants of the industrial valley into a linear park. This required some imagination, since railroad trestles, sewer pipes, settling ponds, and high-tension electric towers are not usually considered part of a park. Vern Hartenburg explained how Metroparks did a media tour for the editorial board of the *Cleveland Plain Dealer* in 1995. Once it convinced the board to take a one-hour tour, the members were loaded into a bus and taken to American Steel & Wire, which had the only access point to the canal. During the trip, they passed a pond covered with a steaming black substance. When questioned as to why Metroparks might want to include such an ugly pond in a park, Hartenburg replied, "Well, we love this pond, because if that pond was not there, all of that oil that is on top and the steam that represents heat, would be going directly into the Cuyahoga River, further degrading the river." The title of the editorial that ran the next day was "An Industrial Grade Park." The reporters had become believers along the way by seeing that you could blend nature and industry. "Virtually every first-time visitor who ends up along the river or the canal, still seeing the smokestacks from Alcoa, then the BP tower off on the horizon, their reaction is always the same. 'My gosh, I had no idea it's down here, and this is incredible.' And then, typically, a blue heron flies by."

Summing up, Hartenburg remarked on several elements that enabled Metroparks to build the Canal Reservation. First, the *North Cuyahoga*

Valley Corridor study was "a key document that gave focus" for the future park. Second, Metroparks' partnership with the national park and the park service's assistance in building the connecting trail both helped immeasurably. And third, the partnerships Metroparks forged with industry, with Cuyahoga County, and with Cleveland and adjacent municipalities empowered Metroparks to implement the vision of the larger group. These collaborations made it possible to begin developing the corridor before national heritage corridor designation was obtained.

While these plans unfolded north and south of the national park, corridor supporters anticipated that Representative Regula would again submit a bill to Congress in 1995 for creation of an Ohio & Erie Canal National Heritage Corridor, which he confirmed in his newsletter to constituents.[23] Congress had changed: it was the start of the 104th Congress, and there were different players involved in the committees and in Congress as a whole. The situation regarding other proposed heritage areas had not changed, with separate areas seeking separate federal designations, and the National Park Service had not resolved the debate over how it would handle such areas. In 1994, two more areas had been added to the collection of heritage areas. The change in Congress and the park service's ambivalence about adding new affiliated areas notwithstanding, 1995 began with great optimism among the corridor's supporters. A January 19 article in the *Massillon Independent*, "Canal Corridor Fever—Catch It!" quoted OECC's executive director, Dan Rice, as saying, "'corridor fever' is contagious . . . you never know where it is going to spring up next." Don Cooke of Navarre, president of the OECC at the time, said, "I'm sure that 1995 . . . will truly be the year of the corridor."[24]

By March 1995, no bill had been submitted, but canal fever raged on. The OECC and the National Park Service cohosted a series of walks along different portions of the proposed corridor, the first taking place in Akron, where 150 people turned out. At the same time, Cleveland Metroparks was working on its new Ohio & Erie Canal Reservation and the extension of the towpath trail between the new reservation and the national park. The City of Massillon was working on its plans for the trail as it passed through the city, and Tuscarawas County, the southernmost one in the proposed corridor, had begun to study its section as well.[25] As an *Akron Beacon Journal* editorial stated: "Perhaps the most difficult part of watching canal fever catch on is keeping up with the pace of change."[26]

One of those changes was the reactivation of the Ohio & Erie Canal Scenic Byway Task Force, under the joint leadership of the OCC and the OECC. The original task force, created in 1993, had submitted a proposal to the Ohio Department of Transportation to create a state scenic byway generally along the route of the historic Ohio & Erie Canal. The reactivated group proposed that the Ohio & Erie route would not be just a scenic byway but would be a prototype for a new state system of scenic byways. These efforts paid off when it was recognized as a state scenic byway in 1996 and then as a national scenic byway four years later.[27]

Such efforts kept corridor supporters busy during the summer of 1995 while Regula's office, in consultation with Debo and Rivers, Trails, and Conservation Assistance Program staff, was fine-tuning a new bill. On August 3, 1995, Representative Regula submitted H.R. 2186, which contained revisions aimed at garnering support and reducing opposition, mainly by reducing the amount of federal funding for development, reducing the length of federal involvement from ten years to six, and increasing the local-state match.[28] Nine other states also had heritage area proposals pending, and, in September, Regula said it was likely that his bill would be folded into comprehensive legislation governing the creation of historic corridors. The National Park Service testified in favor of the Ohio & Erie bill, but recommended that a local organization, rather than a federal commission, should manage the corridor.[29] A generic corridor bill was also moving along in the House, which tightened the federal purse even more than previous bills.[30]

At this point, things stalled on the legislative front, but back home the corridor was still being planned and defined through various local and regional mechanisms, often with the park districts leading the charge. The park districts gained momentum for their own plans from the corridor planning while at the same time helped to facilitate corridor development. In 1995, Bob Fonte had become full-time director of the Stark County Park District (Stark Parks) and recognized that he needed to show the public both that the invested money was being used to good effect and what could be done with more resources. He established a canal task force to review the canal resources in the county, resulting in the Stark County Canal Corridor Master Plan, which specified the route of the spine Towpath Trail; routes for side trails; and sites for three visitor centers, parking areas, and picnic areas.[31] An expanded planning process resulted in the Stark County Trail and Greenway Plan. Tom Long explained that Summit County also embarked on a countywide trail and greenway planning process, partly in response to popular demand for completing the Towpath Trail through the county and creating neighborhood trails to connect to it. Cuyahoga County, led by its planning commission, followed with an extensive planning process.

In August 1996, with still no action on an Ohio & Erie corridor bill, an *Akron Beacon Journal* editorial, "Cruising in High Gear," emphatically stated, "Don't look now, but the Ohio & Erie Canal corridor is no longer a dream. The region's enthusiasm for the project has given it a life of its own."[32] Finally, in September, a bill emerged out of the House of Representatives. It was neither a specific Ohio & Erie bill nor a generic heritage-areas bill, but an omnibus bill—which takes care of many issues and projects all in one piece of legislation. The Senate followed in October, just before the 104th Congress adjourned, with its own bill containing language specifically creating the Ohio & Erie Canal National Heritage Corridor. President Bill Clinton signed the omnibus bill into law on November 12, 1996. Finally, heritage-corridor supporters in northeast Ohio had achieved their goal.[33]

The Omnibus Parks and Public Lands Management Act of 1996 covers such subjects as the creation of the Presidio Trust and additions and changes to the National Wild and Scenic Rivers System and the National Scenic Trails System, among other things.[34] The section of the law dealing with the Ohio & Erie Canal Corridor is referred to as the Ohio & Erie Canal National Heritage Corridor Act of 1996. Nine new areas were established in the Omnibus Parks Act, each with its own management prescription. For the Ohio & Erie Canal National Heritage Corridor, the act specified that a twenty-one-member, unpaid committee would assist federal, state, and local authorities and the private sector in the preparation and implementation of a corridor management plan and would be responsible for annually reviewing its budget. That change from a paid commission to an unpaid committee resolved the problems that some saw in creating and funding a paid commission like the one put in place at the Illinois and Michigan Canal National Heritage Corridor. The act also called for a new entity, the Ohio & Erie Canal Association (OECA), to bridge the two grassroots nonprofits but continue to use existing staff to accomplish heritage corridor goals.

What did not change in the final act is also significant. From the very first public talks and gatherings where the heritage corridor idea was presented, supporters always emphasized that this heritage preservation tool was just that—a mechanism to coordinate and encourage local and regional efforts. The act spells out that nothing in the title is to be construed to change any land-use regulations or laws or to affect local zoning, reiterating what supporters had said all along. The national corridor would not be a new, federally owned and managed park or an expansion of the national park, and it was not intended to supercede in any way local land-use regulations or impair private property rights.

Although it was clear this new "affiliated area" was not simply an extension of the national park in its center, having the park central to the corridor tremendously benefited this corridor over other proposed ones. As explained in the act, in addition to the technical assistance that the park was already providing the corridor in some instances, its superintendent could also now give operational assistance to support the implementation of the corridor management plan, "subject to the availability of appropriated funds."

The authorization of appropriations in the final corridor act was a reduction from earlier bills: it limited them to $1 million per year and placed a cap of $10 million on the amount that could be spent over the life of the legislation to develop the corridor. The local match was set at 50 percent, and federal involvement in the effort was expected to end on September 30, 2012.[35]

The 1996 passage of the Ohio & Erie Canal National Heritage Corridor Act was a milestone for the many grassroots and public organizations working to preserve and enhance the area of the old canal. Even before the bill passed, there had been great confidence that the heritage corridor would be developed, but less certainty about how the project would be funded. The act created access to new funding sources and improved access to existing ones, and it gave the project greater visibility, greater unity in organization, and an enhanced ability to be "sold" to communities along the corridor.

As noted, the legislation called for two entities to be created. One, the Ohio & Erie Canal National Heritage Corridor Committee, has twenty-one members, appointed by the secretary of the interior to represent various constituencies in the community. The committee has two responsibilities: it must approve the Ohio & Erie Canal National Heritage Corridor management plan and review the budget for use of federal funds.[36] The second entity, the Ohio & Erie Canal Association, is a nonprofit organization charged with preparing and implementing the management plan and receiving federal, regional, and private funds on behalf of the corridor to support the management plan. Its responsibilities include making grants to groups engaged in preserving and enhancing the corridor. This includes, but is not limited to, nonprofits, park systems, local governments, and political subdivisions that support the effort. The association must review, disburse, and account for all federal-grant and matching funds used in corridor projects. The management plan also includes specific responsibilities for the OECA, such as conserving the corridor, establishing and maintaining interpretative exhibits, and increasing public awareness and appreciation for the natural, historical, and cultural resources of the corridor.[37]

The newly established fifteen-member OECA board inherited a regional project that was already up and running. It wisely decided not to supplant the existing system but instead facilitated the two existing nonprofits, the OCC and OECC, to continue to manage the projects in their own regions. These groups both had strong and viable partnerships with local organizations in all areas of the region; towpath construction projects were underway; and volunteers were anxious to work on the next phase. Canal fever was already rampant, and the OECA worked to build on the existing base to ensure that new sources of funding, technical assistance, and the overarching corridor management system provided in the legislation were used to encourage its spread.

By June 2000, the OECA had completed a two-and-a-half-year process of creating its management plan. In context of extensive public meetings and in response to local interest, the original boundaries of the corridor were expanded, taking the heritage corridor 110 miles, north to south, from Cleveland to New Philadelphia, and expanding it east to west to include such historic places as Rogues Hollow in Wayne County and Magnolia in Stark and Carroll Counties.[38]

The OECA has an annual call for grant proposals, and the number and size of awards made are determined after the federal appropriation for the corridor is announced. The OECA provides funds to facilitate the work of the two nonprofits (OECC and OCC) who link with the community organizations that do the actual work of building the towpath, creating interpretation waysides and centers, producing signage, and planning connecting trails. The remaining federal funds go to organizations and political entities for use in corridor-related projects. The federal funds require a match of at least one dollar for each federal dollar spent, and this often includes both direct financial investment and critical contributions such as contract and volunteer labor, space, and equipment.

The management plan assigned the OECA the responsibility of helping "local entities to conserve, interpret and develop historic, cultural, recreational, and natural resources for community benefits, while raising regional and national awareness of their unique importance."[39] It recommended three phases for implementation: Establish Identity (2000–06);

Extensive public discussion resulted in this logo, designed to create a regional identity (Ohio & Erie Canalway Association).

Pilot Projects That Use the Regional Framework (2007–12); and The Long Term: A Self-Sustaining Regional Asset (post-2012).[40]

During the first phase, the "Ohio & Erie Canal National Heritage Corridor" name turned out to be a distraction for creating the regional identity—it was too long and people did not understand the concept of "corridor." Thus, the name was changed to "Ohio & Erie National Heritage Canalway," which in common usage became "Ohio & Erie CANALWAY."[41]

OECA subcommittees formed to address interpretation, identity and signage, and marketing. The influence of their work can be seen throughout the Canalway.[42] The subcommittees assist the various entities along the Canalway in telling the story of their particular site and region within the larger historic context of the canal and canal era. They provide guidelines to ensure consistency in the regional use of signs; the logo; and public information, including maps and directional and location signs. A marketing subcommittee promotes the Canalway to attract a wide range of visitors for recreational, educational, and economic purposes. Its goal is to market the Canalway as an experience, suggesting that people "journey back through the building of America by walking our Towpath, driving our Scenic Byway, and riding our historic train [Cuyahoga Valley Scenic Railroad]." It is an invitation to explore the Cuyahoga River and Valley, the national park, the shores of Lake Erie, and little canal towns and urban ethnic neighborhoods along the Canalway.

Even though the OECA provides structure and stability to the process of creating the Canalway, the public is more aware of the results of the many grants that have been made since 1998. These represent many creative and exciting examples of development in the corridor funded by the OECA's federal dollars and investments from community partners. In 1998, the first year, the appropriation of $602,000 was awarded for corridor projects ranging from the $914 given to the Hancock-Carnegie group in southwest Akron for trail cleanup to $375,000 for three towpath construction projects and $100,000 for the Mustill Store restoration. Each project sponsor raised funds equal to or greater than their federal money, thus multiplying the effect of the grants. In many cases, the local park districts, county and city governments, and local foundations provided the match.[43]

Every corridor project has a story to tell—of committee meetings, of late nights spent writing grant proposals, composing budgets, drinking coffee, and discussing what to do if the committee did not get the funds. Then there were the more formal meetings with foundations, business leaders, city councils, park districts, and state officials. Groups had to not only sell the projects but also make sure they were complying with all the federal regulations for use of the funds. Terms like "NEPA" (National Environmental Protection Act) and "Section 106" (the archaeology segment of the National Historic Preservation Act of 1966) became common in discussions.

These next stories are only a sample to illustrate the variety of OECA-funded corridor projects. They demonstrate that the corridor is more than the signature Towpath Trail and that it cuts a wide geographical, educational, interpretive, recreational, and preservation swath from Cleveland to New Philadelphia. These stories also demonstrate creative community partnerships forged among people caught up in canal fever enough to contribute time, energy, and resources.

One such example occurred in 1998: the OECA awarded twelve grants, including the first for a canal education project. It gave $9,980 to the Summit County Historical Society to develop a fourth grade school-outreach program about the Ohio & Erie Canal tied to the curriculum requirements for fourth grade history.[44] The content for this program, "Towpath to the Past," was developed by a committee including fourth grade teachers and curriculum specialists, with resources from the Ohio Historical Society and the University of Akron Archives. It features a travel trunk with canal-related artifacts, clothing, charts and maps, and hands-on student activities. Presenters from the historical society take the trunks to participating elementary schools, where each involved teacher receives a packet of materials to supplement the one-hour classroom presentation. Formally launched in 2003, the program reaches many students yearly in Summit County and Akron public and private schools.

One of the OECA Canalway goals is community and economic development, which is harder to quantify than success in building the Towpath Trail. This is meant to promote "compatible development" along the canal and also to "unify and strengthen connections between communities and neighborhoods and promote regional collaboration."[45] Many early supporters of the heritage corridor concept expressed this ideal, and civic leaders concerned about the loss of industry and jobs in the northeastern Ohio area warmly embraced development. Heritage tourism was seen as one element in plans to bolster the area's economy, but some civic leaders focused on the corridor's potential for attracting talented workers to the region. Many Canalway advocates hoped for something less tangible and more difficult to define. Ernie Lehman, owner of Ernie's Bicycle Shops, expressed it this way: "I don't like Wal-Mart. I just don't—because of the damage I think they do to small towns and communities. I always hoped the heritage corridor would strengthen small towns, strengthen communities, by bolstering locally-owned businesses—small-scale, appropriate businesses. I saw it as saving downtowns, saving community." For Lehman, who had been running bicycle shops in Stark County since 1978, the heritage corridor offered a chance to expand his business and "give back to the community." As he explained, "As soon as I heard about the [Towpath] trail, I wanted my store to be on the trail."[46] His story also illustrates the creative partnering and problem solving that are hallmarks of successful Canalway development projects.

Currently, Lehman owns and operates four bicycle shops. When the heritage corridor grassroots efforts were gearing up in the 1990s, Lehman's Massillon shop was downtown, and there was no Towpath Trail through the city. In fact, the canal had been obliterated, buried under downtown redevelopment. Lehman became involved with the Ohio & Erie Canalway Coalition, eventually serving on its board, and he also helped found an organization specific to Massillon—Massillon Area Greenways Incorporated formed to help coordinate and promote development of the Canalway and Towpath Trail in and near the town (the second-largest city in a county of 378,000). By 1996 Stark County had completed its Canal Corridor Master Plan for the Towpath Trail through the county, including the Massillon section, which would be routed on the historic towpath where it still existed and along the Tuscarawas River on an existing flood levee where it did not.

Lehman saw an opportunity to move his shop nearer to the planned trail and began searching for available properties. In 1999, he purchased two and one-fourth acres situated between State Route 21 and the scenic Tuscarawas River, right where the trail would be. He applied for an OECA Canalway grant, hoping to receive funds to help construct a new building. To his disappointment, he learned that, although the OECA definitely wanted to promote economic development, it granted funds only for projects that clearly served the public. Stark Parks, however, needed a trailhead for the new trail, and Lehman's land was a perfect location. Their partnering resulted in an ample parking lot shared by trail users and bicycle shop customers, public restrooms funded partially by the OECA grant, and a privately funded building for Lehman's shop, with room for two other small businesses.

But one problem remained: one small section of private property blocked the trail from actually reaching the Lake Avenue Trailhead. The owner would not sell to Stark Parks or to Massillon Area Greenways, but he would sell to Lehman. The solution seemed obvious to Lehman, who bought the land and gave the park district an easement for the trail, thus bringing it to his doorstep.

Lehman's wife, Debbie, who for a time ran The Blue Heron Deli next to Ernie's Bicycle Shop, described her joy on seeing families use the trail. Bicycle rentals are popular with families, and Debbie has watched many of them gear up for a ride on the Towpath Trail with apprehensive, even downright-resistant small children in tow. Then a couple of hours later, she'll see them coasting back into the parking lot, all smiles. The Lehmans also operate a very popular canoe livery adjacent to the trail. In addition, the bicycle shop serves a corps of volunteers called the Stark County Trailblazers, who ride the trail providing information and first-aid to visitors. As the Lehmans describe it, there have been little bumps along the way, but overall it is a "win-win" situation.

Cleveland Metroparks' Leonard B. Krieger Canalway Center is another example of an OECA partnership for education and interpretation. Perched on the edge of the industrial valley, the Krieger Center celebrates the industrial and commercial history of the northern Cuyahoga Valley. In a departure from the usual park interpretation of the natural environment, Cleveland Metroparks believed it was critical to the mission of the Canal Reservation to explain the layer of history between the area's agricultural and modern use. Thus, the center tells the story of the industrial valley, describing the role of the valley and the Cuyahoga River in the growth and development of Cleveland's manufacturing and commerce. The exhibits include photographs, maps, interactive educational features, movies, and industrial artifacts, and together they chart the relationship of the river and commerce as well as the early influence of the Ohio & Erie Canal.

As the OECA deliberates about how the federal funds are distributed each year, it must keep in mind all the elements that make up the Canalway. The *Corridor Management Plan* conceptualizes the ways visitors ex-

The Leonard B. Krieger Canalway Center is the heart of Cleveland Metroparks Ohio & Erie Canal Reservation (photo by Ann Donkin).

perience the Canalway as "journeys" and recognizes that these journeys will use various modes of transportation. The Towpath Trail and visitor services have received some of the federal funding, while other funds have been directed to the Scenic Byway and the Cuyahoga Valley Scenic Railroad. The management plan recognizes that the railroad is both a cultural resource, operating as it does on the historic route of the Valley Railway, and an important north-south recreational link within the Canalway. For many years, the train operated only within the national park, but recently, the scenic railroad's board has been dedicated to extending the railroad north into downtown Cleveland and south to Canton. A longer-range goal is to take the train's service even farther south, to Zoar.[47] The train would then help fulfill Superintendent Debo's goal of linking the national park directly to the urban centers north and south of the park, while developing a major transportation role for the Canalway.

To help achieve these things, OECA grants have been awarded to the railroad, for instance for railside shelters. Two major shelters were built between 2001 and 2004: Northside, which serves Akron, and Lincoln Highway, which serves Canton. The National Park Service built them, using a design based on the historic Valley Railway stations. Future shelters will be required when the railroad service is extended into downtown Cleveland.[48]

Preserving historic buildings and structures was another goal of heritage corridor supporters from the very beginning, and federal grants have supported preservation efforts in many ways, from administrative support of historic preservation programs to actual restoration of historic structures, such as the Mill Creek Falls History Center in Garfield Heights, Boston Township Hall in Peninsula, the Mustill House and Store in Akron, and the Zoar Town Hall and the Zoar Hotel in Zoar. OECA funding has played a role in the conservation of natural resources as well, not by funding actual land acquisition (the legislation forbids this) but through various means of encouraging "resource stewardship."[49] Through the OCC and the OECC, federal funding has helped encourage, facilitate, and coordinate local efforts to identify natural resources needing protection and devise ways to protect them. An excellent example is the cooperative effort to create the new Confluence Park in southern Summit County.

The Towpath Trail is the core of the Ohio & Erie National Heritage Canalway, and the public readily identifies it as such. Considerable amounts of the initial OECA funding went to support trail construction, and this is best demonstrated by the miles of completed trail going south from Clinton in southern Summit and Stark Counties. These areas contrast with Cleveland; they are far more rural with little industry, and much of the land was owned by municipalities or by the county. The Village of Clinton in southern Summit County, like much of neighboring Stark County, acquired the canal lands within the village in the 1960s when the state offered them for sale to local governments and park systems. Tom Mayberry, on the village council at the time, remembered that the village had leased the canal lands for some years and then took advantage of the state's offer to transfer ownership to local governments. The council wanted to control the canal land that cut through the middle of the village.[50] The development of the Towpath Trail has moved more quickly, as it has in all areas of the Canalway where the land is owned or leased by the local community.[51]

A grassroots partnership started in Clinton in 1997, when Clinton had just over a thousand residents. When the canal era ended, the historic town was left behind, with a treasure trove of canal history and cultural resources. Less than a half mile north of the village, there was a rare guard lock and two well-preserved lift locks, both with remnants of historic structures beside them. Former mayor Tom Mayberry remembers that he appointed the late Tressie McIntosh, founder of the Clinton Historical Society, to head a canal committee. She had challenged Mayor Mayberry and said, "Do you realize we're about one of the only communities that do not have a canal group?"[52] And so the Clinton Canal Corridor Committee (CCCC) was formed. It and McIntosh were given the task of charting the future of the two and two-tenth miles of the Ohio & Erie Canal right-of-way owned by the village and recommending a strategy for the village.

Two partnerships developed because the CCCC persistently advocated for their section of the old canal; the first was with the University of Akron's Interdisciplinary Anthropology Program and the second with Metro Parks, Serving Summit County. The university program had a summer course in community archaeology and in 1997 created a partnership with the CCCC. The result was four summers of interdisciplinary and archaeology research projects in Clinton. In the summer of 1997, with a grant from the Ohio Urban University Program, the Departments of English, History, Biology, Geology, and Anthropology conducted canal research. Graduate students, undergraduates, and faculty conducted oral histories, located old coal mines, compiled a list of historic resources, identified plants, and conducted archaeological research on village canal lands and at the 1850 Flagel harness shop foundation in McIntosh's garden. CCCC members worked closely with the university committee, and students and faculty participated in Canal Days activities, providing exhibits, artifact workshops, guided walks, and presentations about their work.[53]

The CCCC believed the archaeological work was beneficial not only for the information it gathered but also for the interest it generated in the community. In combinations of field schools where students were trained in archaeological techniques and in sessions where volunteers learned to excavate, process, and identify artifacts, a considerable amount of information was compiled. Over a four-year period, about $95,000 in both Urban University Program funds and university in-kind contributions provided Clinton with research information to comply with Section 106 of the National Historic Preservation Act, at no cost to the village. This research work was used as match for OECA grants and as the basis for interpretation panels along the Towpath Trail.

Although the archaeology generated considerable community interest, it was the partnership with Metro Parks that enabled Clinton to develop its portion of the Towpath Trail. Represented by Dave Whited, chief of planning, Metro Parks engaged in planning with the committee and rebuilt Clinton's stretch of trail. That partnership not only created the venue through which Clinton Village and Metro Parks could request funds from OECA, it also established Metro Parks as a Summit County leader for development and management of the Ohio & Erie Canal Towpath Trail outside the City of Akron.[54]

Both Keith Shy, director-secretary of Metro Parks,[55] and Dave Whited point to Clinton as the real beginning of the park system's commitment to the Towpath Trail. Whited says the towpath itself was not part of their mission, but the park system had two plans that supported the concept. One was the survey of resources and recommendations completed by the Olmsted Brothers in 1925. "That showed the Cuyahoga Valley being protected. But also the [Tuscarawas] valley down in what is now Confluence Park, down through south Akron. And it continues all the way south to the Clinton area, in southern Summit County, trying to protect the Tuscarawas River corridor, some of the canal corridor, and the valley. That was part of the plan for about eighty years." Metro Parks also had an acquisition plan done in about 1970 that suggested the district acquire some land in the Clinton area. Not until the late 1990s, though, was Metro Parks able to buy land adjacent to the canal lands owned by Clinton. Whited noted, in regard to developing the Towpath Trail, that it was amazing how all the pieces came together in Clinton, and that the timing was right with the newly formed Clinton Canal Corridor Committee.[56]

Dave Whited recalls that while construction of the Towpath Trail was overseen by Metro Parks, the committee always worked to facilitate the process whenever possible. The OECA awarded three grants for the Clinton Towpath Trail construction, and these funds were matched by Metro Parks, the Village of Clinton, the State of Ohio, and Summit County. The CCCC grants committee worked closely with Metro Parks to secure additional funds for amenities along the trail, resulting in grants from the Akron Community Foundation, GAR Foundation, and Corbin Foundation for wayside panels, pedestrian bridges, and restrooms. The Ohio & Erie Canal Towpath Trail opened in Clinton in 2000, joining with the Stark County trail on the south. Metro Parks has since extended the trail to the north of Vanderhoof Road.

OECA funds have also supported Towpath Trail development southward into Stark County. Reconstruction of the trail here has been less complicated than in other parts of the Canalway, because the local government acquired canal lands from the state in the 1960s. In Stark County, the historic towpath had been used by Buckeye Trail hikers, horseback riders, and bird-watchers since then.[57] Likewise, south of Stark County, in Tuscarawas County, the county commissioners had also taken the state up on its offer of land and acquired the canal lands that were not already privatized, a stretch which basically included the towpath and canal from Interstate 77 north of Zoar to just short of State Route 800 south of Zoar. However, Canalway supporters and trail advocates in Tuscarawas County were at a disadvantage: even though the county owned most of the canal towpath, Tuscarawas County did not have a metropolitan park district like the counties to the north, and, as a result, did not have an obvious lead agency for extending the Towpath Trail to the southern boundary of the Canalway. To address this problem, Kathy Fernandez, former site manager for Zoar Village State Memorial, and other interested individuals

Communities and park districts, using local and federal funds, have completed nearly a hundred miles of trail. These riders are sharing the trail at Wild Cat Basin in southern Stark County (photo by Rob Bobel).

in the county created the all-volunteer Tuscarawas County Canal Lands Development Committee, which the county government formally recognized in 1996.[58]

The committee was formed to plan and advocate for development of the Towpath Trail in the county. Fernandez was partially motivated by the desire to make the towpath accessible to Zoar Village visitors, and, she explained, "If it hadn't been for the corridor, this local committee . . . might not have come about." In 2005, the county took the next step and created a formal Tuscarawas County Park Department. OECA funding has helped pay for improvements and amenities along the trail north of Zoar, and the OECA, through the Ohio & Erie Canalway Coalition staff, helped citizens and officials create the Tuscarawas County Trail and Green Space Plan, so now all four Canalway counties have trail plans.[59]

Since 1998, OECA has helped implement the Canalway goals in more ways than can be described here, and the effect on northeast Ohio is significant. The success in attaining national heritage corridor designation has brought many benefits for the resources centered around the historic canal. One tangible benefit is the federal funding provided by the Ohio & Erie Canal National Heritage Corridor Act; this is generally cited as the chief benefit of national designation. The federal dollars, however, must

The Ohio & Erie Canalway National Scenic Byway

RORY ROBINSON

The Ohio & Erie Canalway National Scenic Byway is a 110-mile connection to the natural, historic, and recreational resources of the Ohio & Erie National Heritage Canalway. Designated in 1996 as the first scenic byway under Ohio's new program, this route was recognized as a National Scenic Byway in June 2000. This was the result of public officials, businesses, civic groups, nonprofit organizations, community leaders, and individuals working together in the type of partnership so much a part of all successes within a national heritage corridor.

(Ohio & Erie Canalway Association)

In October 1993, the Summit County engineer convened a task force to prepare a nomination for state Scenic Byway designation for the Ohio & Erie Canal. Members included representatives of the engineering departments and planning agencies of Cuyahoga, Summit, Stark, and Tuscarawas Counties and their principle cities; the National Park Service; and several community organizations. The original nomination, submitted to the Ohio Department of Transportation in February 1994, served as the catalyst in the development of an Ohio Scenic Byways Program.

In March 1995, the Ohio & Erie Canal Scenic Byway Task Force was reconvened under the joint leadership of the Ohio Canal Corridor and Ohio & Erie Canal Corridor Coalition to prepare a revised nomination for designation, as a prototype for the new state program. An Ohio & Erie Canal Scenic Byways Advisory Committee—representing the forty-four political subdivisions along the route as well as federal and state agencies, visitor and convention bureaus, metropolitan planning organizations, park districts, chambers of commerce, local historical societies, and others—was established to broaden participation.

Meetings of community leaders were conducted in each of the four counties, and nine additional public meetings throughout the area engaged interested citizens. As a result, the second nomination was submitted in May 1996, and in the following month the Ohio Department of Transportation granted designation to the Ohio & Erie Canal Scenic Byway, the first such designation in Ohio. This nomination included this vision statement: "The Ohio & Erie Canal Scenic Byway is a coordinated local initiative to make related improvements which preserve, protect, and promote the resources of the Ohio & Erie Canal Heritage Corridor for public education and enjoyment. It is intended to provide local residents and visitors with a well-defined and desirable route for vehicular access to all points of interest along the Heritage Corridor."

Four months after the designation, the resources and destinations linked by this route were recognized through national designation of the Ohio & Erie Canal National Heritage Corridor (now the Ohio & Erie National Heritage Canalway).

The Ohio & Erie Canal Scenic Byway route closely follows the remnants of the Ohio & Erie Canal. Because of this, it is composed of many different state, county, and local roads that could easily confuse the new visitor.

be matched by local, county, state, or other federal funds and must be spread over the entire Canalway, so this relatively modest influx of money has been leveraging significant funding from a variety of sources. Debo, commenting on the huge amount of work that has been accomplished in a relatively short time by corridor supporters, said, "If Congress is looking for an example where a modest amount of federal money can have a big impact, and you look for real world, on-the-ground accomplishment, I really would be hard pressed to think there's a better example than the Ohio & Erie Canal National Heritage Corridor . . . , but what impresses me is the amount of local interest and commitment to this project. . . . You really can't find a municipality that isn't firmly behind this project. There have been some really remarkable turnarounds." These include

---

So, in fall 1996, the Scenic Byway Task Force determined to plan and design directional byway approach and identification signs and create and install these as soon as possible. The Summit County Engineer's Office took the lead, writing an application for funding that was successful in securing $240,000 in federal dollars. The four counties provided the required 20 percent match, entered into contracts to complete the work, and developed agreements for installation and maintenance of the signs. The Scenic Byway Task Force coordinated overall implementation.

At the same time, the task force began preparing a management plan for the byway, not only an important document to identify long-term management and enhancement of the byway, but also a key piece of the nomination for National Scenic Byway designation. The management plan identifies strategies for

- enhancement of the road to provide and maintain a safe, attractive, clearly defined, and desirable route for visitor access to all points of interest along the Scenic Byway;
- protection and enhancement of the Byway's special features to optimize visitor appreciation and enjoyment;
- enhancement of the visitor experience, including interpretation of special features and development of visitor services;
- marketing and promotion of the Scenic Byway; and
- involvement and coordination of stakeholders and government.

With the completion of the management plan and sign installation, all was in place for the National Scenic Byway nomination. The designation of the Ohio & Erie Canalway National Scenic Byway occurred on June 15, 2000.

Although the task force has formally disbanded, many of the members and/or the organizations they represented continue to play an important role in implementing the vision for the Scenic Byway as "a well-defined and desirable route for vehicular access to all points of interest along the (National) Heritage Corridor." The Scenic Byway joins the waterways, Towpath Trail, and Cuyahoga Valley Scenic Railroad in providing the visitor a multitude of ways to experience the Ohio & Erie National Heritage Canalway.

---

cities embracing their canal history and using it as a focal point for redevelopment; metropolitan park districts moving into the central, urban parts of their respective counties; and the Ohio Department of Natural Resources moving from divesting canal lands to working as a partner in creating new parks and trails.

Canalway proponents are also quick to cite other, more intangible, benefits associated with the federal designation of the corridor. In addition to the funding, as volunteer Jeff Lennartz explained, "you get all the benefits of that designation . . . the cooperation of government, the creation of the overseeing committee with the various appointees in it—it suddenly becomes a real serious thing that entities have to accept. . . . It's a regional asset to make use of. . . . It carries that weight with it."[60] In addition, the status and impetus that come from federal recognition have also boosted the idea of regional thinking and cooperative partnering. For many of the individuals involved in these projects, reaching out beyond the boundaries of their individual agencies or parks, according to Dave Whited, has "had a unifying effect on the community." Or as Keith Shy, director-secretary of Metro Parks explained, "Before, everybody had done their own thing. They danced their own way. And now, the first thing you think about is, who can I call to collaborate with, and how is this going to be able to help." And in the process of collaboration, friendships have been forged; as some, among them Tom Long and Tom and Phyllis Mayberry, put it, "having fun is what makes it."

In the end, what has been accomplished coalesces around what Richard Sicha calls "re-finding a place." In Cleveland, Akron, and other places along the Canalway, the story is coming full circle as people reconnect to the distinct history of their area. As Vern Hartenburg said about the Ohio & Erie Canal Reservation, "People are fascinated, it's delightful, it's even quiet. It's everything you'd expect in a metro park or the national park. Yet you've got all this stuff around that's—that is . . . distinctly Cleveland." And summing it up: "Maybe that's part of the specialness of the heritage corridor too. Because I think when you're in Akron, the canal sections . . . that feels Akron. . . . And the thing Bob Fonte is doing, you know that is distinctly Stark County. . . . Each spot is distinctively true to the character of the land and the people where it exists. Yet the towpath and the river and the canal are unifying links that kind of say, well, yes, we, as Ohioans or citizens of northeast Ohio, are still all connected."

Heritage Development: The Stewardship Ethic for the Twenty-first Century

DANIEL M. RICE

Today, more than ever, the landscape for resource conservation is changing dramatically for many reasons. The days of one agency owning and managing large regional resources without leveraging assistance from community partners is long gone. Formerly isolated parks and landscapes are being threatened with increased development pressures from urban areas, and planners recognize the value of identifying mutually beneficial green space to maintain balance and a sense of place. However, and most important, elected officials and business leaders understand and recognize the integral relationship between resource conservation and community and economic development. No longer are companies simply looking for communities that offer good schools, water, sewer, police, and fire. Today they seek communities with outstanding quality of-life amenities, including green and open space, community parks, safe hiking and bicycling trails, and venues and programs that celebrate a place's unique heritage.

Heritage areas and heritage development provide a regional framework for resource conservation and collaborative use of natural, historical, cultural, and recreational assets. In partnership with units of government, elected officials, park agencies, nonprofit organizations, chambers of commerce, health care organizations, corporations, schools and universities, and churches, heritage areas celebrate the continuity of community resources and promote an ethic of resource conservation while stimulating community and economic development.

Rather than change the way corporations, county engineers, and hospitals work, heritage development seeks to incorporate the ethic of resource conservation and balance into the usual way of doing business. The choice is no longer one between open space and the industrial park; rather, it is one of how to balance promoting and stimulating community and economic development while conserving precious green space and celebrating a community's unique history. Heritage development demonstrates that one can indeed achieve this delicate balance, and communities that master this approach are thriving and will continue to do so. Through this, we are eliminating outdated paradigms and modeling a new stewardship ethic.

It is no longer a question of whether we can afford to promote the stewardship ethic for the future through heritage development, but rather one of whether we can afford not to. Modeling this essential ethic gives us a unique opportunity to franchise the ethic of resource conservation to new and broader audiences, celebrate the unique heritage of our nation, and create livable communities for all living things. Most important, we have a responsibility to demonstrate to our ancestors that we acknowledge unity with all living things and to leave our world a better place for future generations.

NOTES

1. U.S. Representative Ralph Regula, news release, Sept. 16, 1993.

2. The Ohio & Erie Canalway Coalition (OECC) was founded as the Ohio & Erie Canal Corridor Coalition and changed its name in 2004. The Ohio Canal Corridor (OCC) was founded as the North Cuyahoga Valley Corridor, Inc., and changed its name in 1994.

3. Rory Robinson, interview by Peg Bobel and Lynn Metzger, Mar. 3, 2004. (Further Robinson remarks are from this interview.)

4. Ibid.

5. *A Route to Prosperity: A Study by the National Park Service of the Ohio & Erie Canal Corridor* (Omaha, Neb., U.S. Department of Interior, National Park Service, 1993), 8.

6. The National Park Service's Heritage Areas Program consists of technical support for those areas already established by legislation. In 2006, the National Park Service Advisory Board produced a study that made specific recommendations that would create a legislated foundation for a National Heritage Areas system with the National Park Service.

7. John Debo, interview by Lynn Metzger and Peg Bobel, July 15, 2003. (Further Debo remarks are from this interview.)

8. Congressman Ralph Regula, "Along the Canal: Bill Would Create National Heritage Corridor," news release, Nov. 23, 1993.

9. Ibid.

10. Editorial, "The First Step," *Akron Beacon Journal*, Nov. 30, 1993.

11. Editorial, "Canal Corridor," *Akron Beacon Journal*, Sept. 8, 1994.

12. "Creating a Legacy Park System: Ohio Canal Corridor Builds Partnerships to Deliver a Visionary Project for Northeast Ohio," *Northeast Ohio Avenues* (Oct. 1994).

13. William Hershey, "Congress Sets Aside Canal Corridor Bill," *Akron Beacon Journal*, Oct. 11, 1994.

14. Sabrina Eaton, "Ohio & Erie Canal Bill Defeated in Initial Attempt," *Cleveland Plain Dealer*, Sept. 28, 1994.

15. Editorial, "A Canal Runs Through It," *Akron Beacon Journal*, Oct. 13, 1994.

16. Tom Long, interview by Peg Bobel and Lynn Metzger, Apr. 2, 2003. (Further Long remarks are from this interview.)

17. Jim Quinn, "Popular Canal Trail to Lead Downtown," *Akron Beacon Journal*, Oct. 18, 1994.

18. The seven-and-a-half-mile extension of Towpath Trail from the national park to downtown Akron was funded largely by a $2.5 million ISTEA grant.

19. The City of Akron, Ohio, *Cascade Valley Park Master Plan* (Akron: City of Akron, 1979), prepared by Wallace McHarg Roberts & Todd, Architects, Landscape Architects, Urban and Ecological Planners.

20. Vern Hartenburg, interview by Peg Bobel and Lynn Metzger, May 11, 2004. (Further Hartenburg remarks are from this interview.)

21. Steve Coles, interview by Peg Bobel, Apr. 10, 2003.

22. Richard Sicha, interview by Peg Bobel and Lynn Metzger, Oct. 6, 2004. (Further Sicha remarks are from this interview.)

23. Ralph Regula, "Ralph Regula Reports from Washington," n.d., Rory Robinson private files.

24. Teresa M. Melcher, "Canal Corridor Fever—Catch It!" *Massillon Independent*, Jan. 19, 1995.

25. Editorial, Sarah Vradenburg, "Natural Appeal," *Akron Beacon Journal*, Mar. 17, 1995.

26. Editorial, Sarah Vradenburg, "Cascading Idea Turns Dream to Reality," *Akron Beacon Journal*, Apr. 10, 1995.

27. Bob Downing, "Scenic Byway Plan Is Speeding Along," *Akron Beacon Journal*, Aug. 25, 1995.

28. Bob Downing, "Lawmaker Pushes for Corridor Again," *Akron Beacon Journal*, Aug. 4, 1995.

29. William Hershey, "Regula, Sawyer Boost Canal," *Akron Beacon Journal*, Sept. 8, 1995.

30. Halle Shilling, "Funds for Ohio Canal Lands Urged," *Cleveland Plain Dealer*, Dec. 13, 1995.

31. Bob Downing, "Stark Adopts Plan for Canal Corridor," *Akron Beacon Journal*, Jan. 28, 1996; Bob Fonte, interview by Peg Bobel and Lynn Metzger, Dec. 12, 2003.

32. Editorial, "Cruising in High Gear," *Akron Beacon Journal*, Aug. 12, 1996.

33. Bob Downing, "Canal Gets Key Federal Designation," *Akron Beacon Journal*, Oct. 4, 1996.

34. Omnibus Parks and Public Lands Management Act of 1996, Public Law, 104th Congress, 2d session.

35. The Ohio & Erie Canal Corridor Act of 1996, Division II, Title VIII, of the Omnibus Parks and Public Lands Management Act of 1996. A reauthorization bill was signed into law May 2008, making the Canalway eligible to receive an additional $5 million.

36. "Technical Report," *Ohio & Erie Canal National Heritage Corridor Management Plan*, 2 vols. (Peninsula: Ohio & Erie Canal Association, 2000), 1: app. A, p. A 5.

37. Ibid., p. A 5.

38. Ibid., App. B 2.

39. "Executive Summary," *Ohio & Erie National Heritage Canalway Communication Plan* (Akron: Ohio & Erie Canal Association, 2004), 2.

40. For more information about the Management Plan contact the Ohio & Erie Canal Association.

41. *Ohio & Erie National Heritage Canalway Communication Plan*, 2.

42. Ibid.

43. OECA grant records, files, OECA offices, Brecksville.

44. Summit County Historical Society grant report to the OECA, 2000, in the personal papers of Lynn R. Metzger.

45. *Ohio & Erie Canal National Heritage Corridor Management Plan*, Technical Report, 2 vols. (Peninsula: Ohio & Erie Canal Association, 2000), 1:55.

46. Ernie Lehman and Debbie Lehman, interview by Peg Bobel and Lynn Metzger, Nov. 9, 2005. (Further Ernie and Debbie Lehman remarks are from this interview.)

47. *Ohio & Erie Canal Corridor Management Plan*, 67.

48. Conversation with Robert Bobel (civil engineer, Cuyahoga Valley National Park), Nov. 8, 2005.

49. *Ohio & Erie Canal Management Plan*, 89–91.

50. Tom Mayberry, interview by Lynn Metzger and Peg Bobel, Sept. 15, 2003.

51. Frances Seiberling Bucholzer, interview by Lynn Metzger, Apr. 16, 2004.

52. Tressie McIntosh, interview by Lynn Metzger and Peg Bobel, Sept. 15, 2003.

53. Lynn R. Metzger, Univ. of Akron coordinator of the Clinton research project, personal papers, 1997–2001.

54. Metzger papers.

55. Keith Sly, interview by Peg Bobel and Lynn Metzger, Mar. 11, 2004. (Further Sly remarks are from this interview.)

56. David Whited, interview by Peg Bobel and Lynn Metzger, Feb. 12, 2004. (Further Whited remarks are from this interview.)

57. For a description of preservation efforts for the canal and towpath in Stark County, see Al Simpson, *Along the Towpath: A Journalist Rediscovers the Ohio & Erie Canal* (Akron: Univ. of Akron Libraries, 2003).

58. Kathy Fernandez, interview by Peg Bobel and Lynn Metzger, Feb. 2, 2004. (Further Fernandez remarks are from this interview.)

59. Jon Elsasser, interview by Peg Bobel and Lynn Metzger, Nov. 15, 2005.

60. Jeff Lennartz, interview by Peg Bobel, Oct. 9, 2003.

Chapter 18

Epilogue

The Trail Ahead

PEG BOBEL AND LYNN METZGER

> We are a canal state. . . . It is the canals that began to change this region of the country from frontier wilderness to what we experience today. The canals were built to make the wilderness into an urban state, now we're using the canal or the towpath, to put the wilderness back into an urban state—it's a reversal of roles.
>
> —Congressman Ralph Regula, 2006

When S. S. Dustin wrote about the canal in 1888 as though it were already a historic relic and Pearl Nye sentimentally called it the "Silver Ribbon" in the 1930s, they could never have envisioned the current renaissance of the old canal and towpath. The concept of preserving such historic features developed in the American mind in the 1960s. So the old and neglected Ohio & Erie Canal that began as a transportation system in a wilderness and spurred economic development has become a regional resource for recreation, education, and a new form of economic development. The ribbon is being reconnected through cities, towns, villages, and countrysides, transformed by the reconstructed Ohio & Erie Canal Towpath Trail and serving the same region it did when it was built 150 years ago.

But the Ohio & Erie National Heritage Canalway is more than its signature Towpath Trail; it is a wide swath of geography designated by the Ohio & Erie Canal National Heritage Corridor Act of 1996. It is also more than connected land and trails; it is connected spirit, the rallying point around which diverse neighborhoods and people, ranging from those found in central Cleveland to those in rural Bolivar, came together to develop this multiuse regional resource.

The story of the Ohio & Erie Canal and Canalway is still unfolding. Some think it is a tale of continuous movement and constant improvement. Yes, it will always be subject to change, but that change is actually more about people than the trail. Surely, the story of the current renaissance, the canal fever that began in the 1960s and bloomed in the 1990s, is one of enormous grassroots and regional organizational efforts, which continue to grow. The trail ahead has many challenges, but the same groups that began the movement some twenty-five years ago will guide travelers along it. New voices add expertise to the effort and energy to the journey, but the vision remains constant.

What does the trail ahead look like? What is yet to be accomplished to complete the Ohio & Erie National Heritage Canalway? Many of the advocates and leaders who were interviewed for *Canal Fever* answered that question simply: "Finish the trail." Others reminded us that there is more to completing the Canalway than just redeveloping the core trail; there are visitor centers to complete, stories to tell through interpretation at the centers and in wayside panels along the trail, and historic and natural resources to preserve. Then there must be signs to point directions and identify historic and natural features and amenities. And, finally, the Ohio & Erie Canalway must be marketed as a local, regional, and national heritage area. Although those who live near, use, and love the Canalway are invested in it, its sustainability also depends on people visiting from hundreds of miles away. Those visitors must find their destination easily, enjoy the experience, have a good lunch, and spend time and money here. So the trail ahead includes not only completing the Towpath Trail but also creating a total cultural heritage experience. Further, it includes a commitment to sustain the Canalway in the future, a commitment assumed largely by such entities as the county park systems and local municipalities.

To bring the story of canal fever from the building of a waterway to its makeover as a Canalway, several interesting, challenging, and unique projects illustrate various elements of what lies ahead. These include the completion of the Towpath Trail, Confluence Park in south Akron, and connector trails into neighborhoods up and down the Canalway.

The trail sections and other remaining projects are among the most difficult and expensive along the route, but, again, partnerships forged during the early stages of the Canalway's creation are now helping planners and managers creatively accomplish their goals. Without a doubt, the

This cable-stayed bridge over Granger Road and its look-alike over Warner Road were opened in November 2006 to carry Towpath Trail users safely over the busy roads (photo by Rob Bobel).

most challenging trail ahead for construction of the towpath is the last few miles at the northern end of the Canalway, from north of Harvard Road to Canal Basin Park, a planned visitor gateway in the heart of Cleveland. These last miles lie within the most heavily industrialized section of the Cuyahoga River Valley, containing, for example, steelyards, railroads, major roads, and environmentally damaged and polluted areas. But the Ohio Canal Corridor group has worked toward this since 1984—connecting the heart of Cleveland to Cuyahoga Valley National Park—and now it is less than six miles from the goal.

The project has taken on a significance far beyond simply completing the trail into Cleveland. As the Cuyahoga County Planning Commission declared, "To the future, the Towpath Trail marks the threshold of reinvention: rebuilding a competitive economic center in a distinctive setting based upon the principles of sustainable development; illuminating the industrial grandeur and its significance; enhancing a vital, working, Cuyahoga River; offering a regional recreational amenity; and improving the quality of life by delivering people to the water's edge, where they have not been for generations."[1]

The 2005 Transportation Reauthorization Bill delivered important funding for the final stretch of trail as well as for the Towpath Trail in Akron and a Towpath Trail bridge and tunnel in Tuscarawas County. This was the largest amount of funding in the bill for any trail project in Ohio. The physical and monetary challenges for the trail and Canal

Basin Park are significant, but committed, working partnerships are making it happen. The Towpath Trail Partnership Committee—a gathering of representatives from federal, state, regional, and local government agencies—along with the nonprofit Ohio Canal Corridor group, guides the progress on this final link to downtown Cleveland. To facilitate both planning and fund-raising, the committee is breaking the project into segments; individual parts of the trail will be opened as those pieces are completed. The goal is to complete the entire project in 2014.[2]

Another tangible aim often cited by Canalway proponents is to link east and west neighborhoods to the north-south Towpath Trail at various points along the entire four-county route. According to Jim Kastelic, formerly a planner with the Cuyahoga County Planning Commission and now with Cleveland Metroparks, "We've gotten a lot of people requesting that we link their trail, link their communities with the trail and the [Canal] reservation. And to do that we have to go through some more industrial areas, and it's been a challenge to do that."[3] One such example of a side linkage, the Mill Creek Connector Trail, has been in the works for several years. Mill Creek, full of history and neglected beauty, is a tributary of the Cuyahoga River, entering the river about nine miles south of Lake Erie. It runs through suburbs, along major roads and railroads, and through Garfield Park Reservation and Mill Creek Park before cascading over a forty-five-foot drop, creating a spectacular waterfall that for many decades was hidden from most residents in the area. Just downstream, the creek passes through a surprisingly beautiful gorge, then snakes through more industry and landfills before going under the Mill Creek aqueduct and Towpath Trail, finally reaching the Cuyahoga River. During Canalway planning, it was recognized that the lower creek corridor could potentially connect the popular Towpath Trail to several important places upstream: Mill Creek Falls, the Mill Creek Falls History Center, Garfield Park Reservation, and new and old neighborhoods.

Tom Longo, mayor of Garfield Heights, at the upper end of Mill Creek, was an early proponent of the Canalway idea. As he explained, "There was always this intriguing history of this industrial heartland and the mess they made out of the river. Then, when the talk about bringing it back began, about doing something with our heritage . . . you could just sense this was something that needed to be done." Longo now emphasizes the importance of connecting the city's neighborhoods to the Towpath Trail that has become the connection to that heritage and to the restoration of the environment. "That's the real key, to complete the connection so that it is accessible for the average citizen."[4]

Phase One of the Mill Creek Connector Trail was completed in 2007, and when the entire trail is finished it will provide a trail route and greenway from the Cuyahoga River and Towpath Trail up the Mill Creek Valley to Garfield Reservation.

Longo and Kastelic noted another important aspect of the complex work of connecting people to nature in their neighborhoods. In 2001, the Northeast Ohio Regional Sewer District began a major project that, among other things, has eliminated a combined sewer overflow that used to dump sewage over Mill Creek Falls. As Longo said, "The waterfalls would never have been opened up if the sewer district hadn't taken the overflow and put it down into a tunnel to Southerly [sewage treatment plant]. Don't forget the role of the sewer district. . . . Without the cleanup of the pollution, nothing happens. That's the big one. Without that, none of this takes place."

The positive spirit that pervades these endeavors is illustrated by a story Kastelic tells: "The project I'm working on now, Mill Creek—we're going through some really bad areas," he explained, areas that included an old chemical plant, two closed sanitary landfills, existing construction and debris landfills, and brown fields. "I remember Mayor Bacci came up to me at a recent meeting and he put his arm around my shoulder at this public meeting, and he said, 'You know, what you're trying to do here is a good thing, but you're too late. You should have been here fifty years ago.' I said, 'Mayor, I was six years old. I couldn't do anything then, but I can do something now."

Looking south of Cleveland, the trail ahead for the Ohio & Erie Canalway includes the remaining sections of Towpath Trail through Akron, a five-and-a-half-mile stretch well on its way to completion.[5] That section of trail will link downtown Akron with a proposed 1,300-acre regional park within a 2,300-acre conservation area surrounding the Towpath Trail. The *Confluence Regional Conservation Area Master Plan* grew out of earlier work and illustrates how Canalway planning has spawned related conservation efforts. The master plan credits partnerships formed during work on the Towpath Trail plan and Summit County Trail and Greenway Plan with fostering the vision for the Confluence Regional Conservation Area.[6]

The plan describes the area as one "whose confluence of natural, cultural, recreational, and economic forces defines a region and serves as a gateway to the Portage Lakes, strengthening the relationship among City parks, Metro Park lands, the Portage Trail, ODNR's Portage Lakes State Park, the Ohio and Erie Canal Scenic Byway and the Ohio and Erie

Canal National Heritage Corridor in the process." It references the 1925 Olmsted Brothers plan that showed a regional park along the waterways south of Akron's Summit Lake. The metropolitan park district has made steady progress in eighty-plus years, based largely on that original plan, stating in the Confluence Conservation Area Plan, "It is the natural evolution of that plan to now consider this important missing element."[7]

The master plan envisions a regional park and conservation area, drawing strength and definition from the region's relationship to water: its significance as a prehistoric transportation route, its importance to Akron's industry, and the beauty and recreational value of the Tuscarawas River, the canal, and the Portage Lakes. As the plan states, "By luck and the resilience of nature a remarkable natural resource still exists to be assembled." Like similar efforts in Cleveland in the industrial parts of the Cuyahoga Valley, it envisions working with industry to promote best land-management practices, and it does not shy away from addressing the need to heal and restore damaged lands.[8]

The Confluence Park plan includes a water trail that will provide a route for small, nonmotorized boats and canoes to travel between the Portage Lakes and the Ohio & Erie Canal, re-creating a popular recreational use of the canal that dates back to the early 1900s. Similar to developments north and south of Akron, the new park will include a visitor center and side-trail linkages to nearby neighborhoods.[9]

Moving farther south, the Stark County Park District completed and

The Stark County Park District and the Stark County District Library partnered to open a combined library and Exploration Gateway, a Canalway visitor center (Stark County Park District).

This Towpath Trail tunnel under an active rail line is in southern Stark County in an area known as Wild Cat Basin (photo by Rob Bobel).

opened a major new facility as this book was being finished. The district partnered with Perry Township to construct a combined park education center and branch library at Sippo Lake, halfway between Massillon and Canton. Stark Parks and Perry Township share a lobby, meeting rooms, restrooms, and parking at the Exploration Gateway. Within the Exploration Gateway is the Canalway Center, one of four informational centers planned for in the Ohio & Erie National Heritage Canalway.[10]

The Exploration Gateway is located on a new trail connecting Canton to Massillon and the Towpath Trail. As Stark Parks director Bob Fonte describes it, "The trails are a skeleton on which to hang green space. And they are an economic development tool and a quality of life issue for the community. Our Stark County Trail and Greenway Master Plan was supported because of the quality of life issue."[11]

In Stark and Tuscarawas Counties, the remaining challenges to completing a continuous Towpath Trail have to do with bridging gaps in what remains of the historic canal and towpath. In Stark County, two sections of trail are yet to be completed—one in Massillon at an active rail line, and one at the southernmost boundary of the county. During the canal era, the canal and towpath passed from one county to the next by crossing the Tuscarawas River via an aqueduct. Today, only the stone abutments and piers of the aqueduct remain—its wooden portions are

This trail bridge is the last remaining Fink through-truss bridge in the United States. Its restoration was partially funded by an Ohio & Erie Canalway Association federal grant (photo by Rob Bobel).

long gone. Officials are holding off on completing the last three-quarters of a mile until a river crossing is solved and there is a matching trail across the river, in Tuscarawas County.

In 2007, Tuscarawas County's relatively new park department and the Ohio & Erie Canalway Association completed the Tuscarawas County Trail and Green Space Plan that, similar to plans in the other three Canalway counties, will guide the completion of the Towpath Trail to its southern terminus in New Philadelphia, develop side-trail linkages, and preserve and develop other worthy areas as parks or preserves.[12]

In Bolivar, a few citizen leaders formed a Towpath Trail Committee to find ways to build the trail and reestablish the village's canal roots. To bridge a gap in the trail north of town, where a large chunk of towpath was privately owned, the village bought the property when it came on the market.[13]

The problem of how to get the Towpath Trail from one side of Interstate 77 to the other, between Bolivar and Zoar, which troubled Canalway supporters for years, has been solved. In October 2007, a new Ohio &

Erie Canal Towpath Trail bridge spanning the interstate was dedicated, closing a critical gap.

Also in October 2007, another trail bridge dedication opened an important trail link from Zoar to Camp Tuscazoar. The Zoarville Station Bridge, the last of its kind in the country, is a cast- and wrought-iron Fink through-truss design. The Camp Tuscazoar Foundation, the Tuscarawas County Commissioners, the Ohio Department of Transportation, the Ohio & Erie Canal Association, the OECC, and many dedicated volunteers partnered to restore the bridge and put it to use as part of the trail system. It opens the way for the final miles of Towpath Trail to reach Dover and New Philadelphia.[14]

These are just a few of the many steps being taken on the trail ahead for the Ohio & Erie National Heritage Canalway through efforts fueled by the twenty-first-century's canal fever. With the progress being made, this case of canal fever is likely to last for a very long time, long enough for the plans now in place to be completed, to see generations of folks enjoy the results, and to encourage conservation efforts along the towpath. As we complete this *Canal Fever* journey, we are in awe of the vision and commitment of so many dedicated individuals and organizations. This Ohio & Erie Canalway, like the old canal and towpath on which it rests, connects communities and people, is a recreational resource accessible to the people of the region, and serves as an economic development tool for communities and neighborhoods along the route. And the new Canalway, inspired by its ancestor waterway, preserves the precious heritage of the region and brings joy to those who discover its trails and green places.

The benefits will reach far beyond the people of this story and this time. Keith Shy, director-secretary of Metro Parks, Serving Summit County, articulated the vision of the whole when he said, "You know, this is a once in a lifetime opportunity—we're doing a once in a lifetime thing. You secure the land for this trail, and it is going to be there forever. So—whether Vern can say that, John, I, or Bob, these are once in a lifetime things happening. Now they won't remember our names maybe years and years from now. But my kids, my grandkids, when they are riding the trail, will be able to say, well my granddad helped out sometimes. So that means a little something."[15]

NOTES

1. Cuyahoga County Planning Commission, "Towpath Trail Extension: Alignment and Design Study: Page One," http://www.planning.co.cuyahoga.oh.us./towpath/alignment1.html (accessed Feb. 17, 2006).

2. Tim Donovan, "Building the Towpath Trail," *Trails, Tracks, and Timely Facts* (Spring 2006): 3.

3. Jim Kastelic, interview by Peg Bobel, Oct. 8, 2003. (Further Kastelic remarks are from this interview.)

4. Tom Longo, interview by Peg Bobel and Lynn Metzger, Apr. 14, 2004. (Further Longo remarks are from this interview.)

5. Bob Downing, "Towpath Trail Adds Sections, Funding," *Akron Beacon Journal*, Dec. 25, 2005.

6. Environmental Design Group, *Confluence Regional Conservation Area Master Plan* (Akron: Environmental Design Group, 2003), 1–2.

7. Ibid., 2–3.

8. Ibid., 3–8.

9. Ibid., 19, 30–31, 17, 19–20.

10. Stark Parks, "Planning Underway for Park District-Library Educational Facility," http://www.starkparks.com (accessed Jan. 4, 2006).

11. Robert Fonte, interview by Peg Bobel and Lynn Metzger, Dec.12, 2003.

12. Jon Elsasser, interview by Peg Bobel and Lynn Metzger, Nov. 15, 2005.

13. Dick Lebold, interview by Peg Bobel and Lynn Metzger, Nov. 9, 2005.

14. "Zoarville Station Bridge at Camp Tuscazoar," http://www.tuscazoar.org/ZSB.htm; and "Zoarville Station Bridge Update Page," http://www.tuscazoar.org/ZSBUpdate.htm (both accessed Mar. 9, 2006).

15. Keith Shy, interview by Peg Bobel and Lynn Metzger, Mar. 11, 2004.

Appendix

Interviews for Canal Fever

The following interviews were conducted between December 2002 and December 2005 by Peg Bobel and Lynn Metzger.

Rob Bobel: park engineer, Cuyahoga Valley National Park

Frances Seiberling Buchholzer: former director of the Ohio Department of Natural Resources

Steve Coles: former chief of planning, Cleveland Metroparks

Don Cooke: former president of the Ohio & Erie Canalway Coalition

John Debo: superintendent, Cuyahoga Valley National Park

Tim Donovan: executive director, Ohio Canal Corridor

Kathy Fernandez: former site manager, Zoar Village State Memorial

Bob Fonte: director, Stark County Park District

Virginia Wojno Forney: founder of Cascade Locks Park Association

Christine Freitag: former president, Cuyahoga Valley Association

Ron Gray: canal operations manager, Ohio Department of Natural Resources

Vern Hartenburg: director, Cleveland Metroparks

Ann Henman: founding president, Ohio & Erie Canalway Coalition

Jim Kastelic: planner, Cleveland Metroparks; formerly with the Cuyahoga County Planning Commission

Dick Lebold: Bolivar Canal Committee

Ernie and Deb Lehman: owners of Ernie's Bicycle Shop, Massillon

Jeff Lennartz: founding trustee, Ohio Canal Corridor

Paul Labovitz: superintendent, Mississippi National River and Recreation Area; former outdoor recreation planner, National Park Service, Rivers, Trails, and Conservation Assistance Program

Tom Long: retired, design administrator, Department of Planning and Urban Development, Akron

Tom Longo: mayor, Garfield Heights

Phyllis and Tom Mayberry: current and former mayors of Clinton

Ed Metzger: president, Ohio & Erie Canal Association

Tressie McIntosh (deceased): Clinton Historical Society

Dan Rice: president & CEO, Ohio & Erie Canalway Coalition

Ralph Regula: former U.S. congressman

Rory Robinson: outdoor recreation planner, National Park Service, Rivers, Trails, and Conservation Assistance Program

John F. Seiberling (deceased): former U.S. congressman

Walter Sheppe: retired biology professor, University of Akron; former chairman, Portage Trail Group of the Sierra Club

Keith Shy: director/secretary, Metro Parks, Serving Summit County

Rick Sicha: planner, Cuyahoga County Planning Commission

Tom Tyrrell: formerly with American Steel & Wire; former trustee, Ohio Canal Corridor and Ohio & Erie Canal Association

Ron Thoman: former chief of interpretation, Cuyahoga Valley National Park

Tom Yablonsky: founder, Ohio Canal Corridor, and executive vice president, Downtown Cleveland Alliance

David Whited: planner, Metro Parks, Serving Summit County

Contributors

Chuck Ayers, B.F.A., is a cartoonist and illustrator and cocreator of the comic strip *Crankshaft*. He is also the illustrator of *Joe's Place: Conversations on the Cuyahoga Valley* and *Along the Towpath* and volunteer illustrator for the Ohio & Erie Canalway Coalition.

Peg Bobel, M.S.S.A., is the former executive director of the Cuyahoga Valley Association and a freelance writer. She has edited with her husband, Rob Bobel, the *Towpath Companion* and has written several other books relating to the Cuyahoga Valley.

Robert Bobel, B.S., P.E., is park engineer at Cuyahoga Valley National Park, where he is responsible for canal operations and serves as chief engineer for the Valley Railway. He was project manager for the book *Towpath Companion: A Traveler's Guide to the Ohio & Erie Canal Towpath Trail.*

Robert Downing, journalist, *Akron Beacon Journal*, is author of numerous columns about the region and the Ohio & Erie Canal.

Kathy Fernandez, B.A., is the former site manager of Zoar Village State Memorial. She served as a trustee of the Ohio & Erie Canalway Coalition from its founding until 2009 and currently serves as trustee of the Ohio & Erie Canal Association.

Jack Gieck, P.E., is a retired engineer, photographer, and author of several books, including *A Photo Album of Ohio's Canal Era, 1825–1913*.

Roger Grant, Ph.D., history, Clemson University (formerly at the University of Akron), is author of twenty books, twelve of which are on transportation, including *Ohio on the Move: Transportation in the Buckeye State*.

Joseph Hannibal, Ph.D., curator of invertebrate paleontology, Cleveland Museum of Natural History, is author of *Geology along the Towpath: Stones of the Ohio & Erie and Miami & Erie Canals.*

Glenn Harper, M.A., manager, certified local government program, Historic Preservation Office of the Ohio Historical Society, is a contributor to several works of Ohio history and is an expert on the National Road.

George Knepper, Ph.D., history, professor emeritus, University of Akron, is author of *Ohio and Its People* and other books on Ohio's history.

Lynn Metzger, Ph.D., is a cultural anthropologist at the University of Akron. She coordinated the editing and publishing of *Along the Towpath* and is a volunteer on several Canalway projects. She is the coordinator of this book project.

Russ Musarra, a career journalist, is retired from the *Akron Beacon Journal*. He is author of *Greetings from Akron* and editor of *Along the Towpath* and *Joe's Place: Conversations on the Cuyahoga Valley*.

Dan Rice, M.A., is president and CEO of the Ohio & Erie Canalway Coalition.

Rory Robinson, B.S., is a recreation planner with the National Park Service's Rivers, Trails, and Conservation Assistance Program.

Richard Sicha, M.A., is a planner with the Cuyahoga County Planning Commission.

Sam Tamburro, M.A., is the historian for the Chesapeake & Ohio Canal National Park and former historian for Cuyahoga Valley National Park. He is the coeditor of *The Cuyahoga Valley*, a pictorial essay.

Index